THE *Christian Traveler's Companion:*

The USA & Canada

THE *Christian Traveler's Companion:*

The USA & Canada

AMY S. ECKERT
AND WILLIAM J. PETERSEN

Fleming H. Revell
A Division of Baker Book House Co
Grand Rapids, Michigan 49516

Published by Fleming H. Revell
a division of Baker Book House Company
P.O. Box 6287, Grand Rapids, MI 49516-6287

Printed in the United States of America

Library of Congress Cataloging-in-Publication Data

Eckert, Amy S.
    The Christian traveler's companion : The USA and Canada / Amy S. Eckert and William J. Petersen.
       p.   cm.
    ISBN 0-8007-5721-1
    1. United States—Guidebooks. 2. Christians—Travel—United States—Guidebooks. 3. Family recreation—United States—Guidebooks. 4. Canada—Guidebooks. 5. Christians—Travel—Canada—Guidebooks. 6. Family recreation—Canada—Guidebooks. I. Petersen, William J. II. Title.

E158.E22 2000
917.304'929—dc21
                                      99-059900

For current information about all releases from Baker Book House, visit our web site:
                    http://www.bakerbooks.com

Contents

5

Canada

Introduction

Christian travel is for everyone. Honest—everyone. To do Christian travel you don't have to be a minister or priest or even a member of church leadership. You don't have to be a senior citizen or a parent trying to set a good example. You don't have to be a member of a particular denomination or adhere to certain religious beliefs. You don't need to have "arrived" spiritually or be a daily Bible reader or be a member of the church choir or a Sunday school teacher and you don't even have to attend church each and every Sunday without fail.

Christian travel is not necessarily a trip with a religious theme, like a vacation to the Holy Land or a pilgrimage tour. It doesn't have to be a service trip, where you participate in mission work—building hospitals and churches for the disadvantaged. And you don't have to go on a spiritual retreat unless you want to.

What we mean by Christian travel is travel that rejuvenates your spirit as well as your body, travel that does not leave your spiritual life behind on the coffee table, travel that helps families talk about their faith and that of others in our country's history, travel that encourages appreciation for what God has done and thankfulness for his great gifts. We don't mean to imply that you need to turn your vacation time into an around-the-clock church service. But there are many small things you can do along the way to make all of your travels Christian.

With a little preplanning, you can make faith a focal point of any vacation. Add small side trips to your family's vacation plans. Are you planning to rent a condo in Fort Myers Beach next winter? Consider stopping at St. Augustine on your way and learn of the rich Christian faith that set the cornerstone for our nation's oldest existing settlement. Are you planning to visit San Francisco? This beautiful city traces its beginnings to an old Spanish mission, which you can still tour, and is only one link in a chain of missions strung half the length of the state, from Sonoma to San Diego.

It is inspiring to learn of the faith of the Christians who settled the continent long before we arrived. Montreal was settled by French Catholics who wanted to create nothing less than a new religious colony. And they did quite well, maintaining control of the city until 1854, nearly 100 years after the French lost

AMY'S TEN HINTS ON GETTING READY

1. Learn where the best destinations are. Use the Internet and books from your local library.

2. Learn a little of the local culture before you go.

3. Try preparing a meal that is typical of the place you will visit. Family members will have an idea of what to expect.

4. Plan some surprises on the trip for your kids.

5. Consider every family member's interests, and be sure to visit at least one destination that would score a "1" with each traveler.

6. Pack plenty of travel activities—a deck of cards, some travel games, blank paper, books, music tapes. If possible, select items that relate to your destination.

7. If you're planning a lot of time outdoors, be sure you have an indoor backup plan in case the weather is uncooperative—like museums, shopping centers, or theaters.

8. Pack a book of devotions, your Bible, and a book of choruses (or make copies of a few of your favorite songs).

9. Supply everyone with a small notebook to use as a travel journal. Even very young children can draw pictures of what they did. Recording activities, memories, and thoughts will make the trip real again when you return home.

10. Bring more film and batteries than you think you'll need. You won't want to spend valuable vacation time searching for those items—and you'll likely pay much more if you have to buy them at a souvenir shop.

the territory to the British. Evidence of the faith of those early believers can be seen all through the city in its lavish cathedrals and the names of the city's streets. You can find similar examples in almost every area of the United States and Canada.

Even business trips can include an element of Christian travel. The next time you're sent to Cleveland, check out the Cleveland Museum of Art, known for its fabulous medieval European collection, much of which has religious themes. Take advantage of a free Sunday morning and visit a historic cathedral in a city where you're attending a conference or find a church that is noted for its stunning architecture, artwork, or music. How about worshiping with another denomination to get a sense of their traditions?

By noting places in your travels that are associated with Christianity, you create natural topics for family conversation that focuses on God and what he has done. For instance, as you travel through Shreveport, Louisiana, and learn that James Dobson was born there, it may stimulate an interesting discussion. Or when you visit Baltimore and find that the hymn "Jesus Paid It All" was written in that city, you may break into song right then and there. (Elvina Hall scribbled down all the stanzas on the flyleaf of her hymnal while seated in the choir loft in the Monument Street Methodist Church. You may want to mention to your children that writing in hymnals is not usually a good idea!) It's Christian trivia but it can be stimulating, and you'll find many interesting tidbits in this guide.

Many Christians say they feel closest to God when they are out in nature. And it is true that the handiwork of humans cannot compare with God's creation, whether it is Mount McKinley, the surf off the coast of Bar Harbor, or the wonder of the animals we see in the world or in zoological parks. What better way to add a spiritual element to your trip than to marvel at God's amazing creation? Including every scenic area in the United States and Canada would have been outside the scope of this book, but we point out the must-see locations.

TRAVEL WITH A PURPOSE

Throughout history travel has been an important element of a life of faith. Centuries ago Abraham began the tradition, picking up and moving when God called him. Abraham packed up all of his possessions, his family, and his servants and traveled to a new land. The journey itself was an important part of Abraham's spiritual life. Along the way he encountered trials through which God was able to teach him valuable lessons. And since Abraham had no idea where his destination would be, and no familiarity with the land or its inhabitants, each day must have been a new adventure in his faith walk, relying on God for his every need.

The Israelites learned a similar lesson. Their journeys took much longer, lasting 40 years. Notice that, following the Israelites' disobedience, God commanded his people not simply to camp or to settle and wait for 40 years but to wander, to travel. It must be that God's lessons would be learned through the travel itself, not simply through the waiting.

Christ spent the majority of his ministry traveling and teaching, and when life became too much for him, he headed out into the countryside, walking in the desert of Judea or traveling by boat on the Sea of Galilee. And the disciples followed his example, traveling throughout their world spreading the gospel, visiting believers, and assisting with local projects. Although travel in that day was not only difficult but even perilous, the disciples saw travel as an unavoidable part of spreading the Good News.

For centuries the early church viewed faith-related travel as an important part of Christian life. The faithful would find someone to care for their businesses and farms while they headed off to the shrine of a saint in hopes of receiving a blessing. Travelers were often gone for months at a time, but while the way was difficult and accommodations meager, the journey was not without its pleasures. Family members strengthened relationships, travelers forged new friendships, and the cares of home could be forgotten for a time. When the travelers reached their destination, they were certain to pick up a souvenir before they left—perhaps a shell, a feather, or a container of holy water—that they might never forget their experience. Those early Christian treks formed the basis for modern-day pleasure travel, and many of the ancient traditions survive today.

HOW TO USE THIS BOOK

If you would like to integrate your faith with your travel, then Christian travel is for you. In fact you may already be doing it without putting a label on it. The way in which your family makes its travels Christian will be as unique as you are. *The Christian Traveler's Companion: The USA and Canada* is designed to help you decide what's best for your family.

You may have tried to add Christian sites to your itinerary in the past and been discouraged by the lack of help in the standard guidebooks. That's why this book is special. Sites are included here that would be ignored or glossed over by other guidebooks. *The Christian Traveler's Companion* includes literally thousands of sites within the United States and Canada that offer special inspiration and, yes, fun for Christian families. (After all, most people travel for enjoyment, and Christian travel can and should be fun!) The countries are divided into regions, which are then further divided into states or provinces and then cities. Within each city are listings that are quite varied, just as families' interests and styles are varied.

Look within your desired destination for sites that are worth a special trip, as well as for bits of Christian trivia. You will find listings of historic churches as well as fine arts exhibits that will be especially interesting to Christians. You will find historic sites and places that simply offer good, wholesome family fun.

In addition to each state's listings you'll find boxes that highlight specific locations. We provide a closer look at some of the continent's historic Christian settlements, as well as pointing out great places to enjoy God's creation and sure bets for great family fun.

Because our focus is on Christian sites, we assume that this guidebook will be used in conjunction with other books on the market that offer comprehensive maps and information about lodging and dining.

INTERNET RESOURCES

Visit our Web site: www.christiantraveler.com for updated information on Christian travel. Because addresses can change over time and because new Web sites are continually being created, we have compiled a complete listing of Internet links on our Web site. All of the Web sites included in this book are available on our site and are updated as needed. You will also find many more listings as they become available. This links page serves as a handy reference tool, a clearinghouse for all of the Christian travel sites you will ever need.

QUESTIONS AND ANSWERS
ABOUT CHRISTIAN TRAVEL

Q: It's so hectic when we travel. Is it possible to enhance my spiritual life when we're so busy?

A: Consider packing a good Christian book to read along the way. Take along a tape or CD player and headphones and listen to Christian music, sermons, or a Christian book on tape as you travel. Identify a church for Sunday worship, no matter what city you're in. Take early morning walks alone and use the time for meditation and prayer.

Q: I have young children. Is it possible to add a Christian emphasis to our vacation?

A: Yes! Even very young children can see God's handiwork around them. Tell the story of Noah's ark before visiting a zoo and remind them to look for all the wonderfully unique designs that God parceled out to the animals.

Remind your family of the creation story as you make your way to the Smoky Mountains to enjoy the area's natural beauty. And share with them your appreciation for a healthy and fit body when you head to Utah on a ski trip.

Older children will enjoy reading stories that tie into the day's activities. On your way to San Diego, read about the city's settlement by Spanish padres. Or before visiting Lancaster County in Pennsylvania, read stories about the Amish.

Q: Shouldn't we just skip church when we're away from home? We won't know anyone even if we do find a church to attend.

A: It may be interesting and informative to visit a church of a different denomination while you're away from home. Or you may find visiting a historic cathedral inspiring. If you visit an old church, take time to find out from the members some of its history. You may be surprised by the interesting stories you hear.

Q: My husband never wants to go to church when we're away from home. What should I do?

A: You don't have to be in a formal worship service to worship. The family can gather around a campfire, in a park, or even in your hotel room and read the Bible, sing favorite choruses or hymns, read a devotional, and pray together.

The important thing is for the family to decide what is best for them. You may choose to go to a church one Sunday and do it yourself the next. That's okay.

Q: How can we make our discussions about Christian themes interesting to the kids?

A: With some planning, you can have a theme for each day of your vacation. Your morning devotions could incorporate Bible readings that relate to the theme of the day's activities. For example, if you plan to visit the city of St. Paul, read about the apostle

AMY'S TEN HINTS FOR GOING

1. Learn to go with the flow. Unexpected events are bound to pop up. Think of them as unplanned opportunities rather than as bad luck.

2. Look for souvenirs that are useful and will remind you of your trip.

3. Pick up some recordings of local music at your destination. Once you've returned home, the music can bring you back unlike anything else.

4. Don't be shy—talk with local people. You'll build wonderful memories and learn a lot.

5. Avoid chain restaurants. Eat where the locals eat, and eat what they eat.

6. Allow some space and time alone for family members who need it. Every minute doesn't have to be scheduled. Allow time for rest.

7. Be flexible. If a destination isn't what you'd hoped for, be willing to move on.

8. Take time to enjoy your family as well as the destination. Spend a little time one-on-one with each person.

9. Pick up food at a local grocery or farmer's market and have a picnic.

10. Take the time to whisper a prayer of thanks for God's creation.

Paul in the morning. Select some qualities of the man that the family will look for in the city.

Or read about peace in your devotions before visiting a Quaker site during the day. You may want to pose some questions that the family will consider throughout the day and try to answer together in the evening.

This will take a little research before your trip but it will be worth it.

BILL'S TEN HINTS ON GETTING READY

1. Think of ways that each family member can help in the advance preparation. If someone is a history buff, have him or her do some research. A young child can gather games and books. An older child can search the Internet for the best places to stay.

2. Make a checklist of things that you want to see. Let each family member add to it.

3. Plan enough physical activity to let off steam and get exercise. Even older family members need some exercise.

4. Don't overplan. Always leave room for serendipity. God delights in giving us serendipitous discoveries.

5. Don't forget the binoculars.

6. Know exactly where you are going. There is nothing more frustrating than getting within 20 miles of your destination late at night when everyone is tired and then spending two hours finding the place. Pack detailed maps of all the areas you will visit.

7. Plan your shopping. Make a list of the people you will buy for. Decide in advance how much money the children will have to spend.

8. Make self-stick labels for all the people who should receive a postcard. And buy stamps before you leave home.

9. Plan what you will wear so you can pack lightly and still be prepared for the unexpected. It may rain; it may get cool.

10. At your Sunday meal before the trip, ask family members to think of how the trip may expand their understanding of God and his ways. Every trip is a little bit of a pilgrimage.

Q: Shouldn't a vacation be fun? Why should I expect the children to learn something while we're traveling?

A: Children love discoveries. If you don't tell them it's education, they'll never know! Most children who have read about the Declaration of Independence in a textbook will be fascinated by the real thing in the National Archives in Washington, D.C. Children may be bored reading about the pioneers traveling west along the Oregon Trail, but they will be amazed to see the wagon ruts in the stone and to view an actual Conestoga wagon. You may want to give your children a list of things to look for or discoveries to make on the trip. Make it a contest with prizes at the end.

Learning about the ethnic group that settled an area can be enlightening and help you and your children appreciate people who are different from you. For example, the culture of Louisiana is unique. The Acadians who settled there brought with them a French flair, and African Americans have added a flavor of their own. Before the influence of either of these groups, the culture was Spanish. Add to all of that mix an American spirit of individuality and independence and you get a culture that cannot be found anywhere else in the world.

Before going to an area, whet the family's appetite. Prior to a trip to Louisiana, learn a few words of Creole, listen to some good jazz, read up on the Mardi Gras festivities and their ties to the Christian faith. Read books set in the South or in New Orleans— by Harnett Kane, for example. With a little prior preparation, your children will find their "educational" trip lots of fun.

Q: How can I be sure that a tourist attraction or a restaurant will be appropriate for our Christian family?

A: It can be unnerving to find yourself with your children in a place that may not meet your standards—the restaurant with scantily clad waitresses, the play with suggestive language or scenes, the street fair where drinking is evident. The best possible solution is to assess the appropriateness of a place or attraction before you arrive. This isn't always easy nor is it always foolproof, but it can be done. In brochures and guidebooks, look for hotels and other sites that seem geared to families. Whether you are traveling with children or not, chances are pretty good that a place that welcomes children will be pretty wholesome overall.

Don't hesitate to ask others about their experience at the sites you would like to visit and listen for anything that would suggest inappropriateness.

Many hotels and restaurants have Web sites. If you have concerns about where to eat or stay in a particular city, check them out before you arrive. Some establishments actually offer virtual tours on the Internet, and many provide their menu on their Web site as well. You can also e-mail the location through their Web site and ask questions if you have concerns.

If all your research fails and you find yourself, for one reason or another, in an uncomfortable place, the best thing to do is leave. There's no need to make a scene or insult anyone; just leave.

Q: All the members of our family have different interests. How can we plan a family vacation that everyone will enjoy?

A: You cannot please all of the people all of the time, but there are ways to ensure that everyone in your family is pleased some of the time. Sit down with your family (or other traveling companions) and compile a list of the kinds of things a person could do on vacation. These activities should be general rather than specific. For example, listing a visit to an amusement park is permissible, but listing Knott's Berry Farm is not.

Some of the things that end up on the list may be learning something new, visiting a national park, going to an amusement park, visiting cultural sites like museums and concerts, visiting historic sites, and shopping. Then ask all members of your family to rate those activities on their own sheet of paper in order of preference. The activity that sounds like the most fun will receive a 1 and the activity that sounds the most boring will receive a 10. When everyone is finished, compare the sheets. Then begin planning a trip that will incorporate everyone's number 1, as many 2s as possible, and so on down the list.

This works especially well in families where interests are very diverse and compromising skills are limited. Children can be reminded that while they may have to endure an experience that to them is a 10, at some time on the trip they will have their own personal 1 to look forward to, as will everyone else.

This rating system ensures that some of everyone's desires are met on a vacation, but it does much more. It also teaches young people lessons in compromise and respect for others' interests. And you may all learn more about what other family members enjoy.

Q: We would love to travel, but with a young family, we just don't think we can afford it. What can we do?

A: The first key to affording a vacation is to decide that travel really is important. Over the years Amy's family has traveled over half the globe on vacations that would sound pretty exotic to most people. But she and her husband decided early in their marriage that travel would be a priority for them. Beyond their personal excitement at the prospect of visiting new places, they recognized the educational value of seeing the world and they wanted to give that gift to their daughters as well.

You may have to decide to sacrifice some things to afford the kind of travel you would like to do. Amy's family has given up cable television, movies, and eating dinner out and they carefully save a set dollar amount every payday in order to reach their travel goals.

The way to go for your family may be taking less expensive trips. Buying a tent or camper may be a good choice. While the initial investment may be considerable, campsites are usually much cheaper than hotel rooms. Or consider renting a cottage for a week or two. These options allow you to cook your own meals to further cut costs.

Remember that vacations don't have to be elaborate to be valuable. What is important is that you take time away from your daily environment to rejuvenate mind, body, and soul. Disconnect yourselves from the television, telephone, and fax and focus your attention on one another.

Q: I sometimes feel that travel just for the sake of travel is an indulgence that I as a Christian shouldn't allow myself. What do you think?

A: One of the most meaningful experiences a Christian can have is service travel. But many Christians, especially families, shy away from this type of travel. They don't want to give up valuable vacation time working, they're unsure of their abilities, and they see little opportunity to include children in such a venture.

The fact is that many missions are eager to take any help they can get, even if you are willing to donate just a day or two. And most mission boards have a variety of work opportunities available for a variety of skills, from medical and computer expertise, to carpentry, gardening, and painting. Many missions will offer accommodations or a place to camp as well as meals in exchange for your time. Those who live and work at the mission permanently can share inside information on out-of-the-way places that may not have made it into any travel book.

If you have an interest in a service trip, begin by determining the area of the country or world you would like to visit. The more

BILL'S TEN HINTS FOR GOING

1. Encourage family members to collect things for a scrapbook. It's amazing how quickly you forget if you don't have a reminder.

2. Savor the moment. Maybe you have a schedule; maybe you're late already, but take time to enjoy.

3. Ask questions; be curious. Write down answers to your questions.

4. Think about what will make a good photograph. A mountain 30 miles away may look impressive, but in a photo a small flower may have more meaning.

5. Often postcards are better than your own photos. Buy those that show places you don't want to forget.

6. Take time at the end of the day to review, to help family members recall the highlights of the day.

7. Be an encourager, both in the family and outside of it. Family members may try your patience, but try to be positive. Waitresses may try your patience too, but they also need encouragement.

8. Help your family members respect differences on the trip. You will meet people of varying racial, religious, and ethnic backgrounds. You will visit different kinds of towns and villages. Some may not even have McDonald's! Enjoy the differences; don't fret about them.

9. Note the differences in the religious landscape. How do these people celebrate God?

10. Don't be so wrapped up in your doing that you forget to ooh and aah at what God has done.

flexible you are the greater the likelihood that you will find a good match.

Next, assess your skills. Is your field of employment transferable to the mission field? How about your hobbies? Don't despair if your answer to these questions is no. Many work sites have a place for people who are willing to do odd jobs, and many offer basic on-site training.

Consider how much time you have available and how the entire family can be part of the experience. Some mission projects offer opportunities specifically designed for families, including young children. But you need to be sensitive to the amount and intensity of the work that you plan for younger family members. This is their vacation, too, and if you push them into a project that is too demanding or uninteresting, you may sour them on volunteerism for the rest of their lives.

Finally, contact your denomination's mission board. Ask them for a listing of work opportunities. You will probably receive a lengthy listing or booklet to browse through. If you don't find exactly what you're looking for, don't be shy about asking for additional contacts. Most mission boards want to encourage volunteerism in any capacity and are happy to recommend one another.

This is a good way to travel and at the same time feel that you are doing something worthwhile by helping others.

VALUING TRAVEL

Wherever your journeys take you, whether to a cottage on a local inland lake or across the country by motor home, learn to value travel as a means of spiritual renewal. Avid travelers already know that travel is fun. With a little preparation, your vacation can be more than fun; it can be life-changing.

Travel will allow you the time to deepen existing relationships with family and friends, as well as to foster new friendships. It will also give you the freedom to distance yourself from your ordinary life and to seek God's leading. A visit into nature can remind you of God's incredible creative powers. Service travel through a church can change lives forever—including your own—with opportunities to witness and show Christ's love in action. Travel can also enhance your understanding of other peoples and cultures, and it can remind you of your connections to distant brothers and sisters whom you have never met, who may speak in different languages and worship in different styles, but who all share the same Father.

It is our hope that in this way you will commit to making all of your travels Christian.

UNITED STATES

New England

NEW ENGLAND IS THE BIRTHPLACE of the United States. The region has been blessed to an almost unfair degree. Rich with history and intellectual and cultural sites, New England also has some of the country's most stunning natural beauty, luring travelers to its rocky coastline, great skiing, and blazing autumn foliage.

Massachusetts offers much for Christian travelers to see, largely because so much of early American history was intertwined with Christianity. Plimouth Plantation offers an interesting look at one of the country's earliest settlements and the Christian Pilgrims who founded it. And many of Boston's most famous historic sites are churches, such as the Old North Church and Quaker meetinghouses that served as places of assembly for the early American patriots.

■CONNECTICUT

Tourist Info
Phone 800-CT-BOUND
Web sites
  Connecticut vacation center   www.tourism.state.ct.us
  Fairfield County   www.visitfairfieldco.org
For a complete list of updated links, visit www.christiantraveler.com

Branford For more than two centuries, people have explored the little islets in Long Island Sound, intrigued by the stories of treasures hidden by Captain Kidd or enthralled by the picturesque scenery along the way. The Thimble Islands Cruise is a narrated tour aboard the *Volsunga IV* during the summer that departs from the Stony Creek Dock and takes only 20 to 45 minutes. Reservations are required. Phone 203-488-9978.

Bridgeport Maybe it isn't much of an accolade to say that Bridgeport's most famous resident was P. T. Barnum, but the Barnum Museum here (620 Main St.) is a fascinating place for a family to visit. You won't have any trouble figuring out which building it is. It's the gargoyled, towered, and domed red building in the middle of the city.

The Discovery Museum (450 Park Ave.) is supposed to be for the kids, but adults will love it too. Three stories of exhibits include a planetarium; a "paint with your body" exhibit, where body movement produces light and color; electricity and computer exhibits; films; special events; and workshops. It also has a learning center in which you go on a simulated space mission.

Bristol You may be taking a vacation to get away from the clock but if you are a clock-watcher anyway, you may be interested in the American Clock and Watch Museum with more than 3,000 timepieces (100 Maple St.). Bristol has been famous for clocks since 1790.

Even more unique is the New England Carousel Museum (95 Riverside Ave.) with displays of more than 300 carved, wooden antique carousel figures, including two chariots.

Also located in Bristol (Rte. 229 N and I-84) is Lake Compounce, the country's oldest continually operating amusement park. Highlights include an antique carousel, a classic wooden roller coaster, a water playground, and a lake with a nice beach.

Chester The National Theatre of the Deaf (5 W. Main St.) presents Sunday afternoon storytellings on the green in the month of June. It is done in words and pantomime by this company that tours the world but makes its home in this town.

Coventry Remember Nathan Hale? He was the schoolteacher-patriot who was captured by the British when only 21 years old. Hanged as a spy in 1776, his last words were "I only regret that I have but one life to lose for my country." Coventry was his birthplace and the Hale Homestead is in this town, 20 miles east of Hartford. Admission is $1.

Therefore we will not fear, though the earth give way . . . though its waters roar and foam and the mountains quake with their surging.
PSALM 46:2–3

East Haddam The Gillette Castle State Park (four miles southeast to 67 River Rd.) is one of the state's most popular attractions. It is a 184-acre park surrounding a 24-room castle, incorporating a medieval German design. William Gillette took five years to build his dream house. When you realize he designed all the ingenious locks on his 47 doors, you will be surprised it took him only five years. Admission is $4.

The Nathan Hale Schoolhouse (on Main St., Rte. 149), where the Revolutionary patriot taught in 1773, is a one-room school with period furnishings. The church alongside it has a bell that supposedly was cast in Spain in 815.

Enfield In this town in 1741, Jonathan Edwards preached the sermon "Sinners in the Hands of an Angry God," a key sermon in the Great Awakening of the 18th century.

The Martha A. Parsons House (1387 Enfield St.) was built on land that was put aside for use by parsons (capitalized or not) or ministers, and it holds 180 years of antiques. It was built in 1782.

Essex The Valley Railroad (1 Railroad Ave.) is a scenic 12-mile steam train excursion along the Connecticut River to Chester. There you can connect with a riverboat if you want a one-hour cruise. The equipment is about a hundred years old.

Farmington After you absorb the array of colonial architecture on Main St., you might like to go a few blocks farther to 35 Mountain Rd. and visit the Hill-Stead Museum. It's a country house of an art-loving industrialist, Alfred A. Pope. And what an art collection he put together! His impressionist collection is breathtaking. The residence, by the way, was designed by Pope's daughter, who was an architect at a time when women weren't supposed to be architects. The grounds are noteworthy too, designed by a female landscape architect.

Guilford The Henry Whitfield State Museum (on Old Whitfield St.) preserves the oldest stone house in New England and the oldest building of any kind in Connecticut. It was built by the town's first minister in 1639. The house served as his home and also as the village church, the garrison, and the town meeting hall. Good thing it was built well!

Hartford The Harriet Beecher Stowe House here (79 Forest St.) is where the author of *Uncle Tom's Cabin* and her husband made their home after their retirement. Calvin Stowe's major work was the *Origin and History of the Books of the Bible*. They were good friends of Mark Twain, who lived nearby at 351 Farmington Ave. $6.50 covers entrance to both houses.

Center Church (Main and Gold Sts.), built in 1807 and patterned after London's St. Martin-in-the-Fields, has an ornate white spire that contrasts with the red brick of the facade. It also has Tiffany stained glass windows. The markers in the cemetery go back to 1640. The first pastor of the church was Thomas Hooker, who along with his congregation, founded the city of Hartford. He helped draft the paper that created a government for Connecticut towns and he also wrote an explanation of the polity of Congregational churches. (See Harriet Beecher Stowe also under Brunswick, Maine; Litchfield, Conn.; and Cincinnati, Ohio. See Mark Twain also under Norris, Tenn., and Hannibal, Mo.)

Litchfield This is the town where Henry Ward Beecher and his sister, Harriet Beecher Stowe, grew up, and when you are here, you think that it probably hasn't changed much since that time. Unfortunately the house in which they were raised is no longer here, and only a marker indicates the spot.

The graceful Congregational church (junction of Rtes. 202 and 118) is rated among the finest structures in New England and rightly deserves to have been photographed as much as it has.

If you are into flower gardening, take a short swing south of town (three miles on Rte. 63) and see the White Flower Farm. It's a nationally known nursery with five acres of display gardens and another 30 on reserve.

Mystic The Mystic Marinelife Aquarium (55 Coogan Blvd.) features more than 6,000 live creatures who love the sea, including dolphins, sea lions, and the only whales in a New England aquarium.

Mystic Seaport (50 Greenmanville Ave.) is a re-created 19th-century seaport village, including a church, chapel, schoolhouse, pharmacy, bank, ship's chandlery, and more. Covering 17 acres, it is the nation's largest maritime museum. You can board an 1841 whaler, which made 37 voyages from the South Seas to the Arctic, and you can climb onto a square-rigger. There is also a children's museum where the kids can enjoy games on a 1908 steamboat. A two-day admission is $16, ages 6–12 $8, audio tours $3.45.

GREAT PLACES FOR FAMILY FUN

✔ Bicycling on Cape Cod, Massachusetts

✔ The seaport of Mystic, Connecticut

✔ The beaches on Block Island, Rhode Island

New Haven The Shoreline Trolley Museum (17 River St.) lets you ride a classic antique trolley along a very scenic three-mile route. Admission fee.

Three churches, United (1813), Trinity Episcopal (1814), and Center Congregational (1813), are the only churches on the green and they reflect Federal, Gothic, and Georgian architectural styles. Dwight Chapel off High St. is a Gothic-design structure, named after a remarkable educator-pastor who was president of Yale from 1795 to 1817. Timothy Dwight was a grandson of Jonathan Edwards, a legislator, author of the first American epic poem, founder of Andover Theological Seminary, conservative in theology but progressive in education.

Yale University (in the center of town) was founded by ten ministers in 1701 and named after Elihu Yale, who gave generously to the school. The centerpiece of the campus is Harkness Tower, which is inscribed with the words, "For God, For Country, and For Yale." The tower carillon plays short medleys throughout the day. Yale's campus contains many fascinating exhibits, two of which are the Collection of Music Instruments (15 Hillside Ave.) where they have 850 instruments, and the Beinecke Rare Book and Manuscript Library (High St.), which has a copy of the Gutenberg Bible in its fabulous collection.

After talking about the Gutenberg Bible, it seems odd to mention hamburgers, but if you have a family, hamburgers are never out of place. And strange as it seems, the first hamburger in America was made in this cultured city in 1900. Drive over to Louis' Lunch (261 Crown St., at the corner of Chestnut Ridge Rd.) to find the place. Louis got around to introducing cheeseburgers in 1931.

Norwalk Steps away from restored art galleries, restaurants, and boutiques in South Norwalk is the Maritime Aquarium (10 N. Water St.), which has a huge aquarium, marine vessels, and an IMAX theater. A touch tank allows kids to touch sharks, sea stars, snails, clams, and crabs. Skilled craftsmen build traditional wooden seafaring vessels. It's open every day of the year except Thanksgiving and Christmas.

St. Paul's on the Green (60 East Ave.) is a 14th-century Gothic church containing a Seabury altar and an antique organ.

Old Lyme The First Congregational Church (96 Lyme St.) was built in 1817 and then rebuilt after a fire in 1907. It is a classic New England church with slender Ionic columns and a graceful steeple and spire.

Stamford First Presbyterian Church (1101 Bedford St.) is a relatively new church (1958), but you don't see too many churches shaped like a fish. It has summer concerts in July. Its stained glass comes from Chartres, France, and it has a 56-bell carillon.

The Stamford Museum and Nature Center (39 Scofieldtown Rd.) offers 118 acres of outdoor fun. Here you can visit a working farm and enjoy natural history exhibits and planetarium shows. You can also take a hike on one of many trails and eat lunch at their picnic area. Admission is $5.

Stonington This is a typical northeast fishing community with white-spired churches. It is also the location of the Old Lighthouse Museum (7 Water St.), where you can see shipping and whaling displays. For a great view, climb to the top of the tower. Admission is $4.

Warren Evangelist Charles G. Finney was born here in 1792, taught school in New Jersey, practiced law in western New York, conducted evangelistic crusades in the Midwest and East, and ended up as president of Oberlin College in Oberlin, Ohio.

West Hartford The Noah Webster House and Museum here commemorates the life of the man who spent 36 years developing the dictionary. When he was converted at the age of 40, he became as diligent a student of Scripture as he had been of the English language. The museum is located north of Rte. 84 at 227 S. Main St.

Wethersfield The First Church of Christ (Main and Marsh Sts.) was established in 1735 as a congregation, but the meetinghouse was not built until 1761. It was restored in 1973.

Windsor The Connecticut Trolley Museum (58 North St.) allows you to take unlimited three-mile rides on vintage trolleys to see the historic city.

The First Church in Windsor (75 Palisado Ave.) dates from 1630, but it was redone in 1794 with classic Georgian-style architecture. The cemetery dates from 1644.

Woodbury Glebe House, at 1 Hollow Rd., off US 6, is called the birthplace of American Episcopacy, because it is where Samuel Seabury was elected to become the first bishop of the Episcopal Church of America in 1783. On the first floor is the home; the second floor is the church museum. Open in the afternoons, Saturday through Wednesday. Admission fee.

■MAINE

Tourist Info
Phone 888-MAINE45
Web sites
   Entire state   www.visitmaine.com
   Appalachian Trail   www.trailplace.com
   Bangor area   www.bangorcvb.org
   Sabbathday Lake Shaker Village   www.shaker.lib.me.us/
For a complete list of updated links, visit www.christiantraveler.com

Acadia National Park This national park encompasses 33,000 acres of beautiful countryside on the Atlantic coast. Millionaire John D. Rockefeller, who loved horseback riding, funded all of the park's 120 trails, making this a great place to do some family hiking or mountain biking. Best is the Ocean Trail, which is easily accessible and offers views of some of Maine's most spectacular scenery. The 27-mile Park Loop Road provides a good, although sometimes crowded, overview of the park. Admission is $5 per car.

Augusta If you happen to be in Augusta in late June and early July, you may want to participate in Whatever Week, the festivities of which culminate with the Whatever Race. There are 60 events including tournaments, parades, and whatever.

Bangor Some hymn tunes are named after the town in which the hymn writer was born, but the town of Bangor was named after the hymn tune. The hymn tune is not sung much in churches anymore, but the local pastor in the 18th century was singing it when he went to register the town name. The town was going to be named Sunbury. However, at the registry office when he was asked, "What's the name of it?" he thought they were asking for the name of the tune he was humming, and he replied, "Bangor." History doesn't record how long he stayed as pastor after that mistake.

Bangor Theological Seminary (15 Fifth St.) is housed in the home of Hannibal Hamlin, the man who was Abraham Lincoln's vice president during his first term in office. On the seminary grounds are several old buildings: the Old Commons Building (1827), the Maine Hall (1833), and the chapel (1838).

Bath The Winter Street Church (Washington and Winter Sts.) was built in 1843 and merges Gothic and Greek Revival styles. It dominates the landscape of the town green. And it is typically New England.

However, the Chocolate Church (804 Washington St.) is not typically New England. It was built in 1846 and named for its brown color. It has now been made into an arts center with performance space and an art gallery.

The Maine Maritime Museum and Shipyard (243 Washington St.) has a wonderful nautical collection. Visitors can also watch shipbuilders at work on classic Maine vessels at the restored shipyard. Admission is $7.75.

Bethel This quaint mountain town is a great place to view spectacular autumn foliage, generally the first two weeks in October. In the winter it's a great place to ski.

Blue Hill This town is known for its craft and pottery works, as well as for its historic homes. One of them is the Parson Fisher House (on Rte. 15), dating from 1814. The town's first minister designed and built it and he also made most of his own furniture and household articles. If you wonder about the paintings and the woodcuts inside the house, they were done by Parson Fisher too. Fisher was also a linguist, printer, and inventor. It is not known how well he preached. Admission fee; open in summer only.

Boothbay Harbor At the Boothbay Railway Village (one mile north of town on Rte. 127) you can take a ride on a coal-fired narrow gauge steam train that travels to an antique vehicle display. You will see early fire equipment, antique autos and trucks, and two restored railroad stations. Admission is adults $7, ages 3–12 $3, 2 and under free. Fee includes museum entrance and train ride.

GREAT PLACES TO ENJOY GOD'S CREATION

✔ Hiking the White Mountains, New Hampshire

✔ An autumn drive on Rte. 100, Vermont

✔ Mountain biking in Acadia National Park, Maine

Bristol The Harrington Meeting House (Old Harrington Rd.) has been restored to the way it looked in 1772 with its box pews. That same year the people of Bristol built the Walpole meetinghouse (on Rte. 129) for a sister settlement in South Bristol. They did a good job with it. The roof shingles are still watertight. The Bristol cabinetmakers made the pulpit and box pews.

Brunswick Harriet Beecher Stowe wrote her classic *Uncle Tom's Cabin* while her husband was a professor at Bowdoin College here. The Stowe house on Federal St. is now an inn, so you can sleep there overnight, but you can't go in to look around without staying all night. Incidentally, Harriet Beecher Stowe wasn't the only one who slept here. So did Longfellow and Hawthorne when they were students at Bowdoin College. (See Harriet Beecher Stowe also under Hartford and Litchfield, Conn., and Cincinnati, Ohio.)

Camden From here you can go on sailing vessels for voyages of a half-day to six days along the coast of Maine. Or if you wish, you can simply take a one-to-four-hour sightseeing cruise looking at Penobscot Bay. Contact the Chamber of Commerce (207-236-4404) for names of sailing vessels and cruises in the area.

Damariscotta St. Patrick's Church (west to Newcastle, then north two miles off US 1) is one of the oldest surviving Catholic churches in New England. Built in 1808, it has early Federal architecture and boasts a bell by Paul Revere in the steeple. Irish immigrants founded the parish.

Deer Isle In 1775 when the members of the First Congregational Church (Sunshine Rd.) hired a minister, they gave him a brand-new parsonage. Today the Reverend Peter Powers House, which dates from 1775, is one of the oldest houses on the island. It was a good match for both the Reverend Powers and the congregation. The pastor had lost his previous church because he was outspokenly against the British. The new congregation shared his views.

Eastport Boat excursions leave from here in the summer to view whales in the bay.

The town's Central Congregational Church (Middle St.) was built in 1829.

East Sebago Just 22 miles northwest of Portland, the Retreat Center of Rockcraft is a great place for individual reflection or group retreats. Open year-round, it is situated on Sebago Lake, where you can swim, fish, or canoe. Rockcraft is owned and operated by the Maine Conference of the United Church of Christ. Phone 207-947-5205 for more information and reservations or write P.O. Box 198, East Sebago, ME 04029.

Ellsworth The focal point in the town for more than 150 years has been the Ellsworth Congregational Church (Cross St.). You can't help but admire its spire and colonnade.

Farmington Falls The Old Union Meeting House here was built in 1827 by a Farmington carpenter named Benjamin Butler. The steeple is in the style of the noted London architect Christopher

Wren. Carpenter Butler never realized how many congregations his building would serve. A variety of denominations have used the structure before building their own. Its latest occupant is the Union Baptist Church.

Freeport L. L. Bean started his business here in 1912, promoting a better boot for Maine hunters or your money back. From the crowds in the parking lot alongside the gigantic mall-like building, you can guess that he has been quite successful. The town is now filled with outlet stores to fill every shopper's needs.

Gorham This small community outside of Portland was the birthplace of Ellen G. White, founder of the Seventh-day Adventist Church.

Mightier than the thunder of the great waters, mightier than the breakers of the sea—the LORD on high is mighty.

PSALM **93:4**

Kennebunk Among the stately trees and impressive New England houses, the First Parish Church (on Main St.) stands out. It was built in 1772 and has a bell cast by Paul Revere and Sons.

Kennebunkport The Seashore Trolley Museum on Log Cabin Rd. is unique. It has about 200 antique streetcars, collected from the U.S., Canada, and overseas. Admission is $8.

Mount Desert Island If the weather drives you inside on your vacation, consider visiting the Mount Desert Oceanarium at the end of Clark Point Rd. near Beals St. in Southwest Harbor. When the weather clears up, you may want to try whale watching with a cruise from any number of outfits here. One is Whale Watcher, Inc., at 1 West St., Harbor Place.

Old Orchard Beach This popular beach resort is located 12 miles south of Portland. One of its key attractions is the Palace Playground, an amusement park that features a variety of rides and a restored 1906 carousel.

Poland Spring If the name Poland Spring sounds familiar, it is probably because of its bottled water that is now in stores everywhere. In the 1800s a man claimed to be miraculously cured by the waters of Poland Spring, and the rest is history. Unfortunately tours of the famous spring are not available.

Portland The Children's Museum of Maine (142 Free St.) is a hands-on museum that allows children to become a Maine lobsterman, a storekeeper, a computer expert, or an astronaut. How do you like that for variety?

The Williston Congregational Church (32 Thomas St.) was the birthplace of the Christian Endeavor movement in 1881. The church itself dates from 1878.

The Cathedral of the Immaculate Conception (307 Congress St.) is the seat of the Maine dioceses. The stained glass windows are noteworthy.

The oldest church in the city is First Parish Church (425 Congress St.). It was built in 1825 and 1826 on the site of the parish's wooden meetinghouse where Maine's constitution had been drafted a few years before. The parish itself dates back to 1674 and the congregation tries to keep the church looking as it had when it was built. The pulpit Bible dates back to the 1820s.

The 1828 Mariner's Church (368 Fore St.) is no longer a church but it rates a look because of the thinking behind it. It was a church for sailors in the dock area of a rum-trading town, so survival wouldn't have been easy. The church was built on three levels, with shops on the first floor paying rent that financed the church and its missions. The third floor was where the chapel was set. The building stands mostly unchanged; the shops are still on the first floor, but the church is no longer used for worship.

Henry Wadsworth Longfellow's home and grounds (489 Congress St. in downtown Portland) can be toured along with the Maine History Gallery, which is adjacent. The home is open daily June through October. Admission is $5. (See Longfellow also under Sudbury Center, Mass.; Haddonfield, N.J.; and Grand Pré, Nova Scotia.)

Casco Bay Lines offers a leisurely guided boat tour along the coast of Maine from Portland to Bailey Island from June through September. The cost is $14.50 for adults, $6.50 for children. Phone 207-774-7871 for details and departure times.

From May through October the *Scotia Prince* will ferry you and your car from Portland to Yarmouth, Nova Scotia. The ferry leaves Portland at 9 P.M. and arrives in Nova Scotia at 9 A.M. the next day. A restaurant is available for meals. Phone 800-341-7540 for details and price information. Prices vary according to the season and the number of people in your party.

Sabbathday Lake The Sabbathday Lake Shaker Village is the only remaining active Shaker community in the world. Founded in 1783 by Shaker missionaries, it remains home to the only remaining Shakers, a group of fewer than ten people. While this is a place of work and worship, 6 of the 18 existing structures are open to the public, including the Shaker Museum and a library. Guided tours of the premises are available to visitors. Admission for adults is $6, children $2. During the summer months a variety of workshops, concerts, and lectures are open to the public, and visitors can purchase the community's high-quality herbal teas and culinary herbs in the Shaker store, through a mail order catalog, or over the Internet. There are no dining facilities on site, but a number of restaurants are located within the immediate area. (See Shakers also under Pittsfield, Mass.; Concord and Enfield, N.H.; Chatham, N.Y.; South Union and Harrodsburg, Ky.; Lebanon, Ohio; and Marysville, Wash.)

Saco The Aquaboggan Water Park (four miles north on US 1) offers more than 40 acres of water and land attractions including 5 water slides.

Waldoboro Germans settled this community in 1748 and began building ships and sailing in five-masted schooners. They also built the beautiful Old German Church (Lutheran) on Rte. 32 and conducted services in German for many years.

Waterville At Colby College (two miles west of town) you'll find a Walcker organ that was designed by Albert Schweitzer. It is in Lorimer Chapel. There are also books, manuscripts, and letters of major Maine authors, such as Edwin Arlington Robinson and Sarah Jewett.

Wells At the Wells Auto Museum (on US 1) you can view about 80 antique cars dating all the way back to 1900. Also on display is a collection of nickelodeons, picture machines, and antique arcade games. Admission is $3.50.

Wiscasset The Musical Wonder House (18 High St.) has a rare collection of antique music boxes, victrolas, and talking machines. The owner plays the Steinway player grand pianola and other instruments for you. It is located in a 30-room sea captain's house, which is worth seeing in its own right.

We haven't checked it out, but Wiscasset claims that the first ice cream was made here and served to General Lafayette. Just in case they are right, why not buy a cone or two the next time you stop by?

York York Village (207 York St.) has many historic houses, but perhaps the most intriguing is the Old Gaol, built in 1720 and one of the oldest English public buildings in the United States. You will see its dungeons, cramped cells, jailers' quarters, and an oozing, wet hole in the ground where difficult prisoners were confined. The prison was used until the 1860s. The Pilgrims had established a trading post at this site in 1624.

■ MASSACHUSETTS

Tourist Info
Phone 800-227-MASS
Web sites
  Entire state   www.mass-vacation.com
  Boston   www.bostonusa.com
  Boston Symphony Orchestra   www.bso.org
  Hancock Shaker Village   www.hancockshakervillage.org
For a complete list of updated links, visit www.christiantraveler.com

Amesbury The John Greenleaf Whittier House at 86 Friend St. is worth a visit. The Garden Room, where he wrote *Snow-Bound* and many other works, is unchanged. Whittier was not only a distinguished poet but also a staunch abolitionist and a dedicated Christian. Also worth a visit is the Amesbury Friends Meeting House, which the Whittier family attended. Whittier, chairman of the building committee for the meetinghouse, drew up the plans. A silver plaque now marks the spot where Whittier sat in church.

Andover In the "America House" on Main St., Samuel F. Smith wrote "My Country, 'Tis of Thee." Farther down Main St., the Phelps House marks the place where America's first religious newspaper was founded. Tours are available for a donation.

Barnstable The West Parish Congregational Church on Meeting-house Way in West Barnstable is said to be the oldest Congregational church building in the country. The congregation was actually established in London in 1616 before emigrating to America.

Beverly During the time of the Salem witchcraft trials, the wife of the Reverend John Hale, the local minister in Beverly, was accused of witchcraft. But she was so far above reproach that the case against her collapsed. The Hale House (1694), located at 39 Hale Street, was built by her husband.

Two outstanding evangelical schools on attractive campuses are located in the area: Gordon College at Wenham and Gordon-Conwell Seminary in South Hamilton. Both are denominationally independent.

Boston This city is extraordinarily rich in American history, and that history is interspersed with Christianity. A number of historic churches, for instance, are best remembered not for their worship services but for the roles they played in the colonists' battle for independence.

Take a walk along the historic Freedom Trail, a 2.5-mile walking tour that begins at the visitors center at Boston Common. There you'll find maps and other brochures to inform you on your walk. The actual course of the trail is marked by a red line on the sidewalk, which winds its way past 16 of Boston's most important historic sites. Many, but not all, sites are free.

Park Street Church (1 Park St.) is called "Brimstone Corner," not because of its "fire and brimstone" preaching, but because brimstone for gunpowder was stored here during the War of 1812. William Garrison, the noted abolitionist, preached his first anti-slavery address here in 1829. Samuel Smith's hymn "America" was first sung here in 1831. Old Granary Burial Ground, next to the church, is the resting place of Revolutionary heroes Samuel Adams, John Hancock, Paul Revere, and victims of the Boston Massacre. In the 20th century the National Association of Evangelicals was organized here in 1942. An evangelical bastion in New England, the church was pastored by Harold John Ockenga from 1926 to 1969. Ockenga was the first president of the National Association of Evangelicals. Familiar hymns are chimed from the church's carillon throughout the day.

King's Chapel (Tremont at School Sts.) was the first Anglican church in New England, organized in 1686. The building was built in 1754 and in 1786 it became the first Unitarian church in the nation. Inside the chapel is Paul Revere's largest bell, weighing 2,500 pounds. Revere thought it was also his sweetest sounding bell.

Old North Church (193 Salem St.), founded in 1723, is the oldest church building in the city. More properly known as Christ Church, it is the church connected with Paul Revere's historic ride. From the steeple's highest window were hung two lanterns, sending Revere to warn the Minutemen in Lexington that the British were coming on the night of April 18, 1775. Speaking of Paul Revere, his house is the oldest home in Boston, located at 19 North Sq. It was already 100 years old before its famous occupant took his midnight ride. Admission fee is $2.50.

The Old South Meeting House (310 Washington St.) was built in 1729 and is the city's second-oldest church. Many of the ardent pre-Revolutionary town meetings were held here, including the one called by Samuel Adams regarding the British tax on tea. (And the preferred drink of most Americans ever since that time has been coffee.)

The New Old South Church (which sounds like an anomaly) is where the congregation of the Old South Church moved in 1875, when the previous neighborhood got too noisy. Here (on the corner of Boylston and Dartmouth Sts.) the church has 15th-century stained glass windows depicting the prophets, the evangelists, and the miracles.

The medieval-style Trinity Church, at 2065 Clarendon St., was built in 1877 and was designed by the noted architect Henry Hobson Richardson. It became Richardson's "noblest work." Little wonder; its gigantic tower will remind visitors of the domes of Venice and Istanbul. Inside the church are frescoes and stained glass windows, as well as a statue honoring Phillips Brooks, who was rector of this Episcopal church for 22 years. Trinity Church was the inspired idea of Brooks, who hired Richardson to design the building. Brooks is better known as the author of "O Little Town of Bethlehem."

Copp's Hill Burying Ground (Hull and Snowhill Sts.) is where Cotton Mather is buried. During the Revolution, British cannon on the burying ground were trained on Charlestown and Bunker Hill across the Charles River.

African Meeting House (Smith Ct., off Joy St.) was built by free blacks in 1806 as a religious and educational center. It is the oldest African American church building in the country. In 1832 it was the site of the founding of the New England Anti-Slavery Society. Today it is part of the Museum of Afro-American History. No admission fee but donations are accepted.

For all computer buffs, the Computer Museum (Museum Wharf at 300 Congress St.) will transport you from the past to the present. It includes more than 125 hands-on exhibits, giving you the history of computers, beginning in 1940, and even includes a two-story walk-through computer.

The Children's Museum (300 Congress St.) has many hands-on exhibits, focusing on science, cultural diversity, human biology, and the nature of disabilities. Admission is $7. Also of interest to kids is the New England Aquarium on the Central Wharf. Visitors can

> The LORD your God . . . went ahead of you on your journey, in fire by night and in a cloud by day, to search out places for you to camp and to show you the way you should go.
> DEUTERONOMY 1:32–33

see seals, penguins, lots of sharks, and other sea creatures, including a four-story, 187,000-gallon coral reef tank. Dolphins and sea lions perform in the ship *Discovery,* moored nearby. Admission is $11.

The Bible Exhibit (Belvidere St., opposite the Prudential Center) features rare biblical treasures, audiovisuals, a historic timeline, a children's story corner, and a large Plexiglas wall map with lighted journeys of six biblical figures.

An Italian restaurant named Lucia's (415 Hanover St.) may have more people coming in to see its ceiling frescoes than to try its lasagna. The ceiling frescoes show the twelve apostles and the Last Supper, and because it is an Italian restaurant, it also shows Marco Polo's visit to China. One of the most famous churches in the area is Old St. Stephen's (401 Hanover St.), which was the colonial brainchild of Charles Bulfinch.

Cambridge Christ Church (Zero Garden St. at the Common) is a Georgian-style Episcopal church. Built in 1759, it is the oldest in Cambridge. During the Revolution, it was used as a barracks.

Harvard University was founded in 1636 to train young men for the ministry. The Puritan settlers who had come here in 1630 gave high priority to theological education. A Charleston pastor, John Harvard, had given half his estate and library to the college, and when he died in 1638, the school was named Harvard in his honor. Today its library with more than eight million volumes is one of the world's finest, and its Fogg Art Museum is one of the best university art museums anywhere.

Charlemont Settled in 1749, this town, which is halfway down the Mohawk Trail stretching from Millers Falls to Williamstown, provides "Mohawk Trail Concerts" from May to October in its Charlemont Confederated Church (75 Bridge St.). The concerts feature classic American and European chamber music. Phone 617-625-9511 for information.

Concord The first military encounters of the American Revolution occurred here. You will see Battle Green, a two-acre piece of land where Minuteman John Parker assembled his troops to await the arrival of the British. Parker's role is commemorated by the Minuteman statue. The town's significance in the American Revolution is well-known, but what isn't well-known is that it was named because of a concord the early settlers had with the Native Americans in this place. Nor is it well-known that the famous Concord grape was developed here in 1849.

The Old Manse (Monument St. at North Bridge) was built in 1770 and served as the parsonage for Concord's earliest ministers, including Rev. William Emerson, Ralph Waldo Emerson's grandfather. Nathaniel Hawthorne also lived here for a while and made it the setting for his *Mosses from an Old Manse*.

Orchard House (399 Lexington Rd.) was where Louisa May Alcott wrote *Little Women*.

The Wayside (455 Lexington Rd.) was the home at different times of Nathaniel Hawthorne and Margaret Sidney, author of *Five Little Peppers*.

It won't be as secluded as it was for Thoreau, but you can walk the shores of Walden Pond. A 1.7- mile circuit winds through the woods along the water.

Danvers Rebecca Nurse was a godly woman who was accused of and executed for witchcraft during the Salem hysteria of 1692. Her homestead, here in Danvers (142 Pine St.) is a New England saltbox, and the house includes restored rooms with early New England furnishings. Among the outbuildings is a reproduction of the 1672 Salem village meetinghouse. At 176 Hobart St. is the

Witchcraft Victims' Memorial, which includes names of those who died as well as quotes from 8 of the 19 victims.

Deerfield Main St. in this historic town is one historic house after another. It looks serene now with its 1824 church and its houses dating back to 1720. But it endured Indian massacres and other tensions in those early days. The Ashley House, for instance, dates from 1730 and was the home of the minister during the Revolutionary War period. Pastor Jonathan Ashley was a Tory and supported the British. The congregation, which supported the Revolution, tried to bar him from the church and deny him his salary. If you look at the interior of the house, it appears that he wouldn't have suffered too much as long as he stayed inside.

Dennis The first minister in this town was Josiah Dennis, who began preaching in 1725. He continued his ministry here for 38 years and after he died in 1763, it was decided to name the town after him. You can visit the Josiah Dennis Manse (77 Nobscusset Rd.) and see not only the house but also a maritime wing featuring naval memorabilia. There is also an old schoolhouse on the grounds.

GREAT PLACES TO ENJOY GOD'S CREATION

✔ Biking along the Cape Cod National Seashore, Massachusetts

✔ Picnicking at the Wildlife Refuge, Block Island, Rhode Island

Fall River St. Anne's Church and Shrine (S. Main St., facing Kennedy Park) was designed by a Canadian architect in 1906, using Vermont blue marble and stained glass windows from France.

Haverhill The John Greenleaf Whittier Birthplace (305 Whittier Rd.) was the Whittier homestead since the late 1600s and the setting for some of Whittier's best-known poems. His writing desk and his mother's bedroom are here.

Hingham The Puritan congregation of Old Ship Church first met in 1635. The present building (90 Main St.) is the last remaining Puritan meetinghouse in the United States. Built by ships' carpenters, the church has curved oak roof frames like the knees of a ship,

THE PURITANS IN MASSACHUSETTS

So important are the Puritans to Americans' fundamental beliefs that many stories abound regarding their faith and motives for coming to the New World. There are serious questions about how much of those stories is actual fact.

This much is true. At least some of the early settlers of Massachusetts in 1620 were Puritans, religious people for whom the established church had grown too liberal and who were persecuted for their faith. They were looking for a place in which they could establish a religious community, a place where they could find the freedom to worship as they saw fit. And at least some of those early settlers dreamed of creating a community that would serve as a beacon to others, a "city on a hill."

Visitors to Massachusetts can get a pretty accurate view of how the Puritans lived at Plimoth Plantation. Painstaking research has gone into re-creating authentic buildings, tools, crafts, clothing, even the dialects spoken by interpreters and their knowledge of the world (which stops at about 1627).

But the legacy of those early Pilgrims permeates not only the Cape Cod area, but the entire nation. While the Puritans did not believe in religious tolerance—they condoned only their own beliefs—there is no question that those early seekers of religious freedom set a precedent that has been repeated countless times, by countless believers. The Puritans, in spite of their own beliefs, were instrumental in creating a culture of religious freedom that is uniquely American.

and the roof structure resembles an inverted ship's hull.

Lexington The Minuteman Statue commemorating the place where the first Minutemen died from British bullets stands on Battle Green in Lexington. At the time of the initial fighting, there was a church or meetinghouse on the square (near where the Minuteman Statue stands today). The Hancock-Clarke House (35 Hancock St.) was the parsonage of the Reverend Jonas Clarke at the time and it was here that John Hancock and Samuel Adams hid themselves from the British authorities.

Today the most notable church in town is Grace Chapel, with a vigorous ministry and an average attendance in excess of 2,000. The pastor is evangelical author and speaker Gordon MacDonald.

Marblehead The original *Spirit of '76* painting as well as the 1684 deed to the town from the Manepashemet Indians are displayed at Abbott Hall (Town Hall on Washington Rd.).

Martha's Vineyard Before it became a summer resort, it was a whaling town. During the 1830s Oak Bluffs here was the site of annual summer camp meetings for church groups. The Martha's Vineyard Camp Meeting Association, also known as Cottage City, is known for its tiny cottages, dripping with gingerbread and painted in bright colors. The Cottage Museum, open to the public, is located at 1 Trinity Park, Oak Bluffs. The Old Whaling Church, built in 1843, is now a performing arts center at 89 Main St., Edgartown.

New Bedford Across the street from the New Bedford Whaling Museum on Johnny Cake Hill is Seaman's Bethel. In the seventh chapter of *Moby Dick,* it is mentioned that almost all sailors stop here before going out to sea (see Melville under Pittsfield, Mass.). In the basement is a simple chapel into which sailors could come anytime. Upstairs is the regular New England chapel, often called the Whaleman's chapel. It has a pulpit shaped like a ship's prow.

The Children's Museum (on Gulf Rd. in South Dartmouth) features two floors of hands-on exhibits and 60 acres of nature trails. There are special programs in the summer and on weekends.

Northampton The Great Awakening began here in 1734 as Jonathan Edwards was completing a series of sermons on 1 Corinthians 13, the love chapter. First Church at Maine and Old South Sts. was Edwards's church.

Northfield Evangelist Dwight L. Moody was born in this village in 1837. He was converted at the Mount Vernon Congregational Church in Boston and began his evangelistic ministry in Chicago.

Pittsfield In 1790 the Shakers organized their third settlement in the United States. The Hancock Shaker Village, located five miles west of Pittsfield, captures the Shaker commitment to quality of craftsmanship, love, and simplicity. The religious colony here closed in 1960, so the site is now a museum. Shaker furniture is now housed in 20 restored buildings, including the Round Stone Barn. (See Shakers under Sabbathday Lake, Maine; Concord and Enfield, N.H.; Old Chatham, N.Y.; South Union and Harrodsburg, Ky.; Lebanon, Ohio; and Marysville, Wash.)

Arrowhead (760 Holmes Rd.) is where Herman Melville wrote *Moby Dick* (see also *Moby Dick* under New Bedford, Mass.). This 1780 house is now the headquarters of the Berkshire County Historical Society.

Plymouth Plymouth is the site at which the Mayflower Pilgrims were said to have first set foot in the new land. You can tour the re-created 1627 village of Plimoth Plantation (three miles south on Rte. 3A and Warren Ave.). Costumed actors play the roles of villagers carrying out their daily tasks. The village has 14 houses and the Fort-Meetinghouse. *Mayflower II* is a 90-foot bark, a full-size reproduction of the ship that carried the Pilgrims. When you climb aboard, you can appreciate better what those early settlers endured on their 66-day journey. Admission to the plantation and *Mayflower II* is $18.50, to the plantation only, $15.

The Mayflower Experience, next to the Governor Bradford Motel on Water St., has three theaters to help you experience the historic crossing of the Atlantic by our forefathers.

Nearby, the Wampanoag Summer Encampment re-creates a native village of the same era.

As for Plymouth Rock itself, be ready for a disappointment. First of all, there is some disagreement over whether the Pilgrims' first step in the New World was onto this rock. At any rate, this symbol of liberty has been moved three times and has been chipped away by tourists looking for souvenirs. Today it would hardly be big enough to hold two Pilgrims. But who cares. It's still Plymouth Rock. Visit what's left of it in an extravagant pavilion on Water St. at the foot of North St. There is no fee to view the rock.

Provincetown It was while the *Mayflower* was anchored at Provincetown Harbor, before it landed at Plymouth, that the Mayflower Compact was signed aboard the ship. The document set up the colony's first government. The first party of Pilgrims came ashore here, and a bronze tablet at Commercial St. and Beach Hwy. commemorates that landing. There is also a Pilgrim Monument and Museum here on High Pole Hill. This is a 252-foot-tall granite tower, which provides an excellent view of the area. Admission is $5.

Quincy The United First Parish Church (1306 Hancock St. at Washington St.) was the church of the Adams family. Both John Adams and John Quincy Adams and their wives are buried here. The present church building is dated from 1828.

Roxbury John Eliot, pastor of the Puritan church here from 1631 until his death in 1690, was the first missionary to the Indians and translated the Bible into the local Indian tongue in 1663.

Salem The House of the Seven Gables (54 Turner St.) is the setting for Hawthorne's classic novel by the same name. Hawthorne lived in Salem in the early 1800s.

Salem today is best known for its witchcraft trials. The Witch House (310^1/2 Essex St.) is the 1642 home of the trial judge Jonathan Corwin.

Stockbridge A monument at the corner of Church and Main Sts. commemorates Jonathan Edwards, pastor, evangelist, and philosopher. Across the street stands the Congregational church erected on the site where Edwards preached to the Indians in a much smaller and humbler building.

The Norman Rockwell Museum (Rte. 183) is also worth visiting. The world's largest collection of his original paintings is on display here. Admission is $8. (See Rockwell also under Jaffrey, N.H., and Arlington, Vt.).

The Children's Chimes Bell Tower (Main St.) was erected in 1878 by a noted lawyer, David Dudley Field, to honor his grandchildren. There are daily carillon concerts in the summer.

Mission House (Main and Sergeant Sts.) was built in 1739 by missionary John Sergeant and his wife. He preceded Jonathan Edwards in ministering to the Indians in the area. The house is now a museum of colonial life. It is open for tours only during the summer months.

Sturbridge Old Sturbridge Village (on US 20W, two miles west of I-84, exit 2) is an authentic re-creation of a rural New England community of the early 18th century. Of particular interest are the 1832 Baptist church, the 1735 Stephen Fitch house, and the 1707 Fenno house. Also take a look at the Richardson house parsonage, which dates from 1740. It's a red and white saltbox, and inside are handwoven carpets.

Sudbury Center The Martha Mary Chapel at Longfellow's Wayside Inn (Wayside Inn Rd. off US 20) was built and dedicated by Henry Ford in 1940. It is used mostly for weddings. The Wayside Inn, built in 1702, is a historical and literary shrine and also America's oldest operating inn. The inn was featured in Longfellow's *Tales of a Wayside Inn.* (See Longfellow also under Portland, Maine; Haddonfield, N.J.; and Grand Pré, Nova Scotia.)

Tanglewood Located in the beautiful Berkshire Mountains, this is the summer home of the Boston Symphony Orchestra. The orchestra's concerts feature a variety of music styles, including jazz and pop, as well as classical music.

Williamstown It was at Williams College here that Henry Van Dyke wrote the hymn "Joyful, Joyful We Adore Thee" for the college president. It was also here that the "Haystack Prayer Meeting" was held as four students took shelter under a haystack during a rainstorm and prayed about foreign missions. The first American foreign missionary, Adoniram Judson, was one of the four. The Haystack Monument here has been erected to commemorate the beginning of the American foreign missions movement.

The Sterling and Francine Clark Art Institute here has an outstanding collection, ranging from Botticelli's *Virgin and Child* to works by Monet, Mary Cassatt, and Winslow Homer.

Worcester This is an industrial center with hundreds of manufacturing plants but it also contains the excellent Worcester Art Museum (55 Salisbury St.). The first floor displays Spoleto's *The Last Supper* fresco; the second floor has El Greco's *Repentant Magdalen,* and the third floor, featuring American painters, includes Edward Hicks's *Peaceable Kingdom.*

■New Hampshire

Tourist Info
Phone 603-271-2343
Web site
  Entire state   www.visitnh.com
For a complete list of updated links, visit www.christiantraveler.com

Acworth In New Hampshire you keep saying, "This has to be one of the most beautiful churches in the state." You are sure to say that about the United Church of Acworth, built in 1821. It has a majestic bell tower with a Paladin window.

Charleston The Foundation for Biblical Research (43 Paris Ave.) is located on a historic estate that dates back to 1747. Open all year, it is a nonprofit Bible study center.

Concord The Shakers certainly knew how to choose beautiful sites for their settlements. The Canterbury Shaker Village (15 miles north on I-93) is one of two in New Hampshire and it is the larger and more interesting of the two. The Shaker Village here is a living museum of Shaker crafts, architecture, and inventions. In 1774 two Shakers established this community. More than 20 buildings remain. Among their inventions that you will see here are the circular saw and the clothespin. (See Shakers also under Sabbathday Lake, Maine; Pittsfield, Mass.; Enfield, N.H.; Old Chatham, N.Y.; South Union and Harrodsburg, Ky.; Lebanon, Ohio; and Marysville, Wash.)

Dover In the 1650s and 1660s Quaker missionaries came to this town, and before too long the Puritan authorities had three Quaker women tied to a cart, stripped to the waist, and whipped as the cart was pulled through town. But the women came back the next year and by that time a third of the population had become Quakers. Soon Dover's Quaker Society became one of the largest in New England with two meetinghouses erected. The current Society of Friends Meeting House (141 Central Ave.) dates from 1768. The parents of the poet John Greenleaf Whittier were married here.

Dublin Mark Twain used to spend summers here, but today it is known as the home of *The Old Farmers Almanac* and *Yankee Magazine*.

Enfield The second Shaker site in New Hampshire is in the western part of the state, located in this tiny village. The Enfield Shaker Museum displays Shaker artifacts and crafts, just as you would expect a Shaker Museum to do. (See Shakers under Sabbathday Lake, Maine; Pittsfield, Mass.; Concord, N.H.; Old Chatham, N.Y.; South Union and Harrodsburg, Ky.; Lebanon, Ohio; and Marysville, Wash.)

Fitzwilliam Rhododendron State Park (off Rte. 119, two miles west of town) contains more than 16 acres of (guess what?) rhododendrons and, as you can imagine, it is ablaze in color in mid-July. You won't find a better place to admire this much of this beautiful shrub anywhere around. Admission is $2.50 on week-ends and holidays; free at other times.

Franconia Notch State Park The Old Man of the Mountain was dis-covered in 1805. It really looks like a man's face, but it was formed naturally of five layers of granite and is 40 feet high from the brow to the chin. Sometimes it is called the "Great Stone Face." Nathaniel Hawthorne immortalized it in his story "The Great Stone Face." Daniel Webster said, "Men hang out their signs indicative of their respective trades: shoemakers hang out a gigantic shoe; jewelers, a monster watch . . . but up in the mountains of New Hampshire, God Almighty has hung out a sign to show that there He makes men."

Franklin The Congregational Christian Church at 47 W. Main St., off US 3, is the church that Daniel Webster attended. A bust of Webster is outside.

Glen Heritage-New Hampshire (two miles south on Rte. 16) is a creative park built around 30 theatrical sets. You take a walk through the sets and experience 30 key events in the 300-year his-tory of the state. Each set has animation, sounds, and smells—if your imagination needs some stimulus. There is an admission fee.

Story Land is a village of storybook settings for children. Included are Cinderella's castle, Heidi's grandfather's house, and the old woman who lived in a shoe, plus 17 theme rides on 30 acres.

Hanover Dartmouth College here was one of the results of the First Great Awakening, the revival that swept the colonies in the 18th century. Dartmouth's charter specified the school's intent to reach the Indian tribes and to educate English youth.

The Saint-Gaudens National Historic Site, south of Hanover via Rte. 12A, is the former residence and studio of Augustus Saint-Gaudens, noted sculptor. More than 100 works are on display. Admission is $2.

Jaffrey Cathedral of the Pines is an international nondenomina-tional shrine commemorating American war dead. A couple who lost their son in World War II built it as a national memorial to all Americans who lost their lives during wartime. The Memorial Bell Tower is dedicated to women who died in service. The four plaques above the tower arches were designed by Norman Rockwell. (See Rockwell also under Stockbridge, Mass., and Arlington, Vt.)

The Old Meeting House here was built between 1775 and 1799. What is remarkable is that behind it you will see the 1801 grave of Amos Fortune. Fortune was a slave who bought his freedom, set up a tannery, and then endowed the local church and school. The inscription on his tombstone reads: "To the memory of Amos Fortune who was born free in Africa, a slave in America, he purchased liberty, professed Christianity, lived reputably, and died hopefully."

The Monadnock Bible Conference (78 Dublin Rd.) is a summer Bible conference facility in this historic summer resort community on the eastern slopes of the Monadnock Mountains.

Jefferson It's a long way from the wild West, but Six Gun City (four miles east on US 2) may be the closest you will get to it in New England. It is a re-created frontier village, complete with cowboy skits, a fort, a carriage and sleigh museum, a miniature horse show, pony and burro rides—you get the idea.

Keene An annual event here is a drama presented at The Olde Homestead (four miles south on Rte. 42 in Swanzey Center). Based on the biblical story of the Prodigal Son, the play depicts life in the village of Swanzey Center during the 1880s.

The Pilgrim Pines Conference Center is located in the little village of Swanzey Center. The village also has four covered bridges.

Laconia Surf Coaster (in Weirs Beach about six miles northeast of Laconia) is a family water park on Lake Winnipesaukee. It includes inner tube rides, water slides, and wave pools.

From Weirs Beach you can also enjoy a scenic train ride along the lake on the Winnipesaukee Railroad or you can get on a 46-foot sloop called the *Queen of Winnipesaukee* (don't worry, they won't ask you to spell it). This is a 90-minute lake cruise, or if you prefer, a two-hour moonlight cruise.

Squam Lake, just northwest of Winnipesaukee, was the filming location for the Henry and Jane Fonda movie *On Golden Pond*.

Manchester The Currier Gallery of Art (192 Orange St.) is one of New England's finest small museums. It includes 13th- to 20th-century European and American paintings and sculpture.

Meredith On the shores of Lake Winnipesaukee, you can catch the scenic Winnipesaukee Railroad here as well as at Weirs Beach. But you might want to look around this town a bit first. Annalee's

Doll Museum is a fascinating stop because it stocks every doll imaginable and has a huge Christmas section besides.

Moultonboro The Castle in the Clouds is almost magical. It is fashioned as a medieval castle and it gives the impression that it is floating in air. The builder of the castle spent seven million dollars before World War I to have it built. It has 16 rooms and 8 bathrooms.

Mount Washington Mount Washington is the tallest peak in the White Mountains and the highest north of the Carolinas and east of the Rockies. The top of Mount Washington is said to be the windiest place on earth, so no matter the temperature at the mountain's base, bring warm clothes with you before you begin your ascent. You can drive up the mountain in the summer and fall if the wind isn't too wild and the weather isn't too uncertain. A better choice may be to take the cog railway from the base (four miles east of the junction of US 2 and US 302) to the top (cost is $39). When it was built in 1869, it was regarded as a marvel of modern technology and was the world's first mountain-climbing cog railway. Don't expect the Metroliner. This is a three-hour trip, and it is the second-steepest railway track in the world (see Canon City, Colo., for the steepest). One trestle called "Jacob's Ladder" registers a 37 percent grade.

The earth is the LORD's and everything in it.
PSALM 24:1

Newington The Old Meeting House (Nimble Hill Rd.) is the oldest meetinghouse in the state. It was built in 1712 and it is still used for services. The parsonage (the Old Parsonage) is operated as a museum by the Newington Historical Society.

North Conway The Conway Scenic Railroad (Depot on Main St.) has both steam and diesel trains that leave from this restored Victorian station for an 11-mile round-trip through the Saco River valley. It takes a little less than an hour.

Peterborough The New England Marionette Opera (Main St.) is the largest marionette facility in the country devoted to opera (it may be the only one!). It gives performances from mid-May into December on Saturday evenings and Sunday afternoons. By the way, Peterborough may have been the model for the play *Our Town* by Thornton Wilder.

Portsmouth The Strawbery Banke Museum (Hancock and Marcy Sts.) is the restoration of a ten-acre historic waterfront neighborhood with 42 buildings dating as far back as 1762. The area was first settled in 1630 and named for the wild strawberries that grew everywhere. The name was changed to Portsmouth in 1653. Several historic homes have been made into workshops geared to the family so you can watch or listen to seminars on colonial crafts.

Portsmouth's MacPheadris-Warner House (150 Daniel St.) is the city's oldest brick residence, built around 1716. Most intriguing about the place are the painted murals in its stair hall. They may be the oldest such paintings in the nation. One of them depicts the biblical episode of Abraham about to sacrifice Isaac as he was interrupted by an angel. The others are not biblical: One shows a hawk attacking a chicken and another a British soldier on horseback. No one knows if the murals were meant to relate to each other in some mysterious way.

At 101 Chapel St. is St. John's Church, built in 1807 on the same site where Queen's Chapel had been erected in 1732. The church's Brattle organ, which was imported to Massachusetts from England before 1739, is the oldest operating pipe organ in the nation. On display is a rare copy of the 1717 Vinegar Bible, so named for a misprint of vineyard.

Water Country (off exit 6 of Rte. 85 on Rte.1) is New England's largest water park and it has a new Pirates Cove Kids Adventure area, along with a variety of rides for older kids too.

Rumney The Rumney Bible Conference has a long history as an evangelical Bible conference and retreat center.

■RHODE ISLAND

Tourist Info
Phone 800-556-2484
Web sites
Entire state   www.visitrhodeisland.com
Providence   www.providencevisitor.com
For a complete list of updated links, visit www.christiantraveler.com

Barrington An early settler here was Obadiah Holmes, who founded one of the first Baptist churches (1649). The town is named for Lord Barrington, who was a strong advocate of religious freedom. Barrington College, formerly Providence Bible College, was located here before it merged with Gordon College in Massachusetts. Zion Bible Institute now occupies the campus. (See Gordon College under Beverly, Mass.)

Block Island Located ten miles southeast of Newport in the Atlantic is Block Island. It has great natural beauty, and since it is quite small (seven miles by three miles), cycling is an ideal way to sightsee. Enjoy the beautiful seashore, including the Mohegan Bluffs with their 200-foot-high cliffside view of the ocean. The National Wildlife Refuge located on the island is a great place for a picnic.

Newport Trinity Church (Queen Anne Square) has been in continuous use since it was built in 1726. Its tall white spire is visible for miles. The exterior design is based on a Christopher Wren model. The interior has Tiffany windows, a three-tier wineglass pulpit, and an organ personally tested by Handel before it was shipped from London. The organ was a gift of Bishop George Berkeley in 1733. George Washington attended services here. Patriots stripped the church of its royal insignia but they left the crown on the steeple and the organ. Tours are by appointment only.

Seventh Day Baptist Meeting House (82 Touro St.) is a historic 1729 church built by master builder Richard Munday. The Seventh Day Baptist denomination was founded here in 1671. The church is notable for its wineglass pulpit and fine stairs. The Newport Historical Society is housed here.

Friends Meeting House (Farewell and Marlborough Sts.) was built in 1699, making it the oldest religious building in Newport, and then expanded in 1729 and 1807. The first Quakers to come to America settled here in 1657. Early Quaker costumes are on display. Tours are available by appointment.

The Touro Synagogue Historic Site features the oldest synagogue (1763) in America and contains the oldest Torah in the country. Located at 72 Touro St., its worship services follow the Sephardic Orthodox ritual of its founders.

North Kingston Smith's Castle (located 1.5 miles north of the town on US 1) is one of the oldest plantation houses in the country and the only known existing house where Roger Williams preached. It was burned down in 1676 but then restored in 1678. The furnishings today date from the 17th and 18th centuries.

The Old Narragansett Church (Episcopal) was built in 1707 and is located on Church Lane. Also worth seeing is the Gilbert Stuart Birthplace (815 Gilbert Stuart Rd.). Stuart is perhaps best known as George Washington's portraitist, and his portrait of the first president is one of the most frequently reproduced paintings of all time.

On Main St. in North Kingston are 20 houses all built before 1804, and on side streets there are about 40 more.

Pawtucket What makes the Children's Museum here unique is the fact that it is housed in a fantastic 1841 Queen Anne–style house (58 Walcott St.). Of course, the fact that there's a room-sized floor map of Rhode Island to crawl on and a Narragansett Bay to push boats along and some Amtrak rails for trains to chug along helps too.

Slate Memorial Park (Newport Ave.) is also fun for the kids. It has the oldest "stander" carousel in the world. Built in 1895, it was installed here in 1910 and has been operating ever since.

The First Baptist Church was established here in 1792, although the present building is newer. St. Paul's Church (Episcopal) was built in 1902, the Pawtucket Church (United Church) in 1868, and the Church of St. John the Baptist (Catholic) in 1927.

Portsmouth Children love Green Animals (380 Cory's Lane), a creative garden of more than 80 trees and shrubs sculpted in the European style to resemble dogs, camels, goats, roosters, bears, and even police officers. A Victorian toy collection is housed inside the country estate's 19th-century white clapboard house.

Providence Roger Williams founded the city in 1636 after clashes with the Puritans drove him out of Massachusetts. He dedicated the new settlement to "persons distressed for conscience" and named it "in commemoration of God's Providence." Soon not only members of various Protestant denominations came here, but also Jews and Catholics found refuge here. In essence, freedom of religion was established as a model for the nation to follow. Three years later in 1639, Williams started the first Baptist church in America. At 75 N. Main St., the church has maintained continuous services for more than 350 years. The present church building dates back to 1775. The architect got the idea for the steeple from a book that gave some suggested steeples for St. Martin-in-the-Fields in London. Tours are available.

Farther north on Main St. is the Roger Williams National Memorial, the site of the original Providence settlement in 1636.

Across the street is the Cathedral of St. John, at 72 N. Main St., established in 1722, one of four original parishes in the state. Its box pews and communion silver date to the Queen Anne period.

You can distinguish Providence's historic "Round Top" Church by its golden dome. Officially it is the Beneficent Congregational Meeting House (on Weybosset St.). If you go inside, notice the 6,000-piece chandelier.

■VERMONT

Tourist Info
Phone 800-VERMONT
Web sites
  Entire state   www.travel-vermont.com
  Skiing in Vermont   www.skivermont.com
For a complete list of updated links, visit www.christiantraveler.com

Arlington In this quiet town 15 miles north of Bennington is the Norman Rockwell Exhibition, several hundred *Saturday Evening Post* covers from the 1940s and 1950s housed in an 18th-century church. In addition, you will find that some of the guides at the exhibition were models for Rockwell's paintings.

Rockwell's farm and studio are now the Inn on Covered Bridge Green, 4.5 miles west of Rte. 7A in West Arlington. (See Rockwell also under Stockbridge, Mass., and Jaffrey, N.H.)

Barre The Rock of Ages Quarry has almost nothing to do with the old church hymn, but it has everything to do with granite mining. It is the world's largest granite quarry, going 350 feet straight down. A quarry train will give you a 20-minute ride through the mining complex. Afterward, you can decide for yourself whether there are any parallels between the quarry and the Rock of Ages of the hymn. Admission is free.

Bellows Falls Steamtown USA (two miles north on Rte. 5) was started by Christian businessman Nelson Blount, who liked trains, all kinds of trains. He had made his fortune in the seafood packing business, but his two passions in life were sharing his faith and collecting trains. He collected more than 50 locomotives, the oldest dating to 1887, as well as freight cars and cabooses.

The Green Mountain Flyer is a diesel-engine train with authentic 1930s passenger cars that goes 13 miles to Chester and another 14 miles to Ludlow, both scenic stops. The train leaves from Depot St. at the Amtrak Station.

The Rockingham Meetinghouse (five miles north on Rte. 103) was built in 1787 and restored in 1907. Notice the antique glass windows and walk through the old burying ground with its quaint epitaphs.

Bennington Old First Church (Monument Ave. in Old Bennington), erected in 1805, still has its original box pews and Asher Benjamin three-tiered steeple. Its six tall columns were all fashioned from a single tree. The old burying ground has the graves of those who died fighting the British in the battle of Bennington in the Revolutionary War, as well as the grave of poet Robert Frost. On Frost's tombstone is the epitaph "I had a lover's quarrel with the world."

Next to the Bennington Museum is the Grandma Moses Schoolhouse, which Grandma Moses attended as a young girl. She started painting when she was 70 and continued to paint until her death at the age of 101. The Bennington Museum, on W. Main St. (Rte. 9), has the largest public collection of Grandma Moses' work. Admission is $5.

Brattleboro Harlow's Sugar House (three miles north of town on US 5 in Putney) is an operating sugarhouse. There are maple exhibits and products and you can pick your own fruit when it is in season—strawberries and blueberries in the summer and apples in the fall.

Burlington Lake Champlain Cruises are available from the Burlington Boathouse (College St. at Battery St.). The *Spirit of Ethan Allen,* which is a replica of a vintage steam wheeler, will give you a sightseeing cruise during the day, or if you wish, you can sign up for a dinner cruise in the evening.

You can enjoy a little sacred classical music at the Vermont Mozart Festival held annually in mid-June. Contrary to its name, the festival includes Bach, Beethoven, and others in addition to Mozart. Concerts are held in barns, farms, and meadows throughout the area. Phone 800-639-9097 for information.

At St. Michael's College in Winooski-Colchester is located the Chapel of St. Michael the Archangel. It is worth visiting. There is also a professional summer theater there called St. Michael's Playhouse, which performs at the McCarthy Arts Center on campus.

Grafton This is one of Vermont's most photographed towns and looks as if it were taken directly from the 19th century. It has two steepled churches on Main St.: the 1833 Brick Meeting House and the Baptist church, notable for its Sandwich glass chandeliers.

Isle La Motte St. Anne's Shrine (West Shore Rd.) is located in Vermont's oldest settlement. It includes chapel, gift shop, grottoes, beach, and dock. A statue of Samuel de Champlain, sculpted at Expo '67, is now located here.

Ludlow The Crowley Cheese Factory (five miles west of town in Healdville) is the oldest in the nation and still makes cheese as it did when it was founded in 1882. You can watch the process and sample the product.

Middlebury The Congregational church (on the Common) was built in 1809 and is architecturally one of the finest churches in the state.

At Middlebury College (west of town on Rte. 125) is the Emma Willard House, the location of the first female seminary (high school). In 1814 Emma Willard opened the Middlebury Female Academy, which emphasized math, philosophy, and other scholarly subjects, instead of the normal female curriculum of sewing, singing, and painting.

Old Stone House (11 miles southwest to Brownington Village) is a museum in a four-story 1836 building, built by the Reverend Alexander Twilight, one of the first black college graduates in the country. At the location are period furniture, an early farm, and household and military items.

Newbury You will notice the Methodist Church here but you won't see the Newbury Seminary, which was the first Methodist theological school in the country when it opened in 1834. It lasted for only 34 years. The town's tall-spired Congregational church, built in 1856, replaced an earlier one. The congregation dates from 1764 and was the second in the state.

Newfane This is a picture-book New England town with churches, a town hall, old inns, the Town Green, and everything just as you imagined a New England village should be. The poet Eugene Field often spent his summers here.

GREAT PLACES FOR FAMILY FUN

✔ Skiing in Killington, Vermont

✔ Canoeing Maine's Allagash River

Pittsford The New England Maple Museum, located on Rte. 7, says that it features the "Sweetest Story Ever Told." It gives you the complete story of maple syrup then and now. In addition, the museum allows you to do some free syrup tasting. Admission is $1.

Saint Albans Near the Chester A. Arthur Historic Site (ten miles west to Fairfield, then on an unpaved road to the site) is a replica of the house of the 21st president. Nearby is the 1830 brick church where his father preached.

St. Johnsbury Just east of town on Rte. 2 is the Maple Grove Museum. If you want to learn how maple sugar is produced, this is the place to find out. It is the world's oldest and largest maple candy factory, founded in 1915 by two local women.

Three churches here are worth a look. St. John the Evangelist (2 Winter St.) and North Congregational (72 Main St.) were designed by the same architect, Lambert Packard. Notice the different style of the neoclassical South Congregational, farther down at 11 Main St.

South of the town is the small town of Peacham. With its apple orchards and stately white houses, it is one of the most picturesque of the state. The white clapboard Congregational church, built in 1806, adds to the charm.

Shelburne Shelburne Museum (five miles south of Burlington on US 7) may have the best collection of American folk art in the world. It is spread out over 37 buildings, many of them historic, so you could say it is a collection of collections. The museum even includes a covered bridge, cigar store Indians, a miniature circus train, and the lake steamer SS *Ticonderoga*. Admission is $17.50 for two consecutive days, $7 for one day in winter.

Also in this picturesque town on the banks of Lake Champlain is the 1,400-acre Shelburne Farms (Harbor and Bay Rds.). Here you can tour a working dairy farm, visit farm animals at the children's farmyard, or simply stroll along Lake Champlain's shoreline. The landscaping was designed by Frederick Olmsted, creator of New York's Central Park.

Springfield What was it like to live in a parsonage during the 18th century? Most parsonages weren't like the Reverend Dan Foster House and Old Forge (six miles north on Valley St. in Weathersfield), but this historic home contains period furniture and textiles, and the forge has working machinery and bellows.

The Eureka Schoolhouse (on Rte. 11, Charleston Rd.) is the oldest schoolhouse in the state. Built in 1790, it was recently restored. While you are in the area, you won't want to miss the unique 100-year-old lattice-truss covered bridge nearby.

Stowe The Trapp Family Lodge (on Luce Rd.) is one of many charming lodges and inns in the area, and it is certainly the most famous, because it is run by the family who sang its way into your heart in *The Sound of Music*. The Trapps say the lodge reminds them of their native Austria. It's expensive, so if you don't want to rent one of their 93 rooms for the week, you can just buy a meal there in the evening. There's no charge for just dropping in for a visit.

Waterbury If you're one of those people who believe there must be ice cream in heaven, don't miss the chance to visit Ben and Jerry's Ice Cream Factory (a few miles north of town on Rte. 100). For $2 you can take a 20-minute tour of the factory—painted with spots to resemble a cow—hear about the company's history, and learn of its social consciousness. Best of all, you may even get a scoop of ice cream when you leave.

The Cold Hollow Cider Mill (3.5 miles north on Rte. 100) is one of the largest cider mills in the Northeast. It features a rack and cloth press and is capable of producing 500 gallons of cider an hour.

Woodstock Four bells made by Paul Revere are still alive and well in Woodstock. Well, at least three of them are still alive and well; those three still ring from local steeples. The fourth, slightly cracked, is on display at the Congregational church on Elm St. In the mid-19th century, Woodstock was known as a very literate (five weekly newspapers) and musical (flutes, pianos, and violins were all made here) town.

Mid-Atlantic States

THE MID-ATLANTIC REGION IS DIVERSE. From the crowded streets of Manhattan to the quiet beauty of the Blue Ridge Mountains, this area has something for everyone. Washington, D.C., is a great place for a family to visit. The city's rich history will be of interest to everyone, particularly older children who have studied American history and government in school. One of the great benefits of visiting Washington is that admission to almost everything is free.

Pennsylvania probably has the most to offer Christian travelers in the region, and you can thank William Penn for that. Penn was an English Quaker who longed for religious tolerance. When he didn't receive it elsewhere in the Colonies, Penn founded Pennsylvania as a religious and political haven. The tradition of religious tolerance made the state attractive to a variety of other persecuted religious groups, including the Moravians, the German Protestants at Ephrata, and the Amish.

We begin with Delaware, the first state, in 1787, to ratify the U.S. Constitution. For this reason its nickname is "First State."

■DELAWARE

> **Tourist Info**
> *Phone* 800-441-8846
> *Web site*
>   Entire state   www.state.de.us
> For a complete list of updated links, visit www.christiantraveler.com

Bethany Beach Bethany Beach was founded by the Christian Missionary Society of Maryland in 1901 as a Christian resort, conference grounds, and camp meeting association. A tabernacle was built the same year. While no longer strictly Christian, Bethany Beach's resort atmosphere remains, making it a popular destination for visitors from Washington, Baltimore, and Philadelphia.

Camden This town was laid out in 1783 by a Quaker named Daniel Mifflin. His brother Warner was among the first Americans to free their slaves unconditionally. In the years before the Civil War, the Cooper house became an important stop of the Underground Railroad to assist escaping slaves. (See Underground Railroad under Buffalo, N.Y.; Macon, Ga.; Ottumwa, Iowa; Marshall, Mich.; Ripley, Ohio; and Osawatomie, Kans.)

Delmarva For many years this was the site of the largest Methodist camp meeting site in the state with services broadcast from the tabernacle. Nothing much remains today, but a small town of Delmar still exists across the state line in Maryland.

Frederica Barratt's Chapel and Museum (5352 Bay Rd.) is one of Delaware's most significant religious sites. The church is known as the "cradle of Methodism." Built in 1780, it is an example of traditional Georgian architecture. In 1784 Francis Asbury and Thomas Coke, an emissary of John Wesley, met here and made plans for the organization of the Methodist Church in America. The small town of Frederica is ten miles south of Dover and was originally known as Johnny Cake Landing.

Lewes Settled in 1631 by the Dutch, Lewes is the state's oldest European settlement. Charming Victorian houses and calm shores attract many families looking for retreat from the hustle and bustle of the big eastern cities. Produce stands line the streets, the beaches are clean, and the small-town atmosphere is inviting.

The Zwaanendael Museum at Kings Hwy. and Savannah Rd. was built to replicate the town hall of Hoorn, Holland. The exhibits include a display of the HMS *DeBraak,* an 18th-century ship that was sunk off the Delaware coast and discovered in 1984.

Nearby, Cape Henlopen State Park is a great place to visit, sheltering a seabird nesting colony and offering white sand dunes and a two-mile paved walking trail. Campsites are available. Admission is $5 per car; bikers and walkers are free.

Middletown The Old St. Anne's Episcopal Church was built in 1768 and is one of the finest old churches in the state with original pews and slave gallery.

New Castle This is Delaware's beautifully restored colonial capital. The town still has cobblestone streets.

The Dutch House on the Green is one of the oldest brick houses in the state. It is just about the same as it was when it was built around 1700. A hutch, a 16th-century Dutch Bible, and a courting bench exemplify the lifestyle of the early Dutch settlers.

The Old Presbyterian Church (25 E. Second St.) is thought to have been the direct successor of the original Dutch Reformed Church built here in 1657. Built in 1707, the Presbyterian church is one of several churches that formed the first presbytery in America. The cemetery has marked graves that date back to the early 1700s.

The Immanuel Church (Episcopal) was built in 1703 to 1710 but it houses a congregation that goes back to 1689. The church is located at 32 E. Third St.

If you have time, take the scenic drive down Rte. 9 from New Castle to Dover. The road winds between farm fields and ten-foot-high grasses. The most scenic stretch of Atlantic shoreline is south of Dewey Beach, with beautiful white sand dunes and great swimming.

Rehoboth The name, which was given by English settlers who came to the area around 1675, comes from the Bible and means "room enough" (Gen. 26:22). In 1872 the Methodist Rehoboth

Camp Meeting Association bought the land and plotted out a small town. It remained the site of revival camp meetings for several years. When highways were built into the area in the 1920s, it became a popular tourist resort for residents of Baltimore, Washington, and Philadelphia, anxious to leave the big cities for the beautiful beaches of the Delaware coast.

The Anna Hazzard Museum (17 Christian St.) is one of the original "Tent" buildings erected during Rehoboth's camp meeting era. It is named for a former owner and civic leader.

Wilmington Holy Trinity (Old Swedes) Church (606 Church St.) is the oldest church in the United States standing as originally built and regularly used for church services. It was dedicated in 1698 by Swedish settlers and called Helga Trefaldighet Kyrcka (Holy Trinity Church). The original hipped roof and high wooden pulpit are still intact. It is located in the heart of Wilmington's industrial district. The churchyard dates back to 1638

Your word is a lamp to my feet and a light to my path.

PSALM 119:105

and was used as a burying ground for the original settlers. A nearby reconstructed farmhouse (Hendrickson House), built in 1690, depicts the everyday life of the early settlers. Both buildings are closed to visitors Sundays, Tuesdays, and Thursdays. Admission is free.

The Kalmar Nyckel Foundation at 1124 E. 7th St. is set on the shores of the Christina River. It comprises a museum, a working 17th-century shipyard, and a full-scale working replica of the *Kalmar Nyckel*, the ship that first sailed to this area from Sweden.

The Asbury Methodist Church here was dedicated by Francis Asbury in 1789. The Cathedral Church of St. John (Concord and N. Market Sts.) stands on the site of Old Green Tree Inn, a notorious tavern in earlier days. The first Friends Meeting House was built in 1816 and its burial ground contains the grave of John Dickinson, who drew up the first draft of the Articles of Confederation (1776).

Delaware Toy and Miniature Museum (three miles north on Rte. 52, then follow signs to Hagley Museum) holds a collection of antique and contemporary doll houses, miniatures, and sample furniture from the 18th century to the present.

Delaware Art Museum (2301 Kentmore Pkwy.) houses the Bancroft Collection of English pre-Raphaelite paintings, one of the more important in the country. The museum also includes paintings of outstanding American artists, including Winslow Homer and the Wyeths. A children's gallery has hands-on activities to educate and entertain the kids. Admission is $5.

The Delaware Museum of Natural History (Rte. 52N, five miles northwest) has a children's area where kids can explore Australia's Great Barrier Reef as one of the hands-on, interactive discovery exhibits.

Three large mansions and estates in the area are particularly outstanding. The Nemours Mansion and Gardens on Rockland Rd. is a 102-room, 300-acre layout that is a modified Louis XVI–style chateau. It was built in 1909 to 1910 by Alfred Du Pont. The Rockwood Museum at 610 Shipley Rd. is a 72-acre estate with an 1851 manor house in rural Gothic architecture. In mid-July it celebrates with an Old-Fashioned Ice Cream Festival featuring homemade ice cream. The Winterthur Museum, Garden, and Library (six miles northwest off I-95 on Rte. 52) presents one of the largest and richest collections of decorative arts made or used in America between 1640 and 1860. This Henry Du Pont collection is housed in two buildings, one with 175 period rooms and the other in three exhibition galleries. The museum is set on a 983-acre estate and includes a 60-acre garden of native and exotic plants. Of special interest are the festivals held here: the Crafts Festival on Labor Day weekend and Yuletide at Winterthur, a Christmas-theme tour of the treasure-filled rooms.

■DISTRICT OF COLUMBIA

Tourist Info
Phone 202–789–7069
Web site
 Entire district   www.washington.org
For a complete list of updated links, visit www.christiantraveler.com

Washington New York Avenue Presbyterian Church (1313 New York Ave.) was where Peter Marshall served as minister prior to his being named chaplain of the U.S. Senate. The church was organized in 1803 by the Scottish stonemasons who built the White House. The current building was built in 1951 and contains 19 contemporary stained glass windows. John Quincy Adams and Abraham

Lincoln attended here. Lincoln's pew, his hitching post, and the original manuscript of his proposal to abolish slavery can be seen.

National Presbyterian Church (4101 Nebraska Ave. NW) is where 17 presidents, including Dwight Eisenhower, worshiped. The Chapel of the Presidents, which is dedicated to President Eisenhower, has stained glass windows that depict modern humanity and biblical themes. It was President Eisenhower who prompted the addition of the words "one nation under God" to the Pledge of Allegiance. Concerts take place frequently at this church throughout the year.

National Shrine of the Immaculate Conception (Michigan at 4th St. NE) is the largest Roman Catholic church in the United States and is the headquarters for the Roman Catholic Church in this country. The Crypt Church, which recalls the catacombs of ancient Rome, has been in use since 1926. The Great Upper Church was dedicated in 1959, and additional chapels are still being added. Recitals on the 56-bell carillon in Knights Tower are given Sundays at 2:30.

Franciscan Monastery (1400 Quincy St. NE) is located on the grounds of what is known as "the Holy Land of America." The monastery features a collection of replicas of the principal shrines and chapels found in the Holy Land. The main shrine is a replica of the Holy Sepulcher, the tomb of Christ. Other replicas include the Grotto of Gethsemane, the Chapel of the Ascension on Mount Olivet, and the Nativity Grotto in Bethlehem. The crypt of the church contains replicas of the catacombs of Rome and has some excellent copies of early Christian art and inscriptions.

The United States Supreme Court building at 1st St. and Maryland Ave. NE was erected in 1935. A tableau of the Ten Commandments is one of the emblems above the bench. Moses is included among the great lawgivers in Herman MacNeil's marble sculpture group on the east front. The Supreme Court building is closed Saturdays, Sundays, and holidays.

St. John's Church (16th and H Sts.) is where every president of the country since James Madison has worshiped. This Episcopalian church is located across from the White House. Several of its stained glass windows are dedicated to famous statesmen.

St. Matthew's Cathedral (1725 Rhode Island Ave. NW) was established in 1840 and moved to its present location in 1893. The altar is made of white marble and was a gift, along with the baptismal font, of India. An inscription in marble commemorates the funeral of President John F. Kennedy.

Washington National Cathedral is situated on Mount St. Alban. Completed in 1990 after 83 years of construction, it is purported to be the sixth largest cathedral in the world. Martin Luther King Jr. preached his last Sunday sermon from the Canterbury pulpit. Many famous Americans are buried here. From the Pilgrim Observation Gallery, you can see the District from the highest vantage point in the city. In late September or early October of each year, the cathedral has an open house. It is the only time when visitors can climb to the top of the central tower to see the carillon. Pipe organ demonstrations are given Wednesdays at 12:30. At the Medieval Workshop, children can carve stone, learn how stained glass windows are made, or mold a gargoyle out of clay. Tours are available for a suggested donation of $2, $1 for children under 12.

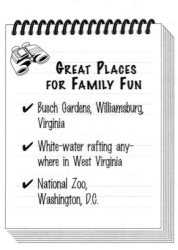

GREAT PLACES FOR FAMILY FUN

✔ Busch Gardens, Williamsburg, Virginia

✔ White-water rafting anywhere in West Virginia

✔ National Zoo, Washington, D.C.

The Capital Children's Museum at 800 3d St. NE (at H St.), a replica of a 30,000-year-old cave, has an interactive TV studio, a maze with optical illusions, and a Mexican pyramid.

Explorers Hall of the National Geographic Society (17th and M Sts. NW) contains Geographic, an interactive geography science center, featuring famous National Geographic–sponsored expeditions. Other hands-on displays relate to sea exploration and tornadoes.

The National Zoological Park of the Smithsonian Institute (entrances in the 3,000 block of Connecticut Ave.) is one of the best zoos in the world. It is best known for its giant pandas, a gift of Chairman Mao to President Nixon, but it has a total of more than 5,000 animals, including Sumatran tigers and Asian rhinoceroses. Admission is free.

The National Museum of Natural History of the Smithsonian Institute (10th St. and Constitution Ave. NW) has a variety of displays about natural history and human culture. It also has a children's discovery room that encourages hands-on learning.

The National Air and Space Museum of the Smithsonian Institute (7th St. and Independence Ave. SW) displays the history and development of air and space technology. It is one of the world's most popular museums. More than 20 galleries deal with all aspects of air and space exploration. You can touch a moon rock and walk through the huge Skylab space station. Films are shown on the five-story screen in the Samuel P. Langley Theater.

The National City Christian Church (Massachusetts Ave. and 14th St. NW) is the national cathedral of the Christian Church (Disciples of Christ). Designed by John Russell Pope in 1930, it houses one of the largest pipe organs in Washington. Half-hour organ recitals are given Thursdays at 12:15.

The United States Holocaust Memorial Museum (entrances on 14th St. SW and 100 Raoul Wallenberg Pl. SW) presents the history of the 11 million Jews and other minorities who suffered and died at the hands of the Nazis in Germany between 1933 and 1945. The exhibit also remembers heroes like Raoul Wallenberg, the Swedish diplomat who risked his life to hide and save Jews. Displays within the exhibit include a rail car thought to have been used for transporting Jews to the killing centers. Arrive early to get free, same-day, timed-entry tickets.

■MARYLAND

Tourist Info
Phone 800-MDISFUN
Web sites
  Entire state   www.mdisfun.org
  Annapolis visit   www.annapolis.org
  Baltimore   www.baltimore.org
  Frederick and environs   www.visitfrederick.org
For a complete list of updated links, visit www.christiantraveler.com

Annapolis The United States Naval Academy's most prominent structure is the U.S. Naval Chapel with its bronze dome. The Revolutionary War hero John Paul Jones ("I have not yet begun to fight!") lies buried here. Visits to the academy are free.

The Maryland State House is the oldest state capitol in continuous legislative use and is the only one that has housed the U.S. Congress. Free 30-minute tours are given daily.

The Banneker-Douglass Museum of Afro-American Life and History is housed in a Victorian-Gothic structure that for nearly a century was the Mount Moriah African Methodist Church of Annapolis. The museum is named for two African Americans who were residents of Maryland. Benjamin Banneker was a mathematician and astronomer; Frederick Douglass, a writer, abolitionist, and U.S. minister and consul general to Haiti. Located at 84 Franklin St., the museum has changing displays in its various halls.

St. Mary's Catholic Church is one of the few churches in the country that can claim to have a special tomb containing the relics of a saint or martyr. The remains of St. Justin, who was beheaded at the age of 26 in the second century, had been kept in a church in Italy for centuries. In the middle of Italy's political turmoil of the 19th century, the remains were sent to Baltimore for safekeeping. Then in July 1989 the brittle bones were placed in a golden urn and laid to rest in a cemetery plot near St. Mary's Church. Visitors should call the church prior to visiting to see when the church gardens are open. Phone 410-263-2396.

Charles Carroll House (107 Duke of Gloucester St.) is the birthplace and dwelling of Charles Carroll, the only Roman Catholic to sign the Declaration of Independence. The restored house, 18th-century gardens, and 19th-century wine cellar can be toured weekends and by appointment. Phone 410-269-1737.

Not far away is All Hallows Church, built in 1727. Here Parson Mason Weems wrote his biography of George Washington, including the apocryphal story of George chopping down a cherry tree.

Baltimore Fort McHenry, which is three miles out of Baltimore on East Fort Ave., is where Francis Scott Key jotted down the words to the "Star-Spangled Banner" on the back of an old letter. Key was an earnest Christian, a teacher of a large Bible class, and one of the founders of the American Sunday School Union. Visitors can tour the fort for $5.

The Star-Spangled Banner Flag House and 1812 Museum (844 E. Pratt St.) is the restored home of Mary Pickersgill, the seamstress who made the flag that inspired Key to write the national anthem. The house is full of period furniture and early American art.

The National Aquarium (Inner Harbor at Pier 3) is home to more than 5,000 marine animals, including dolpins, beluga whales, sharks, and puffins. Children will especially enjoy the coral reef and the rooftop "rain forest."

Port Discovery, the Children's Museum in Baltimore (34 Market Pl.), is an interactive museum that opened in 1999 in the city's old fish market. The Walt Disney Company designed it. Exhibits are packed with fun learning for kids, including a recreated Egypt, complete with the Nile River and pyramids.

E. Stanley Jones, famous Methodist missionary and writer in the first half of the 20th century, was born here in 1884 but spent most of his life in India, where he was awarded the Gandhi Peace prize in 1961.

The Monument Street Methodist Church is the site where Elvina Hall scribbled the hymn "Jesus Paid It All," while seated in the choir loft one Sunday morning. She wrote all the stanzas on the flyleaf of the church hymnal.

Lovely Lane Methodist Church (2200 St. Paul St.), built in 1882, is considered the "Mother Church of American Methodism." It contains a collection of historical materials of special interest to Methodists. Included are John Wesley's personal copy of *The Imitation of Christ*, fragments from his mother's diary, and perhaps the first pulpit used by a Methodist preacher in America.

The Maryland Historical Society (on W. Monument St.) has many interesting exhibits and, as might be expected, has the original manuscript of "The Star-Spangled Banner."

GREAT PLACES FOR FAMILY FUN

- ✔ The Amish attractions in and around Lancaster, Pennsylvania
- ✔ Camping, canoeing, and hiking the Allegheny National Forest, Pennsylvania
- ✔ Swimming, fishing, and boating at Sandy Point State Park, Maryland

Cambridge Old St. Paul's Church (Charles and Saratoga Sts.) was dedicated in 1856 and is the mother church for Baltimore. The parish it represents dates back to 1692. Designed in basilica style, it is noted for its Tiffany windows and inlaid mosaics.

The Basilica of the Assumption (Mulberry and Cathedral Sts.) was built in 1812 and was the nation's first Catholic cathedral. It was visited by Pope John Paul II in 1995.

The Old Trinity Church (eight miles southwest of downtown Baltimore) was built around 1685 and has been carefully restored in recent years. It is one of the oldest Episcopal churches in continuous use in the nation.

Otterbein United Brethren Church is the mother church for the United Brethren in Christ denomination. It was here that

Philip Otterbein in 1789, along with a Mennonite lay preacher, evangelized and started a small group movement that spawned a denomination.

Calvert Cliffs From Calvert Cliffs State Park you get an imposing view of the Chesapeake Bay. Along here are 100-foot cliffs and several miles of beaches. A two-mile walk from the state park brings you to a Miocene period fossil site.

Chestertown Out on Sandy Bottom Rd. is St. Paul's Church, established in 1713 and continually used since that time. Among the notables buried in the church's cemetery is Tallulah Bankhead.

The Emmanuel Protestant Episcopal Church (dating from 1768) housed the meeting in 1780 in which Episcopal churches in America became known as the Protestant Episcopal Church in America as distinct from the Mother Church in England. The church is located at 101 N. Cross St.

Cumberland Emmanuel Episcopal Church on Washington St. was built on the foundations of Fort Cumberland, where George Washington began his military career. The church contains Tiffany-styled stained glass windows and a scale model of Fort Cumberland. The church is open during services only.

East New Market The unique thing about this town, originally called Crossroads, is that at each of the four entrances to the town is a church. At the south entrance on Rte. 16 is Trinity United Methodist, at the north entrance on Rte. 16 is St. Stephen's Episcopal, at the west entrance on Rte. 14 is First Baptist, and at the east entrance on Rte. 14 is the Salem Evangelical and Reformed Church. The first white settler in the area back in the 1660s was John Edmondson, a Quaker. The town is proud of its diverse heritage, and its 75 old buildings are treasured. Many of the brick walks laid in 1884 still exist.

Easton Founded by Quakers in the 17th century, this town features a number of distinctive old homes. Two Quaker brothers, Joseph and James Neall, were both cabinetmakers and their interesting houses still stand. The Third Haven Friends Meeting House on South Washington St. is the oldest known building in Maryland. William Penn once preached here. The pine and oak structure is the oldest frame building dedicated to religious meetings in the United States. It is still in use.

Elkton Until the 1930s this small town was the marriage capital of the world with 10,000 people a year married here. It was the first county seat south of Philadelphia and New York where there was no waiting period or blood test before the ceremony was performed. The Little Wedding Chapel on East Main St. is still ready for business.

Also in Elkton is St. Mary Ann's Church, an Episcopal house of worship founded in 1742, with a cupola and tower added in 1904.

Emmitsburg The National Shrine of St. Elizabeth Ann Seton is at the home of America's first native-born canonized saint. She began her religious community here in 1809 and also started the country's first parochial school. The grounds provide a serene setting for meditation and prayer. The shrine is located at 333 S. Seton Ave. Admission is free.

Faulkner Loyola-on-the-Potomac (Popes Creek Rd.) is a Jesuit retreat house and center located 35 miles from Washington and 60 miles from Baltimore. It is designed as a quiet oasis and does not offer much in the way of recreational facilities nor does it offer accommodations for children.

Frederick The poet John Greenleaf Whittier in his poem "Barbara Fritchie" wrote, "the clustered spires of Frederick stand, green-walled in the hills of Maryland." He was referring to the signature view of the city of Frederick and four of its churches. The octagonal-spired Trinity Chapel, built in 1763; the open-towered St. John's Roman Catholic Church, the construction of which began in 1800; the twin-spired Evangelical Lutheran Church, founded in 1753; and All Saints Episcopal. But there are at least six other churches that are of interest as well. St. John the Evangelist (116 E 2d St.) was, in 1837, the first Roman Catholic church in the United States to be consecrated. A brochure from the Frederick Tourism Council gives the history of each one.

Mount Olivet Cemetery (515 S. Market St.) is the burial spot for more than 25,000 people, including Francis Scott Key, Barbara Fritchie, more than 800 Confederate soldiers, and veterans of the American Revolution. Visitors can't miss the statue of Key, which is 9 feet tall on top of a 15-foot monument. A U.S. flag by his statue waves 24 hours a day. Fritchie was immortalized in John Greenleaf Whittier's poem when, at the age of 95, she said, "Shoot if you must this old gray head, but spare your country's flag." The Barbara Fritchie House and Museum is on W. Patrick St. and features a brief video along with clothing, quilts, and furniture from the period.

The Maryland Christmas Show is held at the Frederick Fairgrounds every year during the last weekend in November and the first weekend in December. Hundreds of visitors come to view and shop.

Schifferstadt Architectural Museum (1110 Rosemont Ave.), the oldest dwelling in the city, was built in 1756 and it provides a window into the life of the early German settlers. In December it features a Christmas market and candlelight tours.

Grantsville This small community is the home of the Spruce Village Forest, which showcases the work of some 2,000 artists. It is also the location of Yoder's Country Market, where a Mennonite family sells Amish, Mennonite, and Pennsylvania Dutch food and craft items.

Hagerstown Jonathan Hager, founder of the town, helped build the Zion Reformed Church here. He was working in his sawmill, dressing logs for the church, when he was killed. He is buried in the church graveyard. The Jonathan Hager House and Museum is located on Key St. on the northern edge of City Park. The house, which Hager built himself, has 22-inch walls, with a large chimney in the center.

LaPlata A number of historic churches are clustered around this town in southern Maryland. Mt. Carmel was the first convent established in the United States. St. Ignatius, founded in 1641, is the oldest active Catholic parish in the nation. Christ Church, William and Mary parish, dates from the 1692 act of the General Assembly establishing Protestant parishes in the state. You can get a copy of the "Historic Churches Tour" brochure from the Charles County Museum Consortium or phone the Department of Tours at 301-645-0558.

Mountain Lake Park The hymn "Power in the Blood" was written at a camp meeting here in 1898 by Lewis E. Jones. At this same place a year earlier, Lelia Morris had written "Let Jesus Come into Your Heart."

Mount Carmel Near the town of St. Charles on Maryland's eastern peninsula is the first convent for religious women in America, founded on October 15, 1790. The Mount Carmel Monastery was begun by four Carmelite nuns who were natives of the area. Two of the original convent buildings have been restored and are open to visitors.

North East Sandy Cove Conference Center (60 Sandy Cove Rd.) was begun as the Morning Cheer Bible Conference a half century ago; then it blossomed into a summer camp for boys and girls, and now it has matured into a full camp, conference, retreat, and resort, with musical events and activities for all ages. Phone 800-234-COVE.

Pocomoke City About ten miles away in the little town of Rehoboth, Francis Makemie organized the first Presbyterian church in America. An Irishman, Makemie immigrated to America in 1683, organizing this church and others in the next two decades. In 1706, joined by two other Irish Presbyterians, he organized the first presbytery and became its moderator. The present Presbyterian church in Rehoboth (built in 1705 and 1706) is the oldest continuously used Presbyterian house of worship in the nation.

St. Mary's City This is where the first colonists, dispatched by Lord Baltimore, settled in 1634. It became Maryland's first capital and it held that distinction until 1694. Reconstructed 17th-century buildings and a replica supply ship are on view. It is not as nice as Virginia's Colonial Williamsburg, but it's far more peaceful and less crowded. There are archaeological digs being carried on to learn more about the early settlers. At the Godiah Spray Plantation (on Rosecroft Rd.) you'll see demonstrations of activities common to 17th-century settlers. The Trinity Episcopal Church, also on Rosecroft Rd., was built with bricks salvaged from the original statehouse.

At the entrance of St. Mary's College here is the Freedom of Conscience Statue, which was erected by the counties of Maryland as a symbol of the religious freedom on which the state was founded. In 1639, at the request of St. Mary's town officials, a guarantee of freedom of conscience to all Christians was enacted by the state legislature.

Sandy Point Beach Most of southern Maryland's beaches are primarily for walking and looking. If you want to go swimming, fishing, or boating, try Sandy Point State Park (Rte. 50, 12 miles east of Annapolis).

Silver Spring The Seventh-day Adventist Church has its international headquarters as well as its North America headquarters and general publication offices here at 12501 Old Columbia Pike. Founded by Ellen G. White in Battle Creek, Michigan, in 1863, the denomination has had its headquarters in the Washington, D.C., area for many years. Guided tours begin in the lobby.

Snow Hill This attractive waterfront town has more than a hundred buildings that date back a century or more. Among them are All Hallows Church, dating from 1756, on Market and Church Sts.

Wye Mills Queen Anne's County is known for its distinguished Georgian mansions, genteel lifestyle, factory outlets, and Amish farmer's market. It is an interesting combination. The farmer's market is operated by Mennonite families who travel from Lancaster, Pennsylvania, every Thursday, Friday, and Saturday to display their wares. Another Amish market, where you can buy shoofly pie, is at the Crumpton Flea Market, near Callister's Ferry.

The Old Wye Church was established in 1722 and renovated in 1948. The Wye Plantation here, overlooking the Wye River, was the home of William Paca, a signer of the Declaration of Independence and twice governor of Maryland. And on Rte. 662 is the Wye Oak, Maryland's 400-year-old, 95-foot-tall state tree.

■ NEW JERSEY

Tourist Info
Phone 800–537–7397
Web sites
  Entire state   www: nj-tourism.com
  Wildwood   www.wildwoods.com
For a complete list of updated links, visit www.christiantraveler.com

Beaches You will find lots of beautiful beaches all along the Jersey shore. Unfortunately some of them may offend Christian sensitivities, with their heavy emphasis on gambling. Ocean City, Ocean Grove, and Point Pleasant Beach are safe choices. Island Beach State Park, some 60 miles north of Atlantic City, is the most scenic natural beach on the Jersey shore. Admission is $6 weekdays, $7 weekends.

Bridgeton This town has New Jersey's largest historic district and one of the best-preserved eighteenth-century churches in the country. The Old Broad Street Church (W. Broad St. and West Ave.) was begun in 1791 and completed in 1795. Bricks were handmade on-site and laid in Flemish-bond style. The pulpit is in the shape of a wineglass.

The first farmers here were Lenape Indians; then came the Swedes and Finns in 1638. The New Sweden Company Farmstead Museum (W. Commerce St. and Mayor Aitken Dr., off Rte. 49) in Bridgeton City Park gives visitors a look at how the early settlers lived.

Burlington Best known as the birthplace of author James Fenimore Cooper and the town where Benjamin Franklin learned the printing trade, the town has a historic district dating back to 1677. In it are the 1703 Old St. Mary's Church (W. Broad and Wood Sts.) and the 1784 Friends Meeting House (300 block of High St.). Tours of both are by appointment.

Cape May At the southern tip of New Jersey is this seashore resort, offering a dramatic change of pace from the amusement piers of the north. This is the state's oldest resort, and its streets are lined with elaborate Victorian cottages. You will find lots of B&Bs here. Victorian Week, held every year in early October, is quite popular. Enjoy the historic house tours and the craft and antique shows. Christmastime in Cape May is lovely, featuring trolley, candlelight, and walking tours of the beautifully decorated Victorian homes. Phone 800-275-4278 for a schedule of events.

The Cape May Point State Park (at the terminus of the Garden State Pkwy.) is the site of the Cape May Point Lighthouse, built in 1859. This is a favorite birding spot, especially during fall and spring migrations. Another popular activity is whale watching. Several boats search the Atlantic for whales and dolphins, spring through fall. Phone the state park at 609-884-2159.

Near the Cape May Point Lighthouse is Sunset Beach, which is a popular place to search for "Cape May diamonds," little sparking pebbles of pure quartz. You can also enjoy beautiful sunsets over the Delaware Bay.

Collingswood Carl McIntire, the fundamentalist radio preacher and editor, pastored the large Bible Presbyterian Church here, edited the *Christian Beacon* magazine, and broadcast the *Twentieth Century Reformation Hour.* For many years Collingswood has headquartered the International Council of Christian Churches, militantly fighting against liberal tendencies in the World Council of Churches. The address of both the church and the council is 1115 Hadon Ave.

Cranberry It was here in the mid-1700s that missionary David Brainerd had his greatest success in his work among the Indians. His diary, published by Jonathan Edwards as *Brainerd's Journal,* has become a Christian classic and has inspired many to missionary service. Brainerd died of tuberculosis at the age of 29.

Delaware Water Gap In Millbrook Village, a few miles north of the Delaware Water Gap, is this reconstructed town in which National Park Service employees dress in period costumes and demonstrate skills from weaving and spinning to blacksmithing. The buildings include a general store and an old Methodist church. The old Millbrook Hotel is now a private residence. Millbrook Village is 12 miles north of the Kittatinny Point Visitors Center along Old Mine Rd.

Farmingdale In 1821 James P. Allaire purchased the property now known as Allaire Village (exit 98 off the Garden State Pkwy.). The Farmingdale area had abundant quantities of a naturally occurring iron, known as bog iron. Allaire employed 500 workers to extricate the iron and fashion stoves, screws, hand irons, and kettles. Eventually his company became one of the largest marine engine shops in the country. But Allaire took his greatest delight in the Episcopal church he built for his workers. The church (with a steeple in the back, not the front) did not require worshipers to pay pew rents, unlike most churches of the day. Allaire Village is now run by the state and includes an operating railroad called the Pine Creek Railroad. The Episcopal church is open to visitors.

Haddonfield This lovely suburban community takes its name from Elizabeth Haddon, a Quaker woman who came from England in 1701 and developed 550 acres of land southeast of Camden, now called Haddonfield. In less than a year she built a house, began a small colony, and proposed marriage to a Quaker missionary, John Estaught. He accepted her proposal. Henry Wadsworth Longfellow wrote of their romance in "The Theologian's Tale" and included it in his *Tales of a Wayside Inn*.

The impressive looking church in the center of town is the Haddonfield United Methodist Church at 29 Warwick Rd.

Harvey Cedars The Harvey Cedars Bible Conference in this seaside community keeps an active program going through the summer. If you're in the area, check it out. The address is 12 Cedars Ave., or phone 609-494-5689.

Hope This village was founded in 1774 by Moravians from Bethlehem, Pennsylvania. They soon built a strong community, and several of the structures remain from that early period. During the Revolution, the Moravians were conscientious objectors and their position was not always appreciated by the Patriot forces, but they did gain respect by the way they cared for sick and wounded soldiers. A smallpox epidemic broke out in the early 1800s, and the survivors returned to Bethlehem, Pennyslvania, to join the larger community of Moravians.

Self-guided tours of Hope's Moravian architecture can be made from brochures available at area banks and stores. (See Moravians also under Bethlehem, Lititz, and Nazareth, Pa.; Bloomington, Ill.; Winston-Salem, N.C.; Gnadenhutten and New Philadelphia, Ohio; and Ephraim, Wisc.)

Jackson Six Flags Great Adventure, located on Rte. 537 at I-195, offers more than 100 rides, shows, and attractions. The shows include everything from trained dolphins and sea lions to a water stunt spectacular. The drive-through Wild Safari Animal Park features more than 2,000 animals on 350 acres.

Jersey City While it might look like a gritty New York suburb to you, this is the location of Liberty State Park, at New Jersey Turnpike exit 14B. Ferries leave regularly from the park for visits to the Statue of Liberty and Ellis Island Immigration Museum.

75

Within Liberty State Park is also the Liberty Science Center with three floors of hands-on exhibits and an Omnimax theater. Phone 201-915-3400 for schedule and fee information.

Kingston Next door to Princeton is the historic town of Kingston, settled by Quakers in 1693. It boasts that George Washington led his troops along the Old Indian Path through the center of town. There are many old buildings here but the two oldest are the Presbyterian church (4561 Rte. 27), established in 1723, and the Jediah Higgins House. Higgins was Kingston's earliest recorded settler in 1714.

Medford Johnson Oatman was an insurance man and Methodist lay preacher who lived in this area a hundred years ago. He wrote more than 5,000 hymns; the best known are "Count Your Blessings" and "No, Not One."

Millville Wheaton Village, off Rte. 552, commemorates Millville's glassmaking heritage. It includes the Museum of Glass with 7,000 glass objects, mostly made in South Jersey. The village also includes several other restored buildings from the 18th-century village. Today the T. C. Wheaton Company employs about 3,000 people.

It was in Millville that Hannah Whitall Smith, author of *The Christian's Secret of a Happy Life,* had a life-changing experience. A glass factory woman led a meeting at a Methodist church, after which Hannah Smith said, "When I got sight of Jesus as my Savior, this great big me melted down to nothing."

Mount Holly There aren't any mountains in this part of the state, but Mount Holly takes its name from a nearby 183-foot hill. The town was begun by Quakers in 1676 and it served as the state capital for two months in 1779. John Woolman, the Quaker abolitionist, known for his *Journal* written in 1774, taught at the Old School House here. Other historic buildings are located on High St. between Garden and Union Sts.

Newark The Catholic Cathedral of the Sacred Heart at Clifton and Park Sts. is a French Gothic cathedral, comparable in size to Westminster Abbey and resembling the basilica at Rheims. It has 200 stained glass windows, bronze doors, and 14 bells cast in Italy. Its towers are 232 feet high.

New Brunswick The 18th-century Presbyterian preacher Gilbert Tennent was the pastor here when George Whitefield came to America stirring up the Great Awakening. Tennent joined Whitefield in his meetings and then went to England to raise money for the founding of the College of New Jersey (later known as Princeton University).

Two old churches—First Reformed Church at Neilson and Bayard Sts. and Christ Episcopal Church at Neilson and Church Sts.—are worth noting. The bell tower and clock on the Reformed church have long been the signals of passing time for tradesmen in the area. The Episcopal church, originally built in the 1740s but rebuilt using the original brownstones in 1852, has a tree standing in its southeast corner that is significant. The tree was planted in the 1930s by Joyce Kilmer's father in honor of his son, who wrote the poem *Trees*. The poet was killed in action in World War I, and the home in which he was raised is open to the public at 17 Joyce Kilmer Ave.

The oldest seminary in the country is New Brunswick Theological Seminary at 17 Seminary Pl. The Gardner A. Sage Library here includes Bibles from every country in the world and also has a room devoted to books of religious art.

Ocean City This neighbor to the south of Atlantic City was established in 1879 as a Christian resort and it was decreed that no liquor be sold in its city limits. That has set the tone for the town ever since. Families flock here. Its music pier holds concerts during the summer, and a Bible conference has been popular as well. The Ocean City Tabernacle, located at 500 Wesley Ave., is open for worship during the summer only and it strives to provide religious services to an interdenominational community of summer visitors. The grounds are beautiful and the guest speakers and musicians are nationally recognized. Speakers have included Elizabeth Dole, Tony Campolo, Lloyd Ogilvie (chaplain of the U.S. Senate), and Jonathan Dupree (a Christian illusionist). Vacation Bible school and children's programs are an important part of the Tabernacle's ministry. For a list of updated speakers and programs, phone 609-399-1915 or e-mail OCTAB@aol.com.

Ocean Grove Ocean Grove, under the leadership of the Camp Meeting Association (Methodist) since 1869, is a family-oriented seaside resort. Its musical performances feature well-known pop and symphony concert artists as well as Christian recording artists. The 6,500-seat Great Auditorium has organ concerts on Wednesday and Saturday on the 1908 Hope-Jones pipe organ. The Victorian architecture of many of the community's homes is well worth viewing. One old cottage, the Centennial Cottage at Central and McClintock Sts. is a restored 1874 vacation home, open to visitors. The tabernacle, chapel, boardwalk, and beach are also popular with vacationers. It is one of only two seaside resorts in New Jersey that sell no alcohol (Ocean City is the other).

Paterson Two beautiful Catholic churches are located here. St. Michael's (at the corner of Cianci and Elm Sts.), built in 1929, has a 96-foot-high dome and beautiful stained glass windows. The sculpture of St. Michael and Lucifer over the entrance was crafted by a local artist, Gaetano Federici. The Cathedral of St. John the Baptist is located in the heart of Paterson's financial district at the corner of Main and Grand Sts. and is Gothic in style. Completed in 1870, the church features a spire rising 225 feet from the ground, beautiful stained glass windows, and a lovely Gothic-style altar.

Plainfield The gospel song "Nothing But the Blood of Jesus" was written here in 1876 by Robert Lowry, pastor of the Park Avenue Baptist Church. The title of the tune, which appears in many hymnals, is "Plainfield." The church is now known as Park Baptist Church and is located at 315 W. 7th St.

Point Pleasant Beach Here is a resort that is family oriented, with shops, amusement park rides, and fireworks. If you tire of the beach or if the rain spoils your fun, check out Jenkinson's Aquarium at Ocean Ave. and Parkway St. Open all year, the aquarium features alligators, seals, sharks, a coral reef, penguins, and exotic birds. Children will especially enjoy the touch tanks, where they can find out what those strange sea creatures feel like.

Princeton Princeton, founded by Quakers in 1696, is best known now for its research and educational institutions. Princeton University, which was originally called The College of New Jersey, had two noted Christian leaders among its earliest presidents: Jonathan Edwards and John Witherspoon, who signed the Declaration of Independence. The University Chapel, near Firestone Library, is one of the world's largest university chapels. It is modeled after King's Chapel, Cambridge. The pulpit and lectern date from the mid-15th century and were brought from Spain. The university library holds more than five million books and magazines.

Somerville The Old Dutch Parsonage State Historic Site at 65 Washington Pl. was built in 1751 and was so named because it was the home of Rev. Jacob Hardenbergh for more than two decades. Hardenbergh became the founder of Queens College in New Brunswick, which later became Rutgers University. Exhibits in the home show local history and early American crafts.

Spring Lake This is a small seaside town, with an uncommercialized boardwalk, spring-fed lakes stocked with swans, and several romantic B&Bs.

Stanhope Waterloo Village along the Musconetcong River has been preserved as it was in colonial days. Founded in 1763, it was originally called Andover Forge. When the forge was abandoned, it found new life as an inland port. When trains took away its shipping business, it was a ghost town again, until it was restored and opened to the public in 1964. One building has always been open and that is the Methodist church, constructed in 1859 and in continuous use since it was built (for 2,300 dollars). There are now 23 authentically restored homes in the village. In the summer you can enjoy the village's concert series with many types of music. A variety of children's programs are offered. For more information, call 973-347-0900.

Wild West City on US 206 is a re-creation of an Old West Town with stagecoach, pony rides, and a miniature frontier railroad ride. There is also a children's petting zoo. Admission is $6.75.

Washington Village State Park Located on Rte. 546 in Titusville, this is the site of Washington's Christmas 1776 crossing of the Delaware (you know, the one in the famous painting). The event is reenacted every Christmas, no matter how cold the weather. Phone 609-737-0623.

Whiting America's Keswick Conference is a summer Bible conference grounds that brings in Bible teachers and preachers from across the country. It is patterned after the Keswick Conference in England. Write Keswick Grove, Whiting, NJ 08759 for more information, or call 201-350-1187.

■NEW YORK

Tourist Info
Phone 800-I LOVE NY
Web sites
  Entire state   www.iloveny.state.ny.us
  Albany   www.albany.org
  Bronx   www.ilovethebronx.com
  Buffalo   www.buffalocvb.org
  New York City   www.nycvisit.com
  Niagara Falls   www.nfcvb.com
  Syracuse   www.syracusecvb.org
For a complete list of updated links, visit www.christiantraveler.com

Albany The First Reformed Church (56 Orange St.) here is the second-oldest Protestant congregation in America, having been organized in 1642. Although the present building is newer, it does contain an old pulpit, an hourglass, a Bible, and a communion service, which had been brought from Holland in 1656.

Auriesville In 1642 a Jesuit missionary, Isaac Jogues, and an assistant were captured by Iroquois Indians here. His assistant was tomahawked, but Jogues was rescued by the Dutch. Later he returned to try to negotiate a peace treaty with the Mohawks. He was murdered by tomahawk-wielding braves. In 1930 he was canonized by the Roman Catholic Church and now he is honored at the National Shrine of the North American Martyrs in Auriesville.

Buffalo The city's oldest African American church is Michigan Street Baptist (511 Michigan St.), where services have been held since 1845. Before the Civil War, it was a station on the Underground Railroad. (See Underground Railroad also under Camden, Del.; Macon, Ga.; Ottumwa, Iowa; Marshall, Mich.; Ripley, Ohio; and Osawatomie, Kans.)

Carmel The home of *Guideposts,* which was founded by Norman Vincent Peale, is in Carmel at 39 Seminary Hill Rd. The publishing offices are in New York City. Tours of the facility are available.

Chautauqua For many years this was a popular Christian conference site, where famous speakers came to address vacationers. Two hymns written here are in most hymnals today, "Day Is Dying in the West" and "Break Thou the Bread of Life." Originally the conference was begun as a school for Sunday school teachers; then it began to offer not only religious instruction but also adult education courses on many subjects. It became so popular that it was copied in many other communities, which began offering summertime courses and concerts, providing instant culture across the nation. Largely secularized today, Chautauqua little resembles the Methodist camp meeting of the 1800s. But for nine weeks every summer the entire town still bustles with concert series, plays, lectures, and demonstrations, often with a religious theme. For detailed information, phone 800-836-ARTS. (See other Chautauqua-inspired sites under Ridgecrest, N.C.; Sac City, Iowa; Lakeside, Ohio; Madison, S.D.; and Boulder, Colo.)

Cooperstown The National Baseball Hall of Fame and Museum is the main reason to come to Cooperstown. On display you will find memorabilia from baseball's greats, including Babe Ruth's bat. There is also a multimedia tribute to the sport, a display on the African American baseball experience, and a history, tracing baseball to ancient Egyptian religious ceremonies. One exhibit explains, "In the beginning, shortly after God created Heaven and Earth, there were stones to throw and sticks to swing."

Houghton Houghton College, associated with the Wesleyan Methodist denomination, was founded in 1883. It is set in western New York's rolling hills and northern hardwood forests.

Lestershire The hymn "God Will Take Care of You" was written here in 1904 by Civilla Martin during an illness.

Lockport The pastor of the First Presbyterian Church here, Maltie Babcock, wrote the hymn "This Is My Father's World," after jogging one morning along the nearby shores of Lake Ontario.

New Paltz Huguenot St. in New Paltz is the oldest street in America that still has its original houses. The stone houses built between 1692 and 1712 are maintained by the Huguenot Historical Society. French Huguenots, after facing persecution for many years, came to southern New York in search of freedom. In 1677 twelve of them purchased land around New Paltz from the Esopus Indians.

New York City *Midtown* Considered the heart of midtown by many is Rockefeller Center, a complex of 19 buildings between 5th and 7th Aves. and 47th and 52d Sts. The outdoor ice rink between 49th and 50th Sts. is Rockefeller Center's trademark. During the warmer months the ice rink becomes an outdoor cafe. The plaza is also the home of the famous gold leaf statue of Prometheus surrounded by jet streams of water. In December the plaza is decorated with a gigantic Christmas tree.

The Empire State Building (5th Ave. and 34th St.) is no longer the world's tallest building, but it is still one of the world's favorite skyscrapers. Go to the concourse level and buy a ticket for the 86th and 102d floor observation decks for fabulous views of the city. The elevators run until midnight, and the view at night will have even the most jaded oohing and aahing.

World-famous St. Patrick's Cathedral, facing Fifth Ave. between 50th and 51st Sts., was inspired by the cathedral in Cologne and is full of fine art. The Gothic-style Roman Catholic cathedral, the largest Catholic cathedral in America with its twin 330-foot spires, was begun in 1858, completed in 1906, and is dedicated to the patron saint of the Irish. Tours are available.

Calvary Church (13428 Northern Blvd.), identified for years as a strong evangelical center in Manhattan, has had a series of outstanding preachers.

David Wilkerson, author of *The Cross and the Switchblade,* preaches regularly at the Times Square Church in Manhattan (1633 Broadway), which he began in 1987.

The American Bible Society (1865 Broadway) has its headquarters here and provides tours for visitors.

The Salvation Army Headquarters is at 120 W. 14th St., between 6th and 7th Aves. On most Friday evenings an inspirational program is presented at the Centennial Memorial Temple. Tours may be arranged if you contact the Salvation Army in advance.

The majestic Gothic structure of the Cathedral of St. John the Divine is located at Amsterdam Ave. and 112th St. It will be the largest Gothic structure in the world if it is ever finished. But don't hold your breath. It was begun in 1812. A fascinating biblical garden is off to the side and shouldn't be missed. Tours are available. Tours are also available at Marble Collegiate Church at 29th St. and 5th Ave. (where Norman Vincent Peale preached for many years) and at Trinity Church on Wall St.

The blind hymn writer Fanny Crosby taught at the Institute for the Blind (which no longer exists), and in her sixties was actively involved at the Bowery Mission.

Calvary Episcopal Church (61 Gramercy Park N) is where Samuel M. Shoemaker ministered. A founder of Alcoholics Anonymous, a leader in the Oxford group, and a writer of numerous books, he was an early exponent of the small groups movement.

Madison Square Garden (4 Penn Plaza) is known for the thousands of athletic and entertainment events it hosts. In 1957 it held Billy Graham's New York Crusade. Singer Ethel Waters was one of the converts. Before her conversion she was most famous for singing "St. Louis Blues"; afterward she became famous for singing "His Eye Is on the Sparrow."

Other NYC churches: Historic Brick Presbyterian Church (62 E. 92nd St.) was pastored from 1883 to 1899 by Henry van Dyke, who wrote *The Story of the Other Wise Man* here. Old John Street Methodist Church (44 John St.), built in 1841, includes a clock from John Wesley. St. Paul's Chapel of Trinity Parish (211 Broadway) is the oldest church building in Manhattan (built in 1764), and was designed by a pupil of the architect who designed St. Martin-in-the-Fields in London. Visitors can see George Washington's pew here. It is the oldest public building in continuous use in Manhattan. St. Mark's in the Bowery (at 131 E. 10th St., originally built in 1788 but rebuilt in 1799) dates to the time when Peter Stuyvesant built a chapel on his farm here. Commodore Perry is buried in the graveyard. Church of the Ascension at 12 W. 11th St. in Greenwich Village (built in 1841) has a mural behind the altar by John LaFarge called *Ascension*, which is considered his finest work. Grace Church (Episcopal) at 10th and Broadway is noted for its stained glass windows (46 in all). At 1 E. 29th St. is the Church of the Transfiguration (Episcopal, built in 1870). Known as the Little Church around the Corner, it is popular for wedding ceremonies.

The Wall Street area features free lunchtime concerts in some of the oldest churches in the city. Both Trinity Church on Broadway and Wall St. and St. Paul's Chapel on Broadway and Fulton St. feature noon concerts.

Central Park: This huge park (bordered by 59th and 110th Sts., 5th Ave., and Central Park W) is a verdant 843-acre oasis in this city of concrete and steel. The park contains grassy meadows, wooded areas, ponds, lakes, and formal gardens, as well as trails for jogging, biking, strolling, or horseback riding. As you explore it, you keep finding things in it you didn't expect to see. It has two zoos, an ice skating rink, ball fields, tennis courts, a castle, numerous fountains, sculptures, a Swedish Cottage Marionette Theater for weekday puppet shows, and the Friedsam Memorial Carousel. Phone 212-260-3444 for information or pick up a free map at the Reception Center inside the Dairy, south of 65th St.

Museums: The Metropolitan Museum of Art (between 80th and 84th Sts. on Fifth Ave.) has an outstanding collection of materials relating to biblical archaeology as well as wonderful art collections. The final 13 galleries of its Egyptian collection opened in 1983, concluding a 25-year project. It now has 40,000 objects covering the full span of Egyptian history. Donations encouraged.

The American Museum of Natural History (Central Park W at 79th St.) has more than 36 million artifacts and specimens and is the largest and most important natural history museum in the world. It's a great place to take your kids. Forty-two exhibition halls display dinosaur skeletons, a 94-foot blue whale replica, and the 563-carat Star of India Sapphire. Closed on Mondays. Admission is by donation.

The Cloisters is a branch of the Metropolitan Museum but is located in Fort Tryon Park just north of the George Washington Bridge (5th Ave. at 82d St.). It was erected in 1938 by Charles Collen, largely from pieces of 12th- and 13th-century French and Spanish monasteries. John D. Rockefeller donated the site as well as many of the works. It features a wide assortment of medieval art in a very restful setting. One spectacular piece is the *Altarpiece on the Annunciation.* Donations encouraged.

Uptown At 114th St. and Morningside Dr. is the Church of Notre Dame of Lourdes. Practically the entire church was imported from France and is an outstanding example of Italian Renaissance architecture.

Riverside Church, long associated with the ministry of Harry Emerson Fosdick, is at Riverside Dr. and 120th St., not far from Union Theological Seminary and the headquarters of the National

Council of Churches at 475 Riverside Dr. It has one of the largest church organs in the world with 13,000 pipes. On the top floor (the 20th) is the largest carillon in the world, a gift of John D. Rockefeller Jr.

At Broadway and 155th St. is the Chapel of the Intercession. Its high altar has stones from the Holy Land and places of early Christian worship.

Brooklyn On Orange St., between Henry and Hicks Sts., is Plymouth Church of the Pilgrims, where Henry Ward Beecher preached against slavery. A statue of Beecher by Borglum is in Memorial Park.

Brooklyn Tabernacle, a multiracial church at 290 Flatbush Ave., has become known through the ministry of the pastor, Jim Cymbala, and the music ministry of his wife, Carol. *Fresh Wind, Fresh Fire* tells the story of how the church has sprung to life in the past two decades.

The Brooklyn Museum (Eastern Pkwy. and Washington Ave.) has an excellent assortment of materials relating to biblical times. Like the Metropolitan Museum, it has an outstanding collection of materials on Egypt. Admission is $4, children under 12 free.

It was in Brooklyn, in 1872, that a housewife, Annie Hanks, wrote the hymn, "I Need Thee Every Hour."

Flushing In this New York City borough is the Bowne House, built by John Bowne in 1661. As a Quaker, he challenged the edict of Gov. Peter Stuyvesant, banning Quakers from holding meetings in his kitchen. He was arrested and deported, and two years later returned, as religious dissent was being tolerated. His stand was an important step in American acceptance of religious freedom.

Ellis Island and Liberty Island Ellis Island was once the main East Coast federal immigration facility. Between 1892 and 1954, 17 million people passed through this historic gateway, the ancestors of more than 40 percent of all Americans living today. The island now houses Ellis Island Immigration Museum, an excellent museum, and admission is free.

The Statue of Liberty is a site you simply can't miss. And few do miss it. Once on Liberty Island you may have to wait up to three hours to take the elevator up 10 stories to the top of the pedestal. Another 12 stories of stairs are available if you are brave enough and hardy enough to climb to Lady Liberty's crown. Admission is free. Visitors to either Ellis Island or Liberty Island can buy ferry tickets in Battery Park at Castle Clinton National Monument ($7 round-trip). If all you want is a great view, take a

85

free ride on the Staten Island ferry, departing from the Staten Island Ferry Terminal at the southern-most tip of Manhattan.

Niagara Falls Actually, you will find a trio of falls here: the American and Bridal Veil Falls in New York and Horseshoe Falls in Niagara Falls, Ontario, Canada, the latter being the largest and most often photographed. The area is surrounded by a lot of cheesy shops and tourist attractions, but go anyway and ignore the kitsch. Niagara Falls didn't become the most famous falls in the world for nothing—they are simply stunning. And while you are there, consider taking a boat ride on the *Maid of the Mist*. The trip takes you as near to the base of the falls as is safe, and the power and noise of the falls will overwhelm you. Phone 716-284-8897 for more information. Admission is $8 for adults, $4.50 for ages 6–12. Don't bring anything that can't get wet.

North Tarrytown The Old Dutch Church in Sleepy Hollow (430 N. Broadway) dates from the end of the 17th century. Adjacent to it is the huge Sleepy Hollow Cemetery, where Washington Irving, Andrew Carnegie, and Robert Ingersoll are buried. A few miles south in Hastings on Hudson is Zion Episcopal Church of which Washington Irving was a member.

Nyack Nyack College, founded as The Missionary Training College by A. B. Simpson in 1883, is located here. It was one of the first Bible colleges in the United States and the world. Simpson also founded the Christian and Missionary Alliance denomination, which had its headquarters here until moving to Colorado Springs in the 1990s.

Old Chatham In 1774 Ann Lee led eight converts to America from England and began the Shaker movement here. They held to celibacy, communal property, and refusal to bear arms, but they are best known for their beautiful handcrafts. Less than ten miles from the Massachusetts border, the village of Old Chatham is home to the Shaker Museum, housing the largest collection of Shaker artifacts in the United States. The landscape around the museum may cause you to think that you are in the English countryside. The Shaker Cemetery is nearby. (See Shakers also under Sabbathday Lake, Maine; Pittsfield, Mass.; Concord and Enfield, N.H.; South Union and Harrodsburg, Ky.; Lebanon, Ohio; and Marysville, Wash.)

Schenectady Although the Dutch First Reformed Church at 8 Church St. dates only to 1862, it has stained glass windows depicting earlier church buildings. The first Reformed church was built here in 1682.

Mohawk Valley's oldest church is St. George's Episcopal Church, at 30 N. Ferry St., built in 1759.

GREAT PLACES FOR FAMILY FUN

✔ Central Park, New York City

✔ Six Flags, Jackson, New Jersey

Schroon Lake Founded by evangelist Jack Wyrtzen as a camp for teenagers, the Bible conference here has become popular for people of all ages.

Setauket The charming, old New England–type village, established in 1651, has two churches of historic interest. The Caroline Church on Strings Nek Rd., to which Queen Caroline donated church silver, was established in 1728. The Presbyterian Church (established in 1714) was where guns were mounted during a Revolutionary War skirmish.

Speculator Camp of the Woods here brings in famous evangelical Bible teachers and preachers from all across the country during the summer months.

Stony Brook Stony Brook School has achieved an outstanding reputation as a private preparatory school with an evangelical emphasis. Headmaster here for many years was Frank Gaebelein, one of the early leaders of the National Association of Evangelicals.

Utica Hamilton College was founded in 1792 by missionary Samuel Kirkland as a school for both Indians and whites. The oldest building on campus is Buttrick Hall, built in 1812.

West Point The U.S. Military Academy here has a beautiful European-style Old Cadet Chapel located near the center of the campus. Erected in 1910 and acclaimed as an excellent example of military Gothic architecture, the chapel also houses the largest pipe organ in the world and outstanding stained glass windows donated by graduating classes. Sunday morning services are open to the public. On selected Sundays free public concerts are performed in the chapel, featuring distinguished artists from around the world. During the summer there are often evening concerts by the Military Academy Band.

Located beside the West Point chapel is the West Point cemetery, final resting place of many distinguished military men, such as Maj. Gen. George Custer and Lt. Gen. Winfield Scott. But not all the cemetery's graves are reserved for the military elite. Two women, Susan and Anna B. Warner, are also buried here.

Anna Warner, who wrote the children's hymn "Jesus Loves Me," grew up near here on Constitution Island and later returned here with her sister Susan to lead Sunday school services for the cadets. Constitution Island, where the Warner sisters lived, is still open to guided tours as is their fifteen-room house. In American history, Constitution Island played an interesting role during the Revolutionary War. In 1776 the Revolutionary army stretched an immense iron chain across the Hudson River from West Point to Constitution Island, preventing the British ships from navigating up or down the river.

■PENNSYLVANIA

Tourist Info
Phone 800-VISIT-PA
Web sites
  Entire state   www.visit.state.pa.us
  The Bach Choir of Bethlehem   www.bach.org
  Bethlehem tourism   www.bethtour.org
  Pennsylvania Dutch country   www.800padutch.com
  Philadelphia   www.libertynet.org/phila-visitor
  Pittsburgh   www.pittsburgh-cvb.org
For a complete list of updated links, visit www.christiantraveler.com

Allentown During the Revolutionary War, the Liberty Bell and the bells of Philadelphia's Christ Church were secretly moved to Allentown and were hidden in Zion Reformed Church (Hamilton Mall at Church St.) for safekeeping. Visitors now see a replica of the Liberty Bell and a mural that incorporates sound and light to describe the Liberty Bell. The Liberty Bell Shrine (located in the basement of Zion Reformed Church) is open every afternoon except Sunday. Admission is free.

Ambridge Old Economy Village here recalls the early German separatists (sometimes called Rappites) who migrated to Harmony, Pennsylvania, in 1804 seeking to set up a society similar to the one the first Christians enjoyed in the Book of Acts. Led by George Rapp, they moved to Indiana in 1814 to found New Harmony, and then ten years later they moved back to Ambridge. So Old Economy Village dates to 1824. Known for their craftsmanship and innovation, they built some of the first prefab houses. Visitors may tour the restored buildings, including the George Rapp House and the Frederick Rapp House. Covering a two-block area, the village has 18 original structures. (See Rappites also under New Harmony, Ind., and Harmony, Pa.)

Beaver Falls Geneva College, affiliated with the Reformed Presbyterian denomination, is located in this lovely community north of Pittsburgh.

Bedford Old Bedford Village, one mile north of town, is a 40-building reproduction of a village between 1750 and 1850. Various crafts, including broommaking, quilting, gunmaking, and tinsmithing are demonstrated. From June through October there are many special events including the Gospel Music Festival in August.

Bernville This is a town of only 800 people but it has a big Christmas celebration on Christmas Village Road. Koziar's Christmas Village (one mile southwest on Rte. 183) claims to be one of the largest Christmas displays in the country with a half million colored lights, tinsel, and replicas of various Christmas themes. The village itself includes a dozen buildings.

Bethlehem This city was a Moravian settlement, named by Count Nicholas Zinzendorf on Christmas Eve 1741. He said it was his fervent desire that "here the true bread of life might be broken for all who hunger." The original Bethlehem has been restored to resemble its appearance three centuries ago. The Yuletide Festival includes a large lighted Star of Bethlehem on the south mountain, hundreds of lighted Christmas trees, and a Moravian Christmas

MORAVIANS IN PENNSYLVANIA

The Unitas Fratrum is more commonly known as the Moravian Church due to its origins in 1457 in Moravia, the Czech Republic. In its early days adherents were followers of the teachings of John Hus, an early Protestant reformer. Religious persecution reduced the group's numbers, but a renewal took place after 1722 in Herrnhut on the estate of Count Ludwig von Zinzendorf in Saxony.

From Herrnhut the Moravians sent small groups of colonist missionaries to the New World. There are a number of small towns that owe their establishment to the Moravian settlers, but Bethlehem, Pennsylvania, was the first, founded in 1741. Bethlehem remains the center of the Moravians in the United States today. Strong reminders of those early missionaries still exist in the historic homes and businesses they left behind, in the exuberant Christmas celebrations, and in the remarkable and world-renowned Bach Choir of Bethlehem.

manger. There is also a live Christmas pageant. Love feasts are featured in the local Moravian church. For complete information, contact Bethlehem Tourism at 800-360-8687.

Described as "one of American Musical Life's best kept secrets" by the *New York Times,* the Bach Choir has been singing—you guessed it— Bach's music since 1898. The oldest Bach Choir in America, this group gave the first performances in the United States of the *Mass in B Minor* and the *Christmas Oratorio.* The choir's home season consists of two Christmas concerts, a spring concert, and the annual Bach Festival over two weekends in May. Contact the Bach Choir at 888-743-3100.

The Moravian Museum of Bethlehem at 66 W. Church St. is in the 1741 Gemein Haus, the oldest building in Bethlehem. Displayed are musical instruments, seminary art, needlework, Moravian furniture, and clocks. Admission is $5 for adults, $3 for students, and free for children 5 and under.

Burnside is an 18th-century Moravian farm, known for being the first privately owned Moravian residence. All other Moravians of that period lived communally in farmhouses built for single men, single women, and married people. (See Moravians also under Hope, N.J.; Lititz and Nazareth, Pa.; Winston-Salem, N.C.; Bloomington, Ill.; Gnadenhutten and New Philadelphia, Ohio; and Ephraim, Wisc.)

Bird-in-Hand This is Pennsylvania Dutch Country and this town is a good introduction to it. The Old Order Amish House (2395

Lincoln Hwy.) shows visitors the Amish way of life. Guided tours are available. The Plain and Fancy Farm (3121 Old Philadelphia Pike) is a shopping village featuring buggy rides and craft and gift shops. The Old Village Store (on Rte. 340) is one of the oldest hardware stores in the country, complete with checkerboards and a potbellied stove. (See other Amish sites in Pennsylvania, as well as in Kentucky, Illinois, Indiana, Iowa, Michigan, Minnesota, Missouri, Ohio, Wisconsin, and Kansas.)

Brookville In its 90-acre historic district are more than 300 buildings dating from the 19th century. During the first weekend in December, citizens dress in 19th-century costumes for the Victorian Christmas celebration, which features Christmas caroling and a children's story hour.

Doylestown The National Shrine of Our Lady of Czestochowa, set on 250 acres, includes a monastery. The stained glass windows of the church depict 1,000 years of Polish Christianity. *The Holy Trinity* is a sculpture above the altar area. The shrine is on Ferry Rd. about five miles northwest of town.

Dublin The Pearl S. Buck House at 520 Dublin Rd. displays the noted author's Nobel and Pulitzer prizes, as well as many personal mementos. Born of missionary parents, Buck wrote many books about China, the country in which she grew up. *The Good Earth* won the Pulitzer prize. (See Buck also under Hillsboro, W.Va.)

Ephrata Ephrata Cloister (632 W. Main St.) was one of America's first communal societies. Members of the cloister were celibate and practiced an austere lifestyle. Known for their music and their unique style of lettering called *fraktur,* the members of the group were pioneers in publishing and printing in Pennsylvania. Ten of the original medieval-style buildings have been restored to resemble the 18th-century village.

At Ten Thousand Villages (240 N. Reading Rd.) you can shop for international crafts. This interesting shop is operated by the Mennonite Central Committee.

Fallsington The first houses in historic Fallsington were built by Quakers who were friends and followers of William Penn. This well-preserved village mirrors nearly 300 years of American architectural history from a primitive log cabin to the Victorian extravaganzas of the 19th century. Three Friends meetinghouses are around a picturesque square. Open from March 15 to November 15.

Gettysburg Gettysburg National Cemetery was the site of one of the most famous, and bloodiest, battles in American history. There were more than 50,000 casualties over three days in July 1863. This was also the site of one of the most famous speeches ever delivered by an American president, Lincoln's "Gettysburg Address." The park and cemetery are open every day from 6 A.M. to 10 P.M. The Visitors Information Center one mile south of town on Taneytown Rd. will provide visitors with a free map for an 18-mile self-guided tour of the park. Or you may join a walking tour, guided by a park ranger, or pay a guide for a personal tour ($30 for up to five people). There is also a museum in the information center.

While the historic battleground gets the most attention, the Prince of Peace Museum (south of Gettysburg Square on Rte. 15) deserves a look. Here artist Paul Cunningham has recreated the life of Christ in a series of colorful life-size three-dimensional scenes.

Grantham Messiah College, which is affiliated with the Brethren in Christ denomination, is located on a spacious 300-acre campus ten miles southwest of Harrisburg. Among its distinctives are the pursuit of justice and peacemaking. The college also has a Philadelphia campus.

Grove City Associated with a Presbyterian background, Grove City College is a growing school with about 2,100 students.

Harmony George Rapp and his Harmony (Rappite) Society established a communal settlement here in 1804 before they moved to Indiana. In 1824 they returned to Pennsylvania and settled in Ambridge. The Harmony Museum here on the town diamond preserves memorabilia of the group. Guided tours are offered. The Harmonist Church tower clock had a single hand pointing to the hour. A working replica is displayed in Grace Church. Mennonites are now responsible for the village. Phone 412-452-7341. (See Rappites also under New Harmony, Ind., and Ambridge, Pa.)

Hershey There is much to see and do in this attractive town, including Hershey Park, the Hershey Gardens, and Hershey's Chocolate World, but the Pastor's Study and Academy at 248 E. Derry Rd. at the Derry Presbyterian Church is one of Hershey's most historic buildings. Erected in 1724, the church's study has been enclosed in glass and can be viewed only from the outside.

Intercourse Amish and Mennonite arts and crafts are displayed at the Old Country Store on Main St. The People's Place Quilt Museum shows a collection of antique Amish quilts. The People's Place at 3513 Main St. is Lancaster County's center for learning about the Amish and Mennonites who live in the area. A three-screen documentary film is shown every 30 minutes during the summer.

> **GREAT PLACES TO ENJOY GOD'S CREATION**
>
> ✔ Cross-country skiing the Allegheny National Forest
>
> ✔ Camping in the Laurel Highlands

The Amish World Museum (3513 Old Philadelphia Pike) presents an inside look at the spirit and the beliefs of the Amish.

Between this town and Bird-in-Hand is the Weavertown One-Room Schoolhouse (2249 Rte. 30 E.), an original Amish school. It is typical of the schools attended by the Amish today, and you can see life-size animated figures re-create actual classroom activities. (See other Amish sites in Pennsylvania, as well as in Kentucky, Illinois, Indiana, Iowa, Michigan, Minnesota, Missouri, Ohio, Wisconsin, and Kansas.)

Jim Thorpe In 1954 the towns of Mauch Chunk and East Mauch Chunk merged to form the community of Jim Thorpe, named to honor the great Indian athlete. (See Jim Thorpe also under Shawnee, Okla.)

St. Mark's Episcopal Cathedral on Race St. was built with the generous gifts of Sarah Packer, wife of financier Asa Packer. It has many unusual features including its Tiffany stained glass windows and one of the oldest operating elevators in the nation.

Kennett Square Longwood Gardens here was once the country estate of Pierre S. Du Pont and it is internationally famous for its beauty, with more than 1,000 acres of outdoor gardens and more

THE AMISH IN PENNSYLVANIA

Amish faith stems from the European Anabaptist movement of the early 16th century. Believing strongly in the importance of separation of church and state, the Anabaptists were frequently persecuted for not supporting the rising nation-states in Europe. They sought asylum in the mountains of Switzerland, eventually coming under the leadership of a Dutchman named Menno Simons (hence the name "Mennonites"). Some 150 years later a group of these believers split off, believing that the Mennonites' ways were becoming too liberal. They came to be known as the Amish, after their leader Jakob Ammann.

During the 1700s, many Amish groups began immigrating to America. William Penn's "holy experiment" in religious tolerance drew many Amish groups to Pennsylvania, settling largely in the Lancaster County area. Other Amish groups would follow, settling primarily in the rural areas of Pennsylvania, Ohio, Indiana, Illinois, Iowa, Missouri, and parts of Canada. But the "Pennsylvania Dutch," as they came to be called, were the first, and perhaps the best-known. They are not the largest Amish community, however; that distinction belongs to the Amish of Ohio.

The Amish presence in Lancaster County is unmistakable. Black horse-drawn buggies carry simply dressed people along gravel roads. Fields are worked with horse-drawn plows. Amish homesteads use no electricity or telephone lines, and laundry is hung to dry in the country breeze. Visitors enjoy visiting restored Amish farms, purchasing homemade baked goods, quilts, furniture, and other crafts. Enjoy Amish country—but please don't photograph its people. The Amish have strong religious feelings against these "graven images."

than 11,000 types of plants. There are organ recitals in the main conservatory on Sunday afternoons in the winter, and performances in the open-air theater during the summer. Longwood Gardens is three miles northeast of the town on US 1.

Lancaster Lancaster County is the heart of Amish country in the state. Although Ohio has a larger population of Amish, the Pennsylvania Dutch are the nation's best known and most visited. For religious reasons, most of the Amish are opposed to being photographed (photos are the same as graven images in their minds), so keep that in mind when you are in the area.

Amish Country Tours (phone 717-768-3600) begin from the Plain and Fancy Restaurant, five miles east of Lancaster on Rte. 30. The Amish Farm and House with a 45-minute lecture tour on the Plain People's way of life is nearby (4.5 miles east on Rte. 30).

Here you can visit several furnished farmhouses, a windmill, and spring house, as well as a blacksmith shop. You will also learn more about Amish worship. (See other Amish sites in Pennsylvania, as well as in Kentucky, Illinois, Indiana, Iowa, Michigan, Minnesota, Missouri, Ohio, Wisconsin, and Kansas.)

The Hans Herr House (four miles south on US 222) is the oldest building in the county and the oldest Mennonite meetinghouse in America. It has been depicted in several paintings by Andrew Wyeth, who is a descendant of Hans Herr.

The Hebrew Tabernacle Reproduction and the Mennonite Information Center are next to each other at 2209 Millstream Rd., about 4.5 miles east, just off Rte. 30. The Hebrew Tabernacle includes lecture tours each hour on the history, construction, function, and significance of the Old Testament tabernacle. The reproduction helps you visualize the worship of the Old Testament. The Mennonite Information Center has exhibits and a video regarding Amish and Mennonite life.

Trinity Lutheran Church (31 S. Duke St.) was originally built in 1730 and then rebuilt in 1761 to 1766. The spire with its statues of Matthew, Mark, Luke, and John dates from 1794.

Lewisburg The Easter hymn "Low in the Grave He Lay" was written by Robert Lowry, pastor of the First Baptist Church here. Lowry was also a professor of rhetoric at Bucknell University.

Lititz The Lititz Moravian Archives and Museum at Church Square and Main St. provides guided tours of the area. In 1756 Lititz was founded as a Moravian community, and until 1855 the entire area was owned by the church. Linden Hall, one of the oldest girls' residence schools in America, was founded by Moravians in the 18th century. (See Moravians also under Hope, N.J.; Bethlehem and Nazareth, Pa.; Winston-Salem, N.C.; Bloomington, Ill.; Gnadenhutten and New Philadelphia, Ohio; and Ephraim, Wisc.)

McSherrystown The Basilica of the Sacred Heart of Jesus (2.5 miles west of Hanover on Rte. 116) was originally constructed in 1741 as a log chapel. It was replaced in 1787 by the present stone structure and designated a minor basilica in 1962. It contains frescoes, statues, and paintings.

Manheim Baron Henry William Stiegel established a glassware factory here, reputed to have produced the finest glassware in colonial America. He also gave to the Zion Lutheran Church the property for its building (2 S. Hazel St.). He stipulated a rental of one red rose per year, which the church still pays. The second Sunday of June the Feast of Roses ceremony is held at the church, with the rent requested by Baron Stiegel presented to a Stiegel heir.

Montrose It was near the Montrose Bible Conference grounds here that in 1958 John W. Peterson and Alfred B. Smith wrote the words and music of the gospel song "Surely Goodness and Mercy Shall Follow Me."

Mount Pocono One mile south on Rte. 711 is the Pennsylvania Dutch farm, featuring an Amish home and farm. The house includes typical Amish clothes and furnishings. In the farmyard are buggies, wagons, sleighs, and farm machinery. (See other Amish sites in Pennsylvania, as well as in Kentucky, Illinois, Indiana, Iowa, Michigan, Minnesota, Missouri, Ohio, Wisconsin, and Kansas.)

Nazareth George Whitefield, the famous English evangelist, purchased a 5,000-acre tract of land from the William Penn family, land that is today the town of Nazareth. He planned to establish a school and he hired a group of Moravians to oversee the project. Financial problems forced Whitefield to sell the entire lot to the Moravians in 1741. The Gray Cottage, a log cabin built in 1740, was the first building in Nazareth and is the oldest Moravian building in North America. The Whitefield House (214 E. Center St.), built in 1743, was the communal church-home of the Moravians and today it is the home of the Moravian Historical Society and the Nazareth Museum. (See Moravians also under Hope, N.J.; Bethlehem and Lititz, Pa.; Winston-Salem, N.C.; Bloomington, Ill.; Gnadenhutten and New Philadelphia, Ohio; and Ephraim, Wisc.)

Palmyra Three miles north of town is the Bindnagles Evangelical Lutheran Church, built in 1803. It is a two-story structure with round arch windows and doors.

Philadelphia William Penn founded the City of Brotherly Love with his Quaker brethren in 1682. Whether you are a history buff or not, you cannot escape feeling tingly at the historic sights in Philadelphia. Independence National Historical Park, the "most historic square mile in America," bounded by Market, Walnut, 2d, and 6th Sts., marks the center of it all. The Declaration of Independence was signed in 1776 in Independence Hall, as was the 1787 Constitution. The U.S. Congress first assembled in nearby Congress Hall. Visitors can take a self-guided tour.

The Liberty Bell in the Liberty Bell Pavilion of Independence National Historical Park is so named because of the quotation on it from Leviticus 25:10: "Proclaim liberty throughout the land."

While Penn founded Philadelphia, Ben Franklin made it what it is today. Franklin's home is the centerpoint of Franklin Court, on Market St., between 3d and 4th Sts. His home is open daily during normal business hours and admission is free. The home contains an extremely creative museum, an informational video, and a replica of Franklin's printing office.

Other historical sites worth visiting are Washington Square, where an eternal flame commemorates the Revolutionary War dead at the Tomb of the Unknown Soldier, and the U.S. Mint, the largest mint in the world, across from Independence Hall. At 239 Arch St. is the Betsy Ross house where Betsy Ross is said to have sewed the first flag of the original 13 states.

Two Quaker meetinghouses are located on Arch St. The Free Quaker Meeting House (5th and Arch Sts.) dates from 1683 and is currently closed. Arch Street Meeting House (4th and Arch Sts.) is the original brick meetinghouse built in 1804 on a site donated to the Religious Society of Friends by William Penn in 1693. Besides the meeting room, there are displays of Bibles, Quaker objects, and a history of William Penn's life and religion.

Bishop White House at 309 Walnut St. was built by Pennsylvania's first Protestant Episcopal bishop. The restored house is part of Independence National Historical Park.

Christ Church on 2d between Market and Arch Sts. was the house of worship of fifteen signers of the Declaration of Independence. Plaques now designate the pews of George Washington, Benjamin Franklin, and Betsy Ross. Christ Church Burial Ground at 5th and Arch Sts. contains the graves of Benjamin Franklin and four other signers of the Declaration of Independence.

Gloria Dei (Old Swedes') Church (Christian St. at Christopher Columbus Blvd.) is thought to be Pennsylvania's oldest church. It was founded in 1700, but its congregation began meeting in 1646.

97

Old St. Joseph's Church (4th St., below Walnut St.) was the first Roman Catholic church in Philadelphia. The Marquis de Lafayette and Comte de Rochambeau worshiped here. The second Roman Catholic church, Old St. Mary's Church (4th St. between Locust and Spruce Sts.) was founded in 1763 and was designated Philadelphia's first cathedral in 1810.

The Presbyterian Historical Society at 5th and Lombard Sts. was founded in 1852 and preserves many artifacts from the colonial period. It also includes a portrait gallery by noted artists.

St. George's United Methodist Church on 4th St. near the Ben Franklin Bridge, was dedicated in 1769 and is the oldest Methodist church used continuously for worship. In 1784 the church licensed the first African American Methodist pastor in America.

The University of Pennsylvania Museum of Archaeology and Anthropology at 33d and Spruce Sts. has an outstanding display of materials from Egypt and Mesopotamia, including Persia and Babylon. Exhibits include a 12-ton granite Sphinx of Rameses II, a lead sarcophagus from Tyre, and the famous treasure trove of the Royal Tombs of Ur, where Abraham came from.

Tenth Presbyterian Church at 17th and Spruce Sts. was pastored by well-known Bible teacher Donald Grey Barnhouse from 1927 to 1960. Today James Montgomery Boice is the pastor, as well as the speaker on the *Bible Study Hour* radio program, originating at 1716 Spruce St.

Perhaps the largest congregation in the city is the Deliverance Evangelistic congregation (2001 W. Lehigh Ave.) with more than 7,000 in attendance on a typical Sunday.

Russell Conwell, Baptist pastor of the largest church in the city in the 19th century, founded Temple University here. His famous "Acres of Diamonds" speech, which he delivered from coast to coast, netted 11 million dollars, which he donated to Temple students.

Philadelphia's Children's Hospital is where Dr. C. Everett Koop was acclaimed for separating conjoined twins, before being named surgeon general of the United States in 1982.

For a century after Joseph Gilmore wrote the hymn "He Leadeth Me," a commemorative plaque was on the sidewalk of the Arch St. location, where the First Baptist Church had stood near Arch and Broad Sts. Pastor Gilmore wrote the hymn after preaching on the Twenty-third Psalm.

"O Little Town of Bethlehem" was written for the Sunday school children of the Holy Trinity Episcopal Church by their pastor, Phillips Brooks. The organist, who was also the Sunday school superintendent, wrote the tune. Holy Trinity Episcopal Church is at 19th and Locust Sts.

Pittsburgh Heinz Memorial Chapel (the University of Pittsburgh at 5th Ave. and S. Bellefield St.) is a modern French Gothic interdenominational chapel with 73-foot-high stained glass windows.

The Carnegie is an opulent cultural center housing the Museum of Art, the Museum of Natural History, the Music Hall, and the Carnegie Library. For years evangelist Kathryn Kuhlman conducted healing and evangelistic services in Carnegie Music Hall (4400 Forbes St.).

The Rodef Shalom Biblical Botanical Garden near the Carnegie Mellon University at 4905 5th Ave. has more than 150 varieties of flora, each with a biblical name or reference. It is on a setting reminiscent of ancient Israel with a stream like the River Jordan running through it.

First Presbyterian Church at 320 6th Ave. has had many notable pastors. Clarence Macartney was pastor here from 1927 to 1953.

The North Way Christian Community Church in nearby Wexford (12121 Perry Hwy.) has one of the larger congregations in the area with about 2,000 in average attendance.

At Calvary Episcopal Church (315 Shady Ave.), Samuel M. Shoemaker launched his Pittsburgh Experiment in the 1950s, training laypeople in personal evangelism. He also started the magazine *Faith at Work*.

St. Davids This lovely Philadelphia suburb, about 15 miles west of the city, is the home of Eastern College, affiliated with the American Baptists. The campus is worth seeing.

Strasburg First settled by French Huguenots, Strasburg was soon home to Amish and Mennonite settlers. Today it is part of Pennsylvania Dutch country. The Amish Village (Rte. 896, one mile south of Rte. 30) contains an 1840 house furnished in Amish style. Guides explain the history, clothing, furniture, and way of life of the Amish. (See other Amish sites in Pennsylvania, as well as in Kentucky, Illinois, Indiana, Iowa, Michigan, Minnesota, Missouri, Ohio, Wisconsin, and Kansas.)

Swarthmore Grace Livingston Hill, described as the "queen of the Christian novel" lived in this college town for many years. She started the Leiper Presbyterian Church south of the town (900 Fairview Rd.).

Valley Forge The Valley Forge National Historical Park contains the Washington Memorial Chapel on Rte. 23 with woodcarvings depicting the history of the country. A bell tower houses the 58-bell Memorial National Carillon. After the 11:15 A.M. service, free recitals are given. In the chapel is the Valley Forge Historical Society Museum with more than 3,000 artifacts from the winter encampment of the Continental Army in 1777 and 1778. The park itself covers 3,600 beautiful acres of rolling hills and forests. It has three picnic areas and lots of free space for kids to run around and play. Entrance to the grounds is free. A visit to General Washington's headquarters costs $2 for adults.

The Freedoms Foundation at Valley Forge (at 1601 Valley Forge Rd., also on Rte. 23) was founded in 1949 to promote responsible citizenship. On its 105 acres are the Medal of Honor Grove, Independence Gardens, and the Faith of Our Fathers Chapel.

■WEST VIRGINIA

Tourist Info
Phone 800-CALL-WVA
Web sites
  Entire state   www.westvirginia.com
  Charleston   www.charlestonwv.com
For a complete list of updated links, visit www.christiantraveler.com

Aurora Just down the road from Cathedral State Park in Horse Shoe Run is Our Lady of the Pines, one of the smallest churches in the nation. The park is so named because of its dense canopy of towering trees, many of them virgin hemlocks and hardwoods, some measuring ten feet in diameter and over a hundred feet tall. It is the state's finest primeval forest, and during the fall, the foliage is magnificent. Our Lady of the Pines is a 16-foot-by-11-foot stone structure with six locally made stained glass windows, a tiny altar, and six pews. Worshipers of any denomination are welcome to stop and pray here.

Beckley Two museums located in New River Park in Beckley will be especially interesting to kids. The Youth Museum of Southern West Virginia features a permanent village of reconstructed or relocated log buildings that depict agricultural life in the area before the advent of mining. Admission is $2. The Beckley Exhibition Coal Mine has 1,500 feet of restored passages open for guided tours. Coal mining has had a great impact on the lives of this area's citizens, and this is a good way to teach children about it. Admission is $7.

Bethany Alexander Campbell, founder of the Disciples of Christ movement, is memorialized here. Visitors can take a walking tour of the historic district of the town and see the Campbell Museum, God's Acre, the Campbell Cemetery, the Old Meeting House, Bethany Church, an old inn built by Alexander Campbell called Hibernia, and several newer residences. The Alexander Campbell Mansion here dates to 1793 and has 25 rooms. For tour information, phone 304-829-7285.

The focal point of Bethany College, founded by Alexander Campbell, is Old Main, built in Gothic style with a 122-foot tower. It was styled after a similar structure at the University of Glasgow in Scotland.

Buckhannon West Virginia Wesleyan College with its 1,600 students is located here. Its Georgian-style campus is especially lovely in the spring and early summer when the rhododendron garden blooms. Wesley Chapel, with its white steeple and Casavant organ (1,500 pipes), holds regular services and, with a capacity of 1,600, is the largest church in the state. Phone 304-473-8510.

Bulltown During the Civil War, a 12-hour battle was waged here between Union and Confederate forces. Today living history demonstrations show how everyday life was lived in the 19th century. St. Michael's Church, one of the first Catholic churches in the state, overlooks the battle site. At 11 A.M. on Sundays during the summer a tour is given that tells how religion developed in Appalachia. In July children can see what school was like a century ago. For three hours they can attend an Appalachian school of the mid-1800s and have the same lessons, games, and homework, using 19th-century texts.

Burning Springs The Ruble Log Church here was built of hand-hewn logs by Aaron Ruble in about 1854. It still retains its original appearance and is one of the oldest structures in the Little Kanawha River Valley.

Charleston The Booker T. Washington Memorial on the grounds of the state capitol honors this African American who was born a slave, spent his boyhood in West Virginia, gained his freedom by the Emancipation Proclamation, and later started Tuskegee Institute in Alabama. He was an advisor to several U.S. presidents and received honorary degrees from Harvard and Dartmouth. A humble Christian, he read his Bible daily. (See Washington also under Hardy, Va., and Tuskegee, Ala.)

The West Virginia Black Sacred Music Festival in February is devoted to praise and worship, from shape-note singing to tambourine shaking to full-scale gospel chorale performances. Founded by gospel legend Ethel Caffie-Austin, the festival seeks to preserve and share African American gospel traditions. Four days of workshops culminate in an "everybody sings" Sunday concert led by nationally acclaimed performers. Contact the Charleston Convention and Visitors Bureau for information and precise dates: 800-733-5469.

On Memorial Day weekend, the Vandalia Gathering draws traditional musicians statewide to the grounds of the state capitol. In addition to music traditions ranging from fiddling to polka, there is a storytelling contest that chooses the "Biggest Liar in West Virginia."

Elkins Each summer many of the nation's most talented folk artists teach 90 weeklong classes at the Augusta Heritage Workshops at Davis and Elkins College (300 Sycamore St.). Here you can learn old-time fiddle playing, log house construction, basketry, weaving, and spinning. In mid-August the festival spills over from the college campus into the city park with dancing, food, and crafts. Phone 304-637-1209 for more information.

Fairmont The Central United Methodist Church here (301 Fairmont Ave.) claims to be the site of the first observance of Father's

Day, on July 5, 1908. The church is now fittingly called the Father's Day Church.

Fayetteville Just outside of town on US 19 is the New River Gorge Bridge, the world's longest steel arch span. It is 3,030 feet long and rises 876 feet above the New River. The river gorge has to be seen to be appreciated, and you can see it beautifully on a short walk from the Canyon Rim Visitors Center. The gorge walls average 1,000 feet in height, the river is rough with plenty of white water, the plant life is extremely dense and green, and you'll wonder how in the world they ever got that bridge up there.

Grafton The founder of Mother's Day, Anna Jarvis, is honored here by an International Mother's Day Shrine. It was in the Andrews Methodist church in 1908 where the first Mother's Day service was held (see also Webster, W.Va., the location of her home). Actually Miss Jarvis was living in Philadelphia at the time and her mother had passed away three years earlier. She thought it would be a good idea if the church where her mother had taught Sunday school for more than 20 years would recognize her on the anniversary of her death. So Mother's Day was celebrated in Grafton in 1908. Six years later, at Anna Jarvis's urging, both houses of Congress passed a resolution calling for a national observance of Mother's Day. It was signed by President Woodrow Wilson. The shrine is located on Main St., one mile south of the intersection of Rte. 50 and US 119.

The whole earth is full of his glory.
ISAIAH **6:3**

Harpers Ferry The Harpers Ferry Historical Park is the largest tourist draw in West Virginia. Admission is $2 per person. It was here in 1859 that abolitionist John Brown raided the national armory and arsenal, trying to seize guns and munitions for his planned slave rebellion. The John Brown Wax Museum within the park chronicles his raid, his capture, trial, and subsequent hanging in nearby Charles Town. Stairs carved into the hillside off High St. follow the Appalachian Trail to Upper Harpers Ferry. The walk will take you past several sites associated with the raid, including St. Peter's Catholic Church, a stone chapel built in 1830 and used continuously until its closing in 1994. During the Civil War, the nervous pastor of this church flew the Union Jack flag to protect the church. You can also visit a living history museum within the park, complete with interpretive guides in period costume.

Old Tyme Christmas is held annually the first two weekends in December. Homes, shops, and historic buildings are decorated with evergreens and ribbons. Festivities include a living nativity scene, musical programs, choral recitals, children's games, tree trimming, candlelighting ceremonies, and more.

Helvetia South of Elkins, off US 250 is the small town that seems to have come directly from the Swiss Alps, which is indeed where its original settlers came from. It is a fairy tale–like village, known for its good food and charm. The Hutte restaurant, which serves Swiss food, bears the sign *Gruss Gott, tritt ein* (Praise God, step in). The town museum and the century-old church are all endearing to the visitor.

Hillsboro The restored home of one of America's greatest novelists, Pearl S. Buck, is here. Although she was raised in China by her missionary parents, she was born in West Virginia. The Pearl S. Buck Homestead was built by her mother's family, who had come from Holland in 1847. It is now set on sixteen acres. Tours are available May through October, showing original furniture and memorabilia. Phone 304-653-4430 for tour information. (See Buck also under Dublin, Pa.)

Hinton The Second Baptist Church, built in a colonial revival–style architecture, is the oldest African American church in the area.

Huntington The Blenko Glass Company (exit 28 off I-64 in Milton) is known for its stained glass. It has supplied stained glass for St. Patrick's Cathedral in New York City and the National Cathedral in Washington, D.C. There is a small museum, and tours are available in which visitors can watch molten glass take its final form, but there is no glassblowing on weekends. Admission is free.

Huttonsville Tygarts Valley Presbyterian Church here, dedicated in 1883, is one of the best examples of High Victorian Gothic architecture in the state. Its ornate style and 105-foot steeple are unusual for its rural location.

Lewisburg The oldest place of worship in continuous use west of the Alleghenies is the Old Stone Presbyterian Church at 200 Church St. Built in 1796, it is a two-story native limestone structure and features an old slave gallery. Architecturally simple, after the meetinghouse style of the 18th century, its thick walls are made of native limestone, essentially unchanged since its original construction, and symbolic to many of a solid faith that survives. It is a landmark in the town's historic district where gas lamps still light the streets and there are no overhead power lines.

Martinsburg The Tuscarora Church (2335 Tuscarora Pike) was established by Scotch-Irish Presbyterians in 1740. The present church, however, was built in 1803 and still contains the pegs where worshipers hung their guns while attending the services. Today it has about 140 worshipers.

Moorefield Three miles north of town is Old Fields Church, which claims to be the second-oldest church in the state. It was built in 1812 and was originally known as the Fort Pleasant Meeting House. What is unusual about it is that both Methodists and Presbyterians used it for more than 100 years. It was also the first schoolhouse in the area. Occasionally services are still held here, under the auspices of the Duffey Memorial United Methodist Church. Old Fields Church is just off US 220, three miles south of Moorefield.

Parkersburg One of the state's unique crafts is glassmaking. From Parkersburg to Huntington you'll find more than a dozen hand-blown glass factories open for touring. Near Parkersburg, in Williamstown, visit Fenton Art Glass (at 420 Caroline Ave.), just over the river from Marietta, Ohio. There is also a museum on site. Admission is free.

Point Pleasant The 50-acre West Virginia State Farm Museum includes more than 30 reconstructed buildings, including a Lutheran church, a general store, and a one-room school. Admission is free.

Romney One mile north of town on Rte. 28 is the Potomac Eagle Scenic Rail Excursions. Passengers are transported in vintage railcars into the beautiful wilderness of the South Branch of the Potomac River. Keep your eyes open for bald eagles. Phone 800-223-2453 for schedule information.

Salem Seventh Day Baptists founded this little city after a 30-month trek from New Jersey. Now their legacy lives on at Fort New Salem, which is a reconstructed pioneer settlement. "The Sign of the Three Barrels" is the visitors center; the blockhouse and the meetinghouse are used for church services and the school. Delila's House is a good example of what slave quarters were like in 1815. It is a living history museum under the patronage of Salem-Teikyo University, about a mile away. Follow Rte. 50 west to the Salem exit, Rte. 23.

Shepherdstown The historic district includes many landmarks. During the Civil War battle of Antietam, the entire town served as a hospital.

The Christ Reformed Church at German and Mill Sts. has bells that were cast in France in 1732 and were dedicated in Shepherdstown in 1795.

Early in December each year, strolling carolers in turn-of-the-century dress walk the town, and peddlers roast chestnuts for Christmas shoppers.

Summersville Music in the Mountains is a June bluegrass jamboree by "the best of the best." One of the country's biggest bluegrass events, it's a family-style feast of familiar names, lightning-fast picking, and close harmonies. Call 304-872-3145 for complete details.

Nearly 2,000 miles of mountain streams have given the state the reputation of being the best white-water rafting location in the East. More than 25 rafting companies operate in West Virginia, many of them along the New and Gauley Rivers. They offer services from basic to luxurious, with levels that range from a leisurely float downstream watching for wildlife to seriously demanding rapids for skilled paddlers. Call 800-CALLWVA for lists of outfitters in the area, or request a free white-water guide.

Union No longer in use is the Rehoboth Church of Union, built around 1785, one of the oldest churches west of the Alleghenies. It is a log church and now designated as one of ten Methodist shrines in the nation. At one time it doubled as a fort against Indian attacks.

Webster A Methodist, Anna Jarvis, started Mother's Day in her church in nearby Grafton. Her home, dating from 1854 or 1855, has been restored to the period and retains its original woodwork and fireplaces. It is open year-round, but there are special observances on Mother's Day.

Southeastern States

PONCE DE LEÓN LANDED on Florida's shores in 1513, and visitors have been flocking to the southeastern corner of the United States ever since. Unlike de León, the multitudes of travelers heading south today are not looking for the fountain of youth, but many find their youth restored in the warm sun, sand, and surf, glad for some relief from brutal northern winters.

There are two must-see destinations in the Southeast for Christian travelers, both of which exhibit the extent to which Christianity played a role in American history. St. Augustine, Florida, the country's oldest permanent settlement, has its roots unmistakably planted in the faith. Ornate historic churches, a 200-foot steel cross, and the city's name itself are clear reminders more than 400 years later of those spiritual origins.

Atlanta, Georgia, offers powerful attractions of another sort, those associated with slain civil rights leader Dr. Martin Luther King Jr. The predominance of Christian sites and memorabilia found within the King National Historic Site serves as a reminder of the degree to which the civil rights movement was rooted in the Christian faith of the African American church.

■FLORIDA

Tourist Info
Phone 888-7-FLAUSA
Web sites
  Entire state   www.flausa.com
  Disney World   www.disneyworld.com
  Fort Myers area and local islands   www.leeislandcoast.com
  Jacksonville   www.jaxcvb.com
  Miami   www.tropicoolmiami.com
  St. Augustine   www.oldcity.com
  Sea World   www.seaworld.com
  Universal Studios   www.usf.com
For a complete list of updated links, visit www.christiantraveler.com

Big Pine Key At the National Key Deer Refuge (north of US 1 on Key Deer Blvd.), you will find the smallest of all white-tailed deer. In fact two-thirds of all key deer live in this refuge. Your best chance of seeing them is early in the morning. Nearby is Blue Hole, an old rock quarry where several alligators happen to hang out.

Boca Raton The Bibletown winter Bible conference and sacred concert complex is located here. Winter concerts are held January through March and feature Christian artists. The auditorium holds about 2,000. For schedules and information, call 561-395-2400.

The International Museum of Cartoon Art (201 Plaza Real) shows 200 years of cartoon history, including comic strips, editorial cartoons, animation, greeting cards, and more. Admission is $6.

Brooksville The Weeki Wachee Spring (on Rte. 50 and US 19) is an underwater amphitheater that allows you to watch underwater performances through 19 plate glass windows. Each performance lasts about 30 minutes.

Cape Canaveral All of NASA's shuttle flights take off from the Kennedy Space Center. If you're fortunate, you may get to see a shuttle take off. And don't worry if you can't get tickets from the Public Affairs Office of the Space Center (call 800-572-4636 if you'd like to try), you'll be able to see the liftoff from many miles away. Kennedy Space Center's Visitors Complex has a huge welcoming center for visitors, as well as an outdoor Rocket Garden, featuring actual spacecraft and their replicas, and the Astronauts Memorial, a beautiful memorial to those who have given their lives in space exploration. The visitors center is also the departure point for two-hour bus tours of the complex. IMAX films portraying the beauty and power of space exploration are lots of fun and worth the money. Admission to the complex is free. Bus tours are $8 and IMAX films are $5.

Cocoa The historic area here covers about four blocks, and on the walking tour (starting at 274 Brevard Ave.) you will see a Gothic church (1886), the Porcher House (1916), and 12 other sites.

Cross Creek The Marjorie Kinnan Rawlings State Historic Site (four miles west of US 301 on Rte. 325) is the restored home of the Pulitzer prize–winning author of *The Yearling*. The area is the setting for several of her books.

Dade City The Saint Leo Abbey (five miles southwest on Rte. 52) is a Benedictine Abbey named for Pope Leo I, with a 21,000-pound cross, carved from Tennessee rose marble.

Daytona Mary McLeod Bethune, an African American Moody Bible Institute graduate, founded what is now Bethune-Cookman College, located here at 640 Mary McLeod Bethune Blvd.

Everglades National Park This is one of the largest national parks in the country, covering 1.6 million acres of one of the world's most beautiful and fragile ecosystems. There are seemingly endless opportunities for fishing, hiking, canoeing, biking, and wilderness observation. But you can forget about swimming—the alligators, sharks, and barracudas make that particular activity inadvisable.

Fort Lauderdale Dr. James Kennedy, creator of the Evangelism Explosion program and speaker on his national TV program, is the pastor of the Coral Ridge Presbyterian Church at 5555 N. Federal Hwy. The church has nearly 5,000 worshipers at its Sunday services. There are also frequent concerts here.

Young at Art Children's Museum (just north of I-585 on University Dr.) is a creative hands-on museum for kids, featuring computer art, a texture tunnel, a giant play space, and an art studio where workshops are held.

Lolly the Trolley leaves from the Galleria Mall and Holiday Inn and gives you a 90-minute tour of historic Fort Lauderdale.

Fort Myers The Christian and Missionary Alliance has a large retirement community at Shell Point Village here. More than 1,000 residents live in this 75-acre village. It is located on McGregor Blvd. 15 miles south of Fort Myers on Route 867.

The Edison-Ford Complex (1 mile southwest at 2350 McGregor Blvd.) gives you the winter houses of two of America's most famous industrialists, Thomas Edison and Henry Ford.

The J. C. Sightseeing Boat Cruises, which leave from the foot of Henry St. in the Fort Myers Yacht Basin, provide jungle cruises and other cruises in which you tour lush wooded areas and/or notable historic sites.

The Seminole Gulf Railway leaves from the Metro Mall Station and gives you a two-hour excursion to Bonita Springs and back in vintage coaches. If you wish, you can sign up for a murder mystery trip, a Sunday brunch, or a New England lobster bake.

McGregor Baptist Church (Southern Baptist) is the largest Protestant church in the city, at 3750 Colonial Blvd.

An organization known as ECHO (Educational Concerns for Hunger Organization), located at 17430 Durrance Rd. in North Fort Myers, is a Christian organization that teaches the poor in foreign countries how to grow their own crops to feed themselves. It invites visitors to check out its 21-acre farm, devoted to raising seeds.

Jacksonville Two large Baptist churches, First Baptist (Southern Baptist) at 124 W. Ashley St. and Trinity Baptist (Independent) at 800 Hammond Blvd., are the largest churches in the city.

The Luther Rice Seminary (Baptist), one of the larger seminaries in the country, has more than 3,000 students enrolled.

The Cummer Gallery of Art (829 Riverside Ave.) contains decorative and fine arts that go back to the time of Abraham in the Old Testament. The formal gardens are modeled after the gardens of the Villa Gamberaia in Florence, Italy.

Jupiter The Jonathan Dickinson State Park (six miles north on US 1) is a 10,000-acre park named after the Quaker who was the first to land here. Dickinson and his party were swept ashore during a storm in 1696, captured by Indians, and then set free. They walked 225 miles to St. Augustine. A book on Dickinson's adventures was widely read both in Europe and in America. Phone 561-546-2771 for information on camping and cabin and canoe rentals.

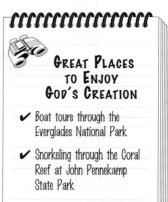

GREAT PLACES TO ENJOY GOD'S CREATION

✔ Boat tours through the Everglades National Park

✔ Snorkeling through the Coral Reef at John Pennekamp State Park

Key Largo John Pennekamp State Park is the nation's first underwater sanctuary, protecting 78 square miles of the 120-square-mile coral reef that runs the length of the Florida Keys. Forty species of coral and more than 650 varieties of fish make this an exceptional place to snorkel or dive. Scuba trips, snorkeling tours, and glass-bottom boat tours are all available. Admission is $4 per vehicle. Phone 305-451-1202 for camping, snorkeling, and boating information.

Key West The Old Town Trolley (leaving from the Trolley Barn at 1910 N. Roosevelt St.) provides you with a 90-minute tour of Key West along with a narrated introduction to the history and pseudo-history of the area.

Kissimmee This area is swarming with attractions like Gatorland (14501 S. Orange Blossom Tr.), the Green Meadows Petting Farm (Poinciana Blvd.), JungleLand (4580 W. Hwy. 192), Reptile World Serpentarium (5705 E. Irlo Bronson Memorial Hwy.), and Water Mania (6073 W. Irlo Bronson Memorial Hwy.). If you're more historically minded, you may want to look at Medieval Life (4510 W. Irlo Bronson Memorial Hwy.), which is a living museum of the Middle Ages, and Old Town, which replicates a turn-of-the-century Florida village.

Lake Wales The Bok Tower Gardens (three miles north of US 27A at 1151 Tower Blvd.) has as its focal point the 205-foot Bok Singing Tower, the highest point on the peninsula. Its 57-bell carillon provides music throughout the day. Surrounding the tower are 128 acres of landscaped gardens.

This isn't the Black Hills, but the Black Hills Passion play takes place in an outdoor amphitheater, two miles south on US 27A. The play is performed from mid-February to mid-April. It portrays the last week of Christ's life before the crucifixion and the play lasts about two and a quarter hours. Phone them in Black Hills, S.D., for information on their Florida performances: 605-642-2646. (For other Passion plays, see St. Augustine, Fla.; Atlantic Beach, N.C.; Gadsden, Ala.; Eureka Springs, Ark.; Ruston, La.; Gatlinburg, Tenn.; Bloomington and Zion, Ill.; and Spearfish, S.D.)

Marineland About 18 miles south of St. Augustine is Marineland of Florida (9507 Ocean Shore Blvd.), which features performing dolphins and much more. The landscaped grounds may be as enjoyable as the 50-minute presentation.

Miami The village of Coconut Grove is the oldest section of Miami, first inhabited in the 1870s. Its residents have included New England intellectuals, bohemians, artists, and writers who established winter homes here. The Plymouth Congregational Church (3400 Devon Rd.) is a lovely coral-rock Mexican mission–style structure dating from 1917. Visitors to the 11-acre grounds will also see natural sunken gardens, the first schoolhouse in Dade County, and the site of the original Coconut Grove water and electric works. The historic village of Coconut Grove is a trendy commercial district with brick walkways and more than 300 restaurants, stores, and art galleries.

The Ermita de La Caridad (Our Lady of Charity Shrine) at 3609 S. Miami Ave. is worth a stop whether you are Catholic or not. This 90-foot conical shrine was built to overlook the bay so that worshipers could face Cuba as they prayed.

The Spanish Monastery (16711 W. Dixie Hwy., in North Miami Beach) is a monastery from Segovia, Spain, that was built in 1141. Publisher tycoon William Randolph Hearst bought it, took it apart, crated it, and shipped it to the United States. It wasn't reassembled until 1954, after Hearst had died. It is now owned by the Episcopal Church.

The Vizcaya Museum and Gardens (3251 S. Miami Ave.) is a 70-room villa in Italian Renaissance style, and the gardens are ten acres of fountains, statuary, and grottoes. The house contains quite a collection of European art and furnishings, some of them five centuries old.

The Bass Museum (2121 Park Ave. in Miami Beach) specializes in religious paintings and sculpture from the Middle Ages.

The Key Biscayne Community Church on the key southeast of downtown (355 Glenridge Rd.) has been known for the outstanding evangelical preachers who have been pastors there.

Fairchild Tropical Garden (10901 Old Cutler Rd.) is the nation's largest tropical botanical garden, and you can take a train ride through its 83 acres. Children under 13 go in without charge.

Miami's Metrozoo (12400 S.W. 152d St.) is the largest cageless zoo in the country and it features some very rare white Bengal tigers. Admission is $14.

Children will enjoy the Miami Seaquarium at 4400 Rickenbacker Causeway. The park features sea lions, dolphins, and killer whale performances as well as a 235,000-gallon tropical reef aquarium. Admission is $19.95, parking $3.

The Latin America Mission has its international office at 5465 NW. 36th St. In nearby Opa-Locka, the World Radio Missionary Fellowship has its offices.

GREAT PLACES FOR FAMILY FUN

✔ Sea World, Orlando

✔ Disney World, Orlando

✔ Kennedy Space Center, Cape Canaveral

Naples Frannie's Teddy Bear Museum (2511 Pine Ridge Rd.) is unique with its display of more than 3,000 teddy bears. Of course, Smokey the Bear and Paddington are there too.

Orlando The Orlando area is full of family amusements, including Sea World of Florida; Universal Studios Florida; Walt Disney World with its Epcot Center, Animal Kingdom, and Magic Kingdom; Wet 'N Wild (6200 International Dr.), the Mystery Fun House (5767 Major Blvd.); and more.

Depending on how old your children are (or how young you feel), Terror on Church Street (at Church and Orange Sts.) may provide a few thrills and chills. It is a high-tech, year-round haunted house. You walk through 23 suspenseful rooms, each with a different theme. Children under ten must be accompanied by an adult.

If you want peace and quiet, visit the Harry P. Leu Gardens (1920 N. Forest St.), which has 50 acres of oaks, flowering shrubs, roses, orchids, azaleas, and more.

Trainland of Orlando (8255 International Dr.) features a one-half-inch scale layout of a model railroad that travels through an indoor garden. Models of toy trains from the 1920s to the present are also displayed.

Theologian R. C. Sproul moved his Ligonier Ministries from Pennsylvania to Orlando in the 1980s. Conferences are conducted here on a regular basis. Ligonier Ministries is located at 400 Technology Park #150. Phone them at 407-333-4244.

Author/evangelist Benny Hinn's church is the World Outreach Church (7601 Forest City Rd.), which has more than 6,000 worshipers each week.

First Baptist Church (Southern Baptist) at 3000 S. John Young Pkwy. has an average Sunday morning attendance of more than 5,000.

Several evangelical parachurch organizations now make Orlando their headquarters. Among them are Campus Crusade, Wycliffe Bible Translators, and *Charisma* magazine.

Palm Beach The Church of Bethesda-by-the-Sea (S. County Rd. and Barton St.) was built in a 15th-century Gothic design with an embattlement tower and an arched main entrance.

It's a nice place to visit, but maybe you wouldn't want to live in the 55-room house (too much cleaning) built in 1901 by Henry Morrison Flagler (Coconut Row at Whitehall Way). Flagler, who developed the Florida East Coast Railroad and also developed Palm Beach, built and opulently adorned this marble mansion, now called the Henry Morrison Flagler Museum. On the grounds you will also see his private railroad car. Donald Trump owns the 118-room place at 1100 Ocean Blvd., in case you're wondering, but it isn't open to the public.

Pensacola The Spanish established a settlement here in 1559, but it lasted only two years. Today the oldest buildings are in Historic Pensacola Village (Seville Square, E. Government and S. Alcaniz Sts.) and include the 1832 Old Christ Church, used as a barracks and hospital for Union soldiers, and the 1805 Charles LaValle House (205 E. Church St.) with a typical French Creole architectural style.

Pompano Beach Butterfly World (3600 Sample Rd., in Coconut Creek) is the largest facility of its kind. Thousands of butterflies flit all around the place.

Punta Gorda The Babcock Wilderness Adventures (8000 Rte. 31) offers swamp buggy nature tours on a 90,000-acre ranch. You will go through cypress swamp and wooded area and have a good chance of seeing alligators, bison, panthers, hawks, and other wildlife.

St. Augustine Founded in 1565, this is the oldest permanent settlement in the nation. The city has preserved its historic past, one that is steeped in Christianity, and flavors of those old Spanish colonial days can still be enjoyed by visitors today. St. Augustine is one Florida city not defined by its beaches, but rather by quaint houses, historic churches, and little shops selling antiques, fudge, rare books, and artwork.

The area that is now St. Augustine was first sighted by the Spaniards during the Christian Feast of St. Augustine under the leadership of Spanish adventurer Pedro Menendez de Aviles. The landing party celebrated mass on September 8, 1565, marking the first Christian ceremony to grace the new world, and remembered yet today by a 208-foot steel cross commemorating the event. The cross was erected in 1965 to celebrate the city's 400th anniversary.

The Mission of Nombre de Dios (27 Ocean St.) further exhibits the history. Here it was that Catholic missionaries ministered to the European settlers and the native Timucuan Indians. The nearby La Leche Shrine is the oldest shrine to Mary in the country.

As you might expect, the nation's oldest city has many historic sights. The historic district centers around St. George St. You won't want to miss the country's Oldest House, which was built in the 1600s and inhabited until 1918 when it was converted into a museum; the Oldest Wooden School House, built around 1755 and now a museum; and the Oldest Store, which—you guessed it—is also now a museum. In the Spanish Quarter you can watch costumed interpreters at work weaving, gardening, and cooking.

Of course, there are several historic churches here too. The grand Cathedral of St. Augustine (36 Cathedral Pl.) features 12 German stained glass windows, which recount the life of St. Augustine, the early church father, and murals that illustrate the settlement of the city of St. Augustine.

115

The oldest Protestant church in America is Trinity Episcopal Parish Church (215 St. George St.), made of a seashell-stucco called coquina. One of its ministers was chased out of town when he prayed for President Lincoln at the height of the Civil War.

The Memorial Presbyterian Church (Valencia and Sevilla Sts.) was built by the railroad mogul Henry Flagler as a memorial to his daughter, and it was Florida's first Presbyterian church. The Ancient City Baptist Church located here (27 Sevilla St.) was Florida's first Baptist church.

Anastasia Island is home to the amphitheater and the nightly presentation of *Cross and Sword,* Florida's official state play. The drama depicts the settlement of St. Augustine. During Lent, a Passion play is presented here. For performance times and reservations, phone 904-471-1965. (For other Passion plays, see Lake Wales, Fla.; Atlantic Beach, N.C.; Gadsden, Ala.; Eureka Springs, Ark.; Ruston, La.; Gatlinburg, Tenn.; Bloomington and Zion, Ill.; and Spearfish, S.D.)

> *[I] shut up the sea behind doors . . . fixed limits for it and set its doors and bars in place, when I said, "This far you may come and no farther; here is where your proud waves halt."*
>
> JOB 38:8–11

St. Petersburg The largest winter Christian conference grounds on Florida's west coast is the Moody Keswick Bible Conference. Located at 7500 100th Way N, it features sacred music concerts from January through April.

Free band concerts are held from September through December in Williams Park in downtown St. Petersburg.

Sarasota The Ringling Museum of Art (three miles north on US 41 at 5401 Bay Shore Rd.) is much more than a circus museum. The Ringling residence, for instance, is patterned after the Doge's Palace in Venice and contains a 4,000 pipe organ. The art gallery contains one of the most distinguished collections of baroque art in the Americas. Of course, there are the circus galleries too with all kinds of circus memorabilia.

The Sarasota Jungle Gardens (3701 Bay Shore Rd.) brings tropical birds together with 5,000 kinds of plants. It also contains the Gardens of Christ, which features eight hand-carved dioramas depicting the life of Jesus. Flamingos, swans, peacocks, and pelicans roam free. There is also a Kiddie Jungle children's playground.

Tallahassee The First Presbyterian Church (Adams St. and Park Ave.) is the oldest public building in the state in continuous use. Built in 1832, it still has galleries where the slaves worshiped.

Tampa Known as the City by the Bay, Tampa capitalizes on its coastal location with the Florida Aquarium (701 Channelside Dr.). The building has an 83-foot-high glass dome, more than 4,300 species of fish, other animals, and 550 native plant species.

Great Explorations (1120 4th St.) has six pavilions of hands-on exhibits, including one for children under seven. Think Tank tests the mind with logic puzzles, and Touch Tunnel challenges the senses in a pitch-black maze.

Tarpon Springs Noah's Ark Chimpanzee Farm (4612 Pinellas Ave. N) has gorillas, chimpanzees, monkeys, alligators, bears, and birds. It also has a separate petting zoo.

St. Nicholas Greek Orthodox Cathedral (36 Pinellas Ave. N), built in 1943, has beautiful iconography and stained glass windows. It is a replica of St. Sophia's in Constantinople. Early in January each year, at its Festival of the Epiphany, it has a very colorful Blessing of the Waters ceremony, followed by an unusual Diving for the Cross ceremony, in which the Archbishop throws a golden cross in the water of the Spring Bayou, and the young men of the area dive in to get it.

West Palm Beach Lion Country Safari (on Southern Blvd., 18 miles west of I-95) is a 640-acre wildlife preserve, in which 1,000 African, Asian, and American wild animals roam free. You can get a closer look on the *Safari Queen,* which gives a narrated boat ride.

White Springs At the Stephen Foster State Folk Culture Center (west edge of city on US 41) a carillon in a 200-foot tower gives daily concerts. Two animated dioramas, musical instruments, and Stephen Foster memorabilia can be seen at the base of the tower. (See Foster also under Bardstown, Ky.)

Winter Haven Five miles southeast on Rte. 540 is Cypress Gardens with more than 8,000 varieties of plants and flowers. New in 1997 is its Biblical Garden with hundreds of plants that are native to the Holy Land and specifically mentioned in the Bible. The Biblical Garden provides a quiet contemplative atmosphere in the busy activity of the larger park. Cypress Gardens also has a Carousel Cove for children, a Wings of Wonder conservatory, a water spectacular featuring its famous waterskiing revue, a 153-foot-high revolving platform, and more. Often, during the week before Easter, Cypress Gardens features concerts by contemporary Christian singers.

■GEORGIA

Tourist Info
Phone 404-656-3545
Web sites
  Entire state   www.georgia.org
  Atlanta   www.acvb.com
  Augusta   www.augusta.org
  Callaway Gardens   www.callawaygardens.com
  Jekyll Island   www.jekyllisland.com
  Savannah   www.savannah-visit.com
For a complete list of updated links, visit www.christiantraveler.com

Americus About 50 years ago, a racially integrated farming commune named Koinonia opened up here and was fiercely condemned by local segregationists. For a while this Christian group sustained itself by a mail-order candy-making business, then gradually made a name for itself by starting a nonprofit organization devoted to replacing substandard housing for those in need. They called the organization Habitat for Humanity. When President Jimmy Carter began promoting it, it achieved national renown. You can see Habitat's first housing development at Koinonia. The community still continues and now numbers about 30 adults and their families. They still farm and make candy. When you stop in, you might buy some candy and get a free tour. If you want to stay longer, ask about their volunteer program. Koinonia is located on Damson Rd., south of Americus.

Athens Whether you are a gardener or not, two gardens in the area are worthy of consideration. One is the Botanical Garden of Georgia at 2450 Milledge Ave. with a three-story conservatory displaying tropical and semitropical plants. In its 313 acres, there are five miles of nature trails and nearly a dozen specialty gardens.

The Founders Memorial Garden is smaller but no less impressive. It was started by 12 local women who founded the first garden club in America. The gardens are especially delightful in spring when the azaleas are in bloom.

Atlanta Some of the most powerful tourist attractions in Atlanta are those associated with Martin Luther King Jr. Many of the sites associated with King are Christian institutions, a reminder of the degree to which the civil rights movement was intertwined with Christian faith. King's birthplace, church, and grave are all part of a 23-acre Martin Luther King Jr. National Historic Site. The visitors center (450 Auburn Ave.) contains poignant displays of photographs, videos, and quotations oriented around King's life and the civil rights struggle. His birthplace offers guided tours starting every hour from 501 Auburn Ave. Admission is free.

Ebenezer Baptist Church (407 Auburn Ave.) is the church where King was pastor from 1960 to 1968. Martin Luther King Jr. was the third generation of Kings to have preached in this church. Plaques lining the Sweet Auburn district point out sites associated with past residents of this historically African American neighborhood. King's grave rests under an eternal flame at the Martin Luther King Jr. Center for Nonviolent Social Change (449 Auburn Ave. NE). The center also contains a collection of King's personal effects and shows a film about his life.

It was while Peter Marshall was pastor of the Westminster Presbyterian Church (1438 Sheridan Rd. NE) that he met Catherine Marshall, a student at Agnes Scott College in nearby Decatur. Shortly after their marriage he took the pastorate of the New York Avenue Presbyterian Church in Washington, D.C.

The largest churches in this city are the Mt. Paran Church of God (89 Ellis St. NE), First Baptist (2200 Cotillion Ave.), which televises its services nationally (Charles Stanley, pastor), and Peachtree Presbyterian (3434 Roswell Rd. NW). Just outside of Atlanta in Tucker, the Rehoboth Baptist Church (2997 Lawrenceville Hwy.) is a large and growing congregation under the ministry of Richard Lee.

The Carter Center is located at 453 Freedom Pkwy. It is from here that former President Jimmy Carter undertakes his work for peace and human rights. At the same place is the Jimmy Carter Library and Museum. Exhibits follow his career from his boyhood in Plains to the presidency. Admission is $5.

The CNN Center at Marietta and Techwood Sts. in the heart of the city, next to the Omni Coliseum, is visited by more than five million people each year. It's the headquarters of the Turner Broadcasting System. Reservations must be made a day in advance. Phone 404-827-2300. Admission is $7. Children under six are not admitted on tours.

Young and old alike will enjoy the World of Coca-Cola (55 Martin Luther King Jr. Dr.). You'll trace Coke's history from its humble beginnings in Atlanta to a soft drink known around the world, even synonymous with America itself. See the print ads of the '20s, a video including "I'd Like to Buy the World a Coke," and a sampling room, where you can taste some of the world's weirdest soft drink concoctions. Admission is $6.

Zoo Atlanta (800 Cherokee Ave. SE) has over 1,000 animals in naturalistic habitats like the Ford African Rain Forest, Flamingo Lagoon, Masai Mara (modeled after Kenya's plains), and the Sumatran Tiger Exhibit.

Among Atlanta's top tourist attractions is Stone Mountain Park, 16 miles east of the city on US 78. It has a number of attractions including the Stone Mountain Scenic Railroad, which goes around the five-mile base of the mountain; the *Scarlett O'Hara*, a paddle wheel steamboat, which cruises the lake; and the Lasershow, a sound and light spectacular with fireworks each evening from early May through Labor Day, and on weekends in April, September, and October. Easter sunrise services are held at Stone Mountain each year, and it is a tradition for many families to celebrate Easter Sunday together on the premises.

Six Flags over Georgia is about 12 miles west of downtown Atlanta and it is rated as one of the best theme parks in the country. It has more than 100 rides and a great many shows.

Augusta Best known as the site of the Master's Tournament in golf, Augusta is a delightful place to visit at any time of the year. Its Garden City Carriage Tours are horse-drawn carriages leaving

GREAT PLACES TO ENJOY GOD'S CREATION

- ✔ Birding in the Okefenokee National Wildlife Refuge, Georgia
- ✔ Climbing the dunes at Cumberland Island National Seashore, Georgia
- ✔ Bellingrath Gardens, Alabama, when the azaleas are in bloom

from the Riverwalk on Friday, Saturday, and Sunday evenings, a fun way to see the city.

St. Paul's Episcopal Church (605 Reynolds St.) is in its fourth building. This one was built in 1918. The first was built in 1750 as part of Fort Augusta, and the Celtic cross that was used to designate the site still stands. Next to the church is the Riverwalk Antique Depot, which is Augusta's finest and most complete antique mall. Also on the Riverwalk is the Morris Museum of Art (1 10th St. #320), which displays more than 2,000 works of art spanning more than two centuries.

One of the oldest African American congregations in the country is Springfield Baptist Church at 114 12th St. The sanctuary dates from 1801, but the congregation was organized in 1787. At that time the church membership consisted of not only slaves but also members of Augusta's large free black community—immigrants or individuals and their families who either had bought their freedom or had been freed by their masters.

The Sacred Heart Cultural Center (1301 Greene St.) was opened in 1900, an ornate cathedral the purpose of which was to provide a beautiful place of worship for its parishioners. Towering silvery twin spires grace the outside of the building. Inside you will enjoy beautiful stained glass, a domed ceiling filled with angels, and an interior of creamy white, intricately carved Italian marble. In 1971 the declining size of the congregation threatened the demolition of the building. Fortunately preservation efforts saved the cathedral, but it is no longer an active church. Concerts, Christmas events, and family cultural festivals are now held there.

Brunswick The Mary Miller Doll Museum at 1523 Glynn Ave. has a collection of 4,000 dolls, dollhouses, miniatures, boats, and toys. It is open every day but Sunday.

MAP International is now located here, having been for several years in Wheaton, Illinois. This interdenominational health organization provides medicine and supplies to Third World countries.

Callaway Gardens Undoubtedly one of the most beautiful spots in the South, and that is saying a lot, Callaway Gardens is a 14,000-acre combination of gardens, woodlands, lakes, wildlife, and outdoor activities, located in Pine Mountain about 70 miles south of Atlanta on US 27. The Callaways wanted not only to revive the land that was once devoted to cotton fields but also to create an oasis of God's creative beauty on earth. In addition to the lovely flower gardens is a beautiful, quiet chapel, the Ida Cason Callaway Memorial Chapel, dedicated in 1962 by Dr. Norman Vincent Peale. Its stained glass windows depict the four seasons in the Georgia woods. The Cecil B. Day Butterfly Center, which houses more than 1,000 free-flying butterflies, is the largest glass-enclosed tropical conservatory of living butterflies in North America.

Decatur Bishop Earl Paulk, charismatic TV speaker, is pastor of the Chapel Hill Harvester Church here. About 8,000 attend on a typical Sunday.

Decatur is also the home of Agnes Scott College, the Presbyterian school that Catherine Marshall attended.

Eatonton This was the home of Joel Chandler Harris, who wrote the Uncle Remus tales, and also of Alice Walker, the Pulitzer prize winner for *The Color Purple*. The Uncle Remus Museum is in Turner Park, three blocks south of the courthouse. Children will like the collection of memorabilia about Br'er Rabbit, Br'er Fox, and Harris's other storybook animals. The log cabin there is a combination of two former slave cabins.

Helen This community resembles an Alpine villa in Bavaria and added to it is the Museum of the Hills (8590 Main St.) in which the rural and village lifestyles in north Georgia at the turn of the century have been re-created.

Babyland General Hospital (19 E. Underwood St.) is nine miles southwest in Cleveland. This is an authentic turn-of-the-century hospital, now home of the original Cabbage Patch Kids, created by artist Xavier Roberts. Tours of the hospital are free.

Jekyll Island Once the preferred retreat of the Vanderbilts, Rockefellers, Morgans, and other American aristocrats, Jekyll Island is today enjoyed by people from all walks of life. Its historic district offers a window into that elegant past with tours of the millionaires' mansions. But the best reason to visit the island is its natural beauty. Visitors enjoy miles of beaches, shell collecting, hiking and biking paths, horseback riding, fishing, miniature golf, and the Jekyll Island Club, which is Georgia's largest public golf resort.

Faith Chapel (Old Plantation Rd.) is open every afternoon from two until four. Stained glass windows in the chapel were made by Tiffany.

Macon The city founders designed the city to be like the ancient Gardens of Babylon that Nebuchadnezzar built. It might stretch your imagination a bit, but the heritage has certainly been preserved. The wide avenues are lined with stately mansions. The Steward Chapel of the African Methodist Episcopal Church at 887 Forsyth St. is where Martin Luther King Jr. made his only major Georgia speech in 1957. The Harriet Tubman Historical and Cultural Museum on Walnut St. commemorates the former slave who led 300 people to freedom via the Underground Railroad. On the Victorian Walking Tour there are several historic churches in town that are worthy of stops. (See Underground Railroad also under Camden, Del.; Buffalo, N.Y.; Ottumwa, Iowa; Marshall, Mich.; Ripley, Ohio; and Osawatomie, Kans.)

Mercer University, affiliated with the Southern Baptists, has more than 6,000 students and is one of the larger church-related colleges in the country. It offers undergraduate and graduate programs in seven schools.

Marietta Both the Roswell Street Baptist Church (774 Roswell St.) and First Presbyterian Church (189 Church St.) are large churches with well over 2,000 in attendance each week.

American Adventures on Cobb Pkwy. is geared to children. It is located next to White Water, an amusement park with various sliding adventures.

Metter This small town (about one hour west of Savannah along I-16 and Rte. 121) is home to Guido Gardens, which is in turn the production home of *The Sower* telecasts. Whether you are interested in seeing the TV production or not, the grounds are a beautiful sight in themselves. Colorful flower beds share space with waterfalls, fountains, flowering trees, topiary, and the Chapel in the Pines, open 24 hours a day for quiet reflection. Conducted tours are held weekdays. Admission is free.

Milledgeville Since this town was the capital of Georgia until 1868, there is a governor's mansion here (120 S. Clark St.). It is now the home of the president of Georgia College, but it is open for guided tours ($3). In the college's library, you can see the Flannery O'Connor Room. Her home is not open to the public, but the room at the library displays many things of interest to those who have read her books. (See O'Connor also under Savannah, Ga.)

Perhaps the easiest way to see the town is to take the Historic Guided Trolley Tour. The two-hour tour introduces you to all the major sights of the town.

Montezuma About one hundred Mennonite families live in this area and operate mostly dairy farms. They use modern machinery in their farmwork but they wear plain clothes; the women wear bonnets and long skirts; the men, in beards, wear caps and suspenders. If you want to get a feel of the community, go to Yoder's Deutsch Haus, three miles east of Montezuma on Hwy. 26, for a cafeteria-style buffet. A gift shop is next door.

Perry The town is full of stately houses and memorable churches, and at Christmastime the town celebrates with a parade and candlelight service. A few miles away, just south of Marshallville, the Massee Lane Garden is a lovely ten-acre camellia garden. It also has a rose garden and Japanese garden. In the colonial-style headquarters are more than 300 Boehm sculptures and porcelains.

Plains James Earl (Jimmy) Carter (president of the United States 1977–1981) teaches a Sunday school class at the Maranatha Baptist Church (148 Hwy. 45 N) every week that he is in town. Visitors are invited to attend. The town isn't much to look at but there are 77 acres here that are designated the Jimmy Carter National Historic Site. Here you will find the Carter home on Woodland Dr. and the Plains Methodist Church (305 W. Church St.), where Jimmy asked Rosalyn for their first date. Two miles west is Archery, where Jimmy Carter lived as a child when his father operated a country store.

Rome Berry College is the vision of a remarkable Christian woman, Martha Berry, who founded the school in 1902 to educate Appalachian youths. Today the facility is housed in 100 buildings on about 26,000 acres. You can't see it all but you can stop at the campus waterwheel to take a picture and then go to the Weaving Room to see a display of handwoven items and other student crafts available for sale. Across from the campus is a small museum that will tell you more about the college founder. Nearby is Oak Hill, which is the Berry family's antebellum mansion. It is open to the public and includes five acres of formal gardens. Admission is $4.

St. Marys Inhabited as long ago as the 16th century, St. Marys was established as a town by the English in 1787. The beauty of the town is in its historic quaintness and its waterfront. Stroll along streets shaded by giant oak and palm trees and you will enjoy the historic landmarks, many of which are surrounded by white picket fences. You will also find a large number of quiet and friendly guest houses and bed and breakfast establishments here.

St. Marys is also the gateway to the Cumberland Island National Seashore, the largest and southern-most barrier island in Georgia. More than 17 miles of secluded white, sandy beaches beg exploring, and the whole family will enjoy watching for the wild horses, birds, and—if you're very observant—deer, armadillos, and alligators.

St. Simons Island Of all of Georgia's barrier islands, St. Simons offers the most complete and commercial resort destination. But the commercial development doesn't mean you won't find lots of natural beauty, like white sand beaches and salt marshes. Fort Frederica National Monument, on the island's north end, contains the ruins of a fort and buildings inhabited by English soldiers and civilians in the mid-18th century. While there, visit the Gothic-style Christ Church on Frederica Rd.

Before Christ Church was built, the Wesley brothers, John and Charles, preached under St. Simons oaks in 1736. The church was almost destroyed when Union troops camped here during the Civil War. They burned the pews for firewood and butchered cattle in the chapel. But in 1886 it was restored. The island has been the setting for a number of Eugenia Price's best-selling novels.

Savannah Savannah is undoubtedly one of the country's most beautiful cities. General Sherman, on his famous Civil War march through the South, spared Savannah. Legend says he found the city too beautiful to burn and even that he presented it as a Christmas gift to President Lincoln. Perhaps the greatest joy you will find in this city is simply walking the streets and visiting the quaint cafés, restaurants, and boutiques. Savannah is known as the City of Festivals. Almost every weekend has some sort of celebration, such as St. Patrick's Day in March, the Riverfront Seafood Festival in April, the spring azalea and dogwood festivals, and concerts at Christmas.

There are a number of memorable churches here. Christ Episcopal Church (28 Bull St.) claims to be the place where John Wesley founded the world's first Sunday school. Wesley Monumental United Methodist Church (429 Abercorn St.) commemorates the Wesley brothers. Also in Savannah is the First African Baptist Church (23 Montgomery St.). Organized in 1773, it is the oldest continually active African American church in the United States. It was begun by a slave, George Leile, whose master allowed him to preach to other slaves when they visited other plantations along the Savannah River. After Leile was granted his freedom in 1777, he raised 1,500 dollars to purchase the present church from a white congregation, and then moved it brick by brick to its present location.

The Cathedral of St. John the Baptist (222 E. Harris St.) is a beautiful late–19th-century structure. The church contains Austrian stained glass windows, an Italian marble altar, and German-made stations of the cross. Tours are by appointment only.

Northwest of Savannah in the community of New Ebenezer is the 1869 Jerusalem Lutheran Church, the oldest public building still standing in Georgia. The church was founded in 1734 by Salzburg Lutherans escaping religious persecution in Germany. Sunday services are held at 11 A.M.

South of Savannah in South Newport you will find what is called the "smallest church in America" but it may be only the smallest church in Georgia. It is a 12-seat cabin endowed by the inheritance of a local woman. It is open twenty-four hours year-round. (See also the "world's smallest house of worship" under Florence, Ky.; the "world's smallest church" in Festina, Iowa; the "world's smallest cathedral" in Highlandville, Mo.; and the Wee Kirk of the Valley in Cedar Vale, Kans.)

The founder of the Girl Scouts, Juliette Gordon Low, lived at 142 Bull St. in a regency-style house that is now a National Program Center. It is open to tourists. The Andrew Low House, 329 Abercorn St., another historic house, was where Low actually founded the Girls Scouts and where she died in 1927. Previous visitors to the house have been William Makepeace Thackeray and Robert E. Lee. Admission is $6.

Savannah was also the childhood home of Christian author Flannery O'Connor. The home, at 207 E. Charlton St., is open during the summers on Saturday afternoons and during the rest of the year Friday, Saturday, and Sunday afternoons. (See O'Connor also under Milledgeville, Ga.)

The Ships of the Sea maritime museum, at 503 E. River St., is a fascinating place to visit. It houses ship models, ships in bottles, scrimshaw, and other sailing artifacts in an old warehouse.

Toccoa Falls In 1977 a 40-year-old earthen dam above Toccoa Falls College collapsed and water came cascading over the falls, inundating the college. What happened to the school is almost miraculous, and if you ask the people there, they will attribute it to God's answer to Christians' prayers. Toccoa Falls College, associated with the Christian and Missionary Alliance, is stronger than ever. The falls, by the way, is 19 feet deeper than Niagara.

■NORTH CAROLINA

Tourist Info
Phone 800-VISIT-NC
Web sites
  Entire state   www.visitnc.com
  Asheville   www.ashevillechamber.org
  Biltmore Estate   www.biltmore.com
  Old Salem   www.oldsalem.org
  Raleigh   www.raleighcvb.org
For a complete list of updated links, visit www.christiantraveler.com

Aberdeen This area near Pinehurst was settled by Highland Scots who still gather in the area for festivals. As you would expect from its Scottish heritage, a Presbyterian church, Bethesda Presbyterian (1002 Sandhills Blvd. N), is the oldest in the area. The congregation began in 1788, but the present wooden structure, which is still used for reunions, funerals, and weddings, was built in the 1860s.

Asheboro About 40 minutes south of Greensboro on US 220 (4401 Zoo Pkwy.) is the North Carolina Zoological Park, home to more than 1,100 animals and 60,000 exotic and tropical plants. This is the nation's largest walk-through natural-habitat zoo.

Asheville Anything was possible at the dawn of the 20th century, and for George and Edith Vanderbilt the sky was the limit. Their home, Biltmore Estate, nestled among 8,000 acres in the beautiful Blue Ridge Mountains, is a marvel in architecture (at exit 50 off I-40E). The estate remains the largest home in America. You can tour the 25-room mansion, many acres of gardens and woodlands, restaurants, shops, and the nation's most visited winery. It is suitable for every member of the family, but the admission is hefty ($29.95). The estate is large enough so that you could stay all day if you like. Arrive early to avoid the crowds, and allow four to six hours to tour the estate.

The Great Smoky Mountain Railway, just 45 minutes west of Asheville in the town of Dillsboro (119 Front St.), is one of the most popular attractions in western North Carolina. Choose from four excursions with diesel-electric and steam engines. Passengers ride in open-sided cars or cabooses, which allow stunning photography of the beautiful mountain scenery.

The Billy Graham Training Center at the Cove sponsors more than 50 seminars during the year. (See Graham also under Charlotte and Montreat, N.C.; Western Springs and Wheaton, Ill.; and Minneapolis, Minn.)

About ten miles east of Asheville at Black Mountain are several religious retreats, including the Montreat Conference Center located at 401 Assembly Dr.

Sliding Rock is a natural water slide located north of Brevard in Pisgah National Forest. Wear old jeans and tennis shoes and make sure you bring your own towel to enjoy a 150-foot wet and wild slide.

The drive along the Blue Ridge Parkway from Asheville to the Boone–Blowing Rock area is breathtaking. This 460-mile road meanders through mountains and meadows and crosses lovely mountain streams. The road may be closed during heavy snows and icy conditions.

Atlantic Beach *Worthy Is the Lamb,* a Passion play incorporating inspirational music, is performed at the Crystal Coast Amphitheater, three miles north of the bridge to Emerald Isle. It may be the only fully orchestrated Passion play in existence. It features ships, horses, and chariots, with the White Oak River behind it pretending to be the Sea of Galilee. The set portrays Jerusalem. Performances are given Thursday through Saturday from mid-June to Labor Day. For more information, contact the Crystal Coast Amphitheater, P.O. Box 1004, Swansboro, NC 18584. (For other Passion plays, see Lake Wales and St. Augustine, Fla.; Gadsden, Ala.; Eureka Springs, Ark.; Ruston, La.; Gatlinburg, Tenn.; Bloomington and Zion, Ill.; and Spearfish, S.D.)

Banner Elk Just south of town on Grandfather Mountain, an outdoor gospel concert called *Singing on the Mountain* is held the fourth Sunday in June each year. It began in 1930. Choirs and singers perform in the MacRae Meadows, and the audience often sings along with them,

Bath Only a couple hundred people live here and the town is only three blocks long but it has a history that is a lot longer than that. In fact it is the oldest incorporated town in North Carolina. St. Thomas Church here, begun in 1734, is the oldest church in the state and is still used by the Episcopal Diocese as a place of worship. It is a simple rectangular brick building with no steeple. In the early 1700s, the church had a collection of 1,000 books and pamphlets and that collection became the first public library in the state.

Charlotte The Paramount Carowinds Theme Park (15423 Carowinds Blvd.) is a 40-million-dollar, 100-acre park with a wide variety of entertainment and inventive rides. You can enjoy roller coasters, water rides, the Animation Station children's area, and the newly expanded water entertainment complex, Water Works. The park straddles the North and South Carolina state line.

Calvary Church (nondenominational) is one of the largest churches in town with a membership of 4,000, an average attendance of 3,600, and a Sunday school attendance of 3,000. The church is located at 5801 Pineville Matthews Rd.

First Presbyterian Church (200 W. Trade St.), which faces E. Trade St., is a Gothic Revival structure built in the 19th century. This impressive building replaced the much simpler meetinghouse where the congregation had previously met.

The headquarters of SIM USA, Inc., formerly known as the Sudan Interior Mission, is here. This interdenominational mission agency now has work in South America and Southern Asia, hence its change to an acronym.

On a dairy farm outside the city, evangelist Billy Graham was born in 1918. He was converted under the evangelistic ministry of Mordecai Ham in 1934 in this city. (See Graham also under Asheville and Montreat, N.C.; Western Springs and Wheaton, Ill.; and Minneapolis, Minn.)

Durham Durham is one-third of North Carolina's Research Triangle, along with Chapel Hill and Raleigh. Duke University is Durham's main draw. Originally called Trinity College, the school changed its name after receiving a gift of six million dollars from the Duke family who had made their fortune in marketing cigarettes in America. Duke's two large campuses have many impressive buildings, but the most impressive is the Duke University Chapel, which James Duke wanted to be placed on the highest ground on the campus. He wanted the central building to be a towering church so that it would have to have a strong spiritual influence on the students. It has a 210-foot tower and a 5,000 pipe organ. The church itself is patterned after the original Canterbury Cathedral. It contains a million pieces of stained glass, depicting almost 900 figures in 77 windows. Check to see if there are any free organ concerts scheduled during your stay in the area. Interdenominational worship services are held each Sunday morning at 11 A.M. Also on the Duke campus are the Sarah P. Duke Gardens near West Campus on Anderson St. Over 20 acres of landscaping, tiered flower beds, and a lily pond are bordered by a pine forest. You will also enjoy the Duke Museum of Art, housing a small but impressive collection of Italian and Dutch oils and classical and African sculpture. Admission to both is free.

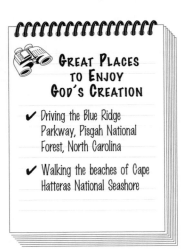

GREAT PLACES TO ENJOY GOD'S CREATION

✔ Driving the Blue Ridge Parkway, Pisgah National Forest, North Carolina

✔ Walking the beaches of Cape Hatteras National Seashore

If you have children with you, or even if you don't, you may want to visit the Museum of Life and Science (433 Murray St.). You (or your kids) can walk through a 50-foot-high tornado, take a one-mile ride on the narrow gauge Ellerbee Creek Railway, "pilot" a completely refurbished Apollo command mock-up, or visit Bio-quest, which has more than 1,000 butterflies flying around you.

Shirley Caesar, black gospel singer and evangelist who won a Grammy for "Put Your Hand in the Hand," was born here in 1938.

Edenton This was the first capital of colonial North Carolina, but today it is a peaceful little town. Here you will see several buildings that were built before the Revolutionary War, the oldest of which is St. Paul's Episcopal Church, built in 1736. Located at Broad and Church Sts., it has the oldest charter and is the second-oldest church building in the state.

Elizabeth City Elizabeth City is not exactly a tourist city but it does have some interesting old buildings in its downtown section. Among them are the Hall's Creek Church (17.5 miles southwest on US 17) and Christ Episcopal Church (200 S. McMorrine St.). The Dismal Swamp Canal, which was dug in 1790, made Elizabeth City into a major port in the area.

About 15 miles southwest of Elizabeth City near Hertford is the Newbold-White House (on Rte. 1336), which may be the state's oldest house. It was built around 1685, and the proprietary government met here in the 1690s. Probably it was built by Joseph Scott, one of the first Quakers to settle in the state. Admission is $2. Quakers still gather here once a year in remembrance of that settlement.

Glendale Springs The Holy Trinity Episcopal Church (Rte. 16, 2.5 miles north of Rte. 163) features a large fresco of the Last Supper by North Carolina native Ben Long. It measures 17 by 19.5 feet. At St. Mary's Episcopal Church (400 Beaver Creek School Rd.) in Beaver Creek the same artist has a smaller fresco, *Mary, Great with Child,* which won the Leonardo da Vinci International award.

Greensboro The *Sword of Peace,* an outdoor drama, is performed throughout the summer at Snow Camp, about 25 miles southeast of Greensboro. It is the story of Can Creek Quakers during the Revolutionary War and it climaxes at the Battle of Guilford Courthouse. Guilford College here is associated with the Friends denomination.

Highlands The Highlands Chamber Music Festival is held each mid-summer in the Episcopal Church of the Incarnation and the Highlands Methodist Church. Phone 828-526-9060.

High Point The Angela Peterson Doll and Miniature Museum on W. Green Dr. is the largest doll museum in the South. It contains some 2,500 pieces, including 1,700 dolls.

Montreat Evangelist Billy Graham and wife Ruth have called this home since 1955. It was also in Montreat, at the Presbyterian Conference Grounds, that the hymn "Ivory Palaces" was written in 1915 by Henry Barraclough. (See Graham also under Asheville and Charlotte, N.C.; Western Springs and Wheaton, Ill.; and Minneapolis, Minn.)

Murphy They call it the Giant Print Edition of the Ten Commandments, because at Fields of the Wood, the Ten Commandments can be seen in letters five feet high and four feet wide, all carved in stone. There is also a 2,210-foot All Nations Cross, the largest of its kind in the world. Fields of the Wood is located west of Murphy off Hwy. 294.

New Bern This is the second-oldest town in the state. Swiss and German Protestants began coming here in 1710 to escape religious persecution in Europe. It became the political center of the colony in 1770. Several churches are of historic note and they are open to visit, along with many homes and commercial buildings in the historic area. Christ Episcopal Church at Middle and Pollock Sts., built in 1715, still uses the silver communion service given by King George II. First Presbyterian at New St. near Middle St., built between 1819 and 1822, was one of many buildings used as a hospital during the Civil War. Don't miss Tryon Palace and Gardens at 610 Pollock St. It was the governor's palace in 1760 and declared the most beautiful building in colonial America.

Ridgecrest The Southern Baptists sponsor a full schedule of Chautauqua-like conferences at the Ridgecrest Baptist Conference grounds here. For a free brochure, phone 615-251-2824. (See also Chautauqua, N.Y., and other Chautauqua-inspired sites under Sac City, Iowa; Lakeside, Ohio; Madison, S.D.; and Boulder, Colo.)

Roanoke Island The Elizabethan Gardens on US 64 are open year-round but are most delightful from April through September. The gardens are a memorial to the English colonists who came here in 1585 and 1587 and disappeared. The bricks used in the gardens predate the Revolutionary War.

Valdese Just east of Morgantown in western North Carolina is the historic town of Valdese, founded in 1893 by Waldensians. These "People of the Valleys" have a religious heritage that reaches back to 12th-century Europe. Theirs is the oldest evangelical church in the world, predating Martin Luther by several centuries. Although faced with religious persecution, the Waldensians persevered, eventually immigrating to other parts of Europe and the United States. Valdese remains a community firmly linked to those early religious pioneers, and there are numerous sites where visitors can learn more about their beliefs and early way of life.

The Waldensian Museum, at 208 Rodoret St., houses exhibits of distinctly Waldensian artifacts relating to the founding of Valdese. Across the street is the Waldensian Presbyterian Church of Valdese, founded at the same time as the village. The early congregants fully intended to remain Waldensian. However, when it became apparent that remaining independent was impractical, the church joined the Presbyterians. The existing Romanesque sanctuary was begun

THE WALDENSIANS IN NORTH CAROLINA

The Waldensian Church of Italy is the oldest evangelical church in existence, dating back as far as A.D. 400. Records of trials for heresy date back to 1183, about the time of the group's formal organization under a man by the name of Peter Waldo.

The Waldensians' beliefs were simple: a Bible to everyone, religious liberty and freedom of conscience and worship, a well-educated corps of ministers, and public schools free from the domination of the church. The Waldensians became part of the Reformation in 1532 and paid for the translation of the first French Bible, the Olivetan Bible. Until the early 1700s the Waldensians were subjected to continuous military persecution. Finally in 1848 these Christians were granted religious freedom by the king of Sardinia.

But that peace and freedom brought with it another problem: Soon overcrowding plagued the traditional Waldensian enclaves in the valleys of northern Italy. Many were forced to emigrate to places where they could find a means of making a living—throughout the rest of Europe and America. One of those emigrant groups were the settlers of Valdese, North Carolina.

Traces of these early Christians' lives can be experienced at a variety of locations throughout town, including the Waldensian Museum, the Trail of Faith, the Waldensian Winery, the Waldensian Presbyterian Church, and the outdoor drama, *From This Day Forward,* an account of the Waldensians' persecution and subsequent emigration to the United States.

only three years later. Stained glass windows carry the seals of the ancient Reformed churches of Europe along with the seals of the Presbyterian churches of Mexico, Korea, and Brazil.

You may also enjoy seeing the dramatic presentation *From This Day Forward* at the Old Colony Amphitheater. This story of the Waldensians' persecution, immigration, and subsequent struggles is presented annually from mid-July to mid-August.

Waxhaw The offices of JAARS, Inc. (Jungle Aviation and Radio Service), which provides training and support for Wycliffe Bible translators around the world, is located at 100 Jaars Rd..

Waxhaw is also a popular center for antique shoppers.

Wilmington St. James Episcopal Church (3d and Market Sts.) was built in 1839, replacing a 1751 church that the British had used as a stable during the Revolutionary War. When you are inside, take a look at the Spanish painting *Ecce Homo*. It was taken from a captured pirate ship in 1748 and is estimated to be between 400 and 600 years old.

Don't miss the St. John's Museum of Art (114 Orange St.). The museum houses a permanent collection of prints by Mary Cassatt, an American Impressionist painter of the early 20th century. Her favorite subject was motherhood. Her prints show the power and love that exist in the mother-child relationship.

Sixteen miles south in Winnabow is the Brunswick Town State Historic Site (8884 St. Phillips Rd.). Founded in 1725, it was a thriving settlement until the British partially destroyed it in the Revolutionary War. All that remains from the original settlement are the walls of St. Paul's Anglican Church.

In the 1890s Madame Chiang Kai-shek's father was ordained in the Fifth St. Methodist Church here.

Horse-drawn carriages and horse-drawn trolleys are the easy way to get a narrated tour of the historic district. Tours begin at the corner of Water and Market Sts. Phone 910-251-8889 for more information.

Winston-Salem The twins were not identical. Winston was an industry-based community; Salem was a Moravian town to which the settlers brought their love of crafts, interest in education, and sense of order.

Salem was settled in 1766 by adherents of the Moravian faith, which was one of the first Protestant denominations. The Moravian denomination was founded in 1457 in what is now the Czech Republic. Many of those who settled in Salem had come from another American Moravian town, Bethlehem, Pennsylvania. Today more than 30 buildings of old Salem have been restored. Historic Old Salem (on Old Salem Rd.) has a visitors center that traces the Moravians' journey from Europe to America and then into North Carolina. Craftspeople in Moravian dress show you how things were done. The Home Moravian Church on the square dates from 1800 and is still an active congregation. In fact it is the largest Moravian congregation in America. Also worth visiting is St. Philips Church, built in 1861. This was the home of the Negro Moravian Church, founded as the first shots of the Civil War were fired. The brick church was used until 1952, when the congregation moved to Happy Hill. There is also a Single Brothers House where teenage boys were apprenticed and Single Sisters House where the girls learned domestic crafts. If you have younger children, age four to nine, consider visiting the Children's Museum of Old Salem. This is a hands-on fun space that encourages exploration and play as a means of learning about life long ago. At Christmas there are strolling brass bands and horse-drawn wagon rides, and the Home Moravian Church sponsors a Christmas Candle Tea. At Easter several brass bands wander throughout the area waking up residents with songs of resurrection at early hours and then they meet with onlookers at Salem Square for an Easter service.

The Salem July Fourth celebrations are a bit quieter than most Americans experience. The community relives the way the early settlers responded to the historic news of independence and its promise of peace, with a somber torchlight procession from church to their homes. The reenactment reminds visitors of the somberness the Moravians felt toward war, even as they embraced peace. (See Moravians also under Hope, N.J.; Bethlehem, Lititz, and Nazareth, Pa.; Bloomington, Ill.; Gnadenhutten and New Philadelphia, Ohio; and Ephraim, Wisc.)

The SciWorks (Museum Dr. off Hanes Mill Rd.) is something to be enjoyed by children of all ages. You can whisper into a parabolic dish and be heard 40 feet away. You can make a shadow and walk away from it. You can see a coin accelerated to 100 miles an hour by gravity, and much more.

■SOUTH CAROLINA

Tourist Info
Phone 803-734-1700
Web sites
  Entire state   www.travelsc.com
  Charleston's Magnolia Plantation   www.magnoliaplantation.com
  Charleston's Spoleto USA   www.spoletousa.org
  Columbia   www.columbiasc.net
  Greenville   www.greenvillesc.org
For a complete list of updated links, visit www.christiantraveler.com

Allendale This county seat was named for its first postmaster, Paul Allen, who was described as being a "pillar in his church, a staunch supporter of all that was good, as well as being an archenemy of all that was evil and corrupt." With those credentials, Postmaster Allen had a town named after him.

Barnwell On Courthouse Square the Barnwell vertical sundial has been giving the correct time for over 150 years. It is believed to be the only vertical sundial in America. The Church of the Holy Apostles (9457 Patterson St.), built in 1856 of cypress in the Gothic style of an English parish church, survived Sherman's march of destruction during the Civil War. However, Sherman used the church as a stable for Union horses, and the large stone baptismal font, believed to date from medieval times, was used as a watering trough.

Beaufort North of Hilton Head on Pritchard's Island is the town of Beaufort, where you will find, at 501 Church St., St. Helena's Episcopal Church, dating from 1724. During the Civil War, this church was turned into a hospital, and gravestones were brought inside to serve as operating tables.

Bishopville If you want to see a different kind of garden, visit Fryar's Topiary Gardens at 165 Broad Acres (one mile north of I-20, exit 116). Nationally acclaimed gardener Pearl Fryar has made this garden into all sorts of unusual shapes, so you will find three acres of trees and shrubs formed into fanciful spirals, pompons, and other creative contortions.

Charleston The first laws of the Carolinas, brought by the settlers, guaranteed the widest measure of religious liberty in all of the thirteen colonies. By 1704 Charles Towne, as it was then known, was a picture of religious freedom with members of the English, French, Quaker, Anabaptist, and Independent churches worshiping peacefully together in a small community.

Residents of modern Charleston have restored many of the city's old downtown homes and commercial buildings. Included in the restoration were over 180 historic churches—so many that Charlestonians often call their home the "Holy City."

One of those historic churches is St. Michael's Episcopal Church (at Meeting and Broad Sts.). It is Charleston's oldest surviving church, completed in 1761. It is modeled after St. Martin-in-the-Fields in London. If you wish, you can climb the 186-foot steeple and get a panoramic view of the area.

First Baptist Church (61 Church St.) is literally first because it is the oldest Baptist church in the South, founded in 1682 by William Screven. The building now used by the congregation was begun in 1819.

St. John's Lutheran Church (Clifford and Archdale Sts.), built in 1817, has notable wrought iron gates and fencing on the outside and an 1823 Thomas Hall organ case on the inside.

The Circular Congregational Church (Meeting St.) is a Romanesque-style church. The first Sunday school in the state was held here. It was said that it is circular so the devil would have no place to hide.

St. Philip's Episcopal Church (148 Church St.) was completed in 1838. In its graveyard, the 19th-century statesman John C. Calhoun is buried. During the Civil War, its bells were converted into cannon. It was also known as the lighthouse church, a light having been put into the steeple to guide ships into port.

The Mt. Zion A.M.E. Church (5 Glebe St.) is the first brick church building owned by African Americans in Charleston. The building was purchased by the congregation in 1882 to relieve overcrowded conditions. Today, with six different choirs, it is the only church in the city offering music ranging from classical to unarranged Negro spirituals dating before the 1900s.

Not far down the block at 110 Church St. is the Gothic-style French Huguenot Church. This is the only church in the country that still follows the original Huguenot liturgy. In fact one French service a year is held each spring.

About 19 miles north of Charleston in Goose Creek is St. James Church, built between 1708 and 1719. Although it hasn't been in use since 1808, it is remarkably well preserved. The original box pews, slave gallery, and pulpit are still there.

The Charleston Museum (360 Meeting St.), one of the major museums of the Southeast, was founded in 1772. It has a half million items in its collection and is especially strong on South Carolina decorative arts. For children, there is a special Discover Me Room with various hands-on exhibits.

The Magnolia Plantation and Gardens (3550 Ashley River Rd., west of the Ashley River on Rte. 61) is a 50-acre informal garden, begun in 1686, which makes it the oldest garden in America. It boasts of having the continent's largest collection of azaleas and camellias. Christians will enjoy its Biblical Garden, which was photographed for *Time* magazine. John Galsworthy called it "the most beautiful garden in the world." For children there is a petting zoo and mini-horse ranch. Highlights of the plantation include the pre–Revolutionary War plantation house, an antebellum cabin, canoe and bike rentals, and bird walks on Saturday mornings.

Charleston is also home to Spoleto Festival USA from late May to mid-June every year. This is America's premier arts festival, filling Charleston's historic theaters, churches, and outdoor venues with over 120 performances. You can enjoy both renowned artists and emerging performers in disciplines ranging from opera, dance, theater, and jazz to symphonic, chamber, and choral music.

GREAT PLACES FOR FAMILY FUN

✔ Paramount Carowinds, Charlotte, North Carolina

✔ Panning for gold and gems, Smoky Mountain Gold and Ruby Mine, North Carolina

✔ Charles Towne Landing State Park, Charleston, South Carolina

At the Dock Street Theatre (135 Church St.) the Society for the Preservation of Spirituals holds an annual concert series during March and April.

Cheraw The old St. David's Episcopal Church (420 Market St.) was the last of the state's churches built under the monarchy of George III. It managed to weather the Revolution and it has the claim to fame that it housed four armies. Gravestones date back to 1720.

Cokesbury This town (eight miles north of Greenwood on Rte. 246) was named for Thomas Coke and Francis Asbury, two trail-blazing Methodist bishops who brought Methodism to America. The former college campus in this community has been restored and is now a city school.

Columbia Columbia is home to several historic churches:First Baptist Church (1306 Hampton St.) was the site of the first Secession Convention, held in December 1860, a year after the church was built. The pulpit furnishings, slave gallery, and brick-pillared portico are as they were then.

The First Presbyterian Church (1324 Marion St.), built in 1853, is one of the few buildings to have survived the burning of Columbia during the Civil War and one of the finest examples of Gothic architecture in the United States.

Trinity Episcopal Cathedral (1100 Sumter St.) is modeled after England's York Minster and was built in 1847. Today it is one of the 20 largest Episcopal churches in the country.

Columbia Bible College and Seminary here was founded in 1923 by Robert McQuilkin, emphasizing missions and a deeper spiritual life. His son, J. Robertson McQuilkin, became president in 1968. Ben Lippen Schools, a highly regarded Christian preparatory school, is now associated with the Bible college.

Forty-five miles southeast of Columbia in the little town of Orangeburg is the beautiful Edisto Memorial Gardens. It is a virtual wonderland of moss-draped oaks, camellias, and azaleas, as well as flowering crabs and dogwoods. It also has 9,500 roses that bloom throughout the summer. The South Carolina Festival of Roses with its golf and tennis tournaments is held here the first weekend of May.

Riverbanks Zoological Park (I-26 and Grayson Blvd.), rated as one of the nation's best, is the award-winning home to more than 2,000 animals, housed in large naturalistic exhibits. Psychological barriers, such as moats, water, and light, create an environment free of bars and cages, and it is noted as a refuge for several endangered species. Just across the Saluda River, you can explore 70 acres of woodlands, gardens, and historic ruins set among the Riverbanks Botanical Garden. Admission is $5.75.

Georgetown This town, which is on the shores of Winyah Bay, was founded in 1729 by a Baptist minister. Before long it became the center of America's colonial rice empire. The Prince George Episcopal Church (Broad and Highmarket Sts.) dates to about 1750, and the congregation has been meeting every Sunday in the church since then, except for the interruptions of the Revolutionary War and the Civil War. The building was erected with bricks brought over from England. Behind the altar is a stained glass window that was once part of the slaves' chapel at a nearby plantation.

Greenville Bob Jones University, founded by the revivalist of the same name, has been located here on a beautiful campus since 1947. The school houses one of the most important art collections in the Southeast. Its Gallery of Sacred Art and Bible Lands Museum contains 30 rooms displaying the art of Europe from the 13th through the 19th centuries. Works of major artists are also included in the collection.

First Presbyterian Church (200 W. Washington St.) currently has the largest congregation in the city with an average attendance exceeding 3,000.

The Christ Episcopal Church (10 N. Church St.) and the John Wesley United Methodist Church (101 E. Court St.) are historic old churches in the city.

Mayesville In this classic small southern town Mary MacLeod Bethune was born. A daughter of former slaves, she was the only one of the 17 children in the family who was able to attend the local school (Mayesville Presbyterian Mission for Negroes). She went on to graduate from Moody Bible Institute. After applying and being rejected twice for missionary work in Africa, she started her own school in Florida, which eventually became Bethune-Cookman College. She served as college president until 1942, was a civil rights leader, and served as advisor to President Franklin D. Roosevelt.

Monck's Corner The Mepkin Abbey (13 miles southeast off Rte. 402 at 1098 Mepkin Abbey Rd.) is now a monastery of great peace and beauty. Its garden and chapel are open to the public. Originally it was Mepkin Plantation, the home of Henry Laurens, a patriot who was imprisoned in the Tower of London. The plantation was burned by the British and then in the Civil War by the Union troops. In this century it was the home of Henry and Clare

Luce, who are buried here. They gave the place to the Catholic church, which has converted it into a monastery.

Myrtle Beach There's no doubt about it; Myrtle Beach is a popular spot to soak up some rays. In addition to white sands, you can expect to find lots of miniature golf, tennis, amusement and water parks. The best time to visit is anytime except spring break and June. At those times, expect to finds lots of tourists, especially teenagers.

For the kids, you can check out the Myrtle Beach Grand Prix, the Pavilion and Amusement Park, and the Myrtle Waves Water Park. The Grand Prix provides every kind of vehicle you can think of, from go-carts and kiddy cars, to Formula 1 race cars and from bumper boats to mini bumper boats. The amusement park has a variety of rides and has the Carolinas' largest flume. The water park includes 17 rides and activities. All the Grand Strand beaches are family-oriented.

If you prefer a quieter seaside location, consider heading farther south. Good bets include Murells Inlet, a picturesque fishing village known for its good seafood, and Pawleys Island. Both have more private homes than souvenir shops. Pawleys Island is known for its hammocks, made by hand here since 1880.

Sheldon Between the towns of Yemassee and Gardens Corner lie the Sheldon Church Ruins, a haunting monument to the tragedy of war. Built in 1753, the church was burned by the British in 1779. After it was rebuilt, it was burned again by General Sherman in the Civil War. On the second Sunday after Easter, memorial services are held here.

Stateburg At Christmas by the Church of the Holy Cross on Rte. 31, masses of poinsettias decorate the grave of Joel Poinsett in the churchyard of this Gothic Revival sanctuary, which was built of blocks of packed earth around 1850. Poinsett, who was a U.S. statesman, died here in 1851 while on his way from Charleston. He discovered the flower, which was later named for him, in Mexico and brought it to the United States. Today it is almost synonymous with Christmas.

Woodruff If you and your family haven't seen an emu ranch lately, you can see one here (exit 16 off I-395 toward Woodruff) at the

S&T Ranch. They will give you a good look as well as an emu education, from incubation to the development of the mature bird.

■VIRGINIA

Tourist Info
Phone 804-786-2051
Web sites
  Entire state   www.virginia.org
  Norfolk   www.norfolk.va.us
  Richmond   www.richmondva.org
For a complete list of updated links, visit www.christiantraveler.com

Alexandria A suburb of Washington, D.C., Alexandria is more than a hundred years older than the capital. Old Town Alexandria has cobblestone streets, brick sidewalks, and quaint shops. Most sightseeing will be along Washington and King Sts.

Two churches are noteworthy here. Christ Church at 118 N. Washington St. is a Georgian redbrick church that has been in use since 1773. Its two most important and distinguished members have been George Washington and Robert E. Lee. Washington purchased pew 60 for 36 pounds and 10 shillings. Lee was confirmed in the church in 1853. Traditionally the president of the United States attends a service here on a Sunday close to Washington's birthday and sits in Washington's pew. In the parish hall is an exhibit on the church's history. Until 1805 the churchyard was the city's only burial ground.

The Old Presbyterian Meeting House (321 Fairfax St.) was built by Scottish pioneers in 1774. It is an active church that has retained its gate pews. During the Revolutionary War, it was the gathering place for patriots. After the death of George Washington, the bell of the meetinghouse tolled continuously for four days, and it was the site of Washington's funeral sermons. Because of rain and mud, it was easier for mourners to walk here than to Christ Church. The original meetinghouse was gutted by a lightning fire in 1835, but it was restored around the old walls a few years later. It looks today much as it did in the mid-18th century.

Bedford About 30 minutes west of Lynchburg is this town that is home to Holy Land USA, approximately 250 acres representing the Bible lands of Israel.

Big Stone Gap John Fox Jr. House and Museum (Shawnee Ave. E) was built in 1888 and is filled with mementos of the author of *The Trail of the Lonesome Pine* and *The Little Shepherd of Kingdom Come*. It is open every afternoon except Mondays.

Blue Ridge Parkway Constructed entirely free of billboards, this 469-mile parkway is a great way to see the Blue Ridge Mountains at any time of year, but especially in spring and fall months.

Blue Ridge Mountain Frescoes are housed in two churches in North Carolina, one in Glendale Springs, three miles north of the parkway's junction with Rte. 16 at milepost 258 and the other in West Jefferson off the junction of US 221 and Rte. 194.

Brookneal Hat Creek Retreat Center, southeast of Lynchburg (at 7141 Hat Creek Rd.), is a retreat and conference center associated with the Presbyterian Church U.S.A. Surrounded by year-round natural beauty, it offers meeting areas, overnight accommodations, and food services.

Charlottesville Near here Charlotte Diggs Moon was born, a name all Southern Baptists know as Lottie Moon. In 1872 she went to China as a missionary, established a church, and within two decades saw more than a thousand converts baptized. She organized a relief service and in the following years the Lottie Moon Christmas offerings raised millions of dollars among Southern Baptists. If Southern Baptists had patron saints, she would be one.

Falls Church The Falls Church (Episcopal) of this town with the same name was reconstructed in 1959 following the original plans of the 1732 church building. The original building was used as a recruiting center during the Revolutionary War and as a hospital during the Civil War. The church is located at 115 E. Fairfax St.

Fort Monroe Named in honor of President James Monroe, this is the largest stone fort ever built in the United States. Of particular interest to Christians is the Chapel of the Centurion, the Protestant chapel within the fort. It was dedicated in 1858 in honor of the Roman centurion Cornelius, the first Gentile convert to Christianity. The chapel has three Tiffany stained glass windows, plus regimental flags of units that have served at the fort.

Fredericksburg St. George's Episcopal Church at 905 Princess Anne St. was originally built in 1732, but the current building with three Tiffany windows was finished in 1849. Martha Washington's father and John Paul Jones's brother are buried in the graveyard. This was the church of Mary Washington, George Washington's mother, and there is a commemorative window in her honor. During the battle of Fredericksburg, the church was hit at least 25 times and in 1863 it was used by General Lee's troops for religious revival meetings. In 1864 it was also used as a hospital.

The Presbyterian Church at 810 Princess Anne St. dates to the early 1800s but the present structure was completed in 1855. It also served as a hospital in the Civil War and it was hit by cannonballs, which left their scars on the walls of the loft and belfry.

Around the city of Fredericksburg are the Fredericksburg and the Spotsylvania National Military Parks covering four Civil War battlefields, including Chancellorsville. Within the park is Old Salem Church, which served as a refuge for civilians fleeing the city during the battle of Fredericksburg. Later, after Chancellorsville, the church was used by the Confederates to tend to the wounded of both sides. It is estimated that 65,000 Union troops and 40,000 Confederates were lost in the fighting.

Fifteen miles south of Fredericksburg is the "Stonewall" Jackson Shrine, honoring the Christian general who died here in 1863.

Hampton St. John's Episcopal Church (100 W. Queens Way) was built in 1728 and houses the oldest English-speaking parish, which was founded in 1610. Its communion silver dates from 1618. The parish museum includes a 1599 Bible and a 1632 prayer book. The stained glass window showing the baptism of Pocahontas was donated by Native American students at Hampton University. A memorial to Virginia Laydon, the first surviving child born in the New World and later a member of St. John's congregation, is located in the churchyard.

The first Christmas celebration held in the New World is said to have been in what is now Hampton. The English settlers, whose leader was John Smith, visited the Kecoughtan Indian village in 1608 to celebrate the birth of Christ.

Little England Chapel (4100 Kecoughtan Rd.) is Virginia's only known African American missionary chapel. Built in 1879, the church was constructed to serve black landowners who had purchased lots and built homes in the "Newtown" section of Hampton. During its 100-year history, it served as a nondenominational church, Sunday school, sewing school, Bible study center, meeting facility, and the base from which extensive missionary work was conducted. The chapel was vacated in 1989 but, after undergoing extensive renovation, reopened in 1993. It offers a permanent exhibit and video program to help visitors understand the religious lives of post–Civil War blacks in Virginia. Admission is free but donations are appreciated.

Hardy What Booker T. Washington called his boyhood home is here and is remembered by the Booker T. Washington National Monument (Rte. 122). You can see the cabin where he was born as well as the plantation kitchen. He and his brother and sister slept on a dirt floor and there was no glass in the windows. Several farm buildings have been reconstructed and programs are given on plantation life, slavery, and Washington's illustrious career from slavery to education and advisor to presidents. (See Washington also under Charleston, W.Va., and Tuskegee, Ala.)

Irvington Historic Christ Church here on Rte. 3 at 420 Christ Church Rd. was completed in 1735 and looks today much the same as it did then. It was a gift to the community by Robert "King" Carter, whose descendants include eight governors of Virginia, two U.S. presidents—the Harrisons, father and son—Gen. Robert E. Lee, and Chief Justice of the U.S. Supreme Court Edward D. White. Inside the church the three-decker pulpit, a Queen Anne holy table, the original communion silver, and all 26 original pews remain. Because heating and lighting have never been added to the church, it is used for services only during the summer.

Jamestown The Jamestown National Historic Site is the home of the remains of the first permanent English settlement in America (1607). Exhibits explain colonial life. It's interesting that the only 17th-century structure still standing is the remains of a church, the Old Church Tower, built in 1639, an addition to a brick church. Over the foundations of that 1639 brick church and the original 1617 frame church, a memorial church was built in 1907 as a reconstruction of the building where America's first elected representative assembly met in 1619. A living history program enables you to "meet" the early settlers. Admission to Jamestown is $4. A ticket to both Jamestown and Yorktown is $7.

The Robert Hunt Shrine is dedicated to the Jamestown Colony's first Anglican minister. Hunt provided spiritual leadership to unite the first settlers' efforts to survive. He celebrated the first recorded Anglican communion in Virginia in 1607.

At the Jamestown Settlement three outdoor living history areas show you what life was like in the early 1600s. Here you will find a reconstruction of James Fort, a Native American village, and full-scale replicas of the three ships that brought the original settlers here in 1607. Special occasions are celebrated throughout the year, and at Thanksgiving there is a three-day event.

Some time later Paul said to Barnabas, "Let us go back and visit the brothers in all the towns where we preached the word of the Lord and see how they are doing."

ACTS 15:36

Lexington Lee Chapel at Washington and Lee University was built in 1867 at the request of Robert E. Lee who served as president of Washington College from 1865 until his death in 1870. Lee's remains are in a crypt below the chapel. In the museum is Charles Wilson Peale's portrait of George Washington wearing the uniform of a colonel in the British army.

Also of interest here is the "Stonewall" Jackson House (8 E. Washington St.), where the general lived from 1859 to his death in 1863.

Lorton Built in the 1770s, the Pohick Church at 9301 Richmond Way was constructed from plans drawn up by George Washington. Now restored to its original appearance, it has an active congregation. During the Civil War, the Union troops stabled their horses in the church and stripped the interior. The east wall was used for target practice.

Lynchburg This is the home of Liberty University, the *Old-Time Gospel Hour,* and the Thomas Road Baptist Church, all founded by Jerry Falwell. Membership of the church has been as high as 18,000. In December the church presents an annual Living Christmas Tree concert. Colorful costuming, spectacular sets, drama, and traditional music with an orchestra and 100-voice choir make this event a sell-out every year. The 36-foot tree is covered with more than 100,000 lights. The Thomas Road Baptist Church broadcasts its services nationally each week, and of course it welcomes visitors.

The South River Meeting House at 5810 Fort Ave. was established by Quakers in 1754; the present stone building was finished in 1798. Because of their opposition to slavery and because of economic hardship, most of the Quakers left the area before the Civil War. In 1899 Presbyterians purchased the ruins of the meetinghouse, restored it as a church, and began holding services there in 1901. In honor of its heritage, it was named the Quaker Memorial Presbyterian Church.

Nearby is Natural Bridge, a 215-foot-high water-hewn stone arch that was once surveyed by George Washington and later owned by Thomas Jefferson. Besides being a natural wonder, the bridge is the site of an annual Easter Sunday sunrise service. Follow the Cedar Creek Trail beyond the Natural Bridge to the Easter Grounds. A 45-minute narrated sound and light show, *Drama of Creation,* is presented nightly beneath the bridge and features the music of Verdi, Rossini, Wagner, Liszt, and Debussy. For specific dates and times, phone 800-533-1410.

Mt. Vernon George Washington's famous estate called Mt. Vernon is the most visited house museum in the country, and easily accessible from Washington, D.C. You can tour George and Martha's home, restored to its appearance during the years when the first president lived here. Admission is $8.

Norfolk Nauticus, the National Maritime Center, is a high-tech interactive museum that combines educational content with entertainment. Major exhibits include the Virtual Adventure, which is a simulated submarine ride, and the Marine Exploratorium, a roomful of large, colorful interactives for children, including a real ship's bridge, periscopes, and a giant wave tank.

St. Paul's Episcopal Church (201 St. Paul's Blvd.) is Norfolk's oldest structure. It was built in 1739 (on the site of a 1641 church known as The Chapel of Ease) and is the sole survivor of a bombardment by the British on New Year's Day in 1776. A cannonball fired by Lord Dunmore of the British fleet is lodged in the southeastern wall.

Other historic churches in Norfolk are First Calvary Baptist (813 Henry St.), erected for an African American congregation in

1915 and 1916; First Baptist (431 Bute St.), dating back to 1800, originally an interracial congregation but increasingly it became an African American membership; the Freemason Street Baptist (Freemason and Bank Sts.), formed in 1816, but the church building dates from 1850 and is in a unique perpendicular Gothic style; St. Mary's Basilica (Chapel and Virgin Sts.), erected in 1857 and proclaimed a minor basilica in 1991; Epworth United Methodist Church (124 West Freemason St.), one of the city's most prominent landmarks; and Christ and St. Luke's Episcopal Church (560 Olney Rd.), with a 130-foot bell tower and a magnificent pipe organ.

GREAT PLACES TO ENJOY GOD'S CREATION

✔ Hiking in Shenandoah National Park, Virginia

✔ White-water rafting the New River Gorge National River, West Virginia

✔ Watching the wild ponies, Assateague Island National Seashore, Virginia/Maryland

Norfolk Botanical Gardens covers 155 acres and contains more than 20 theme gardens, including a rose garden, a healing garden of medicinal plants, a new wildflower meadow, and a 500,000-dollar perennial garden.

Petersburg Old Blandford Church (319 S. Crater Rd.) is a pre–Revolutionary War church that now has 15 magnificent Tiffany stained glass windows, each donated by a southern state. The church has become a memorial to Southern soldiers who perished in the Civil War; about 30,000 Confederate soldiers are buried in the cemetery here. The Memorial Day tradition is said to have begun in this cemetery.

In contrast, First Baptist Church on Harrison St. is believed to be the oldest black church in America. Although the original building was constructed in 1774, its current building dates to 1870. Nearby, Gillfield Baptist Church is the second-oldest black church in America, dating back to 1786.

Portsmouth The Children's Museum of Virginia (221 High St. in Olde Town) offers hands-on attractions in addition to a collection of antique toys and trains, interactive exhibits, and a state-of-the art planetarium.

The restored 1762 Trinity Episcopal Church (500 Court St.) is the oldest building in this town that rapidly became known as a shipbuilding center. Trolley tours highlight the historic Olde Town area.

Richmond King's Dominion is a 400-acre theme park with 50 rides and a 300-foot replica of the Eiffel Tower. Children's rides and games are housed in KidZville, where children can enjoy a tame roller coaster and climb through a full-size cement mixer.

Richmond Children's Museum (740 Navy Hill Dr.) lets children investigate stalagmites and stalactites in a cave. Children can dress up and see what it feels like to be a police officer, a banker, or a shopkeeper.

St. Paul's Episcopal Church (815 E. Grace St.) was designed in Greek Revival style and consecrated in 1845. On the ceiling, the striking plasterwork interweaves Greek, Hebrew, and Christian motifs radiating from the symbol of the Trinity. Eight Tiffany stained glass windows were added beginning in 1890. Behind the altar is a mosaic rendering of da Vinci's *The Last Supper,* also done by Tiffany.

St. John's Church (2401 E. Broad St.) is a white clapboard structure in which Patrick Henry gave his "Liberty or Death" speech at the Second Virginia Convention in 1775. His audience consisted of people like George Washington, Thomas Jefferson, Benjamin Harrison, and Richard Henry Lee. The speech is reenacted on Sunday afternoons from the last Sunday in May through the first Sunday in September. The church actually goes back to 1611 (although the present structure was built in 1741) and the first rector of the church, Alexander Whitaker, ministered to the local tribes and instructed Pocahontas in the Christian faith. Later he baptized her.

About 16 miles from Richmond in the Chesterfield County Courthouse complex on Rte. 10, you will find a Christian monument in the Chesterfield County Museum, a replica of the county's courthouse of 1750. The monument and a painting, *The Apostles of Religious Freedom,* honor seven men jailed on the premises in the 1700s for practicing the Baptist faith in defiance of the established Anglican Church.

Schuyler The Walton Mountain Museum (Schuyler Community Center on Rte. 617) is where author Earl Hamner Jr. grew up and recorded his early memories that became the basis for the long-running TV show *The Waltons.* The museum displays re-creations of sets from that show, including John-Boy's room, the kitchen, and Ike Godsey's store. There is also a 30-minute audiovisual. Admission is $15.

Smithfield St. Luke's Church (two miles southeast on Rte. 10 at 14477 Benns Church Blvd.) is a restored 1632 church, reputed to be the oldest church on an English foundation standing in America. What that means is that this church is built on the foundation of the original walls. In other parts of the country there are Spanish churches that are older, but this one is the oldest on an English foundation. The church is commonly known as the Old Brick Church.

Spotsylvania Francis Asbury, America's first Methodist bishop, died here in 1816. Sent from England by John Wesley, he had logged 270,000 miles of ministry in America.

Strasburg Hupps Hill Battlefield Park has a hands-on Civil War museum that children will enjoy. They can dress up in replicas of Civil War uniforms. Strasburg is known as the "Antique Capital" of Virginia.

Upperville The Trinity Episcopal Church (downtown on US 50) was built in 1955, so it isn't historic in the usual sense. But it was designed as an adaptation of a 12th- and 13th-century French country church, and most of the stone and wood were fashioned by local residents who made their cutting tools in a forge on the grounds.

Virginia Beach The home of the Christian Broadcasting Network, Regent University, and the TV talk show the *700 Club,* all founded by televangelist Pat Robertson, are located here (977 Centerville Tpke.). Tours are available. It is also possible to view the filming of the *700 Club.* A collection of paintings and sculptures depicting biblical scenes is displayed. Admission is free. The adjacent Founder's Inn has formal and informal dining in an alcohol-free and tobacco-free environment. You can eat there and/or spend the night.

Ocean Breeze Park on General Booth Blvd. is an amusement park with attractions for all ages. It has a water park with flumes, slides, tube rides, and activity pools and a Strike Zone batting cage area.

Westover The Westover Church is where Capt. William Perry, who died in 1637, is buried. It is America's third-oldest grave marker. The church itself was constructed in the 1730s.

White Marsh Near White Marsh is the Abingdon Episcopal Church (4645 George Washington Memorial Hwy.), dating from 1755. The first house of worship on this site was built in 1655 and was attended by the grandmother of George Washington, Martha Warner.

Williamsburg Williamsburg was the capital of Virginia from 1699 to 1780, and the present reconstruction gives you a taste of what those early days must have been like. Nearly 90 original 18th- and early 19th-century buildings are located here, as are another 50 that have been reconstructed on their original sites, all fully furnished. Even the gardens and landscaping have been constructed after the fashion of the day. In Colonial Williamsburg is the Bruton Parish Church (Gloucester St. and Parish Green), built in 1712 to 1715. It replaced an earlier church that stood near the present site. The bell that still rings for services dates from 1761. Candlelight recitals are given Tuesday and Saturday evenings at 8 P.M.

Busch Gardens, Williamsburg, features four 17th-century European countries—England, France, Germany, and Italy—and more than 100 rides and shows. So you can experience King Arthur's Challenge, enjoy the Alpengeist roller coaster, see Vesuvius erupt, and take a white-water ride through Roman ruins.

Water Country USA (three miles east on Rte. 199) includes flumes and chutes, a wave pool, inner tube rides, and various swimming pools.

The College of William and Mary is the second-oldest college in the nation (Harvard is older) and was chartered by King William III and Queen Mary II in 1693. The Wren Building dates from 1695 and its design has been attributed to the noted English architect Sir Christopher Wren. The chapel, great hall, convocation room, and a classroom have been furnished to appear as they probably did in the 18th century. This is the oldest academic building still in use in the country.

Winchester Abram's Delight Museum (1340 S. Pleasant Valley Rd., next to the Winchester Visitors Center) is a limestone house built in 1754 by a Quaker, Isaac Hollingsworth. The house is fully restored and furnished as Isaac would have liked it.

Yorktown It was at Yorktown in 1781 that the colonial troops defeated the British, ending the great war. The Yorktown Battlefield, a branch of the Colonial National Park, features a re-creation of the final battle. The museum displays Washington's original field tent.

Grace Episcopal Church, located on Church St. near the river, dates back to 1697 and has been used as a house of worship since then. During the siege of Yorktown, gunpowder and ammunition were stored here. In the Civil War it served as a hospital. The original communion silver, made in England in 1649, is still in use.

South Central States

THE MIX OF CULTURES IN THE SOUTH is not duplicated anywhere else in the country. Like a big pot of gumbo, Native Americans, English, French, Spanish, and Africans have all contributed their influences to the stew. Then the steamy heat has fused the flavors together so that sometimes they are indistinguishable from one another.

Thousands of Christians flock every year to the *Great Passion Play* and other Christian attractions located in Eureka Springs, Arkansas. You will also enjoy the rich religious heritage that belongs to New Orleans—although Mardi Gras will not impress you as a display of the city's spiritual element.

■ALABAMA

Tourist Info
Phone 800-ALABAMA
Web sites
  Entire state   www.touralabama.org
  Alabama Gulf Coast   www.gulfshores.com
  Birmingham   www.birminghamal.org
  Mobile   www.mobile.org
For a complete list of updated links, visit www.christiantraveler.com

Anniston The Church of St. Michael and All Angels (Episcopal) at 1000 W. 18th St., built in 1888, features a magnificent marble altar backed by an alabaster ornamental screen. Bavarian woodworkers carved the entire ceiling of the church by hand. And there are angels on every corner all facing the church at different angles. Lithographs of Christian history are in the assembly room.

Anniston also boasts of its Museum of Natural History, which is situated in the John LaGarde Environmental Interpretive Center in LaGarde Park. It has a bird exhibit with 600 specimens, including many endangered birds. Admission is $3.50.

Ariton Visitors to Christmas City enjoy a 3.5-mile drive through a winter wonderland of more than two million lights and animated scenes of the season. There are also 15 unique craft shops, a pretty white chapel, three restaurants, and nightly entertainment. It is open annually from Thanksgiving through December 31.

Athens If you're around Athens in October, make sure you attend the Tennessee Valley Old Time Fiddlers Convention held at Athens State College (300 N. Beaty St.). Outdoor competitions are held for two days featuring harmonica, banjo, fiddle, mandolin, dulcimer, and guitar.

Athens Bible School (507 Hoffman St.) holds an annual Musical Explosion during the last two weekends in March, featuring mostly country gospel music.

Athens State College, founded in 1822, is Alabama's oldest college. Two interesting sites on the campus are the Altar of the New Testament, which features elegant wood carvings retelling New

Testament stories (on the second floor of Founders Hall) and then Founders Hall itself, which is an 1840s Greek Revival structure.

Birmingham The Birmingham Civil Rights Institute (520 16th St. N) is a thorough and emotional display of the largely Alabama-based civil rights movement. Audiovisual displays, music, and film footage chronicle this painful but poignant period in our nation's history, showing a movement that was clearly intertwined with African American faith traditions.

Across the street is a grim reminder of the movement's innocent victims. The Sixteenth Street Baptist Church (1530 6th Ave. N) is where four little black girls were killed in a September 1963 bombing by white segregationists. There is a plaque here in their memory. During the week the church is open by appointment only, but it has worship services every Sunday.

The Civil Rights Memorial (400 Washington Ave.) was created by Maya Lin, the designer of the Vietnam Veterans' Memorial in Washington, D.C. The memorial has a plaza and a pool from which water flows over a 40-foot black granite wall. Inscribed on the wall are excerpts from Martin Luther King Jr.'s "I Have a Dream" speech. Adjacent are the names of many who gave their lives to the civil rights movement.

Visionland Theme Park (5051 Prince St., Bessemer) is located on 300 acres of rolling countryside in this Birmingham suburb. It includes water rides, a children's area, and thrill rides in four themed areas. The theme park was dedicated to "the glory of God" by Bessemer Mayor Larry Langford.

The Birmingham Botanical Gardens at 2612 Lane Park Rd. has some demonstration gardens maintained by *Southern Living* magazine that can be duplicated in your home. It also features a Japanese garden complete with a 14th-century teahouse reproduction.

The De Soto Caverns (40 miles from Birmingham at 5181 De Soto Caverns Pkwy.) are a network of onyx caves. Tours begin with a sound, water, and laser-light show in the 12-story Great Onyx Cathedral. They end with a sound and light show based on the creation account of Genesis 1. This cave system was used as a Native American burial ground 2,000 years ago. Spanish explorer Hernando de Soto rediscovered the cavern in 1540 (hence the name), and the caverns also served as a Confederate gunpowder mining center and a Prohibition speakeasy.

The Birmingham Museum of Art (2000 8th Ave. N) is noted for its excellent Wedgwood collection, the largest outside England. It also has a great collection of Renaissance paintings.

Dawson Memorial Baptist (1114 Oxmoor Rd.) and Briarwood Presbyterian (200 Briarwood Way) are the two largest Protestant churches in the city. Both have average attendances over 2,000.

Southeastern Bible College (3001 Hwy. 280 E), which began as a night school in 1935, gradually extended its program until it became a degree-granting, four-year college shortly after World War II. It is located in Mountain Brook, just southeast of Birmingham.

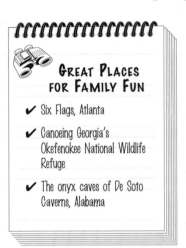

GREAT PLACES FOR FAMILY FUN

✔ Six Flags, Atlanta

✔ Canoeing Georgia's Okefenokee National Wildlife Refuge

✔ The onyx caves of De Soto Caverns, Alabama

Clanton The Southern Baptist leader B. B. McKinney wrote the words to "Take Up Thy Cross and Follow Me" while at a Sunday school convention in this town in 1936.

Cullman On the town's east side (1600 St. Bernard Dr.) you will come to the Ave Maria Grotto on the grounds of the Benedictine monastery. There you will visit a unique garden filled with more than 150 miniature reproductions of famous landmarks. The miniatures, including the Hanging Gardens of Babylon, ancient Jerusalem, Bethlehem, Nazareth, and St. Peter's Basilica in Rome, were constructed by a monk who arrived at the monastery in 1892. The miniatures cover four acres of a terraced landscaped garden. To make his miniatures, the monk used everything he could get his hands on, including marbles, fishing floats, cold cream jars, and cement.

Daphne Malbis Memorial Church (29300 County Rd. 27) is a Greek Orthodox Church of stunning Byzantine architecture opened in 1965 in memory of Jason Malbis, founder of Malbis Plantation. Murals in the church depict the life of Christ. Carved marble and vivid stained glass complete the embellishments.

Decatur Six miles east of the city on Rte. 20 is Mooresville, the state's oldest incorporated town. It features the house of Andrew Johnson, the community brick church, dating from 1840, as well as a Church of Christ, dating from about 1854 in which James Garfield is said to have preached.

Eutaw The First Presbyterian Church (300 Main St.) was organized in 1824 as the Mesopotamian Presbyterian Church and moved into its present location in 1851. Original whale oil lamps, which had been stored for a while in the slave gallery, have been wired for electricity and are now used in the interior. The exterior is one that you will want to photograph.

Nearby is St. Stephen's Episcopal Church (Main St. and Eutaw Ave.), an attractive brick structure. It features a hand-carved lectern and lovely stained glass windows.

Gadsden "Jerusalem's Gate" is an annual Passion play held in March in Wallace Hall at Gadsden State Community College. Unlike most Passion plays, which use traditional hymns or contemporary Christian music, the score for this play is entirely original and performed by the 100-voice Gadsden-Etowah Community Choir. Phone 256-549-0351 for more information. (See other Passion plays under Lake Wales and St. Augustine, Fla.; Atlantic Beach, N.C.; Eureka Springs, Ark.; Ruston, La.; Gatlinburg, Tenn.; Bloomington and Zion, Ill.; and Spearfish, S.D.)

Gainesville The Presbyterian Church here dates from 1837. Its whale oil lamps, pews with doors, and the altar's original chairs are worth seeing.

Hartsville A. J. Showalter, who taught music here, received similar letters from two friends about the deaths of their wives. That prompted the writing of the hymn "Leaning on the Everlasting Arms."

Huntsville Alabama Constitution Village was the site of Alabama's Constitutional Convention of 1819. Today there are demonstrations of woodworking, printing, cooking, and weaving, all performed by costumed artisans. The Center for Early Southern Life on site provides a hands-on history experience in the EarlyWorks Galleries.

The Historic Huntsville Depot offers a view of railroad life in the early 19th century. It is located a few blocks from the village.

Twelve miles southeast in Green Mountain is the Madison County Nature Trail, which will lead you by a covered bridge,

157

a chapel, a 16-acre lake, a waterfall, and the original house on the first homestead.

The U.S. Space and Rocket Center is located at 1 Tranquility Base, with space exhibits, including the Apollo capsule and space shuttle objects returned from orbit. The theater, which seats 280, shows space shuttle and science films photographed by the astronauts. You can enjoy an entire day of space adventure here. Children can ride a cushion of air as they descend to earth on the Lunar Lander in the Kids' Cosmos Energy Depletion Zone. Many visitors are eager to board a device that propels them up a 180-foot tower in less than three seconds. Others want to experience the feeling of weightlessness. The Mission to Mars is the newest space simulator. Here you can "test drive" a new rover over the rocky martian terrain and step on space scales to see how your weight on Mars compares with your weight on the moon.

In Huntsville the largest Protestant church is Whitesburg Baptist at 6806 Whitesburg Dr. S. It has a Sunday school of about 2,000.

Mentone In this area are two unusual churches: St. Joseph's on the Mountain (21145 Scenic Hwy.) has a log structure that serves as the central portion of the church, dating back to 1826; and near De Soto State Park is the Sallie Howard Memorial Chapel (218 Parker Ave. SE), where a 20-foot boulder serves as the rear wall of the church, and stones from a nearby river form the pulpit.

Mobile If you think Mardi Gras sounds like fun but you are reluctant to visit New Orleans during its raunchy festivities, consider Mobile's version. Enjoy the parades, floats, costumes, and "throws" in Mobile, the home of America's original Fat Tuesday. The event is far tamer and more family-friendly than the one in New Orleans.

Christ Episcopal Church (115 S. Conception St.) sits opposite the tourist office at Fort Conde on the site of Alabama's oldest Protestant church. Dedicated in 1842, the church has beautiful Italian and German stained glass windows.

The Cathedral of the Immaculate Conception (2 S. Claiborne St.) features a Roman basilica design and is built on Spanish burial grounds in the heart of Mobile's Old Town. Construction began in 1835. Note the German art glass windows, the bronze canopy over the altar, and the 14 hand-carved stations of the cross.

Cottage Hill Baptist (4255 Cottage Hill Rd.) and Dauphin Way Baptist (3661 Dauphin St.) are probably the largest Protestant churches in the city with average attendances over 2,000.

The magic time in Mobile is spring when the azaleas blaze with color. The annual Azalea Trail Festival follows a 37-mile route past historic homes and magnificent oak trees, trimmed with silvery Spanish moss. The festival is always held the last weekend in March.

Year-round the Bellingrath Gardens and Home (20 miles south of Mobile at 12401 Bellingrath Gardens Rd.) attract visitors to the 905-acre estate, including 76 acres of planted gardens. It is a bird sanctuary too, but because it is known as one of the world's most magnificent azalea gardens, most people come to see the 250,000 azalea plants of 200 varieties, as well as the camellias, roses, water lilies, and hydrangeas. The Bellingrath family, which began the garden in 1917, earned its wealth as a Coca-Cola bottler. The home is furnished with a fine collection of antiques.

Montgomery The legacy of African American activism and faith are obvious at the Dexter Avenue King Memorial Baptist Church (454 Dexter Ave.). This was the first church in which King preached, and also the site where he and other civil rights workers organized the 1955 Montgomery bus boycott. Ten years later King led a nationwide march past the church as he headed toward the state capitol. A mural in the church basement tells the story of King's role in the nation's struggle for civil rights. Call in advance for tours: 334-263-3970. Admission is free but donations are encouraged.

Old Alabama Town (301 Columbus St.) is three blocks north of the church. The reconstructed town depicts urban and rural life in 19th-century Alabama. Visitors can tour a pioneer home-stead, a late 19th-century grocery, a schoolhouse, and an early African American church.

St. John's Episcopal Church, built in 1855, still marks Jefferson Davis's pew. The Gothic pipe organ is also of interest. The church is located at 113 Madison and N. Perry Sts.

In Montgomery the largest Protestant congregation is Frazer Memorial United Methodist (6000 Atlanta Hwy.) with Sunday attendance over 3,000.

Selma The Brown Chapel African Methodist Episcopal Church (410 Martin Luther King Jr. St.), founded in 1866, was the first A.M.E. church in the state. It served as headquarters for blacks during the voting rights campaign and was the starting point for King's historic march from Selma to Montgomery in 1965.

Take a historic walking tour down Martin Luther King Jr. St. Twenty memorials highlight the history of the voting rights campaign in Selma. You will pass First Baptist Church, the George Washington Carver home, the Brown Chapel A.M.E. Church, the Martin Luther King Jr. monument, and others. Contact the visitors bureau for more information on the self-guided tour: 800-45-SELMA.

Tuscumbia In this area south of Florence, Capt. Arthur Keller published his newspaper the *North Alabamian* in the 1880s. And it was here that his daughter, Helen Keller, was born and raised. Ivy Green (300 W. North Commons) marks the birthplace of this remarkable woman who was left unable to hear or see at the age of 19 months. During the summer, you can watch performances of William Gibson's *The Miracle Worker,* which tells the story of Helen's teacher, Anne Sullivan, who worked with her at this place. The family home contains many original furnishings and photographs along with Helen Keller's braille writer.

The Alabama Music Hall of Fame is here, featuring stars of rock, rhythm and blues, and gospel music. A recording studio is available to record personal cassettes or videos.

Tuskegee Booker T. Washington founded the Tuskegee Institute here in 1881. An African American educator and reformer, he built the school into one of the world's leading centers of black education. Daily Bible reading was a key part of Washington's life.

The Oaks (1212 Old Montgomery Rd.) was the home of Booker T. Washington. It is furnished as it was during the time the family lived there, and is part of the Tuskegee Institute National Historic Site.

The Carver Museum, also at 1212 Old Montgomery Rd., pays tribute to the genius of George Washington Carver. His experiments with not only peanuts but pecans, sweet potatoes, and cotton resulted in a more educated approach to farming, as well as hundreds of new products.

The chapel next to the graves of George Washington Carver and Booker T. Washington, built in 1969, has saw-toothed ceilings and deep beams. (See Washington also under Charleston, W.Va., and Hardy, Va.; see Carver also under Joplin, Diamond, and Fulton, Mo.)

▪ARKANSAS

Tourist Info
Phone 1-800-NATURAL
Web sites
  Entire state   www.1800natural.com
  Eureka Springs   www.eurekasprings.org
  Fort Smith   www.fortsmith.org
  Great Passion Play in Eureka Springs   www.greatpassionplay.com
  Little Rock   www.littlerock.com
For a complete list of updated links, visit www.christiantraveler.com

Altus St. Mary's Catholic Church on top of Mount Bethel (R.R. 1) was dedicated in 1879 and is known for its original painting by Fridolin Fuchs, a German painter. From a 120-foot tower hang four bells, weighing nearly 6,400 pounds. There are 29 stained glass windows in the interior.

Arkadelphia One of the older colleges in the state is Ouachita Baptist University, founded in 1886. McClellan Hall on the campus contains the official papers of U.S. Senator John L. McClellan. The school is a Southern Baptist college.

Augusta Woodrow Wilson worshiped in the Presbyterian church here when he lived for a time with his sister, who was the wife of the minister.

Bella Vista The Mildred B. Cooper Memorial Chapel (504 Memorial Dr.), located in the Ozarks of northwest Arkansas, was designed by the architect who created Eureka Springs's well-known Thorncrown Chapel. The Cooper Chapel is nondenominational and is open to visitors of all faiths. The scenic surroundings make the church popular for quiet meditation as well as wedding services.

Blytheville Now a town of about 25,000 residents, it took its name from a Virginia-born Methodist minister, Henry Blythe, who came here in 1853, conducting services and holding camp meetings. The community that grew up around the church became known as Blythe Chapel before eventually becoming modern-day Blytheville.

El Dorado This town got its start when an adventurer named Matthew Rainey had his wagon break down here. He stayed and for some reason called the place El Dorado. Within two years a Baptist pastor had started a school and the First Baptist Church (210 W. Main St.). Both Matthew Rainey and the Baptist pastor are buried in the Old Presbyterian Cemetery, 418 S. Washington St.

Eureka Springs This town is best known as the site of the hugely popular *Great Passion Play,* modeled after Germany's *Oberammergau Passion Play.* Over six million visitors watch a cast of 250 actors and countless live animals reenact the life and passion of Christ every year from late-April to late-October. (For other Passion plays, see Lake Wales and St. Augustine, Fla.; Atlantic Beach, N.C.; Gadsden, Ala.; Ruston, La.; Gatlinburg, Tenn.; Bloomington and Zion, Ill.; and Spearfish, S.D.)

Besides the Passion play, there are at least 14 other activities here of interest to Christians. The Bible Museum (Passion Play Rd.) has a collection of 7,000 old Bibles and 3,000 primitive manuscripts. It has been termed by Dr. Fred McGraw of the Library of Congress the greatest collection anywhere.

Also here, on Magnetic Mountain, is the seven-story concrete sculpture, the *Christ of the Ozarks.* The outstretched arms span more than 65 feet, and the weight is more than a million pounds.

The New Holy Land/Tabernacle (Passion Play Rd.) is a 50-acre tract that re-creates the features of Israel. The Tabernacle is a full-scale reproduction of Moses' tabernacle in the wilderness. On the grounds is also a ten-foot section of the Berlin Wall with a portion of the 23d Psalm written in German on it.

The Sacred Arts Center (Passion Play Rd.) contains more than 1,000 pieces of biblical art, including sculptured marble, mosaics, and needlework portraits.

Nearby is Covenant Gardens (Passion Play Rd.), a unique collection of biblical plants. See for yourself what the various plants referred to in Scripture actually look like. This is open from May to mid-October.

The Hammond Museum of Bells (2 Pine St.) features a large collection of bells and chimes. The tour describes the history and uses of each kind of bell.

Miles Musical Museum (on US 62W) presents a wide variety of musical instruments and machines, including nickelodeons, band organs, player pianos, music boxes, a calliope, and early Edison phonograph machines. The museum also has a chapel, wood carvings, and paintings.

Wings, next to the Queen Anne Mansion on US 62, is an 1898 Victorian home decorated for Christmas year-round. The home also contains glass-enclosed aviaries, housing exotic birds.

St. Elizabeth Church (on Crescent Dr.) is entered through the bell tower, which is unusual. A prayer garden at the side of the church provides a good view of the *Christ of the Ozarks* statue.

Thorncrown Chapel (one mile west, just off US 62) is noted for its innovative architecture. Clear glass windows allow visitors to worship or meditate as they enjoy the beauty of the surrounding Ozarks. The chapel is not an organized church, nor is it affiliated with any denomination, but services are held every Sunday.

GREAT PLACES TO ENJOY GOD'S CREATION

✔ The drive on Rte. 182 along Bayou Teche, Louisiana

✔ Fishing the Buffalo National River, Arkansas

Fayetteville The First Presbyterian Church (406 W. Central St.) with its modernistic architecture is an impressive building. It is faced in redbrick, ribbed with vertical stained glass panes. The panes are deeply set in a brick bell tower, out of which a slender cross rises.

Hot Springs An annual live nativity in early December is held at Park Place Baptist Church (1942 Millcreek Rd.). Admission is free. Visitors relive the birth of Christ in a realistic setting.

Little Rock St. Andrew's Cathedral (Roman Catholic) at 7th and Louisiana Sts. was probably the first large building in Arkansas to be built of the granitelike syenite, quarried nearby. It was completed in 1882.

Philander Smith College was founded by Methodists as a school for African Americans in 1877.

The Children's Museum of Arkansas (1400 W. Markham St.) provides a great opportunity for kids to learn through all their senses. Included are a simulated farmer's market, Victorian house, and changing exhibits on life in other lands.

An annual living nativity is on display in early December at First Church of the Nazarene (1200 N. Mississippi Ave.). Nine outdoor scenes depict the Christmas story with live characters and animals in biblical settings. Visitors may walk or drive through to view the scenes, listen to music, and read the Scriptures placed at each scene. Admission is free.

Mountain View The Ozark Folk Center (two miles north, off Rte. 9 on Rte. 382) re-creates a mountain village and highlights the cabin crafts, music, and lore of the Ozarks. In the Crafts Forum more than 25 artisans display crafts like wheel-thrown ceramics and ironware forging. You can also enjoy original Ozark music in the auditorium at lunchtime and nightly, accompanied by clog-gers. Admission is $7.50 for the crafts center or the evening show. A combination ticket is $13.25.

Pine Bluff Pine Bluff is the second-oldest town in the state, trac-ing its history back to 1819. Twenty-five miles southeast of here on US 79 is Pioneer Village, which transports you back to those early years. The early church, a blacksmith shop, an old Victo-rian home, and a number of other buildings are on display. It is open Monday through Fridays during the summer.

Siloam Springs John Brown University, a nondenominational evangelical college with a strong emphasis on communications, is located here. It was founded in 1919 by evangelist John E. Brown, whose education philosophy can be summed up as "Head, Heart, and Hand." It has a student body of about 1100 students.

Springdale This town was founded in 1840 as a settlement and church named Shiloh. The name of the town has been changed, but the old historic district still carries the biblical name and shows what life was like in the mid-1800s. A museum on W. John-son Ave. displays artifacts of the town's early history.

Van Buren One of the oldest settlements in Arkansas, this town was settled in 1818. A large ten-block downtown area has been restored to its 19th-century appearance, including a courthouse, a schoolhouse, and the old Mount Olive Church.

■KENTUCKY

Tourist Info
Phone 800-225-TRIP
Web sites
  Entire state   www.kentuckytourism.com
  Abbey of Gethsemani   www.monks.org
  Bardstown area   www.bardstowntourism.com
  Lexington area   www.visitlex.com
  Louisville   www.louisville-visitors.com
For a complete list of updated links, visit www.christiantraveler.com

Bardstown My Old Kentucky Home State Park (501 E. Stephen Foster Ave.) is named after the ballad of the same name written by Foster. The song was inspired by Federal Hill, a lovely Bardstown mansion within the park. When you are escorted through the stately mansion by a costumed guide, you feel as if you are stepping into the days of the antebellum South. From Thanksgiving time until mid-December the house comes alive with annual Christmas candlelight tours. During the summer you can see a Stephen Foster outdoor drama in the park. (See Foster also under White Springs, Fla.)

St. Joseph's Proto Cathedral (310 W. Stephen Foster Ave.), begun in 1816, was one of the first Catholic cathedrals west of the Allegheny Mountains. The architect who built it was paid in part with potatoes, most of which rotted. Don't miss the 17th-century European painting collection for which this church is famous. The collection was a gift from Louis Philippe, king of France, who is said to have lived in Bardstown during his exile.

Several other Catholic firsts are located in the Bardstown area. The Loretto Motherhouse in Nerinx was founded in 1812 and is one of the first American women's religious communities. The museum and art gallery are well worth seeing. In nearby Springfield, St. Catherine Motherhouse is the home of the first U.S. community of Dominican sisters. It was founded in 1822. Also in Springfield, St. Rose Proto-Priory was the first Catholic educational institution west of the Alleghenies.

Benton "Big Singing Day" is held each year on the fourth Sunday of May in this town, and it is the only festival that uses the 1835

Southern Harmony Book of shape note tunes. The event has been happening each year since 1843. The songs are mostly Welsh hymns, sung in four-part harmony, with no leader and no instrumental accompaniment. The festival takes place on the courthouse lawn.

Berea In 1853, in the old Glade Church, John G. Fee organized an anti-slavery church, "a union of all spirit-born followers of Jesus Christ," and out of this grew the village and college, which he named Berea because the people "received the word with all readiness of mind" (Acts 17:11). The goal of the school today is "to provide an educational opportunity primarily for students from Appalachia, black and white, who have great promise and limited economic resources." Eighty percent of its 1,500 students come from the southern Appalachian region.

Beverly The Red Bird Mission here is a United Methodist mission complex with a school, hospital, community outreach programs, and a craft shop. It has been operating since 1921. Area craftspeople market their furniture, rugs, and weavings at the Red Bird Mission Crafts. The mission is on Rte. 66.

Chenoa Just west of here in Frakes is the Henderson Settlement, a United Methodist Settlement begun in 1925 as a school and community outreach center. Now it is the only Methodist mission in the country with an agricultural development program, and it includes 1,300 acres of land, livestock, orchards, gardens, and a big community greenhouse. Weavings and other handcrafts are sold in the Log House Craft Shop. Visitors may tour the place or, if they wish, they can stay for a retreat or work camp.

Covington Covington may not be a big city but it sure has a grand and glorious cathedral. The Basilica of the Assumption (Madison Ave. at 12th St.) is modeled after the Notre Dame cathedral of Paris. It has 82 stained glass windows and one of them is the largest in the world. The cathedral hosts a concert series featuring the three pipe organs inside.

Another beautiful church, the Mother of God Church (119 W. 6th St.), has stained glass windows from Germany. Built in 1870 and 1871, the church in Italian Renaissance–style features twin

Why Are There So Many Baptists in the South?

When you drive through the South, you may think there are more Baptist churches than there are people. It is understandable when you realize that the Southern Baptist denomination is the largest Protestant denomination in the country and that two African American Baptist groups, with strong membership in the South, have more than eight million members. And then there are millions of independent Baptists and Baptists of smaller denominations like the Duck River Baptists or the Sovereign Grace Baptists.

But why so many Baptists in the South?

It all began just after the Revolutionary War. Between 1776 and 1820, Baptists and Methodists poured across the Allegheny Mountains into Kentucky and Tennessee and later into Missouri, Arkansas, and Texas.

One Baptist minister, Lewis Craig, led his congregation in a body across the mountains, baptizing new believers in mountain streams and settling at Gilbert's Creek, Kentucky, in December 1781, where they gathered for worship "around the same old Bible they had used in Spotsylvania" in Virginia.

But Baptists didn't wait for congregations to move. Strong individualists, many of them became farmer-preachers like John Taylor who started 10 or 12 Baptist churches in Kentucky and Tennessee. The typical Baptist preacher worked his land five or six days each week and preached on Sunday, though he generally had little education, theological or otherwise.

At first, the small congregations of three or four families would meet in the rude cabin of one of the settlers. Then, maybe a year or two later as others were evangelized, a meetinghouse of round logs was built. Then in another 10 or 20 years, a better meetinghouse of hewn logs and a fireplace would be erected. It was such a church that Thomas Lincoln, father of Abraham Lincoln, helped build in Pigeon Creek, Indiana, in 1819.

Both Baptist and Methodist denominations grew more by evangelism than by people migrations. In 1800, for example, there were 30,000 Methodists west of the Alleghenies. By 1830 that number increased to nearly 200,000, mostly by conversions.

As the population moved west and settlers had to make their own decisions in every area of life, they made their own spiritual decisions too. The neighborhood church and camp meeting evangelism steered the converts to Baptist and Methodist congregations.

Renaissance towers and five murals painted by a parishioner whose works are also in the Vatican.

The Garden of Hope (699 Edgecliff Dr.) in Covington may have the only replica of the tomb of Christ in America.

Danville This lovely little town is the home of Centre College, a Presbyterian school. The architecture of the campus buildings is worth admiring, and there are frequent performances at the Norton Center for the Arts on campus.

Elizabethtown During the month of December, this town is literally lit up like a Christmas tree. Freeman Lake Park is transformed into a display called "Christmas in the Park," as more than seventy lighted Christmas displays sponsored by local businesses illuminate the area.

Elkhorn At Breaks Interstate Park, which lies on the border of Kentucky and Virginia, is a Tri-State Gospel Singing gathering each Labor Day weekend. Breaks Park, known for its 1,600-foot gorge through Pine Mountain, is called the Grand Canyon of the South.

Florence On the campus of Thomas More College off Turkeyfoot Rd., the Monte Casino Chapel, which measures just six by nine feet, is said to be the "world's smallest house of worship." Built in 1810 in a vineyard near Covington by Benedictine monks, it was moved to its present location in the 1960s. You are invited to worship within, but not if you have a large family. (See also the "smallest church in America" under Savannah, Ga.; the "world's smallest church" under Festina, Iowa; the "world's smallest cathedral" under Highlandville, Mo.; and the Wee Kirk of the Valley in Cedar Vale, Kans.)

Gethsemani The Cistercian Abbey, located in this area near Bardstown, is the oldest Cistercian monastery in the United States. Founded in 1824, the Trappist monastery was home to the writer Thomas Merton, who is buried here. There are fewer than a hundred Trappist monks here and, while silence is encouraged, it is not required. Monks make and sell fruitcakes and three kinds of Port Salut Trappist cheese. But watch out for that fruitcake; it's made with real Kentucky bourbon. Visitors are welcome to join in various services. Mass is at 6:15 A.M. on weekdays and there are other prayer services and vespers throughout the day. A retreat house is available for personal or group retreats. Women, however, are welcome only during the first and third full weeks of each month.

Harlan The Little Shepherd Trail extends 38 miles and passes through the Kingdom Come State Park. It was this region that is portrayed in the novel *The Little Shepherd of Kingdom Come* by John Fox Jr., the first American novel to sell a million copies.

Harrodsburg The Shaker Village of Pleasant Hill (seven miles northeast of Harrodsburg) is set on about 2,000 acres and has been restored as a rural Shaker community of the early 19th century. It is America's largest and best restored Shaker village. The 33 structures—some dating to 1809—reflect Shaker simplicity. Don't miss the worship service in the Shaker meetinghouse, held daily. All visitor services are provided in the original buildings. The Shakers, a movement that began in late 19th-century New England, came here in 1805. They formed a communal group and believed in celibacy. The Pleasant Hill community lasted until the death of its last resident in 1923. Accommodations on site are available, and don't worry, the staff won't expect you to live as simply as the Shakers did. TV and air-conditioning are provided. Be sure to eat dinner at the Trustees' Office Inn, specializing in Shaker and regional foods. (See Shakers also under Sabbathday Lake, Maine; Pittsfield, Mass.; Concord and Enfield, N.H.; Old Chatham, N.Y.; South Union, Ky.; Lebanon, Ohio; and Marysville, Wash.)

The first Dutch Reformed church building west of the Allegheny Mountains is the 1800 Old Mud Meeting House in Harrodsburg. Dutch settlers had moved here as early as 1781 and formed a community in which they spoke Dutch and worshiped as they had in the Netherlands. The church they built became known as the Mud Meeting House because massive timber walls are chinked with clay, straw, twigs, roots, and gravel.

Hazard Just north of town in Buckhorn is the Log Cathedral, which is also the Buckhorn Lake Area Church. It was built in 1907 as part of the Witherspoon College campus, although it really wasn't a college. Harvey Murdoch of the Society of Soul Winners had started a Christian elementary and high school and

SHAKERS IN KENTUCKY

The Shakers began as a group of nine dedicated but impoverished followers of Mother Ann Lee, a religious visionary from Manchester, England. She had been part of a group of Christians who worshiped by being literally moved by the Spirit of God, trembling, twirling, and dancing. They called themselves the United Society of Believers in Christ's Second Appearing; their persecutors called them "Shaking Quakers," and then just "Shakers," a name they eventually adopted themselves.

Mother Ann set up a small colony of believers just outside of Albany, New York, in New Lebanon. She claimed to see visions and to hear Christ speaking to her. Revelations convinced her that the only road to salvation lay in celibacy and confession of sin. The Shakers strove to, as far as possible, create a heaven on earth until Christ's second coming. They actively sought converts and established colonies throughout the northeastern United States.

In the early 19th century three missionaries left their mother colony in New Lebanon for the West. They had heard of a great religious revival taking place in Kentucky and were after converts. The result of this Shaker mission trip was seven new colonies in Ohio, Indiana, and Kentucky, including Pleasant Hill, the largest existing Shaker village. Visitors to the Shaker Village in Pleasant Hill can relive the experiences of those early 19th-century believers and will be enamored with the simplicity and beauty of the colony and its setting.

then called it a college in order to make the students proud of their learning. The Log Cathedral is impressive, and inside is a Hook and Hasting pipe organ. Services are held each Sunday at 11:00 A.M.

Hodgenville Near here, 45 miles south of Louisville on US 31 E at Rte. 61 is the birthplace of Abraham Lincoln. This national historic site features 56 steps, one for each year of Honest Abe's life, leading up to a neolithic monument, which shelters Lincoln's small log cabin home. Admission is free.

Hopkinsville About ten miles east in the little village of Fairview on US 68 is the Jefferson Davis Monument Historic Site. This is where the president of the Confederate States was born. A 351-foot monument is said to be the tallest concrete-cast obelisk in the world. The Bethel Baptist Church now occupies the exact place where Davis was born.

This is another area settled by Amish and Mennonite people. Next to the Jefferson Davis monument is Zimmerman Farms produce stand, which is open in the summer months. For dessert you can drive eight miles east to Elkton to another Amish business, Schlabach's Bakery, for their sourdough bread, sweet rolls, or cookies. Nearby is another Amish store, Grandma's Cupboard, run by Elmer and Mary Hochstetler. It is a sales outlet for area women who make quilts and hooked rugs. Part of the profits go to a Christian school. (See other Amish sites in Pennsylvania, Illnois, Indiana, Iowa, Michigan, Minnesota, Missouri, Ohio, Wisconsin, and Kansas.)

Lexington Kentucky is horse country. If Louisville is known for Churchill Downs, then Lexington is known for its horse parks. There are many in the area to see, but the most well-known is the Kentucky Horse Park (4089 Ironworks Pike). It has extensive facilities, a museum tracing the history of horses, and, as you might expect, a few horses as well.

Louisville For anyone who thinks of Kentucky as being culturally deprived, take a look at the glorious Roman Catholic Cathedral of the Assumption (433 S. 5th St.). This Gothic Revival structure was built between 1849 and 1852. Mammoth stone arches support an umbrella of 24 karat gold stars. Tours are available, and the museum is open weekdays.

The Louisville Slugger Museum (800 W. Main St.) is for young and old alike. You'll know it when you see it, because the world's largest baseball bat, 120 feet high, sits out front, and a giant baseball appears to be passing through a plate glass window across the street. Even visitors who aren't baseball fans will feel nostalgic for America's pastime after seeing a movie about the crack of the bat. The big draw is the factory where you can see the famous baseball bats being made.

The Southern Baptist Theological Seminary here houses the Joseph A. Callaway Archaeology Museum and the Eisenberg Museum of Egyptian and Near East Antiquities in its library building. Admission is free.

The Presbyterian Church U.S.A. is now headquartered on Witherspoon Street in Louisville.

Mammoth Cave There is something very spiritual about this place. Apparently others have agreed, as the remains of an old Methodist church are located inside one of the cave's myriad tunnels, and a number of small chapels are located above ground. It's worthwhile discussing just why God would create such an awesomely beautiful site merely to hide it underground.

Apparently he simply enjoys creating, whether he has an audience or not. Mammoth Cave is the world's largest cave system. To date, over 350 miles of underground tunnels have been discovered with another estimated 600 to go. Tours are available for all ages and abilities. There are even wheelchair and stroller-accessible tours. But you must make tour reservations in advance, because this is a very popular destination. Phone 800-967-2283.

Besides the 350 miles of caverns, you may be interested in the Wax Museum in Park City that includes a representation of da Vinci's *Last Supper,* Moses receiving the Ten Commandments, Billy Graham, and more than a hundred other lifelike figures. Not far away at the junction of Hwys. 70 and 255 is Wondering Woods, which is a reconstructed town from the turn of the last century. Sunday morning worship services are held in the Old Community Meeting House.

GREAT PLACES FOR FAMILY FUN

✔ Kentucky Kingdom—The Thrill Park, Louisville, Kentucky

✔ Kentucky Horse Park, Lexington, Kentucky

✔ The amusements around Pigeon Forge and Gatlinburg, Tennessee

Mount Sterling This town of about 5,000 people is best known for its October Court Days when 100,000 people crowd into the center historic area for a big trading festival. Throughout the year, however, others come to see the Ascension Episcopal Church at Broadway and High Sts., with its walnut paneling, carved wood, exposed beams, and stained glass windows. The windows are thought to be the first such windows to cross the Alleghenies by oxcart. Church doors are open during the week.

Owensboro The Mount Saint Joseph Center and Community of Ursuline Sisters is a combination retreat center, museum, and community. In the museum visitors see a variety of musical instruments, art reproductions, and religious articles and displays.

Paris The Cane Ridge Meeting House (1655 Cane Ridge Rd.), eight miles east of the town, off US 460, was built in 1791 as a Presbyterian church. It is said to be the largest one-room log structure in the state. In August 1801 the Cane Ridge Revival broke out here, the largest camp meeting revival on the frontier. Preachers stood on stumps and hay barrels, talking almost continuously to 30,000 people for an entire week. This is also where Barton W. Stone in 1804 formed a group that took the name the Christian Church, later merging with another group to become the Disciples of Christ movement in 1832. The denomination now manages the meetinghouse and museum. A small museum here contains artworks, an old Bible, and a collection of frontier antiques and tools. It is open daily April through October.

Russell Springs This is Mennonite country in Kentucky. Unlike other communities, this one hasn't been commercialized, but two stores give visitors the feel of the place. At Bluegrass Wood and Leather Craft and at Dutchman's Market on Hwy. 910, you may find something that seems unusual to you but is commonplace to the Mennonite farmer.

South Union The Shaker Museum, housed in the 1824 40-room Centre House here, contains hundreds of items depicting life of the South Union colony of Shakers. The museum claims to have the largest collection of western Shaker furniture in the United States. It is open daily. (See Shakers also under Sabbathday Lake, Maine; Pittsfield, Mass.; Concord and Enfield, N.H.; Old Chatham, N.Y.; Harrodsburg, Ky.; Lebanon, Ohio; and Marysville, Wash.)

Tompkinsville The Old Mulkey Meetinghouse State Historic Site is located on 60 acres 2 miles south of town. The meetinghouse may be the oldest in the state and the oldest church in southern Kentucky. The 12 corners of the old church (built in 1804) are said to represent the 12 apostles; and the three doors, the Trinity. Daniel Boone's sister is buried in the churchyard. The building was constructed of half-hewn logs and chinking.

Wilmore Asbury College and Seminary, in this small town south of Lexington, are independent but have strong Methodist roots. The seminary is one of the ten largest Protestant seminaries in the country.

■LOUISIANA

Tourist Info
Phone 800-261-9144
Web sites
  Entire state   www.louisianatravel.com
  Baton Rouge   www.bracvb.com
  Jazzland, New Orleans's newest theme park   www.jazzland2000.com
  New Orleans   www.neworleanscvb.com
For a complete list of updated links, visit www.christiantraveler.com

Louisiana has a clear religious past; the metropolitan New Orleans area alone is home to a whopping 941 churches. And the state is divided not into counties, but into parishes, a holdover from the old days when Catholicism ruled. But most Christians today associate Louisiana with New Orleans, and New Orleans with revelry. They have little interest in visiting during the Mardi Gras season, the annual pre-Lenten festival that has become little more than an excuse for outrageous drinking and debauchery. Still, there is a rich religious heritage in Louisiana, one that will enrich the spiritual lives of Christians of all persuasions.

Alexandria In Pineville, near Alexandria, is Louisiana College, a Southern Baptist college founded in 1906. Set on 81 acres, covered by native pines, oaks, and dogwoods, it has at the center of its campus the attractive columned facade of Alexandria Hall. Musical performances and lecture series are held throughout the year.

Baton Rouge The Samuel Clemens Steamboat has daytime harbor tours of the Mississippi as well as evening dinner cruises from April through August. Departure is from the foot of Florida St. For this and other steamboat information, phone the Baton Rouge Convention and Visitors Bureau: 800-LAROUGE.

Heritage Museum and Village, located at 1606 Main St., features a turn-of-the-century Victorian house along with a rural village, composed of a church, school, store, and town hall.

Television evangelist Jimmy Swaggart continues to preach in his church here—Jimmy Swaggart Ministries, 8919 World Ministry Ave.—although his ministry has been cut back considerably in recent years.

Ferriday Across the Mississippi River from Natchez, Mississippi, is this little town, the birthplace of televangelist Jimmy Swaggart; Jimmy's cousin, rock star Jerry Lee Lewis; and another cousin, country music's Mickey Gilley. On Louisiana Ave. is the Lewis Family Museum, next to Terrell's Drive-Thru. After paying the admission fee, you will see pictures of Lee, Swaggart, and Gilley, plus baby portraits, Bibles, and even sermons written by Jerry Lee in his earlier life.

Gibson James and Betty Provost have a private swamp preserve here, which they call Wildlife Gardens. They keep ostriches and alligators on display in cages, and peacocks roam the grounds. Located at 5306 N. Bayou Black Dr., it gives youngsters the opportunity to observe the swamp landscape on foot.

Grand Coteau Just north of Lafayette, this peaceful little village is a religious and educational center. The entire town is on the National Register of Historic Places. Of particular interest to Christians is the Church of St. Charles Borromeo, a simple wooden structure with a fabulously ornate high-baroque interior.

Houma Known as the "Venice of America," this town is famous for its Cajun food. In bayou country, it also features Annie Miller's Terrebonne Swamp and Marsh Tours, boat trips lasting two to three hours in swamps and wild marshlands, where wild game, alligators, and birds live in abundance. Phone 504-879-3934 for more information.

Lafayette Since Acadians from Nova Scotia settled this area to escape British persecution, there is an Acadian Village here, featuring Acadian architecture with houses, a general store, and a chapel. (See Acadians also under St. Martinville, La., and Grand Pré, Nova Scotia.)

The towering Cathedral of St. John the Evangelist (914 St. John St.) is an impressive cathedral shaded by an equally impressive oak tree called, appropriately enough, St. John's Cathedral Oak. The tree is estimated to be 450 years old and shades the entire lawn with limbs that spread 145 feet. The weight of a single limb is estimated to be 72 tons. The church, which isn't as old as the tree, was built in 1918 and has a 700-seat Romanesque sanctuary.

The Children's Museum of Acadiana (201 E. Congress St.) and Vermilionville (1600 Surrey St.), with guides in period costumes taking you through historic homes, are also worth seeing.

Logansport Each December Logansport becomes the little town of Bethlehem. Several churches cooperate, each presenting a different part of the Christmas story, and visitors are taken on a hayride to each.

Mansfield Seven miles northeast of Mansfield in the community of Carmel stands the Rock Chapel, built by monks from the Carmelite monastery in 1891. The monks carried stones from the surrounding hills and fastened them together with mud plaster. Two monks from France adorned the walls with frescoes and the ceiling with murals. The Rock Chapel was built to give the monks and anyone else a quiet place to pray and study. But in 1904 fire destroyed the monastery and other church buildings. It wasn't until 1961 that the Rock Chapel was restored so that it could be used again.

Many Hodges Gardens (12 miles south on US 171) has 4,700 acres of gardens and greenhouses. In the 1940s A. J. Hodges reclaimed the acreage as a tree farm and experimental arboretum and turned it into formal gardens and a 225-acre lake. Both wild and cultivated plants can be seen all year. Special events include an Easter service, a July Fourth festival, and a Christmas lights festival.

Monroe The Emmy-Lou Biedenharn Foundation on Riverside Dr. sponsors a Bible museum, gardens, and a conservatory. The Biedenharn family house was built in 1914 by Joseph Biedenharn, who made his fortune as the first bottler of Coca-Cola. The house contains antiques, expensive furnishings, and Coca-Cola memorabilia. The Bible museum houses a collection of very old and rare manuscripts, Bibles, maps, portraits, and musical instruments. It also contains some contemporary Bibles with illustrations by renowned artists. The ELsong Gardens are formal gardens, originally designed to be a backdrop for concerts. The EL of ELsong is derived from Emmy-Lou, Joseph's wife. Emmy-Lou had been an international opera singer, who collected antiques from around the world. One of the four fountains in the garden is a porcelain fountain from the garden of Russian empress Catherine the Great.

Morgan City Louisiana's oldest chartered harvest festival is held here every Labor Day weekend—the Shrimp and Petroleum Festival. Yes, the name is odd, but the celebration has some fascinating Christian roots. Dedicated to honoring the local work force—which happens to be primarily shrimp fishermen and offshore petroleum workers—and thanking God for his bounty, this festival is the best down-home fun you'll find in Louisiana.

After a huge outdoor Mass in the Park, local shrimping boats make their way down the river for the Blessing of the Fleet. Afterward, everyone enjoys the Cajun Culinary Classic, with a variety of seafood to sample. Music in the Park offers traditional Cajun, swamp rock, progressive zydeco, country, and rhythm and blues. The Children's Village features an enchanted forest, a fire-breathing dragon, a castle, storytellers, and much more. And when the day is done, you watch the spectacular fireworks display over the Atchafalaya River (you gotta love that name). All events are free.

If you can't make it on Labor Day weekend, you can still enjoy a walking tour of this city, which includes three historic churches in town as well as several historic houses. The three churches are Sacred Heart Catholic Church (1859) at 415 Union St., Trinity Episcopal Church (1877) at 302 Greenwood St., and Pharr Chapel United Methodist (1878) at 517 Federal Ave.

Then to rest up, go to the Brownell Memorial Park and Carillon Tower (located just off Rte. 70 north of Morgan City). This park was the gift of a local woman who wanted to give something back to her community. The result is a quiet park filled with various plants that grow abundantly wild along the ridges of the local swamps. It was her wish that the park be a nondenominational natural setting where a person might retreat to commune with God. In the center of the park is a large carillon tower, which houses one of the world's largest and finest cast-bell carillons. Sixty-one bronze bells ranging in weight from 18 to 4,730 pounds ring regularly.

New Orleans The old part of New Orleans is the French Quarter. This is the original French settlement. Streets are lined with old buildings, embellished with beautiful wrought iron balconies and brightly colored flowers. The city's French and Spanish influences are obvious in its architecture. Jackson Square is the center of activity in the French Quarter. Here you will enjoy watching swarms of entertainers perform, including artists, clowns, mimes, musicians, and magicians.

177

St. Louis Cathedral, dedicated in 1794 as a Catholic church and later as a cathedral, sits right beside Jackson Square as a quiet reminder of the city's richly religious past. It is the oldest active Catholic church (cathedral) in the nation and was awarded the rank of minor basilica in 1964. Behind the cathedral is the Cathedral Garden. Pirate's Alley, which borders the garden, is a favorite spot for painters. On the alley is the house where William Faulkner lived when he wrote his first novel. Next to the cathedral is the Presbytère. Although it was designed to be a rectory, it was never used by the church. Now a museum, it displays exhibits of Louisiana culture and history.

The historic French Market fills several city blocks just east of Jackson Square. Vendors here sell everything from produce to jewelry. This market is not just a tourist's mecca; the complex of shops, offices, and eating places has been here since 1791, located in the very buildings that once housed French and Spanish markets under their rule. You could consider buying a picnic lunch at the Farmers Market, which offers fresh fruits and vegetables and never closes.

St. Augustine's Church (1210 Governor Nicholls St.) was designed by the same architect who virtually rebuilt St. Louis Cathedral in 1849 to 1851. St. Augustine's opened in 1842 and is the second-oldest African American Catholic church in the country. One of its stained glass panels shows the Sisters of the Holy Family, an order of black Creole nuns that was founded in 1842.

Another notable Catholic structure is Ursuline Convent at 1100 Chartres St. Built between 1745 and 1752, it is the oldest structure in the French quarter. Next door is the Chapel of Archbishops with a stained glass window paying tribute to the battle of New Orleans. Andrew Jackson credited his victory in that battle to the Ursuline sisters' prayers for divine intercession.

Christ Church Cathedral (Episcopal) at 2919 St. Charles Ave., also known as the Fourth Episcopal Cathedral of New Orleans, is a majestic Gothic-style church that dates from around 1887. Most of the 100 stained glass windows were made between 1950 and 1970. Free classical music concerts are held in the sanctuary on selected Sunday afternoons.

The St. Charles Avenue Streetcar is a 13-mile line begun in 1835 and is the oldest continuously operating street railway in the world. Along with the Riverfront Streetcar, it offers some of the best tours of the city. And for $1, you can't beat it.

The Louisiana Children's Museum has hands-on exhibits like a supermarket, complete with stocked shelves and check-out registers, and a TV news studio where young news anchors can see themselves on the monitors. The museum is spread over 45,000 square feet at 420 Julia St. Admission is $5.

Jazzland, New Orleans' newest attraction, is a 140-acre theme park located about 12 miles from downtown. The park offers entertainment, regional food, a variety of music, games, and more than 25 rides. Visitors can enjoy open-air concerts, sample crawfish, and get a peek at the New Orleans of the past. For opening dates, times, and prices, call 504-586-8305, or find them on the Web.

GREAT PLACES FOR FAMILY FUN

✔ Searching for diamonds at Crater of Diamonds State Park, Arkansas

✔ The Aquarium of the Americas in New Orleans

✔ Swimming and island-hopping, Gulf Islands National Seashore, Mississippi

Gospel singer Mahalia Jackson was born here and sang with the children's choir at her home church, Mount Moriah Baptist Church (2403 Louisa St.), before moving to Chicago in 1927.

There are many ways to see the city of New Orleans. Mule-drawn carriage rides are available; bicycles can be rented for an afternoon exploration. You can also have your choice of various riverboat cruises: a paddle wheeler, a sightseeing cruise on the *Cajun Queen,* or a two-and-a-half-hour cruise on the *Creole Queen* to visit the 1815 battle of New Orleans site.

It's not the usual sight-seeing attraction, but the Metairie Cemetery is one of the most beautiful—and most unique—cemeteries in the world. Because the city sits about six feet below sea level, underground burial had been a problem—bodies didn't stay put. So building tombs above ground became the practice. The wealthiest of families built extraordinarily ornate memorials to their loved ones, making Metairie Cemetery a place to see some spectacular artwork. It's located on the Metairie Rd. exit off I-10.

Ruston Both Louisiana Tech and Grambling University are in the area. Tech's Horticulture Center with more than 600 species of native and exotic plants is south of town, and each summer the Louisiana Passion play is held here. (For other Passion plays, see Atlantic Beach, N.C.; Lake Wales and St. Augustine, Fla.; Gadsden, Ala.; Eureka Springs, Ark.; Gatlinburg, Tenn.; Bloomington and Zion, Ill.; and Spearfish, S.D.)

St. Francisville In the area are numerous plantations and historic buildings, one of which is Oakley where John James Audubon painted 32 of his *Birds of America.* The plantation is open daily except Thanksgiving, New Year's Day, and Christmas, and is a part of the Audubon State Commemorative Area, which is a wildlife sanctuary.

Also of interest is Grace Episcopal Church, built in 1858, located in the town on Hwy. 10.

St. Martinville Known in the 17th century as Petit Paris, this quiet town was a refuge to exiled Acadians and aristocrats fleeing the French Revolution. On the town square is St. Martin of Tours Catholic Church, the mother church of the Acadians, and the Petit Paris Museum. Inside the church is a replica of the Grotto of Lourdes. The baptismal font was a gift of Louis XVI of France. (See Acadians also under Lafayette, La., and Grand Pré, Nova Scotia.)

Shreveport In 1974 the American Rose Society decided to move its headquarters from Columbus, Ohio, to a 118-acre plot on the west side of Shreveport (8877 Jefferson Paige Rd.). Today on this plot you will find 20,000 rose bushes in 64 gardens. Something is always in bloom except in December and January.

For flower lovers, the R. S. Barnwell Memorial Garden and Art Center on Clyde Fant Parkway is well worth a visit too.

For the children, there is Water Town, a 20-acre activity theme park, featuring speed slides, adventure slides, and a wave pool.

Shreveport was the birthplace of James Dobson, president of Focus on the Family, which he established in Pomona, California, and later moved to Colorado Springs.

■ MISSISSIPPI

Tourist Info
Phone 800-WARMEST
Web sites
  Entire state   www.decd.state.ms.us/tourism
  Jackson   www.visitjackson.com
  Natchez   www2.bkbank.com/ncvb
For a complete list of updated links, visit www.christiantraveler.com

Canton Mount Zion Baptist Church (514 W. North St.), one of Canton's oldest churches, dates back to 1865. Originally, prior to the Civil War, members worshiped in a white Baptist church, but after the war the blacks were told they had to organize their own church. The members found a place on Freedom Hill and built the church. The present church building was built in 1929.

On the Fourth of July weekend, Canton celebrates not only with a Championship Hot Air Balloon Festival but also with their annual Gospelfest Homecoming, held in Canton Square. The balloon race is the oldest balloon race in Mississippi and includes over 50 balloons in competitions, balloon glows, and a variety of entertainment.

Clarksdale The Delta Blues Museum opened in 1979 upstairs at the Carnegie Public Library at 114 Delta Ave. Hundreds of blues and gospel artists have sprung from this area, so it is appropriate for the museum to be located here. The historical background of blues is detailed here, including a diagram showing the roots of sacred and secular styles from field hollers to hip hop. Admission is free.

Author Tennessee Williams spent a good part of his childhood in Clarksdale, living at the rectory of St. George's Episcopal Church at First and Sharkey Sts. The city hosts a Tennessee Williams Festival the second weekend in October.

Hattiesburg East of town in Petal is the Checkers Hall of Fame, which features one of the world's largest game boards. International tournaments are occasionally played here. It is housed in a Tudor-style mansion off Lyn Ray Rd.

Jackson Mynelle Gardens (4736 Clinton Blvd.) is a five-acre display garden with thousands of azaleas, camellias, and day lilies along with reflecting pools and statuary. The turn-of-the-century Westbrook House is also available for viewing.

The Voice of Calvary Ministries (begun by John Perkins) continues as a ministry of Christians seeking to express the love of Christ in the poor communities in and around Jackson. (See Perkins also under Mendenhall.)

Also in Jackson are several Christian institutions of higher education. Among them are Reformed Theological Seminary, located on Clinton Blvd.; Belhaven College, a Presbyterian school; and Millsaps College (Methodist).

Lucedale The Palestinian Gardens in Bexley provides an authentic scale model of the Holy Land at the time of Christ. Twenty acres are scaled one yard to a mile. When you walk through the gardens, you become acquainted with Holy Land geography. It is located 12 miles north of Lucedale and 6.5 miles east of US 98.

Mendenhall John Perkins founded his Voice of Calvary Ministries here and in nearby Jackson. He moved to Pasadena, California, in 1982, before moving back to Mississippi in the 1990s, believing God had called him to minister in his hometown. Mendenhall Ministries continues to minister to this poor, rural area of the state and to develop models that can be replicated in other communities and countries.

Natchez Natchez is famous for its annual Spring and Fall Pilgrimages, held in March, April, and October. The pilgrimages have no Christian associations, but rather give visitors an opportunity to tour the many stunning examples of antebellum plantation houses, and there are lots of them in the area. Unlike other areas of the South, Natchez and its stylish homes survived the Civil War nearly untouched. A number of these houses are open year-round, but others are open only during pilgrimage time. Carriage tours are also available. Phone 800-647-6742 for ticket information.

These commandments that I give you today are to be upon your hearts. Impress them on your children. Talk about them when you sit at home and when you walk along the road, when you lie down and when you get up.

DEUTERONOMY 6:6–7

Among the plantation houses you certainly wouldn't want to miss is Longwood on Lower Woodville Rd. It is a huge, Italianate-detailed, "octagonal" house crowned with an onion dome. It was under construction at the start of the Civil War. A few years older is Dunleith (84 Homochitto St.), which is also an inn where adults can stay (no children under 18 are allowed). Located on 40 acres of land, Dunleith is a Greek Revival mansion with French and English antiques.

Trinity Episcopal Church (306 S. Commerce St.) is the oldest church building surviving in downtown Natchez. Constructed in 1822 in a Federal style, it was remodeled in 1838 into a Greek Revival appearance. It includes two rare art glass windows designed and installed by Tiffany.

The First Presbyterian Church at Pearl and State Sts. was built in 1828 and 1829, with the Stratton Chapel added in 1901. The church is in Federal-style architecture, while the chapel is in a Romanesque Revival style.

The Zion Chapel A.M.E. Church (N. Martin Luther King St.) was originally the Second Presbyterian Church but was sold after the Civil War to this African American congregation. Its first minister, Hiram Revels, was the first black man to serve in either house of Congress. He was chosen to serve the unexpired term of Jefferson Davis.

The Holy Family Catholic Church (28 St. Catherine St.) is the oldest African American Catholic church in Mississippi and is an outstanding example of 19th-century Gothic Revival architecture.

The Grand Village of the Natchez Indians is a historic park commemorating the presence of the area's first inhabitants. The village includes a visitors center with a museum as well as outdoor exhibits, such as reconstructed dwellings and a nature trail set among the ceremonial mounds.

The Natchez City Cemetery is one of the South's most beautiful burial places, featuring exquisite statuary and stately old trees and plants. If you are a rose lover, you will enjoy the many varieties of antique roses here.

The Natchez Trace The Natchez Trace Parkway is a long, thin park running for almost 450 miles from Nashville to Natchez, crossing early paths worn by the Choctaw and Chickasaw, flatboatmen, outlaws, itinerant preachers, post riders, soldiers, and settlers. More than 300 miles of the park lie within Mississippi, with the remainder in Alabama and Tennessee. The drive is beautifully manicured and free of billboards. Commercial traffic is banned. The park's visitors center is located in Tupelo, offering exhibits and the official map and guide, with detailed information on places from Nashville to Natchez. Admission is free.

Philadelphia In 1964 three young men were invited by local churches to organize literacy campaigns and voter registration drives among African Americans. Arrested for a traffic violation, they were taken to a local jail and then released. Shortly afterward they were fatally shot by sheriff's deputies and by Klansmen. Mt. Nebo Missionary Baptist Church, one of the churches that had invited the three men, has a memorial in front of the church with photos (257 Carver Ave.). The firebombing of Mt. Zion Methodist Church had prompted the men to come to the town. A simple granite memorial stands in the front of this church, which is located ten miles east of the courthouse at 1119 Rte. 747.

Port Gibson Along Church St. you will find many old, restored houses and churches. One of the most interesting is the First Presbyterian Church (Church and Walnut Sts.), built in 1859. On top of the steeple is a ten-foot gold leaf hand with a finger pointing to heaven. The interior features an old slave gallery and chandeliers taken from the steamboat *Robert E. Lee.*

Tupelo For better or for worse, this town is best known as the birthplace of Elvis Presley. Off Veterans Ave. is a 15-acre park complex that serves as a shrine to Elvis. Included is the shack in which he was born, a museum of personal memorabilia, and a tiny chapel, which contains Elvis's Bible, donated by his father. At 909 Berry St. is the First Assembly of God Church, which the Presley family attended.

Yazoo City About 26 miles east of Yazoo City is the site of the Casey Jones train wreck in 1900. Now, the Casey Jones Railroad Museum, maintained by the state, recalls that wreck with railroad artifacts and history on display. Also on display is a 1923 steam locomotive. The museum is at 1 Main St. in Vaughn.

■TENNESSEE

Tourist Info
Phone 615-741-2159
Web sites
  Entire state   www.state.tn.us
  Gatlinburg   www.gatlinburg-tennessee.com
  Knoxville   www.knoxville.org
  Memphis   www.memphistravel.com
  Nashville   www.musiccityusa.citysearch.com
For a complete list of updated links, visit www.christiantraveler.com

Chattanooga The Tennessee Aquarium (1 Broad St.) is the world's largest freshwater aquarium. The facility houses the world's largest turtle collection, as well as 7,000 other animals, including 350 species of fish, mammals, birds, reptiles, and amphibians.

First Presbyterian Church (554 McCallie Ave.) where Ben Haden serves as minister, has its morning services televised nationally. It has been known for years as a strong bastion of evangelical faith in the city.

Covenant College, situated on scenic Lookout Mountain, is associated with the Presbyterian Church of America.

Highland Park Baptist Church (1907 Bailey Ave.), with an average worship attendance of more than 6,000, is one of the largest churches in the state.

Cleveland Lee College, a growing school in a lovely setting, is associated with the Church of God, which has its national headquarters here.

Cordova Adrian Rogers, who is seen frequently on TV, pastors the Bellevue Baptist Church here in the Memphis area (at 2000 Appling Rd.). The church has been well-known both in Southern Baptist circles and elsewhere for decades.

Dayton The 1925 Scopes trial, during which William Jennings Bryan argued against the teaching of evolution in the public schools, was held here in the Rhea County Courthouse. You can visit the courtroom where the trial took place. The 1892 courtroom remains much as it was during the trial and is still used today. The museum, two floors below, exhibits articles relating to the trial and traces the proceedings from beginning to end. Bryan University, an evangelical liberal arts college established in his honor in 1930, is not far away. (See Bryan also under Salem, Ill., and Lincoln, Neb.)

Franklin In 1864 Franklin was the site of a Civil War battle in which 6,000 Confederate soldiers and 2,000 Union soldiers were slain. In addition, seven Confederate generals were killed and seven others were wounded or captured, making it one of the war's most decisive and bloody battles. This historic town features St. Paul's Episcopal Church, built in 1831. It is at the corner of 6th and Main Sts.

Gatlinburg The *Gatlinburg Passion Play* is an indoor musical drama about Jesus that traces his life from birth through the ascension. It is performed nightly (except Sundays) from June until the Saturday before Labor Day, as well as on Easter and Memorial Day weekends. There is also a Christmas drama presented in December (322 Airport Rd.). (For other Passion plays, see Atlantic Beach, N.C.; Lake Wales and St. Augustine, Fla.; Gadsden, Ala.; Eureka Springs, Ark.; Ruston, La.; Bloomington and Zion, Ill.; and Spearfish, S.D.)

Christus Gardens (510 River Rd.), near the entrance to the Smoky Mountains, is of interest to all Christians, but children will enjoy it most of all. It depicts life-size beeswax scenes of the nativity, the Sermon on the Mount, and the Last Supper. It also depicts Jesus saying, "Suffer the little children to come unto me." The rotunda houses the nation's most complete collection of coins of biblical times. There are also beautifully landscaped floral gardens, an award-winning Winterfest lighting display, and much more.

The Gatlinburg Convention Center hosts many Christian-oriented events throughout the year, including Christian concerts. For a schedule of upcoming events, call 800-267-7088 or contact them on the Web.

Also to be seen in this busy tourist city is the National Bible Museum (510 River Rd.) with 300 rare volumes of the Bible in 120 languages. Artifacts dating back to 1500 B.C., including a lamp believed to be from Old Testament times, can be found here. The museum is located between the Christus Gardens and Aerial Tramway, which goes from Main St. up 2,300 feet to the top of Crockett Mountain.

Great Smoky Mountains National Park This park covers 500,000 acres of Appalachian peaks and is misty, not smoky, but there's no reason to change the name now. The park welcomes more visitors every year than any other park.

Hendersonville The Johnny Cash Museum is located three miles east of town on Gallatin Rd. The museum is dedicated to the career of the born-again country singer and is set in a Georgian-style mansion. It contains many of his awards and personal belongings as well as antiques and a guitar display.

Trinity Music City USA is at 1 Music Blvd. in Hendersonville. Formerly this was the estate of Conway Twitty but now it is owned by the Trinity Broadcasting Network. Live TV shows are performed here. During the weeks from Thanksgiving to New Year's Day a spectacular light exhibit (more than 350,000 lights) is displayed. You might consider worshiping in the Trinity Music City auditorium, the state-of-the-art theater home of Trinity Music City Church. This elaborate auditorium holds services Sundays, Tuesdays, and Thursdays. Some of the evening services are broadcast over TBN, featuring some of America's best-known preachers. Also on the premises is the Virtual Reality Theater where you can view films about Christ and the apostles. The Gold, Frankincense and Myrrh Gift Shop and the Solid Rock Bistro are also open for shopping and light meals at Trinity Music City. On weekends young people enjoy the First Planet on the Rock (1 Music Blvd.), the latest in contemporary Christian music offered up with food and soft drinks.

The Greek Parthenon is an exact replica of the one in Athens, Greece. Built in 1896 for the state's centennial, it is located in what is now known as Centennial Park on West End Ave. Art exhibits are now displayed here.

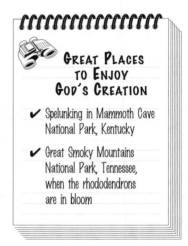

GREAT PLACES TO ENJOY GOD'S CREATION

✔ Spelunking in Mammoth Cave National Park, Kentucky

✔ Great Smoky Mountains National Park, Tennessee, when the rhododendrons are in bloom

Lebanon Because of the tall red cedars in this area, the founding fathers named the city Lebanon after the biblical land of Lebanon. Cedars of Lebanon were used to build Solomon's Temple, and the state park seven miles south of town is called Cedars of Lebanon State Park. The wood from Tennessee's cedar trees has been used for many purposes including construction, paper products, and pencils.

Maryville Maryville College here, established in 1819, is a Presbyterian liberal arts college. The buildings represent various architectural styles from 1869 to 1922. Tours of the campus are available, and the school presents many plays, concerts, and exhibits in its Fine Arts Center.

Memphis Memphis Memorial Park (5665 Poplar Ave.) contains the Crystal Shrine Grotto. Paintings of events in the life of Christ are set in onyx. The work was done by Mexican artist Robert Rodriquez during the Depression.

The National Civil Rights Museum (450 Mulberry St.) contains exhibits and displays of the key events in the civil rights movement in the 1950s and 1960s. It is housed in the Lorraine Motel where Martin Luther King Jr. was assassinated in 1968. The Montgomery Bus Boycott display details the events leading up to the 1955 arrest of Rosa Parks. Visitors can sit in a restored bus and listen to a dramatic recording.

The Pyramid (Auction Ave. downtown at the waterfront) links Memphis to the ancient capital of Egypt of the same name. The 32-story stainless steel structure is fashioned after the Great Pyramid of Cheops and houses an arena seating up to 22,500 for music and sporting events. Guarding the entrance to the facility is a 20-foot statue of Pharaoh Rameses the Great.

How would Elvis have celebrated Christmas? It's hard to say, but those who carry on his memory at Graceland decorate his estate as if they were celebrating every day. Graceland is located at 3734 Elvis Presley Blvd.

Memphis was home to Elvis, of course, but there is much more to Memphis's musical heritage than the King. The Music and Heritage Festival will prove that to you every Labor Day weekend on Beale St. Featured are gospel, country, blues, and jazz music as well as dance troupes and craft booths. Admission is free.

Central Church (independent) at 6655 Winchester Rd. is probably the largest Protestant church in the city with more than 4,000 attending worship services and more than 2,500 in Sunday school.

For a different style of worship, you may want to visit soul music legend Al Green's Full Gospel Tabernacle. Located at 787 Beale St., Sunday services feature powerful music, dancing, preaching, and sometimes speaking in tongues.

Nashville The city is sometimes called the Protestant Vatican or "the buckle on the Bible Belt." More than 700 churches are here, and it is known for Bible publishing. But perhaps it is best known as the home of the Grand Ole Opry (2804 Opryland Dr.). This is the setting for America's longest-running radio show, first airing in 1925. Live music is performed Fridays and Saturdays, featuring primarily country music, of course, but gospel music is pretty common. The Opry is broadcast from the world's largest broadcast studio, seating 4,424 people (at last count, anyway). Advance ticket purchasing is recommended. Call 615-889-6611.

The Opryland Hotel (2800 Opryland Dr.) is always beautiful but especially at Christmas. The hotel is aglow with more than two million lights, and the indoor gardens are decorated for the holidays as well. Of course, you can stay there if you wish or you can eat there, or you can just walk through the facilities, but make sure you have your walking shoes on. The hotel is huge.

Downtown Nashville is the headquarters of the Southern Baptist Convention, the largest Protestant denomination in the United States. The Baptist Sunday School Board features tours with audiovisual presentations weekdays. It is located at 127 Ninth Ave.

The Methodist Publishing House is also located in Nashville (201 8th Ave. S). This is where *The Upper Room* devotional magazine is produced. Tours are available daily. The Upper Room Chapel and museum at 1908 Grand Ave. is in the Upper Room Building. The chancel depicts the upper room in da Vinci's *Last Supper.* The rear wall is Ernest Pellegrini's wood carving of the da Vinci work. The museum also offers seasonal displays.

Three other major denominations have their headquarters here: National Baptist Convention of America, the African Methodist Episcopal Church, and the National Association of Free Will Baptists.

Sam Jones, who was called the "Moody of the South," was a Methodist circuit rider in the 19th century who made Nashville the center of his ministry. A local riverboat captain, Tom Ryman, built a building (originally the Union Gospel Tabernacle, but now known as Ryman Auditorium at 116 5th Ave.) to house Sam Jones's ministry. Later this became the home of the Grand Ole Opry from 1943 to 1974. The building, renovated in 1994, contains a small museum.

Downtown Presbyterian Church at Church St. and 5th Ave. was built in 1849 and served as a Union hospital during the Civil War. The building is built in Egyptian Revival style (and how many Egyptian Revival buildings have you seen?). The stained glass windows have a papyrus motif. Nondenominational services are often conducted at noon. Tours are offered daily.

Caffe Milano (176 3d Ave. N) features a gospel brunch on Sundays, and Christian recording artists frequently sing and play for the guests.

Norris The Museum of Appalachia is considered a must-see by anyone who's been there. Located on Hwy. 61, just north of Knoxville on I-75 at exit 122, this is not your typical museum but rather a vast village with authentic houses, a church, a mule-powered molasses mill, barns, a school, a Hall of Fame building featuring a large dulcimer exhibit, livestock, and even the cabin where Mark Twain is said to have been conceived. "Christmas in Old Appalachia" is re-created every year at the museum. (See Twain also under Hartford, Conn., and Hannibal, Mo.)

Pigeon Forge Just inside Dolly Parton's Dollywood is the newly opened Southern Gospel Music Hall of Fame and Museum. The Hall of Fame honors more than 40 gospel musicians, and the museum displays memorabilia relating to the artists. Dollywood is located at 700 Dollywood Lane.

Sewanee The University of the South, established in 1857 as an Episcopalian college, is set on 10,000 acres of forests, lakes, and cliffs. Its All Saints' Chapel is noteworthy with an interior height of 51 feet, a length of 233 feet, and a 5,000 pipe Casavant organ. Services are held almost daily. The 56 bell Leonidas Polk Carillon is housed in Shepard Tower. Free concerts are given most Sunday afternoons. Breslin Tower is an 1886 clock tower modeled after the Magdalen Tower in Oxford, England.

Midwestern States

CLUSTERED AROUND THE GREAT LAKES and the upper Mississippi River, the midwestern states are a sportsman's paradise. Thousands of tourists flock to the area every year to enjoy swimming, boating, fishing, hiking, skiing, and canoeing.

Modern-day midwesterners are largely the descendents of solid hardworking farm families who took their work and their faith very seriously. From the Scandinavians in Minnesota to the Dutch in Michigan to the Germans in Wisconsin and Indiana, you'll find locals are still genuine and honest people. Quintessential examples of this solid faith tradition can be enjoyed in the various Amish communities located throughout the region, the largest of which are in northern Indiana and central Ohio.

■ILLINOIS

Tourist Info
Phone 800-2-CONNECT
Web sites
  Entire state   www.enjoyillinois.com
  Chicago   www.ci.chi.il.us/Tourism
  Southern Illinois   www.sitc.org
  Southwest Illinois   www.illinoissouthwest.org
For a complete list of updated links, visit www.christiantraveler.com

Altamont The Altamont Living Museum (102 S. Main St.) was once an active church built in 1912. Today it is used as a theater for live performances of music and drama or for exhibiting fine art. It still retains its beautiful stained glass windows, curved oak pews, and a sloped wooden floor.

Arcola This is the center of Amish country in Illinois. Five miles west of the town at Rockome Gardens, Old Bagdad Town is a re-created frontier village with Amish furniture and crafts. The Rockome Family Style Restaurant features Amish cooking, including shoofly pie. In nearby Arthur, also an Amish center, you will find the Arthur Cheese Company, which features Amish Swiss. An annual cheese festival is held the end of August. (See other Amish sites in Pennsylvania, Kentucky, Indiana, Iowa, Michigan, Minnesota, Missouri, Ohio, Wisconsin, and Kansas.)

Belleville The National Shrine of Our Lady of the Snows (442 S. DeMazenod Dr.) is one of the largest outdoor shrines on the continent. The most popular of the events at the 200-acre expanse is the annual Way of Lights during the Christmas season, which features nearly one million lights, a Christmas village, horse-drawn carriages, and open-air tram rides. Dates and listings of acitvities are available at www.oblatesusa.org.

Bishop Hill In 1846 Swedish immigrants built a religious communal society here. By 1861, however, dissension set in and the commune dissolved. But a generation ago Bishop Hill was restored. It now has more than a score of gift and craft shops as well as the original churches, restored as museums. Restaurants serve Swedish and American food. Just northwest of Bishop Hill in Andover is a small chapel, endowed by Jenny Lind, the famous Swedish opera singer. The chapel is open to the public.

Bloomington This is the home of Illinois Wesleyan University with its Evelyn Chapel, a Moravian-style building in Flemish bond patterned brick. Each spring since 1924, the *American Passion Play* is presented at the Scottish Rite Temple, performed by a cast of 350. (For other Passion plays, see Atlantic Beach, N.C.; Lake Wales and St. Augustine, Fla.; Gadsden, Ala.; Eureka Springs, Ark.; Ruston, La.; Gatlinburg, Tenn.; Zion, Ill.; and Spearfish, S.D. See Moravians also under Hope, N.J.; Bethlehem, Lititz, and Nazareth, Pa.; Winston-Salem, N.C.; Gnadenhutten and New Philadelphia, Ohio; and Ephraim, Wisc.)

Cahokia This is the oldest town in Illinois and the home of the oldest church in Illinois as well as the oldest house in the state. The town was founded by a French Catholic missionary in 1699, and the oldest house still standing dates from 1735. The oldest church is the Historic Holy Family Mission Log Church, completed in 1799 and restored in 1949. The original walnut logs stand upright in Canadian fashion.

Carbondale The Bald Knob Cross on Bald Knob Mountain (Illinois' second-highest peak, in Shawnee National Park) is a lighted white marble structure that is visible day and night. Completed in 1963, this is one of the largest Christian monuments in the country. When illuminated at night, the cross (111 feet tall) can be seen over an area of 7,500 square miles.

Charleston Near this town and just west of the Lincoln Heritage Trail is the Indian Church, the first church built on the Little Indian Creek in 1832.

Chicago The Art Institute (Michigan Blvd.) is one of the world's finest. The immense exhibit of medieval and Renaissance paintings focuses almost exclusively on biblical themes, bringing to life stories that have long been common to most Christians.

The Oriental Institute Museum (1155 E. 58th St.) on the University of Chicago campus, has an outstanding collection of archaeological material relating to biblical times.

Fourth Presbyterian Church (126 E. Chestnut St.), a beautiful Gothic-style church, offers a change of pace from the N. Michigan Ave. shopping scene. The church has a quiet courtyard, and on Fridays is often the venue for organ recitals and concerts.

The Chicago Temple (First Methodist Church at 77 W. Washington St.) has the highest church spire in the world. From street level to the tip of its Gothic tower, it measures 568 feet.

The Chicago Historical Society (1601 N. Clark St.) is a great place for children as well as adults. It contains history galleries where you can see Lincoln's deathbed and the abolitionist John Brown's Bible. Children will enjoy climbing aboard the Pioneer locomotive, Chicago's first train.

A. W. Tozer, pastor and author, ministered at the Southside Christian and Missionary Alliance Church in Chicago from 1928 to 1959. His best-known book is *The Pursuit of God,* which has sold over a million copies. The church is no longer in the area.

In 1886 baseball player Billy Sunday was invited to go to the Pacific Garden Mission on S. State St., where he was converted. Within a few years he had quit baseball and become an evangelist. The best times to visit the historic Rescue Mission are late afternoon and early evening. Located at 646 S. State St., it is neither near the Pacific nor a garden. But it got its name from an old-time beer garden located on the site. (See Billy Sunday also under Dundee, Ill.; Winona Lake, Ind.; Marshalltown, Iowa; and Canton, Ohio.)

Moody Memorial Church (1609 N. LaSalle Dr.) and Moody Bible Institute (820 N. LaSalle Dr.), located about a mile apart on Chicago's near north side, are two of evangelist D. L. Moody's legacies. Moody Bible Institute has a museum of Moodyana. A half-hour multimedia show is available, as well as tours of the facility. The church is located across from Lincoln Park at North and Clark Sts.

Near Moody Church is the LaSalle Street Church (1111 N. Wells St.), which has been working to meet the spiritual needs of both professionals in the high-rise apartments nearby and the lower-income residents of the city. The church is nondenominational.

On the University of Chicago campus at 57th St. and Woodlawn Ave. is Rockefeller Chapel, one of the outstanding examples of Gothic architecture in the country.

The Holy Trinity Orthodox Cathedral and Rectory at 1117 North Leavitt St., built in 1903, resembles Russian provincial churches. The interior is lavishly decorated with Russian ecclesiastical art.

Columbia Toddhall (350 Todd Center Dr.), located on 45 scenic acres of rolling hills, trees, and a meandering creek, is a retreat and conference center affiliated with St. George's Episcopal Church. A wide variety of recreational facilities are available.

Deerfield Trinity University and Seminary here are major evangelical schools related to the Evangelical Free Church.

Dundee Evangelist Billy Sunday owned a farm in the area known as Sleepy Hollow just west of Route 72. (See Billy Sunday also under Chicago, Ill.; Winona Lake, Ind.; Marshalltown, Iowa; and Canton, Ohio.)

Elgin David C. Cook founded a Sunday school publishing plant in the 1870s that was a fixture on Grove St. in Elgin until it moved to Colorado Springs in the 1990s.

Elmhurst Theologians Richard and Reinhold Niebuhr both graduated from Elmhurst College here. They are credited with the development of American neo-orthodoxy.

Evanston Willard House (at 1730 Chicago Ave.) is the headquarters of the Women's Christian Temperance Union. Frances Willard, president of the WCTU for the last two decades of the 19th century, was a strong advocate of both Prohibition and women's suffrage. The Willard family home, Rest Cottage, is a gabled Victorian Gothic structure built in 1865. It contains many of the house's original furnishings as well as Willard's personal possessions. It is open daily.

GREAT PLACES TO ENJOY GOD'S CREATION

✔ Exploring the canyons at Starved Rock State Park, Illinois

✔ Watching the sun set at Indiana Dunes National Lakeshore, Indiana

Fulton Dutch Days are celebrated here the first weekend in May each year. Townspeople wear native costumes from the various provinces of the Netherlands. More than 10,000 tulip bulbs are planted each year. The festival ends with worship in a local church. Men and women sit on opposite sides of the church, and part of the service is conducted in the Dutch language.

Greenville Founded in 1892, Greenville College, associated with the Free Methodist denomination, is located here. On the college campus is the Bock Museum, which houses a collection of works by sculptor Richard W. Bock, who worked on a number of Frank Lloyd Wright buildings. Each spring the college hosts Agape, one of the largest Christian music festivals in the Midwest. The two-day festival, planned entirely by students, draws about 5,000 visitors each year. For the exact dates, check their Web site at www.GreenvilleIllinois.com.

Kankakee Olivet Nazarene University is composed of 29 major buildings on a 160-acre campus here. Tours are available.

GREAT PLACES FOR FAMILY FUN

✔ Children's Museum of Indianapolis

✔ Navy Pier, Chicago

✔ Viewing Chicago from the top of the Sears Tower

Libertyville The Lambs (on Rte. 176, east of I-94) is a nonprofit organization dedicated to helping mentally handicapped adults. It is both a residence and a workplace, and more than 150 residents work in eight businesses here. The Country Inn is an old-fashioned restaurant on the grounds, and there are many other buildings on the grounds that make a stop here worthwhile.

Marshall The First United Methodist Church (702 Plum St.) houses the Hinners Track Action Pipe Organ, which dates from 1909.

Naperville This booming Chicago suburb features Naper Settlement (523 S. Webster St.), which is a living history museum documenting the life of a 19th-century prairie town. Many buildings have hands-on exhibits and activities. Don't miss the 1864 Gothic Revival chapel.

Norway Twelve miles northeast of Ottawa is this first permanent settlement of Norwegians in the area. Because of religious persecution, they came to America in 1834. The leader, Cleng Peerson, became known as the Norwegian Daniel Boone. The Norsk Museum (off Rte. 71 on Rte. 2631) is open weekends from May to October.

Ottawa Christ Episcopal Church (113 E. Lafayette St.), an example of English High Victorian Gothic architecture, opened its doors in 1838. One of Germany's most noted artists designed the Wallace Window, a depiction of the resurrection.

St. Charles The Old Church Inn (N. Fourth St.) is now a restaurant but originally was St. Patrick's Catholic Church. A limestone structure built in 1851, it allows diners to sit in the original church pews and of course features fish on Friday.

Salem William Jennings Bryan's birthplace (408 S. Broadway St.), a white frame house near the town library, contains many of his personal possessions, including his Bibles and family pictures. It is open every afternoon except Thursday. A statue of Bryan by Gutzon Borghum, the famous sculptor of Mount Rushmore, stands at the Marion County Courthouse in Salem. Admission is free. (See Bryan also under Dayton, Tenn., and Lincoln, Neb.)

South Barrington Willow Creek Community Church is a unique seeker-friendly church with an average attendance of more than 15,000. It is one of the largest churches in the country and is pastored by Rev. Bill Hybels. Its amazing growth has been contagious. Other churches, seeking to reach unchurched people in their communities, are following the Willow Creek format, and several thousand have now become Willow Creek Association churches.

Springfield This city owes much to its most famous former resident, Abraham Lincoln. Sites associated with his life and death are throughout the city, including the Lincoln Home Visitors Center (426 S. 7th St.). The major attraction is Lincoln's Home (8th and Jackson Sts.), the only home Lincoln ever owned. But also here is the Lincoln-Herndon Law Offices (6th and Adams Sts.); the Old State Capitol, where Lincoln gave his "House Divided" speech, warning the nation that its slave policy would destroy the country; and the Lincoln Tomb (1500 Monument Ave.) in the

Oak Ridge Cemetery. Lincoln; his wife, Mary Todd; and their three sons are all buried in this impressive monument.

A few miles south of Springfield near the town of Auburn, Haldor Lillenas, pastor of the Nazarene church there, wrote several hymns, including "Wonderful Grace of Jesus."

Wadsworth The Gold Pyramid House (37921 Dilleys Rd.) near here may be the most unusual residence in the state. It is a goldplated pyramid, with a 200-ton statue of Ramses II standing guard. Around it is a spring-fed moat. The house is modeled after the Great Pyramid of Cheops in Egypt. Visitors who overnight in the Pyramid's hotel are welcome to tour the residence.

Western Springs Evangelist Billy Graham was pastor of the Western Springs Baptist Church (4475 Wolf Rd.) before entering his evangelistic ministry. (See Graham also under Asheville, Charlotte, and Montreat, N.C.; Wheaton, Ill.; and Minneapolis, Minn.)

Wheaton This suburban town west of Chicago is home to Wheaton College, founded in 1853, and is the headquarters for many religious publishing houses and organizations.

Wheaton College houses the Billy Graham Center with its Walk through the Gospel and its Evangelism Museum, which presents a panoramic view of American evangelism since 1700. The college, which is Billy Graham's alma mater, also has the valuable Marion E. Wade Collection of books and papers by C. S. Lewis, J. R. R. Tolkien, Dorothy Sayers, and others. One of the college's more unusual residents is the giant Perry Mastodon, which was found locally and is now housed on campus.

Tyndale House Publishers (351 Executive Dr.), the publisher of the Living Bible and the New Living Translation, along with a full line of fiction and nonfiction books, is located in Carol Stream, on the north side of Wheaton. Kenneth Taylor began publishing his New Testament paraphrases in 1962.

Among the many other Christian organizations here are Crossway Publishing, Hope Publishing, the National Association of Evangelicals, Christianity Today Publications, The Evangelical Alliance Mission, and Pioneer Clubs.

Zion Almost on the Wisconsin border, Zion may seem like other suburban towns, but it was founded as a theocracy. A Scotsman from Australia, John Alexander Dowie, founded the Christian Catholic church here in 1896, and his combination of evangelism and faith healing won thousands of converts. With a city planner, he designed the city with full water and sewer service, lighting, and a rapid transit system. He appointed himself as general overseer, governing all aspects of the residents' lives. In the center of town was the 6,000-seat Zion Tabernacle. In 1901 Dowie declared that he was the Old Testament prophet Elijah.

Dowie's successor, Wilbur Glenn Voliva, began the first religious radio station in 1923 and originated an annual Passion play, which for more than 40 years was held outdoors. Now it is held in the Christian Arts Auditorium every Saturday in April and May. For more information, write to the Christian Catholic Church, Zion, IL 60099. (For other Passion plays, see Atlantic Beach, N.C.; Lake Wales and St. Augustine, Fla.; Gadsden, Ala.; Eureka Springs, Ark.; Ruston, La.; Gatlinburg, Tenn.; Bloomington, Ill.; and Spearfish, S.D.)

Of interest today are Shiloh House, at 1300 Shiloh Blvd. (originally Dowie's family home), which houses a museum on the history of Zion, as well as a large collection of manuscripts on divine healing; Zion Industries, Inc. (part of Dowie's original economic plan), where fig bars are still made; and the Old Lace Factory building (also part of Dowie's plan).

■INDIANA

> **Tourist Info**
> *Phone* 800-291-8844
> *Web sites*
>   Entire state   www.state.in.us/tourism
>   Amish Acres   www.amishacres.com
>   Amish country in northern Indiana   www.amishcountry.org
>   Anderson/Madison County   www.madtourism.com
>   Anderson University   www.anderson.edu
>   DuBois County   www.duboiscounty.org
>   Indianapolis   www.indy.org
> For a complete list of updated links, visit www.christiantraveler.com

Anderson Anderson University, affiliated with the Church of God denomination, is known for its church music program and features many musical programs throughout the year. Several well-known contemporary Christian musicians got their start here. In addition, its School of Theology (1100 E. 5th St.) has a collection of Holy Land artifacts in its Gustav Jenninga Museum of Bible and Near Eastern Studies. The headquarters of the Church of God denomination is also here.

Paramount Theatre (1124 Meridian Plaza), a stunning movie palace from the 1920s, is the center of the arts in town. One of only 12 such theaters in the nation, the interior re-creates an outdoor amphitheater, complete with a starlit night sky, constellations, and drifting clouds projected onto the dome-shaped ceiling. The stage is reminiscent of an ancient Spanish villa. The Anderson Symphony Orchestra calls the theater its home.

Alexandria Just northeast of Anderson in Alexandria is the Gaither Family Resources and the Latte Coffee Bar (1617 S. Park Ave.). Created by the songwriting and performing team Bill and Gloria Gaither to welcome and serve musicians and fans, it is located right next to the Gaither Recording Studio. Here you can shop for music, books, and gifts or relax with a snack and a cappuccino. Special events often feature celebrity recording personalities.

Berne Amishville U.S.A. (four miles southeast of town) features a restored Amish farmhouse, barn, and buildings as well as horse-drawn buggy rides. You can also watch the authentic mid-1800s gristmill grind corn or wheat into flour. The Essen Platz family restaurant is located on the premises and offers hearty country cooking. You can also camp at Amishville, and on Sundays you are invited to worship at Berne's Mennonite Church, the largest in the United States. (See other Amish sites in Indiana, as well as in Pennsylvania, Kentucky, Illinois, Iowa, Michigan, Minnesota, Missouri, Ohio, Wisconsin, and Kansas.)

Bloomington On the Indiana University campus, the Lilly Library contains rare books and manuscripts, including a copy of the 1454 Gutenberg New Testament and a copy of the first complete Bible in English, dating from about 1535.

Bristol This small town, east of Elkhart, features the St. John of the Cross Episcopal Church (601 E. Vistula St.), built in 1851. It is unusual because it is held together by wooden pegs, and you don't find too many churches built like that.

Columbus The town is known for its architecture. Included among the buildings that tourists visit are the First Christian Church at Fifth and Lafayette Sts. Its 166-foot tower, designed by Eliel Saarinen, can be seen for miles. Saarinen's son, Eero, designed the North Christian Church (850 Tipton Lane), a simple hexagonal structure tapering to a spire and topped by a gold leaf cross.

Crawfordsville The Ben Hur Museum here was built at the home of the author, Gen. Lew Wallace. He wrote most of the famous novel on the grounds here. Tours are available.

Crown Point Near Crown Point is the Cedar Lake Conference Center, a Christian interdenominational facility that brings in noted speakers during the summer.

Ferdinand The Immaculate Conception monastery is one of the largest communities of Benedictine women in the United States. You can't miss the monastery—the huge Romanesque dome is visible for miles around. The church's solid oak panels and pews were hand carved in Oberammergau, Germany. Known for their hospitality, the Sisters welcome all who wish to tour their 190-acre campus or join them for prayer. The monastery also has a gift shop named For Heaven's Sake. Also on the property is the Kordes Enrichment Center, which is a retreat and conference center open to all faiths.

In Ferdinand, Christmas is celebrated in the old style. The town follows the German tradition, when it was customary for craftsmen to set up booths in front of the largest church in the weeks leading up to Christmas. The Christmas market, or Christkindlmarkt, is accompanied by chapel concerts, tours, and lights at the monastery. Most festivities begin around Thanksgiving.

Fort Wayne The Concordia Theological Seminary here, associated with the Lutheran Church, Missouri Synod, was designed by architect Eero Saarinen to resemble a North European village. Open to visitors.

Fountain City A state historic site, the Levi Coffin house was the first building in Indiana to be named to the National Register of

Historic Places. In 1831 Levi Coffin, a Quaker businessman, decided to limit his merchandise to goods made by free workers. When the Civil War began, he helped freed slaves find jobs in the North, and during a twenty-year period, he helped more than 2,000 of them. Consequently, this small town became a stopover for thousands of former slaves.

Gary The City Methodist Church at 577 Washington St., a Gothic building of Indiana limestone, was dedicated in 1926. Judge Elbert Gary of U.S. Steel was the primary benefactor. The church still stands but has not been used for several years.

Goshen In the heart of Amish country is this town that houses Goshen College. The college, a four-year liberal arts college, owned by the Mennonite Church, is home of the Mennonite Historical Library, which contains genealogical resources as well as Anabaptist, Mennonite, and Amish research materials. (See other Amish sites in Indiana, as well as in Pennsylvania, Kentucky, Illinois, Iowa, Michigan, Minnesota, Missouri, Ohio, Wisconsin, and Kansas.)

Greencastle The town is the home of DePauw University, a Methodist college founded in 1837. On the campus is the state's oldest Methodist church.

Hammond One of the largest, if not the largest, Sunday schools in America is part of this city's First Baptist Church (523 Sibley St.), pastored by Dr. Jack Hyles. For years it has emphasized its bus ministry, bringing children to Sunday school from miles away.

Hammond's St. Joseph's Roman Catholic Church at 5304 Hohman Ave. was built in 1879 and is the oldest church in the area. Its Italian marble altars, stained glass windows from Munich, Germany, and mosaics by Venetian artisans are noteworthy features of the interior.

Huntingburg A Victorian Christmas is in store here, beginning in early November. Spirited carolers wander from shop to shop and merchants' windows are elaborately decorated for the holiday season. You can tour exquisite hundred-year-old homes and enjoy holiday music at the Old Town Hall.

Indianapolis The oldest church building in continuous use in the city is Christ Church Cathedral on Monument Circle. Built in 1857, it is a Gothic Revival building, designed by William A. Tinsley, featuring Tiffany stained glass windows. Tours are available by appointment.

The oldest Catholic church is St. John Catholic Church on South Capitol St., dedicated in 1871.

There are two can't-miss destinations in Indianapolis if you have children. The Children's Museum of Indianapolis (3000 N. Meridian St.) is one of the nation's best. Four stories of hands-on fun will entertain and educate family members of all ages (including adults). The Indianapolis Zoo (1200 W. Washington St.) offers lots of opportunities to view animals up close. Be sure to feed the colorful lorikeets.

Jasper St. Joseph Church (on Kundek St.) is a massive Romanesque structure that you would expect to see in Europe instead of in southern Indiana. But there is a story that explains it. In the early 1800s the Reverend Joseph Kundek, a Catholic priest, came from Germany to minister to German immigrants who had recently settled in the area. Kundek not only ministered to existing settlers, he recruited others to come. As a result, three villages in this area, Huntingburg, Ferdinand, and Jasper, all share the same German Catholic roots. So in 1867 the Jasper settlers built a church that reminded them of the old country. It has German stained glass windows and three Austrian mosaics that contain more than 23 million stones.

If you are in the area in December, visit Jasper's German Feiertagmarkt or Christmas market. Local artisans create one-of-a-kind stocking stuffers, and the merchants' window decorations are elaborate.

Merrillville The only Greek Orthodox Church in the state is St. Constantine Orthodox, located at 8000 Madison St. Situated on 37 acres, it features a rotunda 100 feet wide with 25 stained glass windows and Byzantine mosaic work. A Greek festival is held the second weekend of July.

Michigan City First Congregational Church (6th and Washington Sts.) was built in 1881, in a Gothic style. The bell is thought to be the one placed in the city's Congregational Mission Church in 1843.

St. Paul's Lutheran Church (9th and Franklin Sts.), also in Gothic style, was built in 1875 and 1876.

Middlebury Set in the middle of Indiana's Amish country, Middlebury's claim to fame is Das Dutchman Essenhaus, a grand eat-till-you-burst family-style restaurant specializing in country cooking. The place is so popular that you should expect to wait 30 minutes or more in the summer months or consider eating a late-afternoon supper. But—not to worry—while you wait, there are ample opportunities to spend your money. You can visit local gift shops to purchase souvenirs, quilts, candles, or even books on Amish theology. While you shop, Christian music is played. The Essenhaus Bakery on the premises features homemade bread, pasta, cheese, desserts, and apple butter. The Essenhaus also has accommodations at the inn.

THE GERMANS IN SOUTHERN INDIANA

In the 1830s the Catholic bishop of Vincennes noted an increasing number of German immigrants settling in the area of DuBois County, Indiana. In an effort to minister more effectively to them, the bishop sent the Reverend Joseph Kundek, a German-speaking priest, to the area.

Kundek did more than just minister to the Germans already there. He recruited more German Catholics to settle in the area. In fact Father Kundek himself purchased several hundred acres of farmland and wrote to families in Germany's Black Forest, encouraging them to relocate to Jasper, Indiana. Eventually Kundek plotted a new town, called Ferdinand, placing a church in the middle of town to reflect Christianity's central role in the community's life. This time Father Kundek recruited German Catholics through advertisements in a German Catholic Cincinnati newspaper and in Europe. When the towns' populations grew large enough, Father Kundek determined to create a German convent, with nuns who could instruct the children in their native language.

Evidence of Father Kundek's German Catholic influence in southern Indiana exists still today. The town of Jasper, with its Black Forest settlers, is still known for its woodworking industries. The Immaculate Conception Monastery, founded by the German Benedictine Sisters in Ferdinand, is one of the largest Benedictine communities of women in the United States. DuBois County is still marked by its German-style Christmas festivals. And the monastery and cathedrals in the area look like European structures—not what you would expect to see in America's heartland.

About halfway between Middlebury and Shipshewana on Rte. 250 is the Deutsch Kase Haus, where you can see skilled Amish cheesemakers at work and purchase a variety of cheeses, baked goods, and gifts to take home.

Montgomery The center of another Amish community, Montgomery has a variety of Amish craft shops and bakeries. The Gasthof is the largest restaurant, featuring hearty Amish cooking—as though there were another kind! Upstairs is the Heuboden Gift Shop where you can purchase homemade quilts, rag rugs, antiques, dolls, and more.

Nappanee Many Amish families live in northern Indiana. If you want an inside look into their lives, visit Amish Acres (Rte. 19, 1600 W. Market St.). It's an 80-acre complex that depicts the religious beliefs and customs of a people who still follow the lifestyle of 17th-century Europe. It includes an Amish family-style restaurant, a 19th-century farm, and 18 restored buildings. You can tour the historic home and its outbuildings, try riding in an Amish horse-drawn buggy, and pet farm animals. During the summer months, artisans craft brooms, quilts, and rag rugs as they were made years ago. Try the Thresher's Diner, an all-you-can-eat family-style meal that will guarantee you loosen your belt when you're finished. The Amish Arts and Crafts Festival is held in mid-August.

The historic round red barn at Amish Acres was built in 1911 and has been converted into a repertory theater. *Plain & Fancy,* a musical comedy about the Amish, plays every season, as well as half a dozen other musicals like *Hello, Dolly!, Brigadoon,* and *Fiddler on the Roof.* (See other Amish sites in Indiana, as well as in Pennsylvania, Kentucky, Illinois, Iowa, Michigan, Minnesota, Missouri, Ohio, Wisconsin, and Kansas.)

New Harmony In 1814 a German religious communal group, led by a Lutheran separatist, George Rapp, moved here and purchased 30,000 acres of forest. They were called Harmonists or Rappites. They planned to build a perfect community before the new millennium came. By perfect community, they meant they were to live in perfection and celibacy. By 1824 more than 150 buildings had been erected and 20 different products were marketed. But by then Rapp was discouraged by a nationwide depression and the fact that Christ had not returned yet, so he sold New Harmony to Scotsman Robert Owen, who had similar utopian views. Today it is one of America's most illustrious and best preserved utopian communities. Plenty of activities are available throughout the year. The Athenaeum serves as a visitors center and features a film about the community's history. Visitors can also see the Roofless Church at North and Main Sts., designed by Architect Philip Johnson. The bronze sculpture *Descent of the Holy Spirit* by Jacob Lipchitz is featured. The burial place of German theologian Paul Tillich is located in Tillich Park here. Engraved stones contain selections of Dr. Tillich's writings. (See Rappites also under Ambridge and Harmony, Pa.)

Pigeon Creek Abraham Lincoln's father helped build a log cabin Baptist meetinghouse here in 1819.

Richmond Earlham College, associated with the Friends denomination, is located here. It is perhaps best-known as the school where Elton Trueblood taught philosophy from 1946 to 1970 and where Trueblood founded the Yokefellow Movement and wrote such books as *The Company of the Uncommitted*. On campus is the Lilly Library and the Stout Memorial Meetinghouse.

The Wayne County Historical Museum (1150 N. A St.) occupies the 1865 Quaker meetinghouse of the Whitewater Society of Friends.

Rockville Billie Creek Village is a turn-of-the-century settlement that includes three covered bridges, two churches, a general store, farmhouse, craft shops, and costumed artisans. Next to it is Billie Creek Inn, which has 31 rooms and accommodates travelers as well as retreat groups. Church group rates are heavily discounted.

Saint Meinrad In 1854 the Abbey of Einsiedeln founded a monastery here to meet the needs of German immigrants in southern Indiana. The Abbey Church, built of local sandstone, is a Romanesque structure. The monks operate a graduate-level theological school and the Abbey Press, an international marketer of religious and inspirational products. Guests are invited to join the monks in prayer.

The Abbey Press Gift Shop features many inspirational products for purchase, including a wide assortment of books and Bibles. Notice their line of greeting cards. The shop also serves sandwiches and homemade soups and pies. The gift shop is located just south of the intersection of Rtes. 62 and 545. A guest house and visitors center are nearby.

Santa Claus As you can imagine, this little town is very busy in December. Back in 1946 Santa Claus Land was opened here as the first theme park in the nation. Recently its name was changed to Holiday World, but it is still in the same place, with an animal farm, lots of toys and rides, a wax museum, and a 17-acre water park, which just happens to be the largest such park in the state. If you want more information, you can find it at www.holiday-world.com. By the way, if you want to stay overnight, Santa's Lodge is also here. It's a two-story inn resembling a huge barn complete with hand-hewn timbers in the lobby.

Shipshewana One of the largest Amish communities in the world is located in this area. It is also the home of one of the largest flea markets in the world. If you enjoy flea markets, Shipshewana is the place to be. It is open every Tuesday and Wednesday from May through October. You can buy just about anything here, including local produce, flowers, and lots of Amish crafts and baked goods. You can even purchase livestock if you want to tote home a cow in your backseat.

Across the street from the flea market is a more serious stop— not that flea markets aren't serious business. The Menno-Hof Museum (US 20 and Rte. 5) was built by local Amish and Mennonites and it uses multi-image presentations, historical environments, and colorful displays to explain the world of the Mennonite and Amish people. You'll visit a 16th-century dungeon, escape on a 17th-century sailing ship, survive a tornado, and learn about the power of faith. Admission is by donation. (See other Amish sites in Indiana, as well as in Pennyslvania, Kentucky, Illinois, Iowa, Michigan, Minnesota, Missouri, Ohio, Wisconsin, and Kansas.)

South Bend The Notre Dame University campus is adorned by the Basilica of the Sacred Heart, built in the late 1800s. Ornately decorated with gold and brass, the structure has on its walls and ceilings rich, detailed murals by artist Luigi Gregori.

Also on the campus is the Grotto of Our Lady of Lourdes, which is a reproduction of the Grotto in Lourdes, France; and the Log Chapel on the edge of St. Mary's Lake, which is a replica of an 1830 chapel built by Father Stephen Badin, the first Roman Catholic priest ordained in the United States.

North of the football stadium is the Snite Museum of Art. Here you will find rare religious artworks as well as masterworks by European and American artists.

Tell City This is near the place where the Lincolns landed when they first moved to Indiana. Young Abe Lincoln worked for a year on a ferry that crossed the Anderson River.

Near the juncture of the Ohio River and the Anderson River is Camp Koch, a summer camp for handicapped young people. A large statue called the *Christ of the Ohio* overlooks the camp on Fulton Hill. It was cast by sculptor Herbert Jogerst.

Upland In this small village south of Fort Wayne is the impressive campus of Taylor University, an evangelical, four-year liberal arts college.

Valparaiso The Chapel of the Resurrection on the Valparaiso University campus is one of the largest chapels on a college campus anywhere in the country. A 140-foot campanile houses bells that chime several times each hour. Valparaiso University is affiliated with the Lutheran Church, Missouri Synod.

Vevay In this small southern Indiana town is the home of Edward Eggleston, novelist and preacher of the 19th century. His home, at Ferry and Main Sts., is one of 28 vintage buildings in downtown Vevay. Eggleston, a Methodist minister, wrote *The Hoosier Schoolmaster* and *The Circuit Rider,* as well as a half dozen other works.

Vincennes The town was established in 1732 by the French to combat British expansion in the area. The Old Cathedral (St. Francis Xavier Church at 205 Church St.) dates back to 1826 and was built on the site of the first log church here. Behind the Old Cathedral is the Old Cathedral Library and Museum, which is the oldest library in Indiana. It contains 10,000 volumes dating from the 12th to the 18th centuries.

Winona Lake This has been a nationally known Bible conference grounds since the days of Billy Sunday and songleader Homer Rodeheaver. Also in Winona Lake are Grace College and Seminary. A liberal arts college, Grace is affiliated with the Grace

Brethren Church. (See Billy Sunday also under Chicago and Dundee, Ill.; Marshalltown, Iowa; and Canton, Ohio.)

■ Iowa

Tourist Info
Phone 888-472-6035
Web sites
Entire state   www.state.ia.us/tourism
Amana Colonies   www.jeonet.com/amanas
Des Moines   www.desmoinesia.com
For a complete list of updated links, visit www.christiantraveler.com

Amana The Amana Colonies are actually a cluster of seven villages just west of Iowa City: Amana (Main Amana), West Amana, South Amana, High Amana, East Amana, Middle Amana, and Homestead. Founded in the mid-1800s by a group of Swiss and Germans who faced persecution in their homeland, the Community of True Inspiration fled first to Buffalo, New York, and then to the rolling countryside of Iowa when their numbers demanded more space. Here they shared work, meals, and all their worldly goods as well as their deep pietistic faith. Their quiet, communal settlement was named Amana, which means "to remain true."

In 1932, in the Great Depression, the Amana Colonies were forced to make changes and they became a profit-sharing corporation. They voted to end their communal way of life and their community kitchens were disbanded. Of all of America's utopian communities—and there have been many—Amana held together for the longest time.

Although the communal way of life is a thing of the past, much remains the same. Even today many of the townspeople know and speak German, and descendents of those first settlers still run the local shops. The Amana colonies are known for their quality woolen goods, furniture, wine, cheese, baskets, and more recently, appliances. The original Amana Appliance Store (836 48th Ave.) is still open for business.

Today Amana Colonies is Iowa's most popular tourist attraction. Throughout the colonies are scattered four museums: the Museum of Amana History (220th Trail in Amana), the Communal Kitchen and Cooper Shop Museum (Middle Amana), the

Communal Agricultural Museum (South Amana), and the Community Church (Homestead). The Museum of Amana History is located in Main Amana and is filled with historic artifacts relating to the surrounding area. The exhibits will give you a better understanding of the beliefs and religious life of the original Amana Colonies residents. In Main Amana is the Heritage Wine and Cheese Haus, featuring locally made products. Also worth visiting are the High Amana Store in High Amana, which hasn't altered its interior since 1857, and the Amana Colonies Nature Trail, where you can hike, cross-country ski, and view Native American mounds.

But first go to the Amana Welcome Center (38th Ave., just west of Amana near the intersection of US 151 and Rte. 220). Among other things, you can find out where the restaurants are, and that's important, because restaurants here are noted for their delicious food.

Burlington St. Mary's Catholic Church at 420 W. Mount Pleasant St. in West Burlington was built with thousands of imported and native stones and features split rock sidewalks and crystal rock walls. In the garden can be found forty different kinds of trees. The church was completed in 1931.

Burr Oak After grasshopper plagues in Minnesota, Laura Ingalls Wilder, author of the *Little House* series of children's books, spent a year in this community. Laura's father managed the hotel that has now become a Laura Ingalls Wilder Museum (3603 236th Ave.), while the women, including Laura, waited tables, cooked, and cleaned. The museum is open daily during the spring and summer. (See Wilder also under Spring Valley and Walnut Grove, Minn.; Mansfield, Mo.; Pepin, Wisc.; Independence, Kans.; and De Smet, S.D.)

Clermont The Union Sunday School houses a rare pipe organ, donated by a former governor of Iowa, William Larrabee. Larrabee ran for office on the slogan, "a schoolhouse on every hill and no saloons in the valley."

Decorah One of the most scenic campuses in the Midwest is Luther College. On the edge of the campus is the Farm Park, which tries to preserve some farm animals that are almost extinct. It gives visitors a rare opportunity to see a Norwegian fjord horse, a Navajo-Churro sheep, or a mulefoot hog, for instance.

The Vesterheim Museum (502 W. Water St.), which includes 13 buildings in the complex, tells how Norwegian immigrants settled here. Some consider it one of the best ethnic museums in the country.

Just north of Decorah on Hwy. 52 is the Seed Savers Heritage Farm (3076 N. Winn Rd.), which does for fruits and vegetables what the Farm Park is doing for farm animals— saving endangered species. Here you will find 300 kinds of tomatoes, 330 varieties of beans, 125 different peppers, etc. These are offered for sale in the Amish-built barn. In all, the farm has over 15,000 rare vegetable varieties.

Des Moines The Salisbury House (4025 Tonawanda Dr.) resembles a mansion from Tudor England more than it does one from 19th-century Iowa. Modeled after a historic residence in Salisbury, England (hence its name), and built by a wealthy cosmetics manufacturer, the home features many fine English furnishings as well as a 3,500-volume library, including a page from the Gutenberg Bible.

Dubuque The University of Dubuque and its theological

THE AMANA COLONIES IN IOWA

The Community of True Inspiration left their homes in Germany in 1842, settling near Buffalo, New York. Persecution from church and government authorities had forced the group to seek religious freedom in America. But after only 12 years the Germans found themselves in need of more space. The Community headed west to the rolling green fields of Iowa. Almost half of the 25,000 acres they acquired were forested with valuable walnut, oak, and cherry trees. They called their new home Amana—"to remain true."

Before long there were actually seven villages making up the Amanas: Amana (sometimes called Main Amana), East Amana, West Amana, High Amana, Middle Amana, South Amana, and Homestead. The founders established the colonies as a commune, with all but the individual members' personal effects owned by the society. Eventually, however, difficult times forced the colonists to engage in commerce with the outside world to support themselves, and finally in 1932 the community members voted to abolish the communal system altogether.

This didn't change everything about the Amanas, however. While the stores are now all privately owned, most of them remain in the hands of the colonies' faith-driven descendants. Life is still simple, faith is still fundamental, and German is still spoken by many townspeople. Visitors can see nearly 500 restored buildings within the 25-mile circuit that takes in the Amanas. And the members of the community are known for making quality products, including Amana appliances, prized woolen goods, furniture, baked goods, and cheese.

seminary are related to the Presbyterian Church U.S.A. Its historic Alumni Hall, built in 1907, is a replica of a 15th-century English structure. Blades Hall has impressive stained glass windows. The campus carillon plays frequent concerts. Tours are available.

Dyersville Only three miles away from the Field of Dreams Baseball Diamond, the movie set where *Field of Dreams* was filmed in 1988, is the Basilica of St. Francis Xavier (104 3d St. SW), which has been termed one of the best examples of Gothic architecture in the Midwest. The twin towers reach 212 feet, and the church's main altar is of Italian marble and Mexican onyx.

Festina The St. Anthony of Padua Chapel is known as the "world's smallest church," even though it isn't. It is 14 by 20 feet and holds four small pews. It was built to fulfill a promise that a mother made. If God would let her son survive Napoleon's Russian campaign, she would build a chapel. The son returned home and the chapel was built of local stone. Behind the church is a small cemetery containing the son's grave. (See also the "world's smallest house of worship" under Florence, Ky.; the "smallest church in America" under Savannah, Ga.; the "world's smallest cathedral" under Highlandville, Mo.; and the Wee Kirk of the Valley under Cedar Vale, Kans.)

Guttenberg At the Guttenberg Library on S. 2d St., a facsimile of the Gutenberg Bible is on display. It was purchased and brought from the Johannes Gutenberg Print Shop in Mainz, Germany.

Kalona This is Amish country in Iowa. In the area visitors can find seven Amish churches and seventeen Mennonite churches, plus a few hundred horse-drawn buggies. In April the Kalona Quilt Show and Sale attracts more than 4,000 people to see what has been made by local Amish and Mennonite women. The Kalona Quilt and Textile Museum (415 B Ave.) has three or four special shows each year on the history of quilting, and the Kalona Kounty Kreations (3 miles north, off Hwy. 1) is one of the largest quilt supply stores in the Midwest. Nearby is the Community County Store (Jones St.), which is an Amish-owned general store that sells a variety of items; and the Stringtown Grocery (540th St.), also an Amish-run store.

The Kalona Historical Village and the Iowa Mennonite Museum and Archives (both at Hwy. 22 and Ninth St.) give more background on Mennonite and Amish life. (See other Amish sites in Pennsylvania, Kentucky, Illinois, Indiana, Michigan, Minnesota, Missouri, Ohio, Wisconsin, and Kansas.)

Marshalltown Evangelist Billy Sunday came from this area of Iowa. As a teenager, he worked in Nevada, Iowa, then took a job as an undertaker's assistant in Marshalltown and played baseball on the side. When his team won the state championship, he attracted the attention of the manager of the Chicago Whitestockings, who immediately signed him up. (See Sunday also under Chicago and Dundee, Ill.; Winona Lake, Ind.; and Canton, Ohio.)

Milford Treasure Village Children's Theatre (2033 Hwy. 86), three miles northwest of the town, has a wide variety of programming through the week from the end of June through Labor Day weekend. Gospel concerts are featured on Sunday nights.

Nashua The Little Brown Church in the Vale (2729 Cheyenne Ave.), about 40 miles northeast of Waterloo and 2 miles northeast of Nashua, draws nearly 150,000 visitors a year. It was immortalized by an old hymn, "The Church in the Wildwood," written in 1857. Hundreds of couples come from all over the world to be married here.

The author of the hymn, William Pitts, a native of Wisconsin, came to Iowa to see his girlfriend. When he stopped along the Little Cedar River, he saw a spot that he imagined would be a wonderful place for a church. On the way home he wrote the song, "Oh, come to the church in the wildwood. Oh, come to the church in the vale." Years later Pitts returned to the place to teach music at a local school and he was stunned to find that a small church was being built in the very place he had earlier visualized. When the church was dedicated, Pitts's song was sung for the first time.

Next to the Little Brown Church is the Old Bradford Pioneer Village, which is a reconstruction of the 19th-century village. There are 13 buildings in the complex, including the building where William Pitts had his office.

Ottumwa Southeast of the town and north of Floris is Mars Hill Church, the oldest log church in the United States still in use. Built in 1857 of oak and walnut logs, it was one of Iowa's earliest religious buildings. Services are held once a year in the month of June. During Civil War times, it was also a stop on the Underground Railroad. (See Underground Railroad also under Camden, Del.; Buffalo, N.Y.; Macon, Ga.; Marshall, Mich.; Ripley, Ohio; and Osawatomie, Kans.)

Pella In 1847 early Dutch settlers came here seeking freedom and named the area "Pella," which means "city of refuge." The Dutch heritage is still apparent through its architecture, windmill in the city square, flower beds, and Klokkenspel, a musical clock that performs four times daily. Tulip Time is the second weekend in May. The Pella Historical Village includes more than 20 buildings. Among them are the church and boyhood home of Wyatt Earp. The Historical Village is open from April through December.

Sac City This is the home of Iowa's only complete existing Chautauqua building. Founded by religious leaders in the 1800s, the Chautauqua mission was to educate and enrich individuals spiritually and otherwise, holding workshops for all members of the family. Sac City holds its annual Chautauqua Days over the July Fourth weekend. (See also Chautauqua, N.Y., and other Chautauqua-inspired sites under Ridgecrest, N.C.; Lakeside, Ohio; Madison, S.D.; and Boulder, Colo.)

St. Donatus Not too many communities in America were started by immigrants from the little European country of Luxembourg, but this one was. St. Donatus is still famous for its Old World architecture and traditions. Perhaps its main attraction is the Outdoor Way of the Cross, built in 1861, featuring 14 brick alcoves, winding behind St. Donatus Catholic Church (97 E. 1st St.). At the top of the hill is the Pieta Chapel, which is a replica of a church in Luxembourg.

Spillville Settled by Czech immigrants, this community takes pride in the fact that Czech composer Antonin Dvorak spent a summer here in 1893, composing his *New World* symphony. While here he played the organ for the daily mass at St. Wenceslaus Church (207 Church St.). The building where Dvorak stayed that summer is now the Bily Clocks Museum, featuring hand-carved clocks ranging from a few inches tall to ten feet and made of a variety of woods. Visitors will also see an apostle clock from which the twelve apostles parade every hour. The museum is located at 323 S. Main St.

Stanhope For the past 20 years Varlen and Fern Carlson have been building the Country Relics Village, which is a one-third to two-thirds scale model of an early 1900s village. The church, for instance, contains four small pews, an organ, and stained glass windows. The general store is loaded with hundreds of miniature supplies.

Stanton This Swedish town has all its homes painted white and so is known as the "little white city." The whole town is built around the gray-stoned Mamrelund Lutheran Church (410 Eastern Ave.) with its towering steeple. Also in the skyline is the town water tower, which residents say is the world's largest Swedish coffeepot. They make this claim because little Stanton was the birthplace of Virginia Christine, the woman who played Mrs. Olson on the Folger's Coffee commercials for many years.

Urbandale Living History Farms (2600 111th St.) in Urbandale just west of Des Moines got national attention in 1979 when Pope John Paul II delivered a sermon here to a crowd of about 400,000 people. Now there is an interfaith Church of the Land on the site.

West Bend The site of the Grotto of the Redemption (300 N. Broadway Ave.) attracts more than 100,000 visitors each year. It contains what is believed to be the largest collection of minerals and semiprecious stones in any one place in the world, estimated to be worth more than 2.5 million dollars. Begun in 1912 by a young seminary student, who vowed that if he recovered from a serious illness he would build a shrine to the Virgin Mary, the grotto contains a Brazilian amethyst weighing more than 300 pounds. Next to the grotto is the St. Peter and Paul's Church, with a memorable Christmas chapel.

West Branch This small town was the birthplace of President Herbert Hoover and is now the location of the Herbert Hoover National Historic Site. In addition to the Presidential Library, there are several other 19th-century buildings, including the 1853 schoolhouse and the Quaker meetinghouse that he attended.

Winterset Robert James Waller made almost everyone aware of the bridges of Madison County, whether by means of his best-seller or the film starring Clint Eastwood and Meryl Streep. Even before the film, the covered bridges of the area (and there are six of them still remaining) were a tourist attraction. For film fans, the John Wayne birthplace is located here on S. Second St. But don't overlook the Madison County Historical Complex (815 S. Second St.) with its 12 buildings on an 18-acre site. One of the structures is the Zion Federated Church built in 1881. Another is the only outhouse listed in the National Register of Historic Places.

■MICHIGAN

Tourist Info
Phone 800-543-2937
Web sites
  Entire state   www.michigan.org
  Detroit   www.visitdetroit.com
  Grand Rapids   www.visitgrandrapids.org
  Holland   www.holland.org
  Southwestern Michigan   www.swmichigan.org
  Traverse City   www.tcvisitor.com
  West Michigan Tourism   www.wmta.org
For a complete list of updated links, visit www.christiantraveler.com

Albion In 1913, while George Bennard was staying here, the inspiration came to him to write the beloved hymn "The Old Rugged Cross." It was first sung in nearby Pokagon. A bronze marker, commemorating the writing of the hymn, has been placed at College Ct. and Michigan Ave. By the way, Albion College was where the old song "The Sweetheart of Sigma Chi" was written. So you can sing both as you travel through. (See Bennard also under Niles and Reed City, Mich.)

Alma Each Memorial Day weekend Alma and Alma College host the annual Alma Highland Festival and Games, featuring everything Scottish, from kilts to bagpipe music.

Ann Arbor One of the attractions on the campus of the University of Michigan is the Kelsey Museum of Archaeology, which features art and artifacts of biblical times, including Egyptian, Greek, Roman, and classical Mediterranean cultures.

The U. of M. Museum of Art, with a permanent collection of over 13,000 pieces, is rated as one of the top ten U.S. university art museums, and if you are involved in church music, you might like to see the Stearns Collection of Musical Instruments, with over 2,200 instruments.

Also in Ann Arbor is the Ann Arbor Hands-on Museum (Huron at N. Fifth Sts.) with more than 80 displays on four floors. It is recommended for children eight years old and older.

Battle Creek The Sojourner Truth Grave is located on Fifth St. in the Oak Hill Cemetery here, commemorated by a plain square monument. Truth was born a slave in the 1790s, gained her freedom in the 1820s, and crusaded against slavery until her death in 1883.

Battle Creek, known as the cereal capital of the world, was the home of both John Harvey Kellogg and C. W. Post. Kellogg's Cereal City, U.S.A., at 171 W. Michigan Ave., is a worthwhile visit for the entire family.

Not as well known is the fact that the Seventh-day Adventist Church was founded here in 1863 by Ellen G. White and that John Harvey Kellogg, the father of corn flakes, was one of 16 children of an early Adventist.

Bay View The Methodist Church founded this community, north of Petoskey, in 1875 as a summer retreat, citing as reasons the area's lakeside location, its healthful climate, and its proximity to a railroad steamer line. The community sponsored programs, including lectures, concerts, recitals, and Sunday evening vespers. Over time Bay View expanded its lecture topics to include science and literature and has hosted such speakers as Helen Keller, William Jennings Bryan, and Booker T. Washington. Sunday vesper concerts are still a mainstay as well as musical and theatrical performances by the Conservatory of Music and the Bay View Theater Arts Department. All are open to the public. The neatly kept Victorian houses, adorned with gingerbread, cupolas, and towers, that line the highway are an attraction in themselves. Some 440 of them have been designated as a National Historic Landmark. The local historical museum is open during July and August.

Benton Harbor Shiloh House on Britain Rd. is the administration building and dormitory for the House of David colony. The House of David was founded in 1903 as a Christian commune, following the teachings of Joanna Southcott of England. During the middle of the 20th century, the communal group had an amusement park, a band, and a very successful baseball team. All the ballplayers sported long beards, which was a trademark of the group. Only a few members of the group remain. The Benton Harbor Public Library (213 E. Wall St.) has a House of David Room, which is one of the most unusual and thorough special-interest archives of its kind.

Berrien Springs In 1901 the Seventh-day Adventists moved their college here from Battle Creek and later moved their seminary here as well. Today Andrews University and seminary are a mainstay in the community's economic life. The school now covers more than 1,300 acres. Of particular interest is the Horn Archaeological Museum on site, which houses over 9,000 artifacts. Pottery, coins, jewelry, tablets, and other pieces from Bible lands span more than 5,000 years of history. The museum's mission is not only to explore the cultures of these ancient people but to "spark a vision of the God whose role is evident through history." The museum is free and open to the public during regular business hours as well as Saturday afternoons.

Also located on the Andrews University campus is the school's Natural History Museum. The museum houses the only complete mastodon skeleton discovered in Michigan, as well as collections of insects and shells and exhibits of both native and exotic birds and mammals.

The Old Berrien County Courthouse (Old US 31 and Union St.), built in 1838, is now a museum and is open daily.

Bloomfield Hills Christ Church Cranbrook (470 Church Rd.), an Episcopal church built in Gothic style, contains sculptures of men of science and religion, as well as antique and modern paintings. Its bell tower has a carillon of fifty bells. Concerts are given each afternoon in the summer. The church is open daily.

Charlevoix The Greensky Hill Mission was a Methodist church built here by Peter Greensky to reach the Chippewa Indians in the 1840s. It was made of boughs and bark. The church that is still in use is a log church built by the Chippewas in the 1850s. Located on Susan Lake just off Boyne City Rd., it is the oldest continually operating Indian congregation in Michigan and still holds Sunday services.

Charlotte Called the Maple City because the area is a leading producer of maple syrup, Charlotte is also the home of Olivet College, a campus blending old and new architecture. Olivet College was founded to educate the clergy but quickly expanded to accommodate anyone.

Clare The Amish of Michigan live clustered primarily around this village. If you'd like a free map of the area, stop by the Chamber of Commerce. Several local businesses, including The New Wood Store, Benchley's Oak Furniture, Yoder's Country Bakery, and the Surrey Road Quilt Shop, sell Amish-made crafts, furniture, and baked goods. Yoder's Amish Quilt/Craft Shows are held in May and September every year. (See other Amish sites in Pennsylvania, Kentucky, Illinois, Indiana, Iowa, Minnesota, Missouri, Ohio, Wisconsin, and Kansas.)

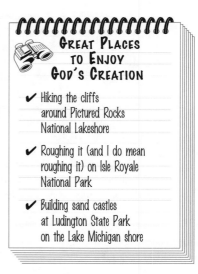

GREAT PLACES TO ENJOY GOD'S CREATION

✔ Hiking the cliffs around Pictured Rocks National Lakeshore

✔ Roughing it (and I do mean roughing it) on Isle Royale National Park

✔ Building sand castles at Ludington State Park on the Lake Michigan shore

Dearborn Greenfield Village, comprised of more than 80 18th- and 19th-century buildings, moved here from all across the country, is located in Dearborn. On this 254-acre site is also the Henry Ford Museum with its indoor-outdoor panorama of American life. Also here is the Henry Ford Estate—Fair Lane.

Detroit Mariner's Church (170 E. Jefferson Ave.), completed in 1849, is the oldest stone church in the city. It was made famous by Gordon Lightfoot in his song "The Wreck of the Edmund Fitzgerald." The church is dedicated to the memory of the crew who lost their lives in the Great Lakes' most famous shipwreck. Tours are available.

Another interesting church is the Historic Trinity Lutheran Church at 1346 Gratiot Ave. The Luther Tower is a copy of the tower in the Erfurt, Germany, monastery where Luther was schooled.

Second Baptist Church (441 Monroe Ave.) was organized in 1836 by 13 former slaves and is Detroit's oldest black congregation. African Americans gathered here to celebrate the Emancipation Proclamation.

Old St. Mary's Church (646 Monroe Ave.), built in 1885, began in 1833 as a parish of German and Irish immigrants.

Christ Episcopal Church (960 E. Jefferson Ave.) is a Gothic Revival church built in 1863. It is one of 15 members of the Detroit Historic Churches Association. The entire list is available from the church.

Flint Just north of the city is Penny Whistle Place (5500 Bray Rd.), a unique and creative play park for children. It features Punch Bag Forest, Buick Bounce, Cable Glide, Net Climb, and Ball Crawl. It is open from Memorial Day through Labor Day weekend.

Crossroads Village and Huckleberry Railroad (6140 Bray Rd.) is a museum village where you can combine family fun with history. There are vintage amusement park rides, an experience with 18th-century train travel, a staged train robbery, and several 19th-century industries in action.

Frankenmuth The Bavarian village makes it seem like Christmas all year-round with its quaint shops and restaurants. A German Lutheran missionary, August Craemer, led 15 immigrants from Bavaria to Frankenmuth in 1845 to set up a base for mission stations throughout the area. St. Lorenz Lutheran Church (140 Churchgrove Rd.), built in 1880, is one of the largest Missouri Synod Lutheran churches in the world. Across the road from the church are the Church Bells in the Forest, the original church bells brought from Nurnberg, Germany, by the first settlers. Alongside the bells is an authentic replica of the log cabin that was the first dwelling in the community. It was used as a parsonage, church, and school.

This is what the LORD says: "Stand at the crossroads and look; ask for the ancient paths, ask where the good way is, and walk in it, and you will find rest for your souls."

JEREMIAH 6:16

Frankenmuth is one of Michigan's top tourist attractions. Its two huge restaurants, Zehnder's and the Bavarian Inn (both on S. Main St.), are famous for their home-style chicken dinners. The Zeesenagel Italian Village (780 Mill St.) presents the Christmas story in a unique way, and Bronner's Christmas Wonderland—all

200,000 square feet of it—is an experience in itself (25 Christmas Lane). At the south end of Bronner's parking lot is the Silent Night Memorial Chapel, a replica of the church in Oberndorf, Austria, where "Silent Night" was written.

Frankfurt There are arguments about where Father Marquette was buried, but Frankfurt, on the shore of Lake Michigan, has put up a historical marker claiming the honor for their town. They say that his remains were later removed to St. Ignace, in the Upper Peninsula. (See Father Marquette also under Mackinac Island and St. Ignace, Mich.)

Near Frankfurt in the town of Benzonia, Rev. Charles E. Bailey had dreams of building a college, church, and colony to meet the needs of settlers in the area. He led a small group of settlers there in 1858 and started Grand Traverse College in 1863. It existed until 1918. Its best-known graduate was Civil War historian Bruce Catton. All that remains of Bailey's dreams are Mills Cottage and the Congregational church. The church (one block west of US 31 on River Rd.) is no longer used for worship but it houses the Benzie Area Historical Museum. The cottage is now called the Mills Community House (Michigan Ave.), which serves as a local library.

Grand Haven The Scriptorium, Center for Christian Antiquities (926 Robbins Rd.), part of the Van Kampen Collection, houses a world-famous collection of Bibles and other Scripture-related artifacts. It has one of the largest cuneiform and papyri holdings in the United States.

Grand Rapids This is a city of church-related colleges and evangelical publishing houses. Among the colleges are Aquinas College (1607 Robinson Rd.), set on 107 scenic acres. Self-guided tours and nature trail maps through the campus and the Holmdene estate are available. Calvin College, related to the Christian Reformed Church, which has its denominational headquarters here, is located on a large campus in the southeast quadrant of the city. Cornerstone College (General Association of Regular Baptists), Grace Bible College, and Reformed Bible College are also located here.

Evangelical publishing houses include Zondervan, Baker, Eerdmans, Kregel, and Discovery House. Two of these publishers, Baker

(2768 E. Paris Ave.) and Kregel (525 Eastern Ave. SE), have excellent bookstores with some of the largest supplies of used religious books in the country.

Several mega-churches are also located in Grand Rapids. Calvary Church (interdenominational) at 777 East Beltline is the largest, but First Assembly of God (2100 44th St. SW) and Sunshine Community Church (related to the Christian Reformed Church at 3300 East Beltline) also have weekly attendances of several thousand worshipers.

Mel Trotter, an alcoholic who was converted in Chicago's Pacific Garden Mission, moved to this city, where he established a rescue mission to provide food and shelter, as well as spiritual guidance, for the needy. The Mel Trotter Mission is at 225 Commerce SE.

While you are in Grand Rapids, don't miss Meijer Gardens and Sculpture Park at 3411 Bradford St. off East Beltline. Its 15,000-square-foot conservatory makes it the largest in Michigan, and the large outdoor area of colorful flower gardens, creative sculpture, ponds, and woods deserve an admiring visit as well. Admission is $5.

In the town of Ada, five miles east of the city, is the international headquarters of Amway, one of the area's largest employers. The Amway building is more than a mile long, and one-hour tours are available. The company was started in a garage, by two Christian businessmen who thought of a different way to sell laundry soap, and is now international.

Holland Since 1929 this town on the shores of Lake Michigan has been known for its annual Tulip festival, which attracts thousands of visitors each May. At the festival each spring visitors see one of the largest tulip plantings in the country, tour a Netherlands museum, enjoy folk dances, and watch a Festival Musicale, with its mix of hymns, anthems, and spirituals.

Holland's oldest church, built in 1856, is the Pillar Christian Reformed Church. A fine example of Greek Revival architecture, it has massive Doric columns.

Hope College, at College and 10th Sts., related to the Reformed Church of America, sponsors a summer repertory theater series each year that is considered one of the best in the state. Tours of the campus are available.

Just north of town on US 31 is Dutch Village, Windmill Island, and a Wooden Shoe Factory.

Holland was the birthplace of Samuel Zwemer, one of the most influential leaders in the area of missions in the 20th century. A graduate of Hope College, he was a cofounder of the Arabian Mission and worked in Muslim lands from 1890 to 1930.

Holland has some of the most beautiful beaches in Michigan. Take your family to Holland State Park (at the western terminus of Ottawa Beach Rd.) and enjoy the beautiful sand and surf of Lake Michigan.

Holly This small town had a reputation as a wide-open brawling town in the last part of the 19th century. Then, Carry Nation, the militant Prohibitionist, was summoned and she went through the town smashing every whiskey bottle she could find. The town still celebrates a Carry Nation Festival the first weekend after Labor

The Dutch in West Michigan

In the 1840s droves of settlers began heading into Michigan, a new and unsettled frontier. Among those settlers were large groups of Dutch immigrants, frustrated by the lack of religious freedom in their homeland and eager for the opportunity to establish a new colony where they could worship as they saw fit.

The Dutch settlers were attracted to the western shore of Lake Michigan, where the moderate temperatures, shoreline, and fertile hills reminded them of home. The majority of them founded the lakeshore town of Holland and its neighboring communities of Zeeland, Vriesland, Overisel, and Drenthe. And one of the first buildings they constructed was a church.

Faith has continued to be an important foundation to life throughout the west Michigan community. Locals joke about the churches on every street corner, and the exaggeration is only a modest one. While the Reformed tradition is no longer the only religion in town, that first Dutch Reformed church is still an active congregation, First Reformed of Holland.

Over the years the Holland area has become more ethnically diverse, but the town's original Dutch heritage is remembered every spring during Tulip Time, one of the country's largest flower festivals. More than one million visitors flock to Holland to see city streets lined with a quarter of a million tulips, Klompen dancers dressed in traditional clothing and wooden shoes, theatrical performances, Dutch organ recitals, and three days of parades. And for a taste of what life was like during those early years, visit Pillar Christian Reformed Church, the community's first frame sanctuary, during Tulip Time for a Dutch worship service.

Day. Battle Alley in the downtown area is now a restored 19th-century village.

Huron City Established in the mid-1850s by a wealthy lumberman, this town became a ghost town in the early 1900s until a noted minister, William Lyon Phelps, began holding revival meetings in the local church each summer. Soon the church expanded from 250 to 1,000. After his death in 1937, the town was on its way to becoming a ghost town again until a granddaughter of the minister decided to preserve the community as a museum

FRENCH MISSIONS IN THE GREAT LAKES

In the 17th century the Jesuits began sending missionaries to the New World. Heading first to the French colony of New France, which is now Québec, the Jesuit priests received training and learned native languages, after which they accompanied explorers to claim land for France. While the Jesuits were frequently excellent chroniclers, cartographers, and explorers themselves, their chief goal was clearly the spread of the gospel.

Many Christian missionaries believed that everything the natives believed was wrong. Not the Jesuits. They believed the native peoples already knew God and that their cultures were inherently good. However, they also believed the Indians could benefit from Christian teaching.

The best known of these Jesuit missionaries in the Great Lakes area is Father Jacques Marquette. His first mission was in Sault Ste. Marie, Michigan, to the Ojibwa people. Later Marquette was sent to the Huron people at Chequamegon Bay, Wisconsin, and then to the Huron in the Straits of Mackinac. He came to love the native people there, and they loved him in return.

In 1673 Marquette set out to explore the Mississippi with Louis Joliet. Marquette's journal was the only chronicle that survived that expedition. Shortly after establishing a mission for the Illinois Indians, Marquette became ill. As he neared death, he asked his friends to return him to the Huron mission in the Straits of Mackinac. Marquette would die before reaching St. Ignace, but his body lies buried there. He was not yet 38 years old.

During the 17th and 18th centuries, the French and British would battle for the valuable lands of the Great Lakes, seeking to control land, waterways, and trade routes. They would not have had success without the aid of Jesuit priests like Father Marquette—part cartographer, part chronicler, part explorer. But a missionary first.

town. Today there are 12 buildings on the site, 9 of which are open to the public, including the Phelps Museum, built in honor of the minister.

Indian River The world's largest crucifix is the attraction at the Cross in the Woods at the Indian River Catholic Shrine (7078 Rte. 68). Built by sculptor Marshall Fredericks, the crucifix is a 55-foot-high redwood cross overlooking a pastoral setting. A new church sanctuary was constructed in 1997 with beautiful plate glass windows framing the famous crucifix. Also on the grounds are statues of St. Francis of Assisi and other Roman Catholic saints. A gift shop and museum feature 500 dolls dressed in nun's habits from almost every Catholic order.

Interlochen The Interlochen National Music Camp and Interlochen State Park are located about 14 miles south of Traverse City. Daily concerts are offered at the music camp during the summer. The music camp has been functioning since 1931. The state park next to the camp is one of Michigan's first state parks and contains a beautiful stand of giant white pines.

Kalamazoo Kalamazoo College sponsors a Bach Festival each March and a Festival Playhouse each June and July. In Stetson Chapel is a 3,023 pipe organ.

St. Luke's Episcopal Church (247 W. Lovell St.), with Gothic Revival architecture, and First Presbyterian (just west of City Hall at 321 W. South St.), built in 1930, are both picturesque houses of worship.

North of Kalamazoo is the Gull Lake Bible Conference Grounds (Gull Lake Rd.), where outstanding speakers and musicians come throughout the summer.

Livonia The Evangelical Presbyterian Church (on Buckingham St.) is probably the largest Presbyterian church in terms of regular attendance in the state. It is also the largest church in the Evangelical Presbyterian denomination.

Ludington White Pine Village here has historic buildings that recreate Michigan life in the late 1800s. Included are a general store, trapper's cabin, courthouse, town hall, and a one-room school.

Mackinac Island Father Jacques Marquette, a French Jesuit priest, was the first European settler on Mackinac Island when he came to serve the native Huron population in the late 17th century. Tourists have been flocking here ever since. The island is a favorite with Great Lakes boaters. Its beautiful beaches and its view of nearby Mackinac Bridge also make it a favorite romantic getaway.

Visitors to Mackinac Island arrive by ferry from one of three mainland outfitters: Arnold Transit, Shepler's, and Star Line. (Billboards throughout Mackinaw City and St. Ignace ensure that you won't miss them.) All charge $13.50 per adult, $7 per child, and $5.50 per bicycle. And you may want to take your bicycle. Since 1898 Mackinac Island has forbidden the use of automobiles. Transportation is by horse or bicycle, either of which you can rent from numerous places at the boat dock. Quaint shops also make for a fun afternoon. Be sure to buy a box of Mackinac Island's world-famous fudge at numerous stores throughout town.

Three interesting churches on Mackinac Island include the Bark Chapel, which is actually a reconstruction but is much like the one built by Jesuits in 1670. Mission Church, built by a Presbyterian missionary in 1829, and St. Anne's Church, just down the street, built about 50 years later, show the efforts of early missionaries to reach out to the Native American population. All are on Huron St. (See Father Marquette also under Frankfurt and St. Ignace, Mich.)

Manistee Settled by Irish and German settlers in the mid-19th century, this town has a block or two of elegant homes built by its successful businessmen. The Guardian Angels Church (371 5th St.), built in 1890, combines Gothic and Romanesque styles and is worth a look. Our Saviour's Evangelical Lutheran Church (32 Walnut St.) dates from 1868 and was erected by Danish Lutheran settlers. It is a more modest structure than the Catholic church.

Marshall When you consider that Marshall has a population of only 7,000, it is quite remarkable that the town has over 800 historic buildings. Take your time strolling through this picturesque town; you can get a copy of the city's walking tour map from the Chamber of Commerce (Michigan and Madison Sts.). The annual historic home tour is held the weekend after Labor Day. Marshall is also especially beautiful at Christmastime. Extraordinary decorations are illuminated on the Friday after Thanksgiving and continue through New Year's Day. The annual Christmas Candle-light Walk is held every December and features historic homes decorated for the holidays.

The Underground Railroad marker at 120 South Eagle St. com-memorates the time when people of the town helped slaves on their journey into Canada. When one former slave, Adam Cross-white, was captured here in 1846, the entire town rose up to defend him and his family, sending him along the Underground Railroad to freedom. Crosswhite returned to Marshall after the Civil War and lies buried in the local cemetery, only a few hun-dred feet from several of his rescuers. (See Underground Railroad also under Camden, Del.; Buffalo, N.Y.; Macon, Ga.; Ottumwa, Iowa; Ripley, Ohio; and Osawatomie, Kans.)

Muskegon St. Paul's Episcopal Church (1006 3d St.), is a grayish greenstone structure, built in 1892. The interior is adorned with fine stained glass, marble, mosaics, and the wood carvings of Alois Lang, a wood carver from Oberammergau, Germany.

The Muskegon Museum of Art (296 W. Webster Ave.) is called one of the finest of the small art museums in the United States. It has an excellent collection of works by American painters as well as prints from major European artists.

The Maranatha Bible Conference facility is located south of the city on Lake Harbor Rd. Nationally known pastors, authors, and musicians can be heard here throughout the summer. Founded in 1936, the facility features Saturday night concerts throughout the summer and Sunday services at 10:30 A.M. and 6 P.M. It is open year-round and about 25,000 people take advan-tage of the programs each year. During a typical summer week, about 500 guests are lodged on the premises.

Niles Don't be confused. There are three places in Michigan that remember George Bennard's famous hymn, "The Old Rugged Cross." One is Albion, where he wrote it; one is Reed City, where he lived; and the third is Niles, where it was first sung. Actually it was first sung in the nearby community of Pokagon in 1913. To commemorate the famous hymn and its composer, a local inter-denominational group established a memorial garden in Niles complete with rocks, trees, flowers, a large rock altar, and a 13-$^1/_2$-foot cross. Future plans include a shelter, walkways, foot bridges, and more plantings.

227

Old Mission Peninsula The main drive north of Traverse City into the Old Mission Peninsula is lined with old maple trees, behind which are cherry orchards and vineyards. Grand Traverse Bay can be seen much of the way. Old Mission Church (Old Mission Rd.) was built in 1839 by Peter Dougherty, a Presbyterian missionary to the Native American population here. The church is about a mile south of the village of Old Mission, and the bell in the church is the original. Exhibits and displays are inside.

GREAT PLACES FOR FAMILY FUN

✔ Mackinac Island

✔ Ludington State Park

✔ Hiking and skiing in the Porcupine Mountains

Petoskey Andrew Porter, a Presbyterian missionary, established an Indian school here in 1852, and a Roman Catholic Indian mission began a few years later. The oldest building in Petoskey today is probably the St. Francis Solanus Indian Mission (on W. Lake St.), built in 1859 of square hand-cut timbers, held together by dovetailed corners.

Plymouth With a name like this, you would expect the town to do something special on Thanksgiving, and it does. Each November, this handsome suburb reenacts the first Thanksgiving.

Reed City The Old Rugged Cross Historical Museum is the outgrowth of a memorial cross erected to the memory of Rev. George Bennard, who composed the famous hymn. Rev. and Mrs. Bennard lived nearby and many relics from their lives and music are located here. The museum is not solely dedicated to the Bennards, however. About two-thirds of the space is dedicated to more general history of the Reed City area. Admission is free. (See Bennard also under Albion and Niles, Mich.)

St. Ignace Father Jacques Marquette founded a mission to the local Ojibwa Indians in 1671 and named it St. Ignace de Michilimackinac in honor of St. Ignatius Loyola, founder of the Jesuit order. Two years later he left with Louis Joliet for a journey down the Mississippi. He died on the way back. The Old Mission Church is in Marquette Park at 500 N. State St. and located very close to what is thought to be the site of the original mission. It is now a museum of Ojibwa culture. Admission to the outdoor park and Marquette's grave is free. There is a $2 fee to visit the museum and reconstructed long house. (See Father Marquette also under Frankfurt and Mackinac Island, Mich.)

Zeeland Dutch influence is strong in western Michigan and the town of Zeeland was one of the earliest Dutch settlements in the area in 1847. First Reformed Church (148 E. Central Ave.) was built in 1866 and stands on the site of Zeeland's second log church, built in 1849. The site of the first log church and first schoolhouse is in Pioneer Square, where a monument now stands. The Dekker Huis and Zeeland Historical Museum (37 E. Main Ave.) are open in spring and summer on Friday and Saturday.

■Minnesota

Tourist Info
Phone 800-657-3700
Web sites
   Entire state   www.exploreminnesota.com
   Duluth   www.visitduluth.com
   Minneapolis   www.minneapolis.org
   St. Paul   www.stpaulcvb.org
For a complete list of updated links, visit www.christiantraveler.com

Albert Lea The Freeborn County Historical Museum and Pioneer Village (two miles south of the intersection of Rte. 89 and I-35) has an outstanding display in its 13,000-square-foot museum and library and its very large pioneer village. In addition to the Norwegian Lutheran Church and an 1853 log cabin are more than a dozen other buildings dating from the nineteenth century. Guided tours are available by appointment.

Cold Spring Assumption Chapel (one mile northeast on Rte. 23) was built as a tribute after the townspeople were saved through prayer from a devastating plague of grasshoppers that had invaded their crops. The "Grasshopper Chapel" was ravaged by a tornado in 1894 and then rebuilt again in 1952.

Faribault Shattuck-St. Mary's School (1000 Shumway Ave.), founded by Episcopal bishop Henry Whipple in 1865, is located here. Whipple was a strong defender of the Dakota Indians and established his church headquarters here as well as his base for missions to the Indians. Many of his proposals for Indian relations were later adopted. Worth seeing is the historic Cathedral of our Merciful Savior (515 2d Ave. NW), which includes the bishop's chair and a stained glass window depicting a peace pipe superimposed on a broken tomahawk, which was a gift from the Sioux Indians in appreciation of Whipple's efforts.

The Ivan Whillock Studio (122 N.E. First Ave.) is also of interest, not only because it is housed in an 1865 limestone structure, one of the oldest in the state, but also because of the religious wood carvings and sculptures.

Harmony This area is the center of Minnesota's Amish country, and guided tours are available to show you the neighborhood Amish farms and the first church, built in 1856. Several country markets are also of interest. (See other Amish sites in Pennsylvania, Kentucky, Illinois, Indiana, Iowa, Michigan, Missouri, Ohio, Wisconsin, and Kansas.)

Hutchinson In 1855 three brothers who loved to sing started a church here, and the town of Hutchinson has been named in their honor. Because the people of Martha's Vineyard in Massachusetts heard of their need for a church bell and contributed to the cause, the people of Hutchinson named the church the Vineyard United Methodist Church (1395 S. Grade Rd.). The church bell still rings.

Little Falls The Linden Hill Conference and Retreat Center (608 Highland Ave.) is housed in two elegant Victorian-era mansions. Originally owned by the lumber magnate families Weyerhaeuser and Musser, the houses are open for conferences and retreats with overnight accommodations for small groups. Linden Hill features beautiful antiques and original heirlooms.

Minneapolis The Mississippi's Falls of St. Anthony were discovered and named by Father Louis Hennepin in the late 1600s. The falls drop 15 feet at the eastern edge of downtown, diminished somewhat by dams and the Upper St. Anthony Lock, which bypasses the falls. Guided walking tours of the St. Anthony Falls Historic District are available from April through October. Phone 612-627-5433.

Central Lutheran Church on 12th St. S is the largest Lutheran church in North America, seating 2,500. The windows are similar to those of Westminster Abbey and the organ has 5,791 pipes and 78 speaking stops. On the south commons is a sculpture by Paul Granlund, *Resurrection.*

First Covenant Church (810 S. 7th St.) is associated with Paul Stromberg Rees, evangelical leader and early president of the National Association of Evangelicals. He was pastor from 1938 to 1958.

Westminster Presbyterian Church (83 S. 12th St.), seating 1,500, is one of the 25 largest Presbyterian churches in the country. A large rose window faces the mall.

Bethany Fellowship on Auto Club Rd. is a complex containing a Christian school, factory, church, mission society, and publishing house. The publishing house has been very successful with Jeannette Oke's novels in recent years.

Near Loring Park is the Basilica of St. Mary (88 N. 17th St.). The basilica was the first in the nation, celebrating its first Mass in 1914.

Northwestern Schools, consisting of a liberal arts college, a Bible school, and a seminary, was founded by fundamentalist leader William B. Riley in 1902. Riley was pastor of the First Baptist Church (1021 Hennepin Ave.) from 1897 to 1947. Billy Graham was named president of Northwestern after Riley's death.

The international headquarters of the Billy Graham Evangelistic Association is located on Harmon Pl. in the city. (See Graham also under Asheville, Charlotte, and Montreat, N.C.; and Western Springs and Wheaton, Ill.)

The Minneapolis Institute of Arts (2400 3d Ave. S) is a cultural highlight in the Twin Cities. It is internationally renowned as one of the great American museums. Here you can see 100,000 objects representing 5,000 years of the arts.

Mountain Lake In the 1870s this community was established by Mennonite and Lutheran immigrants from Russia. Today Heritage Village (on County Rd.) commemorates the settlement. A collection of 18 historic buildings, including an 1884 Mennonite house-barn combination welcomes visitors. A festival "Utschtallung" or Heritage Fair is held the second Saturday of September. Russian Mennonite foods are served and demonstrations of pioneer activities are given.

New Ulm The Way of the Cross on 5th St. N has 14 stations that portray the life of Christ. At the top of the hill is a chapel dedicated to Our Sorrowful Mother. From the top, visitors can also get a view of the city and the Minnesota River Valley.

New Ulm is known for its Glockenspiel, one of the few carillon clocks in the world (4th and Minnesota Sts.). Cast in the Netherlands, it contains 37 bells weighing a total of 2.5 tons. Animated figurines that depict the history of the town come out of sliding doors three times each afternoon.

WHY SO MANY SCANDINAVIANS IN MINNESOTA?

The mid-1800s were years when Scandinavians—Swedes, Norwegians, and Danes—were increasingly disillusioned. Populations were burgeoning, and land was limited. A new Swedish king had taken the throne and instead of improving the lot of the lower and middle classes, he had made it more difficult. Instead of giving more religious freedom, he had given less. In Norway, where only a small percentage of the land is arable, only the eldest son of a family had a chance to make much of a living. Besides, Norway was ruled by the Swedish king. A religious revival was also sweeping the area, and converts were increasingly uncomfortable in the state church.

Just at that time, news came that land was opening up in the states of the Great Plains—and particularly in Minnesota. So the mix of small farmers hungry for more and better land and people who desired to worship freely began the flow of emigration to America. Some came to New York, then took an Erie Canal barge west to Buffalo, then around the Great Lakes to Chicago. Others came by ox-team across Ohio, Indiana, and Illinois. In Chicago they found a vigorous Scandinavian population. By 1900, Chicago had more Swedes than any city in Sweden except Stockholm. But if they were farmers, they didn't stay in Chicago long; they often went west to Moline, Illinois, another growing Scandinavian area, and then up the Mississippi River into Minnesota.

If the Minnesota and Dakota winters were harsh, they were no more severe than winters in Scandinavia. Land was cheap, and they, especially the Norwegians, had never seen soil so productive. Quickly churches were begun. The congregants usually continued to worship in Norwegian or Swedish and in short order they established the Augustana Synod of the Lutheran Church (now American Lutheran), the Swedish Covenant Church (now Evangelical Covenant), and the Swedish Baptists (now Baptist General Conference). They also started colleges, seminaries, and publishing houses in Chicago, Moline, and Minneapolis.

Often when the immigrants' children had children, they moved on to North Dakota, Montana, Saskatchewan, and Manitoba, continuing the move west and northwest.

Northfield This town is the site of both Carlton College, a private liberal arts college founded in 1866, and St. Olaf College, an Evangelical Lutheran school known for its choral groups and glee clubs. St. Olaf's beautiful 350-acre campus is atop a wooded hill in the town.

Owatonna Owatonna's Village of Yesteryear (1448 Austin Rd.) has been listed as one of the top ten attractions in southern Minnesota. It now has nearly a dozen 19th-century buildings, including an old church, relocated to its present site.

Red Wing Originally it was the site of a Dakota Sioux farming village. Red Wing's first white settlers arrived in 1837 when the Evangelical Missionary Society of Lausanne (Switzerland) arrived. Today the town has a charming historic district, including a number of beautiful churches. You can get a walking tour guide from the Red Wing City Hall (on Fourth St. between Plum and Bush Sts.).

Rochester Noted for its Mayo Clinic, founded in the 1880s by the Mayo brothers, this town was the home of noted evangelical writer and theologian Francis Schaeffer in his later years. He received treatment at the clinic.

Assisi Heights (1001 14th St.), which very closely resembles the Basilica of St. Francis of Assisi in Italy, is situated on 100 acres on one of the highest hills in the county. Visitors are welcome to tour the facility, which is the central location of the Sisters of St. Francis. Of special interest are the ornate lobby and the hand-blown stained glass windows. Housed within Assisi Heights is the Assisi Community Center,

> *He said to them, "Go into all the world and preach the good news to all creation."*
> MARK 16:15

which is a conference and retreat center, resembling a beautiful European monastery. The center has overnight accommodations for individuals as well as large groups. A spirit of solitude prevails for those looking for some quiet time to pray and reflect.

St. Cloud St. Johns University, 14 miles west of the city on I-94 in Collegeville, features its Abbey Church, a modern structure designed by Bauhaus School architect Marcel Breuer. The bell tower is a 112-foot-high concrete slab, supported by two concrete parabolas. It contains the original monastery bells. The school was founded in 1856 by Benedictine monks to minister to German immigrants in the area.

St. Paul The Cathedral of St. Paul (239 Selby Ave.) took nearly 50 years to build. Modeled after St. Peter's Basilica in Rome, it is 307 feet long, 216 feet wide, and seats 3,000. The dome rises 306 feet from the floor to the tip of the cross. Inside are magnificent stained glass windows, paintings, statues, and other works of art. A small historical museum is located on the lower level. Admission is free.

The Minnesota Children's Museum (W. 7th St.) is a great place to take the younger children. Kids explore six interactive galleries and enjoy the building's colorful architecture. Touching is not only allowed, it's expected.

The Penumbra Theatre (270 N. Kent St.) in the Hallie Q. Brown/Martin Luther King Center is Minnesota's only professional African American theater company. Every December a gospel rendition of the Christmas story is performed, *Black Nativity*.

Both the James J. Hill House on Summit Ave. and the Landmark Center on W. 5th St. have something to delight music lovers. The Hill House features a three-story pipe organ as well as changing art exhibits. The Landmark Center, which is the restored Old Federal Courts Building, contains the Schubert Piano Museum as well as the Minnesota Museum of Modern Art.

Bethel College and Seminary, associated with the Baptist General Conference denomination, attract evangelical students from many denominations.

St. Peter The town grew up around the historic Episcopal church at 118 N. Minnesota Ave. built in 1857. Stained glass windows for the church were transported by oxcart and steamboat from New York. But the town today is known as the home of Gustavus Adolphus College, which was established in 1862. The Old Main, which was built the year the school was founded, still stands. Adolphus, the Swedish king who fought the Thirty Years War to preserve Protestantism in the 1600s, has long been a heroic figure for Swedish Lutherans. The school's Nobel Hall of Science contains the Nobel Gallery dedicated to inventor and humanitarian Alfred B. Nobel. The school hosts the Nobel Conference, which has been held annually for more than three decades.

Sauk Centre Sinclair Lewis, who wrote *Elmer Gantry* and numerous other novels, grew up here and used this town as the backdrop for many of his novels. Visitors can see the Sinclair Lewis Boyhood Home and the Sinclair Lewis Museum, both of which display memorabilia of the novelist.

Scandia This Swedish community preserves many of the early immigrant structures in the Gammelgarden Museum, located in an outdoor park at 20880 Olinda Tr. N. Among the structures is the 1856 Elim Lutheran Church, a log sanctuary that is regarded as the oldest extant church building in the state. Admission is $2.

Shakopee The Minnesota Renaissance is a bustling 15th-century village filled with hundreds of costumed villagers and nobles. Musicians, jugglers, and mimes provide continuous entertainment on stages. More than 270 international artisans display and sell handcrafted wares in an authentic marketplace. Full-contact armored jousting and medieval feasting take families back in time. The village is open daily from mid-August to late September, weekends, and Labor Day.

Springfield This community celebrates Christmas in July as well as December. On the fourth Wednesday of July each year, Christmas in July is held with all the sounds and sights associated with Christmas. It is concluded by Christmas music, a Christmas dinner, and a talent show. In December a nativity pageant is held with a 75-voice community choir, a live manger scene, and many live animals, including camels. Some 200 community and area volunteers are included in the production.

Spring Valley The Methodist Church (221 W. Courtland St.), built in 1876, has at least one claim to fame. It was the home church for Laura Ingalls Wilder and her husband in 1890 and 1891. The building is no longer used as a church but is a museum, featuring displays of the Wilder family, religious artifacts, and other items of local historical significance. (See Wilder also under Burr Oak, Iowa; Walnut Grove, Minn.; Mansfield, Mo.; Pepin, Wisc.; Independence, Kans.; and De Smet, S.D.).

Taylors Falls North of St. Paul is a scenic area called the Historic Angel Hill District, which is a New England–style village with white frame houses and a prim, tall-steepled 1861 church.

Walnut Grove The Wilder Museum here on Hwy. 14 interprets Laura Ingalls Wilder's life in the little house on the prairie. The popular Wilder pageant is held on three weekends in July. A few miles away is the actual site of the dugout where Laura and her family lived on the banks of Plum Creek. (See Wilder also under Burr Oak, Iowa; Spring Valley, Minn.; Mansfield, Mo.; Pepin, Wisc.; Independence, Kans.; and De Smet, S.D.)

Willmar The Green Lake Bible Camp Chapel (9916 Lake Ave. S) is perched on a hill overlooking Green Lake. The Norwegian-style stave church was constructed in 1940, a replica of the historic stave churches of Norway. This rustic structure has become a popular wedding chapel and sight-seeing stop.

The SonShine Festival, an outdoor Christian music festival, features three days of solid Christian rock 'n' roll and is held each July. It draws about 12,000 people each year to hear nationally acclaimed performers. The annual event is held on the grounds of the Willmar Civic Center. Phone 800-233-3378 for more information.

This Scandinavian town also features Kaffe Fest in June, celebrating the people's love for Scandinavian coffee.

■Missouri

Tourist Info
Phone 800-887-1234
Web sites
  Entire state   www.missouritourism.org
  Branson   www.branson.com
  Kansas City   www.kansascity.com
  Precious Moments Chapel Center   www.preciousmoments.com
  St. Louis   www.explorestlouis.com
For a complete list of updated links, visit www.christiantraveler.com

Ava At Assumption Abbey on Rte. 5 in the Ozark hills, Trappist monks have a special fruitcake recipe. They produce and sell more than 18,000 fruitcakes a year, each weighing two pounds and each filled with raisins, cherries, and pineapple and marinated in burgundy.

While the monks work in quiet, the Assumption Abbey bakery does a big business, both at the bakery here and by direct mail.

In addition, the abbey extends hospitality to men and women of all faiths who are seeking rest. Home-cooked meals are provided. Advance reservations are necessary for overnight stays. Phone 417-683-5110.

Bethel In 1844 Bethel was founded as a German religious community and operated as a communal colony. Today, located just west of Hannibal, it is a charming art colony with special agricultural and cultural festivals throughout the year. There are also a number of bed and breakfast accommodations here.

Bowling Green A sizable Amish community lives in this area. Unlike the larger Amish communities in Indiana, Ohio, and Pennsylvania, there are no visitors centers, museums, or tourist-oriented attractions in Bowling Green, which is roughly midway between St. Louis and Hannibal. However, you will find numerous shops where the Amish sell quality products for which they've become known, including candy, dolls, baked goods, furniture, and rugs. (See other Amish sites in Missouri, as well as in Pennsylvania, Kentucky, Illinois, Indiana, Iowa, Michigan, Minnesota, Ohio, Wisconsin, and Kansas.)

Branson This is the nation's second country music capital, topped only by Nashville. It attracts some five million visitors a year to its star-studded theaters. And it isn't only country music that you'll find here; you can enjoy lots of variety.

Silver Dollar City, just west of Branson, features thrill rides and music as well as Ozark artisans demonstrating traditional crafts.

The New Promise Theatre (755 Gretna St.) is home to the award-winning musical *The Promise*. Recounting Christ's life from his birth in a stable to his death and ascension, *The Promise* is a powerfully inspirational presentation. You can find the theater on the Web at www.thepromise.com.

One of this tourist city's big attractions is its Old Time Country Christmas, held each December.

Near Branson, off Hwy. 65 on Rte. 1, is the Shepherd of the Hills Inspiration Tower. It is 230 feet tall and contains 92,000 pounds of steel and 4,400 square feet of glass. From it, visitors have a breathtaking view of the entire area. *The Shepherd of the Hills,* written in 1907, is the best-known work of author Harold Bell Wright, who spent his summers here for many years. The book was later made into a movie starring John Wayne, but the plot of the book was not recognizable in the movie.

Just south of Branson is the College of the Ozarks (100 Opportunity Ave. in Point Lookout), where each student works his or her way through college. The Friendship House and Gift Shop has an all-you-can-eat smorgasbord, and children under five eat without charge. Visitors may enjoy the quiet of the Williams Memorial Chapel here or the view from Point Lookout at dusk when the campus carillon is sounding.

Carthage This town has become a haven for artists with about 18 artists now residing here. But most people come to visit the Precious Moments Chapel (4321 Chapel Rd.) and gift shop and to buy the popular Precious Moments figurines. The Precious Moments Chapel features 30 stained glass windows and 52 murals designed by Sam Butcher, creator of the Precious Moments dolls and figurines. It's quite an impressive display. But this isn't just a chapel, rather a chapel center, including an art museum and the Fountain of Angels, with over 250 bronze figurines spouting water. Also there are music shows, a hotel, an RV park, and dining facilities.

Conception Junction Conception Abbey, which produces greeting cards and colorful notes, is located here on Rte. VV. The business is known as The Printery House, run by Benedictine monks. This is a 1,000-acre site and tours are available. Guests can also arrange in advance to stay for a day or two.

Concordia Kathryn Kuhlman, charismatic evangelist whose slogan, "I Believe in Miracles," attracted a nationwide audience, was born here.

Diamond The George Washington Carver Monument here commemorates the birthplace of the slave who rose to fame as a godly educator and agriculturist. The visitors center traces his career and achievements. It's located about two miles west of Diamond on Hwy. V. (See Carver also under Tuskegee, Ala., and Fulton and Joplin, Mo.)

Eolia About halfway between St. Louis and Hannibal, the little village of Eolia boasts St. John's Episcopal Church, the oldest Episcopal church west of the Mississippi.

Excelsior Springs The Church of St. Luke, the Beloved Physician (Episcopal, on Elms Rd. and Regent St.) is located across the street from the Elms Hotel. The interior of the church is so lovely that it is frequently requested for weddings.

Fleming Park Missouri Town 1855 has more than 35 buildings dating from the mid-19th century, including an old church, a blacksmith shop, and old houses. Special reenactments are performed at various times throughout the year.

Florissant The Old St. Ferdinand's Shrine (on rue St. Francis) and St. Stanislaus Jesuit Museum (on Howdershell Rd.) are picturesque sites. The museum has an excellent collection of rare Greek and Latin books dating to 1521.

> **GREAT PLACES FOR FAMILY FUN**
>
> ✔ Silver Dollar City, Branson, Missouri
>
> ✔ Six Flags, St. Louis, Missouri
>
> ✔ The Wild West town and Boot Hill Cemetery in Dodge City, Kansas

Fulton Westminster College (Presbyterian) here is where Winston Churchill delivered his famous "Iron Curtain" speech, and the college has maintained close ties with Great Britain ever since. The college purchased the Church of St. Mary the Virgin from Aldermanbury, England. They dismantled it stone by stone, then shipped it across the Atlantic and reconstructed it on the Westminster campus. It now houses the Winston Churchill Memorial and Library. The church itself was built in 12th-century England and redesigned by Sir Christopher Wren in 1677. It was damaged in World War II but it has now been restored by Westminster College.

There is also a George Washington Carver Memorial here at 906 Westminster Ave., although his main memorial is in Diamond, Missouri. (See Carver also under Tuskegee, Ala., and Joplin, Mo.)

Hannibal What was once an unknown village became immensely popular when a certain author made his debut. Samuel Clemens, more commonly known as Mark Twain, was born here in 1835, and the town has never been the same.

There are numerous tourist sites for those who enjoy this quintessentially American author. His boyhood home is preserved at the Mark Twain Boyhood Home and Museum (208 Hill St.).

The Mark Twain Museum includes a collection of *Tom and Huck,* Norman Rockwell's paintings. The Mark Twain Riverboat (Center St. Landing) offers visitors a one-hour steamboat ride down the Mississippi, recounting the history and folklore of this region. And the Mark Twain Cave (1 mile south of town on Rte. 79) is supposedly the one in which Tom Sawyer and Becky Thatcher got lost in the classic *The Adventures of Tom Sawyer.* (See Twain also under Hartford, Conn., and Norris, Tenn.)

Hazelwood The Museum of Western Jesuit Missions (900 Howdershell Rd.) recounts the story of the first Indian school west of the Mississippi and the great missionary Father Pierre Jean de Smet. In the museum you learn of the school and its people through displays, artwork, church items, and pioneer tools. (See de Smet also under De Smet, S.D.; Casper, Wyo.; and Kettle Falls, Wash.)

Highlandville It's called the "world's smallest cathedral." It's the Cathedral Church of the Prince of Peace, three miles off Hwy. 65. Containing the lovely Garden of Saints, it displays statues of saints among the flower beds. Inside the cathedral is a well-known oil painting, *Cristo de Espaldas (The Back of Christ).* It shows Christ, immediately after bidding his disciples, "Follow me." So Christ has turned, expecting the viewer to follow, walking in his steps. The cathedral, which is only 14 feet by 17 feet and is mentioned in the *Guinness Book of Records,* seats fifteen and contains the world's smallest cathedral organ, with 42 pipes. (See also other "smallest" churches under Florence, Ky.; Savannah, Ga.; Festina, Iowa; and Cedar Vale, Kans.)

Independence If you are an angel collector, you will love The Angel Lady (216 S. Spring St.), a unique shop specializing in— you guessed it—angels. Crafted by artisans from around the world, you can add to your collection with angels of every ilk and also find books and memorabilia on the subject.

Jackson The oldest Protestant church west of the Mississippi is the Old McKendree Chapel, a Methodist church that dates back to 1819. The chapel is just off Rte. 306.

Jamesport This is the largest Mennonite and Amish settlement in Missouri. Like Bowling Green on the other side of the state, this town offers no visitors centers or museums. However, there are numerous shops that offer Amish-made goods. For instance, Ginerich Dutch Pantry and Bakery, owned by Mennonites, has a variety of food and baked goods, and just out of town is Sherwood Quilts and Crafts with a large selection of handmade quilts. (See other Amish sites in Missouri, as well as in Pennsylvania, Kentucky, Illinois, Indiana, Iowa, Michigan, Minnesota, Ohio, Wisconsin, and Kansas.)

Joplin Just outside of Joplin is the George Washington Carver National Monument, remembering a Christian man who revolutionized how Americans think of soybeans and peanuts. An educator, botanist, and agronomist, he taught children of ex-slaves how to improve land exhausted by cotton. Carver became known as the "Peanut Man," because he urged small farmers to grow protein-rich and soil-regenerating soybeans and peanuts and then found many uses for the crops. The Carver Nature Trail leads from the birthplace site through two springs and ends at the Carver family cemetery. The monument is just off Hwy. V on Carver Rd. (See Carver also under Tuskegee, Ala., and Diamond and Fulton, Mo.)

Kansas City Swope Park is the home of the Kansas City Zoo (I-435 and 63d St.). Recently added were a 5,000-acre African plains exhibit and an IMAX theater. Worlds of Fun and Oceans of Fun are two adjoining theme parks, with shows, rides, and attractions for people of all ages. A recent advertising campaign says, "If you want to see skyscrapers, go to New York. If you want to ride them, go to Kansas City," touting its new 205-foot Mamba, one of the fastest, tallest, longest coasters in the world.

The Cathedral of the Immaculate Conception on W. 12th St. was built in 1856. The architecture is called neo-Baroque with a Romanesque influence.

The Hallmark Visitors Center in the Crown Center Complex (2501 McGee St.) presents the history of the greeting card company.

The Church of the Nazarene, a denomination with about a half million members, has its headquarters at 6901 The Paseo. Also located here are its publishing house and the Nazarene Theological Seminary (1700 E. Meyer Blvd.).

The Fellowship of Christian Athletes, which ministers to athletes and coaches, has its offices here on Leeds Rd.

Kimmswick In this town there is a shop called It's a Small World Christmas Haus that is stocked with European Christmas miniatures. Open year-round, it attracts visitors from across the country.

Kingsville The Powell Gardens (1609 N.W. US Hwy. 50) is an 807-acre garden and natural resource center where visitors can wander among flowers and plants to their heart's content. A new chapel here provides visitors with a place to get apart from the crowd and meditate.

Lawson The Watkins Woolen Mill Historic Site is a historic experience. Part of Watkins Mill State Park, it was originally a mill, providing woolen fabrics for the area. Now the mill and a number of other buildings, including a church and a schoolhouse, have been restored to their 19th-century condition. The elegant home on the hill as well as the mill can be toured. During the year, there are a number of living history weekends, and one of them is called Victorian Christmas Liberty.

William Jewell College, a Baptist college founded in 1849, is one of the oldest liberal arts colleges in the state. It is known throughout the area for its music and dramatic performance series. Nearby on N. Water St. is Lightburne Hall, the 26-room mansion built in 1852 by a founder of the college.

The James Inn Bed and Breakfast on N. Water St. occupies the facilities of the Saint James Catholic Church, built in 1913 and used as a church until 1981. In 1997 it was converted into a bed and breakfast. Its high ceilings make it a unique facility.

Mansfield About 40 miles east of Springfield on US 60 is the Laura Ingalls Wilder and Rose Wilder Lane Museum and Home, where the much-loved children's author wrote all of her *Little House* books. Laura Ingalls Wilder and her daughter Rose Wilder Lane, also an author, are both buried here. The Wilder home is exactly as Rose left it, and the museum connected with it has four hand-written manuscripts. It was her daughter who encouraged Laura to write her books. A Laura Ingalls Wilder Festival is held each September. The museum and home are both closed from November through February. (See Wilder also under Burr Oak, Iowa; Spring Valley and Walnut Grove, Minn.; Pepin, Wisc.; Independence, Kans.; and De Smet, S.D.)

Perryville St. Mary of the Barrens Church (off Hwy. 61) dates back to 1827. Visitors are invited to walk through its grounds, and the church has a museum displaying its history.

Potosi Located about 80 miles south of St. Louis on Rte. 2 is the YMCA of the Ozarks, one of Missouri's favorite family getaways. Situated on a secluded lake among rolling hills and tall pines, this 3,000-acre retreat and conference center has accommodations for groups of 2 to 300. And there are lots of activities available including swimming, canoeing, paddleboating, softball, and volleyball. Phone 573-438-2154 for more information.

St. Joseph When the Catholic Diocese of Kansas City–St. Joseph decided to close the Queen of the Apostles parish and raze the cathedral, school, rectory, and convent, local parishioners and neighbors protested loudly. But they did more than just protest. They raised money to save and restore the buildings. Today the beautiful Twin Spires (501 S. 10th St.) houses a multifaith religious museum and its sanctuary is in demand as a concert hall and wedding site.

GREAT PLACES TO ENJOY GOD'S CREATION

✔ Driving the Great River Road along the Mississippi River, Iowa

✔ Spring at the Lake of the Ozarks, Missouri, when the dogwoods are in bloom

St. Louis The first thing you'll see when you arrive in St. Louis is the gleaming Gateway Arch, the nation's tallest monument at 630 feet. St. Louis was truly the gateway to the West for many pioneers, who stocked up on their provisions in this city before heading out. Visitors can take an elevator ride up to the top of the arch for a spectacular view of the city and the Mississippi River, but think twice about it if you're claustrophobic. Those cars are tiny. Riding to the top is popular, nonetheless. If you arrive midday or during peak tourist seasons, prepare for a lengthy visit. Admission is $6.

While you're waiting, visit the Museum of Western Expansion, located at the base of the arch. Here you can learn about the Louisiana Purchase and its exploration. The 40-minute film *Monument to the Dream* chronicles the arch's construction and is shown once every hour. Admission is free.

243

Dwarfed by the arch, which stretches overhead, is St. Louis's oldest church, the Old Cathedral Basilica of St. Louis, the King, otherwise known simply as the Old Cathedral (209 Walnut St.). The simple Greek Revival structure was built in 1834, and masses are still held daily. The Old Cathedral Museum, located on the west side of the cathedral, has some of the most outstanding ecclesiastical art in the country, as well as some works by the old masters.

Don't get confused by the cathedrals. There is also the beautiful Cathedral Basilica of St. Louis, sometimes called the New Cathedral (4431 Lindell Blvd.). This massive building is a combination of Romanesque, Byzantine, Gothic, and Baroque styles. Its most stunning feature is its 83,000 square feet of mosaic art, the world's largest collection, depicting 19th-century church history in Missouri. Over 41,500,000 tesserae in more than 8,000 colors cover the walls, ceilings, and three domes. Check to see if a concert is scheduled to perform at the cathedral while you're in town.

The Black Madonna Shrine and Grottoes (1 St. Joseph Hills Rd.) are a galaxy of multicolored rock grottoes. The ornamental works of religious art were created out of Missouri tiff rock and seashells and have become famous nationwide.

Historic Union Station (18th and Market Sts., one mile west of downtown) was once the nation's largest and busiest railroad terminal. Today the building houses a shopping mall, food court, and entertainment center in a beautiful old building.

The Magic House (516 Kirkwood Blvd.) is not a house of magic as its name suggests, but a thoroughly wonderful children's museum. Located in a restored Victorian house, the building is packed with interactive learning experiences. Especially fun is the giant, enclosed twisty slide that children (and adults) enter on the house's third story and exit on the ground level.

Forest Park, the country's largest urban park, was originally the home of the 1904 World's Fair and St. Louis Exposition. Today the park is a tourist's paradise, home to three museums, a zoo, a planetarium, a 12,000-seat amphitheater, a grand canal, as well as countless picnic areas and pathways, almost all of which are free. The St. Louis Zoo is the best of all the park's options. It's a world-class zoo where you'll want to spend the entire day. It's also free. The St. Louis Science Center, in the park's southeast corner, has tons of hands-on exhibits that will appeal to all ages, an Omnimax theater, and a planetarium. The science center is free, but the planetarium and shows charge admission. Also located within the park are the Missouri History Museum and the St. Louis Art Museum with masterpieces of Asian, Renaissance, and Impressionist art. Admission to both is free.

The headquarters of the Lutheran Church–Missouri Synod is on South Kirkwood Blvd. here. Founded in 1847, it has a North American membership of 2.6 million.

Walter A. Maier, famed as the radio preacher on *The Lutheran Hour* from 1920 to 1930, founded the St. Stephen's Lutheran Church at 515 Pendleton Ave.

The superintendent of the Sunshine Rescue Mission always ended his prayers with the phrase, "And that will be glory for me," which inspired hymn writer Charles Gabriel to write the gospel song "O That Will Be Glory for Me."

In Warrenton, about 50 miles west of St. Louis at 2300 E. Hwy. M, is the headquarters of Child Evangelism Fellowship, a ministry that emphasizes an outreach to neighborhood children.

St. Patrick This little town of fewer than 20 people has a busy post office on March 17 and a Shrine of St. Patrick that has visitors throughout the year. The shrine is patterned after the Church of Four Masters in Donegal, Ireland. It has a round bell tower and a circular staircase. Its stained glass windows were made in Dublin and are patterned after the famous illuminated manuscript, *The Book of Kells*.

Smithton A charismatic revival broke out in the Smithton Community Church in the mid-1990s that has attracted visitors from across the nation. The church is located on Rte. 1.

Springfield The headquarters of the Assemblies of God is located here, as is their denominational school, Evangel College.

The Ozark Mountain Christmas Festival of Lights is a town highlight each December.

Tipton This is Mennonite and Amish country. An easy introduction to the area is at the Dutch Bakery and Bulk Food Store on the west end of Tipton at 709 Hwy. 50W. Pies are homemade and the breads include a delicious oatmeal bread. Nearby is the Butterfield Inn at Hwys. 50 and 5, run by Mennonites Carl and Anna Mary Lehman, where dinners are served Thursday, Friday, and Saturday nights, but never on Sunday. (See other Amish sites in

Missouri, as well as in Pennsylvania, Kentucky, Illinois, Indiana, Iowa, Michigan, Minnesota, Ohio, Wisconsin, and Kansas.)

Versailles Old Order Mennonites live here, and that means horse-drawn buggies are on the roads. It also means that eating and shopping are good. Pleasant Valley Quilts is run by the Brubaker family and is located about six miles south of town at 15050 Hopewell Rd. in Barnett. A tea shop adjoins the store. Dutch Country Store is a popular place for local Mennonites because they carry a great assortment of bulk foods. Weavers Market in nearby Excelsior Springs carries farm produce, homemade pies, and other goods. Clearview Mennonite Church on Hwy. E and Bethel Mennonite Church are local churches. In between the two is Martin House, at 731 S. Main St. in Brookfield, which serves Amish meals.

Webb City In King Jack Park here, a 32-foot concrete and steel structure atop a 40-foot high hill was created by local art instructor Jack Dawson. The huge structure is the *Praying Hands,* and the artist simply wanted to remind passersby of the importance of prayer in their daily lives.

■OHIO

Tourist Info

Phone 800-BUCKEYE

Web sites

  Entire state   www.ohiotourism.com

  Cincinnati   www.cincyusa.com

  Cleveland   www.travelcleveland.com

  Columbus   www.columbuscvb.org

  Erie County   www.visit-lake-erie.com

For a complete list of updated links, visit www.christiantraveler.com

Akron The Chapel in University Park (135 Fir Hill Rd.) is the largest church in the state with average attendance around 9,000. The pastor is Knute Larson. Another large church in the city, only slightly smaller, is the Akron Baptist Temple (2324 Manchester Rd.), associated with the ministry of Charles Billington. The House of the Lord (1650 Diagonal Rd.), pastored by Joey Johnson, is one of the largest and fastest-growing interracial churches in the area.

Bellevue Historic Lyme Village is located two miles east of town. It contains a number of restored 19th-century buildings, including a log church, a schoolhouse, and a post office. Tours of nearby Historic Lyme Church are also available.

Berlin This is the heart of Amish country in Ohio and may possess the largest Amish population in the world (between 35,000 and 45,000). One mile east of town at 4363 Rte. 39 is Amish Farm, where visitors can see an Amish home and enjoy a slide presentation on Amish life. Baked goods are prepared daily, and buggy rides are available. *Behalt,* located five miles east, is a 265-foot cyclorama illustrating the Amish and Mennonite heritage. The cyclorama is within the Mennonite Information Center at 5798 County Rd. 77. On Fridays and Saturdays Holmes County's Amish Flea Market is open in nearby Walnut Creek. Handmade Amish items are usually available. (See other Amish sites in Ohio, as well as in Pennsylvania, Kentucky, Illinois, Indiana, Iowa, Michigan, Minnesota, Missouri, Wisconsin, and Kansas.)

Bowersville Norman Vincent Peale, father of "positive thinking," was born here in 1898. He is known for his best-seller *The Power of Positive Thinking* and for *Guideposts* magazine, which he founded.

Cambridge This town is known for its Cambridge Glass, and the Cambridge Glass Museum features more than 5,000 pieces of it. It is also known for its *Living Word* outdoor drama, which portrays the life of Jesus. Performances are held outdoors in an amphitheater three miles northwest of Cambridge on Rte. 209 on Thursday, Friday, and Saturday evenings from mid-June through Labor Day weekend.

Canton Located here is the Christian Hall of Fame, sponsored by the Canton Baptist Temple (515 Whipple Ave. NW). It consists of 100 original oil portraits of Christian leaders from New Testament times to the present. Included along the 260 feet of corridors are paintings of Tertullian, Luther, Calvin, Knox, and Billy

Sunday. (See Sunday also under Chicago and Dundee, Ill.; Winona Lake, Ind.; and Marshalltown, Iowa.)

Malone College (515 25th St. NW), affiliated with the Evangelical Friends, is also located in Canton.

The National First Ladies' Library (331 Market Ave. S) is housed in the family home of Mrs. William McKinley (25th first lady of the United States). Opened in June 1998, this bibliographic library has collections of books, letters, papers, and furniture pertaining to the first ladies of the United States. Admission is $5.

Cedarville Cedarville College, associated with the General Association of Regular Baptists, is located on 300 acres on the north edge of the village. The college is known nationally as a leader in campus networking and instructional technology.

Cincinnati At 2950 Gilbert Ave., you will find the Harriet Beecher Stowe house. Although *Uncle Tom's Cabin* was written after the Stowes moved to New England, the inspiration and the research came while Harriet was living in Cincinnati. In the house are Stowe memorabilia and exhibits on black history. (See Stowe also under Hartford and Litchfield, Conn., and Brunswick, Maine.)

The hymn "I Am Thine, O Lord," was written by Fanny Crosby in the home of William H. Doane, who lived here.

Hebrew Union College (3101 Clifton Ave.) displays fascinating exhibits relating to archaeology, Jewish life cycles, and the Torah. The American Jewish Archives are also located here and the rare book room is noted for its collection of ancient manuscripts.

The Museum Center at Union Terminal contains a natural history and a historical museum. It also has a Helen Steiner Rice room, dedicated to the Christian poet who lived most of her life in Cincinnati.

St. Peter in Chains Cathedral at 8th and Plum Sts. is an outstanding example of Greek Revival architecture. It was dedicated in 1945 and then renovated in 1958. Guided tours are available.

From the yard of the Immaculata Church (Pavillion and Guido Sts.) you can get a wonderful view of the city.

Cleveland The Cleveland Museum of Art (11150 E. Blvd.) is a beautiful white marble temple housing a world-renowned medieval European collection with a strong religious emphasis. Also worth seeing is the Egyptian art and the European and American paintings. Admission is free.

The Great Lakes Science Center features more than 350 interactive exhibits that will intrigue families with children of all ages. The museum also has an Omnimax theater (super-sized images combined with a state-of-the-art sound system) and is the ninth largest hands-on museum in the nation.

SeaWorld Cleveland, one of four Sea Worlds in the country, is located in Aurora, 30 minutes southeast of downtown. The 90-acre marine entertainment park is open from mid-May through early September.

Lake Farmpark is a unique 235-acre open-air science and cultural center located in Lake County. It is open year-round and offers farm animals, wagon rides, festivals, and shows. The park is at 8800 Chardon Rd. in Willoughby.

St. Theodosius Russian Orthodox Cathedral (733 Starkweather Ave. in Cleveland's Tremont district) is one of the best examples of Russian Orthodox church architecture in the country. Built in 1911, it has a striking onion-shaped central dome and 12 smaller surrounding domes, representing Christ and the twelve apostles.

Karamu House (E. 89th St. and Quincy Ave.) is the nation's first multicultural arts center and theater celebrating African American culture. Every year from late November until early January, the theater presents the *Black Nativity,* a gospel version of the Christmas story.

In the mid-19th century a Lake Erie vessel was heading for port in Cleveland. It was a stormy night, and some of the lighthouse lights—the lower lights—were not working. In the darkness the pilot missed the channel to the harbor and crashed into the rocks, causing the loss of many lives. Songwriter Philip P. Bliss, hearing the story, wrote the gospel song "Let the Lower Lights Be Burning."

Columbus World Harvest Church (4595 Gender Rd.), led by Rod Parsley, is a charismatic assembly averaging more than 5,000 in attendance. It is the largest church in the city.

Defiance AuGlaize Village features 17 reconstructed or restored buildings dating from 1860 to 1920.

The Chapel of Crosses Church, a Lutheran church built in 1975, contains an antique wooden pump organ manufactured in 1892. It is located three miles west of Defiance.

East Liverpool Will Thompson, called the Bard of Ohio, was born and lived most of his life here. He wrote both secular and sacred songs in the 19th century and also established a music company here. Perhaps his best-known hymn is "Softly and Tenderly Jesus Is Calling."

East Palestine The hymn "All to Jesus I Surrender," by Judson Van DeVenter, was written while he was conducting a series of meetings here.

Gnadenhutten In 1782 a volunteer militia of American patriots massacred more than 90 Christian American Indians at a Moravian mission here. Today there is a nine-acre memorial, the Gnadenhutten Museum and Park (Walnut and Main Sts.), which includes a log church and a cooper's cabin. The museum contains relics and American Indian artifacts. Gnadenhutten is Ohio's oldest existing settlement. (See Moravians also under Hope, N.J.; Bethlehem, Lititz, and Nazareth, Pa.; Winston-Salem, N.C.; Bloomington, Ill.; New Philadelphia, Ohio; and Ephraim, Wisc.)

GREAT PLACES TO ENJOY GOD'S CREATION

✔ The frozen waterfalls in Hocking Hills State Park in the winter

✔ Hiking in Cuyahoga Valley National Recreation Area

Jackson The Noah's Ark Animal Farm was not founded by Noah but it does contain more than 150 animals and birds on its 35 acres. Included are bears, llamas, lions, and zebras.

Kidron Because of the Amish population here, Lehman Hardware has become successful as the nonelectric appliance and equipment store of the area. The bulk of the floor space is given to wares like gas-powered washing machines, wood-burning stoves, and kerosene lamps. Now Lehman's has an 80-page catalog called *Lehman's Non-Electric Good Neighbor Heritage Catalog*. (See other Amish sites in Ohio, as well as in Pennsylvania, Kentucky, Illinois, Indiana, Iowa, Michigan, Minnesota, Missouri, Wisconsin, and Kansas.)

Lakeside Located on the Marblehead Peninsula between Toledo and Cleveland, the Lakeside Association bills itself as "the Chautauqua on Lake Erie." Its mission is to foster traditional Christian values in a Chautauqua setting and to provide programs and services for enrichment and spiritual, cultural, intellectual, and physical growth. Programs are diverse, designed to attract all ages and interests. You may hear music, ranging from a program by a former Monkees member to a choral festival featuring Bach's *Magnificat,* and spend a day discussing ecumenical advances or how to talk to your children. Accommodations are also available. Internet address is www.lakesideohio.com. (See also Chautauqua, N.Y., and other Chautauqua-inspired sites under Ridgecrest, N.C.; Sac City, Iowa; Madison, S.D.; and Boulder, Colo.)

Lebanon On South Broadway, the Warren County Museum exhibits a collection of furniture and other artifacts from the Shaker movement. The Shakers, whose proper name is the United Society of Believers in Christ's Second Appearing, broke off from the Quakers and started communities across America in the early 1800s. Also on South Broadway is the Golden Lamb Shaker Museum. On the first floor is the Golden Lamb Inn, a famous restaurant that had been frequented by such notables as Mark Twain, Henry Clay, and Charles Dickens. There is a Charles Dickens Room on the second floor. The Shaker Museum is on the fourth floor. (See Shakers also under Sabbathday Lake, Maine; Pittsfield, Mass.; Concord and Enfield, N.H.; Old Chatham, N.Y.; South Union and Harrodsburg, Ky.; and Marysville, Wash.)

Mansfield The Living Bible Museum, located at 500 Tingley St., contains two museums. The Life of Christ presents 21 dioramas with an audio text. The Miracles of the Old Testament show 19 dioramas depicting the works of God in the Old Testament. There is also a display of rare Bibles and immigrant American religious folk art here.

Mentor Lawnfield (8095 Mentor Ave.), which was the home of President James A. Garfield, is open to the public from April to November. Garfield, the only president who was an ordained minister, preached frequently and once baptized 40 people after an evangelistic campaign.

Middlefield About 16,000 Amish live in Geauga County. The Dutch Country Kitchen Restaurant here specializes in Amish-style meals, and the Middlefield Cheese House (16942 Kinsman Rd.) is where many of the Amish bring their milk to be made into Swiss cheese. The cheese plant is a cooperative and one of the largest producers of quality Swiss cheese in the United States. The film *Faith and Teamwork* is shown at the plant, describing the steps in the cheese-making process. A museum at the plant features old-world carvings and Amish artifacts. The Chalet Shop makes it easy for visitors to make purchases. (See other Amish sites in Ohio, as well as in Pennsylvania, Kentucky, Illinois, Indiana, Iowa, Michigan, Minnesota, Missouri, Wisconsin, and Kansas.)

Mount Pleasant For nearly a century in the 1800s the Friends Meeting House here housed the annual meeting of the Ohio and Pennsylvania Quakers. Today the interior is exactly as it was 170 years ago, although the Quakers haven't met here since early in the 20th century. It is located just off Rte. 150.

New Philadelphia The Schoenbrunn Village State Memorial on East High Ave. commemorates the coming of David Zeisberger in 1772 as a Moravian missionary to the Delaware Indians. The town quickly grew to 60 buildings and 300 inhabitants. It was here that Ohio's first civil code was drawn up and Ohio's first church and schoolhouse were built. However, the Revolutionary War caused the village of Schoenbrunn to be abandoned in 1777. Today there are 17 reconstructed log buildings here as well as the original mission cemetery.

Trumpet of the Land is a historical drama held in an outdoor amphitheater, telling of the coming of the Moravian missionaries here. It is performed Monday through Saturday from mid-June to late August (exit 81, off I-77). (See Moravians also under Hope, N.J.; Bethlehem, Lititz, and Nazareth, Pa.; Winston-Salem, N.C.; Bloomington, Ill.; Gnadenhutten, Ohio; and Ephraim, Wisc.)

Oberlin Charles G. Finney is best known as a 19th-century revivalist but he also was professor of theology at Oberlin College from 1835 to 1875. He became president of the school in 1851 and continued to hold revival meetings throughout his lifetime. From its founding in 1833 the college was strongly antislavery and coeducational. Between 1836 and 1910 it awarded degrees to more African American students than the rest of America's predominately white colleges combined. It was the first coeducational college in the world. The school today is known for its music conservatory, and concerts are presented throughout the year.

Oxford While a professor at Miami University here in the 1830s, William Holmes McGuffey established his first reading audience. McGuffey's Readers became the staple of American elementary education in the latter half of the century. His home is now the McGuffey Museum on campus.

Pennsville Hymnwriter Lelia Naylor Morris, who wrote more than 1,000 hymns, was born here. Among her compositions are "Nearer, Still Nearer," "Sweeter as the Years Go By," and "What If It Were Today?"

> **GREAT PLACES FOR FAMILY FUN**
>
> ✔ Cedar Point, Sandusky
>
> ✔ Sea World, Cleveland
>
> ✔ King's Island, Cincinnati

Portsmouth Portsmouth was the birthplace of Christian cowboy movie star Roy Rogers, who died in 1998. In the first week of June each year, the town holds a Roy Rogers Festival, with entertainment and Roy Rogers memorabilia. (See Roy Rogers also under Victorville, Calif.)

Ripley The Rankin House State Memorial (off US 52 on Liberty Hill) is the restored home of an early Ohio abolitionist, the Reverend John Rankin. The house was a station in the Underground Railroad and thought to have been the home where Eliza, the character in *Uncle Tom's Cabin,* found refuge after crossing the Ohio River. Rankin used an elaborate system of lanterns to communicate the "all clear" message to townspeople. In the museum his personal Bible as well as other memorabilia can be seen. (See Underground Railroad also under Camden, Del.; Buffalo, N.Y.; Macon, Ga.; Ottumwa, Iowa; Marshall, Mich.; and Osawatomie, Kans.)

Sandusky Cedar Point Amusement Park along the Lake Erie shore was voted the best amusement park in the world by *Amusement Today* magazine. It holds three Guinness world records: greatest number of roller coasters (13) and rides (67) and the tallest freestanding ride (Power Tower at 300 feet). As for the steel roller coaster Magnum XL200, it isn't for the faint of heart.

Springfield Wittenberg University, associated with the Evangelical Lutheran Church of America, is situated here. Its Weaver Chapel is known for its leaded stained glass windows.

Sugarcreek Known as the "Little Switzerland of Ohio" because of its Swiss settlers and architecture, the area is also known for its Amish heritage. At the Alpine Hills Historical Museum, visitors can view the Amish heritage and also see an 1890s Amish kitchen. The Ohio Central Railroad (Depot at 111 Factory St.) provides a guided tour of the Amish countryside in vintage coaches pulled by a 1912 steam locomotive. (See other Amish sites in Ohio, as well as in Pennsylvania, Kentucky, Illinois, Indiana, Iowa, Michigan, Minnesota, Missouri, Wisconsin, and Kansas.)

Toledo The old Sunday school song "Brighten the Corner Where You Are" may have been the most popular gospel song in the early part of the 20th century. It was written by Ina Ogdon, a Toledo woman, who had been a gifted speaker and lecturer on the Chautauqua circuit. When her father suffered a stroke, her personal career was set aside and she became a caretaker for him. It was then that she wrote the song with the line, "To the many duties ever near you now be true, brighten the corner where you are."

Waynesville Known for its antiques, this small town has more than 30 antique shops. It also boasts of Pioneer Village, a re-created 19th-century town that includes a Quaker meetinghouse. Christmas in Waynesville is celebrated every weekend after Thanksgiving as more than 1,500 lights illuminate the village.

Zoar In 1817, 300 German Separatists came to East Central Ohio along the Tuscarawas River to begin a new society. Soon it became a communal society and it prospered with a wide variety of businesses and shops. The community lasted until 1898 when it lost its competitive edge and finally disbanded. Much of the community has now been restored. In the Number One House, an audiovisual presentation gives the complete history of the colony. In the greenhouse, visitors see spiritual significance in all the details, with the large Norway spruce symbolizing Christ and the twelve slip junipers representing the apostles.

■WISCONSIN

Tourist Info
Phone 800-432-TRIP
Web sites
  Entire state   www.tourism.state.wi.us
  Green Bay   www.greenbaywi.com
  Madison   www.visitmadison.com
  Milwaukee   www.milwaukee.org
For a complete list of updated links, visit www.christiantraveler.com

Apostle Islands National Lakeshore The islands were named by French missionaries who miscounted. Thinking there were 12 islands, the missionaries named them the Apostle Islands; there are 22. The Apostles encompass 42,000 acres of land spread over 600 square miles of Lake Superior. Primitive camping and hiking are allowed on most islands. Favorite pastimes are sailing and charter-boat fishing for lake trout and whitefish.

Baileys Harbor The Bjorklunden Chapel, on Chapel Lane just south of town, is a unique building established by Mr. and Mrs. Donald Boynton of Highland Park, Illinois. After having traveled to Norway, where they admired an old Norwegian-style church (*stavkirke*) in Lillehammer, they decided to build one at their summer home in Baileys Harbor. The 41 murals on the inside were painted by Mrs. Boynton, and both of them worked to carve interior and exterior works of art for it. The 325-acre estate is now owned and operated by Lawrence University.

Beloit In an old redecorated downtown church is the Angel Museum (656 Pleasant St.), featuring some 11,000 angels, mostly from a private collection. Oprah Winfrey has recently donated 600 African American angels to the collection.

Boscobel The Boscobel Hotel (1005 Wisconsin Ave.) was where the International Gideon organization got started. In 1899 two traveling salesman, both Christians, were housed in the hotel, discussing how they could spread their faith in their traveling profession. They decided to start the Christian Commercial Travelers Association, placing Bibles in hotels across the country. The group's

255

name was soon changed to the Gideons. Within 15 years 250,000 Bibles had been placed in hotels. Today the number is in the millions. The old stone hotel still stands. Tours are available.

Cedar Grove Dutch settlers began arriving here and in nearby Oostburg in 1845. To commemorate their arrival, an annual Holland Festival is held the last weekend of July. The program includes a parade, street scrubbing, and dances performed in colorful Dutch costumes.

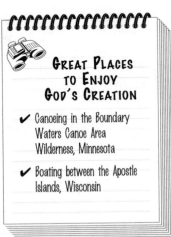

GREAT PLACES TO ENJOY GOD'S CREATION

✔ Canoeing in the Boundary Waters Canoe Area Wilderness, Minnesota

✔ Boating between the Apostle Islands, Wisconsin

Coon Valley Norskedalen is a re-created Scandinavian pioneer village, offering tours of the Bekkum Pioneer Log Farmstead museum, an arboretum, and trails for hiking and skiing. Also here is the Skumsrud Heritage Farm, open weekends from Memorial Day through Labor Day. The farm features an open-air museum with artisans demonstrating and selling their wares. Both the village and the farm are on Rte. 1.

Elkhorn The Webster House here is the restored 19th-century home of Joseph Philbrick Webster, composer of the hymn "In the Sweet Bye and Bye." He also penned about 1,000 others. The home displays a mounted-bird collection and Civil War books and documents. The quaintness of the town itself has earned it the nickname "the Christmas card town."

Ephraim In 1853 Scandinavian Moravians founded this town, which is now a quaint resort community. Despite hardships, they were soon able to build a school and a church. A number of buildings, including the pioneer schoolhouse, the Iverson Parsonage, and the Moravian Church, can be visited. (See Moravians also under Hope, N.J.; Bethlehem, Lititz, and Nazareth, Pa.; Winston-Salem, N.C.; Bloomington, Ill.; Gnadenhutten and New Philadelphia, Ohio.)

Fond du Lac St. Paul's Cathedral on West Division St. is an English Gothic limestone structure with wood carvings from Oberammergau, Germany, and rare ecclesiastical artifacts. Information for self-guided tours is available.

Green Bay When you pick up the brochure "The Green Bay Area European Settlement Church Tour" from the Green Bay Area Visitor Center (1901 S. Oneida St.), you will be directed to nine different historic churches in the city. Featured churches include St. John the Evangelist, built by French Catholics; St. Patrick, built by Irish Catholics; Willebrord, built by Dutch settlers; and St. Francis Xavier, built by Germans.

Heritage Hill State Park (2640 S. Webster Ave.) is a reconstructed village spanning 150 years of Northeastern Wisconsin history. Here you will visit a fur trader's cabin, a frontier fort, and a brick farmhouse. You may also meet a Jesuit missionary, a printer, or a soldier as you explore four different time periods between 1762 and 1905. Summers at the park feature Music on the Green. In December, Heritage Hill hosts "The Spirit of Christmas Past," showcasing historic buildings decorated for the holidays. For more information, go to www.netnet.net/heritagehill.

Green Lake The Green Lake Conference Center (American Baptist) is a 1,000-acre, year-round conference facility. A variety of activities are available from cross country skiing and tobogganing in the winter to tennis and golf (36-hole course) in the summer.

Kenosha Carthage College, a Lutheran liberal arts college established in 1847, is located here on a picturesque campus (2001 Alford Dr.). The campus houses the Palumbo Civil War Museum in the college's art gallery. It's open daily.

Also in Kenosha is Kemper Center (6501 3d Ave.), originally an Episcopalian school and now an arboretum with over 100 species of roses, besides other flowers and herbs.

La Crosse The city of La Crosse was named by French fur traders in the 1700s. They had seen a group of Winnebago Indians playing a ball game using a long-handled racquet that resembled a cross, and the name stuck. The game of lacrosse has changed little since that time.

St. Rose Convent (715 S. 9th St.) is the Mother House of the Franciscan Sisters of Perpetual Adoration. The convent's Chapel of Angels is recognized as one of the most beautiful in the United States. Since August 1, 1978, at least two Franciscan sisters have maintained a 24-hour prayer vigil for the church, community, and the world.

Christ Episcopal Church (111 N. 9th St.) has the traditional features of a European cathedral, including Romanesque architecture, a Gothic cruciform shape, and Italian Renaissance interior. The cathedral also has a magnificent Tiffany window.

St. Joseph the Workman Cathedral (530 Main St.) is a traditional Gothic cathedral with a relief carving of St. Joseph the Workman above the main entrance, depicting the saint with a carpenter's square, symbolizing his labors. The cathedral also has a 1,500-pound bronze canopy over the Botticiano marble altar and stained glass windows depicting Wisconsin's Catholic heritage.

GREAT PLACES FOR FAMILY FUN

✔ The Minnesota Zoo, Minneapolis

✔ The Milwaukee Public Museum

La Farge The area around this town and the nearby town of Ontario are the centers of Amish culture in Wisconsin. Their numbers are estimated at about 8,000 in the state. The Amish are known for their agricultural abilities and also for their old-world craftsmanship. Homemade furniture, quilts, and baked goods draw in visitors to this area from miles away. (See other Amish sites in Pennsylvania, Kentucky, Illinois, Indiana, Iowa, Michigan, Minnesota, Missouri, Ohio, and Kansas.)

Little Norway Located between Blue Mounds and Mount Horeb, this small town contains the restored 1856 homestead of Norwegian immigrant Osten Haugen (3576 Hwy. JG North). In addition to pioneer artifacts, it also has a replica, built in 1885, of a 12th-century Norwegian church, which was used as an exhibition building in Chicago's Columbian Exposition of 1893.

Manitowoc Five miles west of Manitowoc is the Pinecrest Historical Village of Manitowoc County. The County Historical Society has gathered about a dozen 19th-century structures, including distinctly different log cabins, built by Norwegian, German, and Austrian pioneers, and a Presbyterian mission church, built in 1864.

Milwaukee The Mitchell Park Conservatory (524 S. Layton Blvd.) is comprised of three 85-foot-high glass domes housing tropical, arid, and seasonal plants and flowers. At Easter and Christmas the lilies and poinsettias are stunning.

The various ethnic backgrounds of Milwaukee spawned a number of fascinating churches. Calvary Baptist Church on North Teutonia Ave. is the oldest black Baptist congregation. Dating from 1895, it now has about 1,200 members and has built a 72-unit housing project for its senior members.

St. Jehosaphat's Basilica (601 W. Lincoln Rd.) was built for Polish Catholic parishioners. To build it, the pastor purchased marble, paneled mahogany, wrought iron, and copper—500 freight carloads—from the Chicago Post Office, which was being torn down at the time. Its dome is larger than that of the Taj Mahal. Tours are available.

Trinity Evangelical Lutheran Church (2500 S. 68th St.) was built in 1878, although the congregation was formed three decades earlier. It is the mother church of the Missouri Lutheran Synod in Wisconsin. The building has been called one of the state's finest examples of Victorian Gothic design.

Annunciation Greek Orthodox Church was the final major work in the life of Frank Lloyd Wright. He called it "My little jewel—a miniature Santa Sophia." It is located on W. Congress St. It can be seen only on Tuesdays and Fridays by prearranged group tour.

St. John's Cathedral, dedicated in 1853, was the first Roman Catholic cathedral built in Wisconsin. It is located on Cathedral Square, across the street from Cathedral Square Park (N. Jackson St. between Wells and Kilbourn Sts.). Normally it's a quiet park, built on the site of Milwaukee's first courthouse. But if you are there on a Thursday in the summer, you may not find it quiet, because that's the night of the free jazz concerts, Jazz in the Park.

At Marquette University two churches are major attractions: St. Joan of Arc Chapel, which was transported stone by stone from the Rhone Valley of France; and the Gesu Church, with its spires and rose stained glass. In the Haggerty Museum of Art on N. 13th St. on campus is a fascinating Bible series of more than 100 hand-colored etchings by Marc Chagall.

New Glarus In the Swiss Historical Village (612 7th Ave.), you can relive Swiss history. It contains a replica of the first Swiss log church built here for worship in 1849. Also included are a blacksmith shop, schoolhouse, store, cabin, and cheese factory. It is located at Rtes. 39 and 69.

Pepin The Laura Ingalls Wilder Little House (where she was born in 1867) is located 7 miles north of town (Cty. CC) and the Laura Ingalls Museum (the Pepin Historical Museum) is in the town itself (306 3d St.). It is full of displays and memorabilia. William Cullen Bryant said that Lake Pepin "ought to be visited in the summer by every poet and painter in the land." (See Wilder also under Burr Oak, Iowa; Spring Valley and Walnut Grove, Minn.; Mansfield, Mo.; Independence, Kans.; and De Smet, S.D.)

Peshtigo In October 1871, at the same time that the Great Fire ravaged Chicago, Peshtigo was destroyed by a conflagration that consumed 2,400 square miles of timberland. About 1,000 citizens perished, and the town virtually disappeared. Today the town is a small manufacturing center and commemorates the fire with the Peshtigo Fire Museum (400 Oconto Ave.), housed in the Congregational church that was built immediately after the fire.

Racine The DeKoven Foundation for Church Work (600 21st St.) was formerly Racine College, founded in 1852 as an Episcopal school. Since 1935 it has served as a retreat and conference center, a summer camp, and a center for Episcopal activities. Eight buildings on the 40-acre property were all built between 1850 and 1870 and include the centrally located St. John's Chapel. The original interior of the chapel with its oak pews, trusses, and stained glass windows has been preserved.

Also built in 1852 is the First Presbyterian Church on College Ave. It is the oldest church building in Racine and has been praised by architectural historians for its simple Greek Revival architecture.

St. Francis St. Francis Seminary (3257 S. Lake Dr.) was founded in the mid-19th century to train priests for the German Catholic immigrant community. Henni Hall, the original seminary building, still stands. During the half century after its founding, a convent, an orphan asylum, and a school for the deaf were begun as well.

St. Nazianz In 1854 a group of 113 German Catholic immigrants came here and established a communal settlement. Its founder,

Father Ambrose Oschwald, was too independent to find favor with either Catholic authorities or the Wisconsin state officials. But within 20 years, the colony had built a stone church, convent, monastery, school, orphanage, hospital, seminary, numerous cottages, a central kitchen, and a variety of shops. After Oschwald's death, the group associated with the Salvatorian Order of the Catholic Church. Most of the original buildings are now gone, but about a half dozen remain.

Shell Lake The Museum of Woodcarving features the largest collection of wood carvings in the world created by one man. The figures are extraordinarily beautiful in their detail and portray a strong religious theme. Joseph Barta claimed that divine help enabled him to create over 100 life-size figures and over 400 miniature carvings in about 30 years time. The most stunning is a life-size carving of Leonardo da Vinci's *The Last Supper.*

Shullsburg This small town near Platteville has streets named Charity, Friendship, Justice, Mercy, and Hope, and still looks like a 19th-century village with about 50 buildings dating back a century or more. Friar Samuel Mazzuchelli, who named the streets, also designed many of the local buildings. His 1844 masterpiece, the Church of St. Augustine, is in New Diggings, a half dozen miles southeast, and he was buried in Benton in a cemetery behind St. Patrick Church.

Waukesha The Elmbrook Church (777 S. Barker Rd.), pastored by Stuart Briscoe, may be the largest Protestant church in the state with about 6,000 in attendance each Sunday. Briscoe and his wife, Jill, are prolific writers of Christian literature and are much in demand as speakers.

Wausau Salem Lutheran Church on Sixth St. has a pipe organ designed after a 17th-century Bach favorite. The pipes are from Germany, but the intricate oak woodwork is from the United States.

Wisconsin Dells The Biblical Gardens on Clara Ave. has handcrafted statues depicting the life of Christ in 15 tableaux. Open May through October, it is located in a sandstone canyon with a brook and flower gardens.

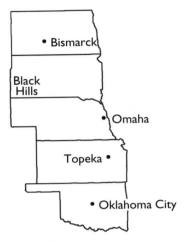

Great Plains States

THE CONTRIBUTIONS of the Great Plains states to American history lie largely in providing the means to get somewhere else. This vast prairie was the crossroads of many of the historic trails used by pioneers heading west for better lives and by cattle drivers on their way to market. The Oregon Trail, the Lewis and Clark Route, the Mormon Trail, the Chisholm and Santa Fe Trails, and others were the highway system of a long-lost era.

But don't be mistaken. There is great beauty in this fertile land and plenty to see and do along the way. Visitors can enjoy great scenic beauty in the Black Hills, visit frontier forts built to protect and provision travelers, and see historic sites associated with the pioneer trails. Christian travelers will especially enjoy a variety of Indian missions located throughout the region, sites that explore the sometimes uneasy relationship between native peoples and the ministers who tried to educate and serve them.

■KANSAS

Atchison The strong Catholic heritage of this town dates back to within a few years of the city's founding. Benedictine monks first came here in 1858, four years after the town was settled, and established St. Benedict's Abbey. The Benedictine Sisters arrived just a few years later. Both communities established schools: St. Benedict's College for men and Mount St. Scholastica College for women. In 1971 they were merged to become Benedictine College (1020 N. 2d St.). Today the abbey and convent, with their beautiful chapels, are fascinating places to visit. The Benedictine Sisters have transformed some of their former school buildings into the Mount Conference Center (710 S. 9th St.), which hosts religious retreats, conferences, and meetings.

Don't miss Trinity Episcopal Church (300 S. 5th St.) and St. Patrick's Church (two miles west of US 73 on 234th Rd.). Trinity, built in 1868, is the church in which native daughter Amelia Earhart was baptized in 1897. The interior features walnut woodwork and beautiful stained glass windows.

St. Patrick's is the oldest structure in continuous use in the Roman Catholic Archdiocese of Kansas City. The beautiful stone church was also built in 1868 and stands on a hill overlooking the scenic valley settled by Irish farmers in the late 1850s.

Baldwin City Baker University (United Methodist) is the state's oldest four-year college. Besides the Old Castle, which houses a museum containing many antiques and historical exhibits, the university library has the Quayle Bible Collection with clay tablets from Old Testament times, a synagogue scroll, a Gutenberg leaf, 15th-century Bibles, and more. Guided tours are available.

Cedar Vale The Wee Kirk of the Valley may be the smallest church in the United States. Its six pews seat two persons each, symbolizing all that would have been needed for the twelve disciples. It is located in south central Kansas, six miles south of Cedar Vale. (See other "smallest" houses of worship in Florence, Ky.; Savannah, Ga.; Festina, Iowa; and Highlandville, Mo.)

Council Grove Located on the Santa Fe Trail, the Kaw Mission was established in 1851 by the Methodist Episcopal Church South. Built of native stone, the two-story building contained eight rooms and was designed to accommodate 50 students. Only male students who were orphans or dependants of the Kaw tribe were sent to the mission. While the site operated for only three years before the Kaw were moved to an Oklahoma reservation, the Kaw Mission State Historic Site (500 N. Mission) features an interesting history of the lives and cultures of Native Americans in this area as well as the history of the Santa Fe Trail.

Elk Falls The entire town of Elk Falls calls itself a "living ghost town." Located in the Kansas Ozarks, it has a visitors center in the middle of town with walking maps that will take you to the Little White Church built in 1880, the 1893 Iron Truss Bridge, as well as Tiffany's Gallery (for collectibles) and the Cape Cod Bakery and Restaurant.

Fairway In this Kansas City suburb, visitors can tour the Shawnee Indian Mission (3403 W. 53d St.). Begun in 1839 by the Methodist missionary the Reverend Thomas Johnson, the mission sought to teach basic academics, trade skills, and agriculture to Native American children and young adults. The mission closed in 1862. You can learn more about the Johnson family and their students through exhibits and furnishings at the mission.

Fort Scott The fort was established by the U.S. Army in 1842 to protect the Permanent Indian Frontier. In 1853 the Army abandoned the site as the frontier moved westward, and the buildings became the town of Fort Scott. Today Fort Scott National Historic Site (Old Fort Blvd.) contains 20 major historic structures, 33 historically furnished rooms, museum exhibits, and a bookstore. Interpretive programs, guided tours, and special events are offered throughout the year.

Goessel This small town was founded a century ago by Russian Mennonites who bought land from the Santa Fe Railroad for $2.37 an acre. The Mennonite Heritage Museum on Poplar St. includes a replica of an immigrant house built by the railroad for new arrivals. The museum also contains items from early farms, schools, and churches and a six-foot Liberty Bell fashioned from Turkey Red wheat. Admission is $2.50.

Great Bend The Barton County Historical Society Museum and Village, located just south of the Arkansas River bridge, has nine historic buildings, including St. Paul's Lutheran Church (built in 1898), the post office, schoolhouse, and Santa Fe depot.

Hays The Ellis County Historical Society Museum on W. 7th St. is housed in a 19th-century church building. In it you'll find a replica of an early schoolroom and changing exhibits of the possessions of early settlers.

Highland The Highland Presbyterian Mission, three miles east of town on Rte. 1, was built for Iowa, Sac, and Fox Indians in 1837. It was the first white settlement in the county. Today the mission houses the Native American Heritage Museum

THE INDIAN MISSIONS IN KANSAS

If there is one dark blot on American history's textbook pages, it is surely its treatment of Native Americans. Eventually the U.S. government forced the country's native tribes to relinquish nearly all their lands, substituting smaller parcels that were frequently as worthless to the new inhabitants as they were to the U.S. government.

But whatever the political climate, missionaries did their best to minister to Native Americans and improve their lot. The Kaw Mission in Council Grove was a Methodist Mission dedicated to caring for male orphans or dependants of the Kaw Indians, providing them with room and board, education, and religious and vocational training. The Shawnee Mission in Fairway provided the same amenities to the children of the Shawnee and Delaware tribes. And the Native American Heritage Museum in Highland was originally a Presbyterian Mission providing education and training to the Iowa, Sac, and Fox Indians. By 1870 nearly all of the missions were closed as Congress authorized the extinction of native land titles in Kansas and the resettling of displaced tribes in Indian Territory.

Visitors traveling through Kansas today will have many opportunities to visit historic American forts like Fort Larned, Fort Leavenworth, and Fort Scott. Travelers will also have opportunities to visit traditional Native American sites like the Pawnee Indian Village. But the opportunities to experience sincere attempts at reconciliation between Americans and Native Americans will generally be found in only one place—the Indian Missions.

State Historic Site, which highlights the cultural heritage of many different area tribes. Admission is free, but donations are appreciated. It is open Tuesday through Saturday.

Hillsboro The headquarters of the Mennonite Brethren Church of North America and Tabor College, the denominational school, are both located in this community. The area was settled by immigrants from Russia and Poland in the late 1870s. The denomination has a doctrinal position similar to that of other Mennonites but the Mennonite Brethren have a stronger emphasis on the importance of a religious experience.

The Pioneer Adobe House Museum (at 501 Ash St.) was built in 1876 by a Mennonite family, using adobe bricks and mud and slough grass on the roof. A windmill is also on the grounds.

To get a taste of German cooking, stop in at The Olde Towne Restaurant on N. Main, where you can sample cherry mos, zwiebach, verenika, and homemade German sausage.

Holton The Sanctuary is an ecumenical Christian ministry committed to providing a quiet place for prayer, solitude, and spiritual growth. The cozy quarters are located in a quiet setting on a lake (720 Iowa St.). While it is operated by a Presbyterian minister, it is open to all faiths.

Hutchinson This is Mennonite country. Eight miles west of town is the Mennonite Dutch Kitchen Restaurant, where you can get fresh pies and go bonkers over bread or spicy cinnamon rolls. Doesn't that make your mouth water?

South of Hutchinson in the little town of Yoder is the heart of Amish country. Several interesting stores that reflect the Amish heritage are located here: Dutch Mill Bakery, Home Place, Koffahaus, Yoder Cafe, and Yoder Furniture factory are among them. (See other Amish sites in Pennsylvania, Kentucky, Illinois, Indiana, Iowa, Michigan, Minnesota, Missouri, Ohio, and Wisconsin.)

Independence Little House on the Prairie, 13 miles southwest of town on US 75, is a reconstructed log cabin showing the place where Laura Ingalls Wilder lived from 1869 to 1871. Also displayed at the site are a post office and a one-room schoolhouse. (See Wilder also under Burr Oak, Iowa; Spring Valley and Walnut Grove, Minn.; Mansfield, Mo.; Pepin, Wisc.; and De Smet, S.D.)

Junction City St. Paul's Lutheran Church (six miles southeast, located at 5805 Clark's Creek Rd.) is a light-colored stone church. It was organized in 1861 after a missionary came by horse and buggy to preach the first Lutheran sermon in the area. That sermon was repeated to the settlers in the entire Clark's Creek valley, and soon a congregation began meeting. The church is still in use today; it includes a small museum.

Larned Fort Larned (six miles west of Larned on Hwy. 156) was built to protect travelers along the Santa Fe Trail, and today it has nine restored sandstone buildings as they appeared in 1860. The restored fort is regarded as one of the best preserved vestiges of the Santa Fe Trail–Indian wars era. Within four miles of the fort is the Santa Fe Trail Center on Rte. 3, which chronicles the history of the trail and the settlement of the region.

Liberal This town is known for at least three things. First is its annual Shrove Tuesday pancake race against the housewives of Olney, England. According to tradition, an Olney housewife in the year 1445 was in such a rush to get to church that she forgot to leave her cooking at home. Ever since then, Olney housewives, and more recently in competition with Liberal housewives, have been engaged in an annual skillet-wielding race.

Liberal is also known for the Mid-America Air Museum (2000 W. 2d St.), the largest aviation museum in Kansas. More than 80 aircraft are on display. Additional facilities include the 6,000-square-foot Aviator's Memorial Chapel.

Dorothy's House (567 E. Cedar St.) is a simulation of the farmhouse from which Dorothy and Toto were whisked away by a twister into the Land of Oz. Dorothy's room is restored to resemble the set of the 1939 movie. If you believe in Dorothy, you'll have to believe in the farmhouse.

Lindsborg Bethany College (421 N. 1st St.) is a Swedish Lutheran school here with a strong music emphasis. Each year, since 1882, the Messiah Festival of Music and Art is held during Easter week. At first the choir was composed of untrained villagers and farmers who practiced long and hard to sing Handel's *Messiah,* and now the choir has become the Bethany Oratorio Society, one of the oldest continuously active oratorio societies in the country.

The Birger Sandzen Memorial Gallery on the Bethany College campus features the works of the Swedish-American painter of the same name.

The McPherson County Old Mill Museum Complex (120 Mill St.), five blocks south, displays historic buildings, pioneer exhibits, and Swedish costumes.

Lucas Back in 1904 a disabled Civil War veteran, S. P. Dinsmoor, built a cabin out of stone and cement and around it created his idea of the Garden of Eden (2d and Kansas Sts.). It features cement figures on the ground and perched in trees. In all, he used more than 113 tons of cement to make his statues, which include a combination of biblical characters and allegorical figures that express his theological and political views. Above his Garden of Eden flies a red, white, and blue American flag.

Lyons Four miles west of town on US 56 is a large granite cross commemorating the first Christian martyr on the North American continent. When Coronado explored the New World, he had with him a Catholic priest named Juan de Padilla. About a year after Coronado had completed his exploration, Padilla returned as a missionary, but shortly after beginning his missionary work, he was attacked and killed.

Medicine Lodge Carry Nation's Home at Hwy. 160 and Oak St. commemorates the temperance leader of the past century who used her hatchet, Bible, and loud-voiced prayers to put many taverns and saloons out of business. Her first demonstration for temperance occurred in Medicine Lodge in 1899 when she and several other women held a prayer meeting in front of one of the town's seven saloons, after which she attacked the front door with an umbrella. Her home is now a museum.

Mission Hills The Shawnee Indian Methodist Mission on West 53d St. was established in 1830 by Thomas Johnson as a school for Indian children. It also housed the first territorial legislature when it met in 1855. Both the Oregon and Santa Fe Trails passed through the complex.

Newton In the 1870s Mennonite groups began leaving Russia in fear of religious persecution. Among them was one of Kansas' most famous Mennonite immigrants, Bernhard Warkentin. His letters home to Russia described the fertile Kansas prairie and the promise it held for farming the Turkey Red hard winter wheat. Ultimately those letters home persuaded more than 5,000 Mennonites to settle in Kansas, and the state has been up to its armpits in wheat ever since.

The Mennonite influence in Kansas is more obvious than the wheat fields. The Warkentin House (211 E. 1st St.) will convince you that Bernhard Warkentin was not a simple man when it came to housing. His home could more accurately be described as a Victorian mansion.

You can learn more about the Mennonite influence at the Kauffman Museum (N. Main and 27th Sts.). The museum highlights Central Plains culture and natural history with a special emphasis on the immigration of the Mennonites.

If you're looking for a souvenir to take home with you, consider shopping at Ten Thousand Villages (625 N. Main St.). Sponsored by the Mennonite Central Committee, this nonprofit shop features crafts from 30 developing countries around the world.

Newton is the headquarters of the Mennonite General Con-

THE RUSSIAN MENNONITES IN KANSAS

Bernhard Warkentin was born in the village of Altonau of the Molotschna Mennonite settlement in the Ukraine in 1847. When he was 25, he arrived in the United States to study this country's agricultural, economic, and political climate.

Once here, Warkentin realized that Mennonite farmers would be a great benefit to the development of the Great Plains states. He encouraged his Mennonite brethren to settle in Kansas and to bring with them Turkey Red hard winter wheat. His efforts, coupled with the advertising campaign of the American railroad companies, resulted in about 15,000 Mennonites coming to the United States, the vast majority of whom settled in Kansas. In the fall of 1874 the Kansas countryside was first sown with Turkey Red wheat, the hardy high-yield grain that has given Kansas its enormous productivity and has helped make this region the breadbasket of the world.

The Mennonite influence in Harvey County, the area with the highest Mennonite concentration, is clearly visible. Nearly two dozen Mennonite churches, two colleges, a nationally recognized mental health center, several halfway houses, the Mennonite Press, and the Mennonite national headquarters are located here, each founded and supported by Mennonites. Visitors to Kansas today will also see signs of the early Mennonites' settlement of the area. In Newton visitors can tour the Kauffman Museum, with its special emphasis on the local Mennonite population, and the Warkentin House, an elaborate Victorian mansion that proves not all Mennonites live simply.

And the wheat fields are unmistakable.

ference (722 N. Main St.) and also the location of the denomination's Bethel College (27th and N. Main Sts.). This group of Mennonites does not incorporate foot-washing as an ordinance of the church nor does it require women to have their heads covered.

Osawatomie The Old Stone Church (Sixth and Parker Sts.) is a restoration of one of the first pioneer churches in the state. Dedicated in 1861, the church was started by Samuel Adair, brother-in-law of abolitionist John Brown. The Samuel Adair Historic Site (at Tenth and Main Sts.) contains a statue of John Brown, who sometimes stayed here. The cabin was a station on the Underground Railroad, helping African Americans flee slavery. (See Underground Railroad also under Camden, Del.; Buffalo, N.Y.; Macon, Ga.; Ottumwa, Iowa; Marshall, Mich.; and Ripley, Ohio.)

Oskaloosa Old Jefferson Town on Hwy. 59 contains a collection of vintage buildings moved from other locations. Included is the Edmonds Church, built in 1891 and still used for Easter sunrise services and weddings.

Pawnee Rock Heartland Farm (Rte. 1) is an 80-acre farm and organic gardens owned and operated by Dominican Sisters. Organic produce is sold to the community and to area restaurants. A silo has been converted into a chapel, and a granary is now an art studio. Cottages on the farm may be used by individuals for retreats or quiet vacations.

Pleasanton The St. Philippine Duchesne Shrine, six miles west of town, preserves the site of a Pottawatomie Indian settlement, founded with the help of Jesuit priests and nuns. An elderly nun, Sister Rose Philippine Duchesne, was devoted to the Pottawatomies in the mid-1800s. The 168-acre park also includes nature trails and picnic facilities.

Topeka Charles Fox Parham, a founder of modern Pentecostalism, founded Bethel Bible School here in 1890 to train missionary evangelists. (The school is no longer in existence.) The modern-day Pentecostal movement is often traced to the day in 1901 when one of the students spoke in tongues. Parham taught that speaking in tongues was the sign of Spirit baptism.

Charles Sheldon, author of *In His Steps,* which has sold more than 20 million copies, became the first pastor of the Central Congregational Church at 1248 S.W. Buchanan St. in 1898. The book was developed from messages he preached in his church. There has been a new surge of interest in the book recently because of the popular question, "What would Jesus do?"

Victoria The Cathedral of the Plains (900 Cathedral St.), erected in 1908 to 1911, was built mostly by hand labor. Officially it is the St. Fidelis Church, 220 feet long and 141 feet high. It was built from native limestone, but the stained glass windows were imported from Germany.

Twelve miles south of Victoria in the little town of Pfeifer is the Holy Cross Shrine, completed in 1918. Its red and blue stained glass windows are supported by delicate vaulted arches and pillars. It has been called the "two cents church," because each family in the parish was asked to donate two cents on each bushel of wheat they grew while it was being built.

Wamego This Dutch settlement celebrates its annual Tulip Festival the third weekend in April when thousands of Holland tulips are in bloom. In the Wamego City Park is an Old Dutch Mill and Wamego Museum complex remembering the period of the 1870s when the city was getting its start. The park also contains the White Chapel School, a jail, and a log cabin.

Wichita The city of Wichita has a number of historic churches where you may want to worship. First Presbyterian Church (525 N. Broadway St.), begun in 1870, has extraordinary stained glass windows that depict the lives of early Wichita settlers. St. John's Episcopal (402 N. Topeka St.), begun in 1887, is a magnificent Gothic-style building. Also worth visiting are First Baptist Church (216 E. 2d St.), the First United Methodist Church (330 N. Broadway St.), and the Cathedral of the Immaculate Conception, also known as St. Mary's Cathedral (307 E. Central Ave.).

Friends University (2100 W. University St.), associated with the Mid-America Yearly Meeting of Friends, is located here, and is one of the largest of the Friends' colleges.

Calvary Baptist Church on North Water St. houses the First National Black Historical Museum and Cultural Center of Kansas. In addition to year-round exhibits, the museum is also the site of holiday caroling and spiritual assemblies that make the place burst with gospel music.

If you enjoy gardens, visit Botanica, the Wichita Gardens (701 N. Amidon St.). More than nine acres of perennials and woody plants grace the grounds, as well as dozens of fountains and pools.

■NEBRASKA

Tourist Info
Phone 800-228-4307
Web sites
  Entire state   www.visitnebraska.org
  Lincoln   www.lincoln.org/cvb
  Omaha   www.visitomaha.com
For a complete list of updated links, visit www.christiantraveler.com

Aurora The Plainsman Museum (two miles north of town at 210 16th St.) has exhibits that date back to 1859. Of special interest are its plains sod house and its prairie chapel. Thirteen shops are located on the boardwalk.

Bellevue According to historians, the first sermon in Nebraska's history was preached here in 1833 by Moses Merrill, a Baptist minister. He was authorized by the Baptist Missionary Union to build a "dwelling house and a school" at a cost not to exceed 500 dollars. The Presbyterians came shortly afterward, and the oldest church in Nebraska was built here by Presbyterians in 1856 to 1858. But the most common type of Sunday services in the area was at a wagon trail encampment, as described by a Bellevue newspaper in 1854. A tin horn would call the worshipers together in a corral, where they would sit under wagons to take advantage of the shade. A young theological student, who was also the ox driver in the train, officiated as the preacher.

Blair Dana College (2848 College Dr.), begun by Danish Lutherans, is located here, and the Danish influence is strong throughout the area. The 250-acre campus is landscaped with gas lamps from Copenhagen, and the library's heritage room displays Bing and Grondahl and Royal Copenhagen Christmas plates. The first Sunday in December the college hosts a Danish Christmas Festival.

Boys Town A National Historic Site, Boys Town (just west of Omaha at Dodge Rd. and 137th St.) was founded by Irish-born Father Edward Flanagan in 1917. Today its 900 acres are home to more than 550 troubled young boys and girls and headquarters for its nationwide youth care programs. Annually tens of thousands of visitors enjoy the All-American Rose Garden and the Garden of the Bible, which are tended by resident youths. Two lovely Gothic chapels, one Catholic and one Protestant, are open for services, a reminder of Father Flanagan's ecumenism. ("Every boy must learn how to pray. How he prays is up to him," he said.) Flanagan House was the home where Father Flanagan lived and worked, and various displays demonstrate why the famous priest believed, "There's no such thing as a bad boy or girl."

Bridgeport Twelve miles west on Rte. 2 is the Oregon Trail Wagon Train. This is a re-creation of an 1840s wagon train with authentic covered wagons. You can sign up for a one- to four-day trip and enjoy the chuck wagon cookouts and the other activities that the early settlers experienced. Reservations are essential. Phone 308-586-1850.

Fremont The Fremont and Elkhorn Valley Railroad (N. Somers Ave.) features train rides on vintage rail cars. Reservations recommended. Phone 402-727-0615.

Grand Island Railroad Town is part of the Stuhr Museum of the Prairie Pioneer (3133 W. US 34). There are 60 buildings here that were built nearly a century ago, including the cottage where actor Henry Fonda was born.

Hastings Asmat Museum at Crosier Monastery (223 E. 14th St.) houses a collection of rare art forms preserved by American missionaries who have worked with primitive Asmat people of New Guinea. The works are mostly wood carvings from various areas.

Hastings College (800 Turner Ave.), a Presbyterian school with slightly more than 1,000 students, is located here. Situated on 88 acres, it offers a variety of cultural events throughout the academic year. Its art gallery is open every day, and its theater and music departments put on productions and recitals frequently.

Keystone The Little Church at Keystone was the brainstorm of 11 teenage girls. Built jointly by Catholics and Protestants, the church was erected in 1908. The girls saw the shared building as the ideal means of providing a necessary meeting place for both congregations. At the north end was a Catholic altar, and at the south end a Protestant one. Pews had reversible backs. During Catholic Masses, worshipers faced the Catholic altar. Then the pew backs were flipped over so the Protestant congregation could face its altar. The church was in use until 1949. You can tour the little church if you phone ahead: 308-726-2281. Admission is free.

Lincoln In 1939 Theodore Epp launched the first *Back to the Bible* broadcast in this city and he directed the broadcast for the next 45 years. Now Woodrow Kroll is the speaker and three other broadcasts are also produced, including one with Elisabeth Elliot called *Gateway to Joy*. In addition, the organization now has offices and agencies in 15 countries around the world and produces original programming in 25 languages.

> Consequently, you are no longer foreigners and aliens, but fellow citizens with God's people and members of God's household.
> EPHESIANS 2:19

Early in its history, Lincoln was called "the Holy City" because it contained 100 churches, and at that time a population of only 70,000. Because Methodism was strong here, the St. Paul Methodist Church had several enlargements before its present structure took form.

As a young lawyer, William Jennings Bryan went to Congress from Lincoln, and the Old Bryan House (a private dwelling on D St.) was where he received one of his presidential nominations. (See Bryan also under Dayton, Tenn., and Salem, Ill.)

Among the many attractions of Lincoln, one of the most unusual is the National Museum of Roller Skating (on South St.), the only museum in the world dedicated to roller skating.

Minden At the Kearney County Courthouse in the town square each Christmas, *The Light of the World* Christmas pageant is presented, telling the story of Christ's birth. The outdoor pageant, performed by local citizens, is illuminated with 10,000 lights.

Harold Warp's Pioneer Village (at US 6, US 34, and Hwy. 10) will give you a taste of what pioneer living was all about. This amazing collection of early Americana covers three city blocks with more than 30 buildings. Also included are locomotives, 350 antique autos, and 22 historic airplanes. The crafts demonstrations and the horse-drawn covered wagon ride are popular attractions.

Omaha The world's largest indoor rain forest has made the Henry Doorly Zoo (3701 S. 10th St.) the number one tourist attraction between Chicago and Denver. Also on site are the Kingdom of the Seas Aquarium and the Lozier IMAX Theater.

St. Cecilia's Cathedral at 701 N. 40th St. is a Spanish Renaissance cathedral with a white Carrera marble altar from Italy. Its Our Lady of Nebraska Chapel contains stained glass windows from a 16th-century cathedral in Pamplona, Spain.

One of the most respected Christian radio stations in the nation is KGBI of Omaha. It is a ministry of Grace College of the Bible (840 Pine St.).

Red Cloud This is Willa Cather–land, the town in which she grew up. Her novels *O Pioneers!, My Antonia,* and *One of Ours* all tell of life in this part of Nebraska. Many Cather landmarks are scattered throughout the town. One that might be overlooked is Grace Episcopal Church (325 N. Webster St.), which she joined when she was 49 years old. Another church that figures in her writings is Dane Church on Bladen Rd., south of town. (See Cather also under Santa Fe., N.M.)

Scottsbluff The clay and sandstone highlands of Scotts Bluff National Monument were landmarks for travelers along the Mormon and Oregon Trails in the 1940s. For many years the bluff was too dangerous to cross, but in the 1850s a route was opened through Mitchell's Pass, where scores of wagon trains wore deep ruts in the sandstone. Evidence of these early pioneers can still be seen on the half-mile stretch of the original Oregon Trail preserved at the pass. Twenty miles east on Rte. 92 is another pioneer landmark, Chimney Rock. Those pioneers must have been tired of the flat prairie; they described Chimney Rock as "towering to the heavens." You won't be quite as impressed, but then you're probably traveling by air-conditioned automobile. Nonetheless, the 500-foot tower served as an important inspiration and is visible from more than 30 miles away.

York Near here is the historic Mennonite village tracing the Mennonite religious heritage from when they fled Russia in 1874 to their religious freedom in York County, Nebraska.

September in York is fun for the family at Yorkfest with everything from hot air balloon rides to a children's fair and a quilt show.

■NORTH DAKOTA

Tourist Info
Phone 800-HELLO-ND
Web sites
  Entire state   www.ndtourism.com
  Bismarck   www.bismarck-mandancvb.org
For a complete list of updated links, visit www.christiantraveler.com

Bismarck The 19-story state capitol (600 E. Boulevard Ave.) is visible for miles across the flat Dakota landscape. Free tours of the limestone and marble art deco capitol are available weekdays all year-round, as well as summer weekends.

Across the street from the capitol is the North Dakota Heritage Center, the state's largest museum and archive. Exhibits include pioneer and Native American artifacts and national history displays. Admission is free.

To get to the history-rich Fort Abraham Lincoln State Park, you can take the Fort Lincoln trolley from the town of Mandan (phone 701-663-9018) or the Lewis and Clark paddle wheeler from Bismarck (N. River Rd., phone 701-255-4233). Either one will get you to the place where Gen. George Custer was stationed before he initiated his fateful last stand.

Bottineau In this town near the Canadian border is the Monument to the Four Chaplains in memory of the chaplains who sacrificed their lives during World War II when the ship *Dochester* went down. The monument is at 4th and Sinclair Sts.

Dickinson Once an oil town, Dickinson is now known for its great dinosaur deposits. Children especially will enjoy the Dakota Dinosaur Museum (200 Museum Dr. off I-94 at exit 61), with its ten full-scale dinosaurs and other fossil, mineral, and animal collections.

Dunseith Thirteen miles north of town on the Canadian border is the International Peace Garden, a 2,300-acre garden that straddles the border between the United States and Canada. The stone tablet states the purpose: "To God in His Glory . . . we two nations dedicate this garden and pledge ourselves that as long as man shall live we will not take arms against one another." More than 120,000 annuals grace both sides of the line. The border walk extends 1.5 miles past fountains, pools, cascades, the Perennial Garden, Arbor Garden, arboretum, Sunken Garden, and the bell tower. In addition, the International Music Camp, which is held here annually, features Saturday concerts.

Fargo Bonanzaville, USA, is a restored pioneer village with more than 45 buildings on "fifteen acres of valley heritage." Included are a train depot, the Plains Indian Museum, and log cabins.

The Children's Museum at Yunker Farm (28th Ave. N) is open year-round and is a hands-on museum that children will enjoy.

Jamestown Frontier Village here is open from May through September and includes an 1881 church, trading post, fire department, post office, and barber house among its many buildings. Admission is free.

The 1914 Basilica of St. James (First Ave. S) is the only basilica in North Dakota and one of only 34 in the nation.

Medora Medora in western North Dakota is the state's biggest tourist attraction. Founded in 1883 by the Marquis de Mores, it soon became a ghost town after facing repeated disasters. It was resurrected about four decades ago. Today it has a 2,750-seat amphitheater and 13 family attractions. The Medora Musical, dedicated to Theodore Roosevelt, runs from mid-June through Labor Day. Guided tours of the 26-room chateau built by de Mores are given daily.

Minot Eastern North Dakota is Scandinavian country. Each fall the Norsk Hostfest in Minot attracts 60,000 Scandinavians to the celebration. In addition to traditional Norwegian foods, big-name entertainers are featured in the All Seasons Arena.

The Scandinavian Heritage Center on South Broadway claims to be the world's only outdoor living museum that is dedicated to preserving the ethnic heritage of all five Scandinavian countries. On the premises are a storage house and a 225-year-old house, both from Norway.

Richardton The Assumption Abbey (418 3d Ave. W) here is a Benedictine monastery known as the Cathedral of the Northwest. Its library contains some priceless 16th-century volumes, which can be viewed. St. Mary's Catholic Church (418 3d Ave. E), built in 1884, is open daily.

GREAT PLACES TO ENJOY GOD'S CREATION

✔ A picnic at Painted Canyon Overlook, Theodore Roosevelt National Park, North Dakota

✔ Exploring Badlands National Park, South Dakota

Sentinel Butte West of Medora is the site of Father Cassedy's Home on the Range for Boys (16351 I-94), which is a nonsectarian establishment similar to Boys Town.

Walhalla The town is known as home to North Dakota's largest concentration of moose as well as one of the state's best ski areas, but it also boasts some historic sites, including an 1851 trading post and a log-hewn oak house and store, said to be the oldest remaining structures built by whites in North Dakota. Eleven miles south of the town is a marker that indicates it is the Oak Lawn Church State Historic Site. It was the location of a Presbyterian church built in 1885 by Rev. Ransom Waite. Unfortunately it burned in 1954.

Washburn North of Bismarck about 40 miles is this town where famed explorers Meriwether Lewis and William Clark endured the severe winter of 1804 and 1805. A number of attractions relate to Lewis and Clark's commission to map the new territory acquired in the Louisiana Purchase of 1803. The Lewis and Clark Interpretive Center (junction of Rtes. 83 and 200A) describes the expedition's stay in North Dakota, where they were joined by the guide Sacajawea, her husband, and her infant son. Bicentennial celebrations of the historic journey will center around the Interpretive Center in 2004.

Several miles west of Washburn in the town of Stanton is the Knife River Indian Villages National Historic Site. A museum on site examines the history and culture of the local Hidatsa, Mandan, and Arikara tribes, who helped Lewis and Clark survive the difficult winter. (See Lewis and Clark also under Great Falls, Mont., and Astoria and Portland, Ore.)

■OKLAHOMA

Tourist Info
Phone 800-652-6552
Web sites
Entire state   www.travelok.com
Oklahoma City   www.okccvb.org
Tulsa   www.tourism.tulsachamber.com
For a complete list of updated links, visit www.christiantraveler.com

Ardmore St. Phillips Church (East and McLish Sts.) is a small copy of the design of Merton College, Oxford University, England. The stained glass windows tell the story of Christ's ascension, Christ the Good Shepherd, Paul before Agrippa, and the angel with the women at Christ's empty tomb.

Bartlesville Twenty miles south of Bartlesville on Rte. 123 is Woolaroc, once a ranch, now a drive-through wildlife preserve that is home to bison and 40 other species. The preserve surrounds a museum of western memorabilia, including gun and rifle exhibits, Native American artifacts, and western art by artists like Remington and Russell.

Chouteau Oklahoma's first printing press and first publications can be traced to this place and date about 1835. A Presbyterian missionary, Samuel Worcester, came from Georgia with the Cherokee Indians and produced a book called *The Child's Book* in the Creek language. An earlier Presbyterian missionary had begun a school here in 1821.

Clinton The Oklahoma Route 66 Museum (2229 Gary Blvd.) honors the traveler, and that's what you are. So consider yourself honored. Exhibits are grouped by decade, beginning with Route 66's construction in the 1920s, the Dust Bowl of the '30s, the military highways of the '40s, and the family vacation days of the '50s, complete with a diner and drive-in movie theater.

Colony On the first and third Saturdays of each month a country, bluegrass, and gospel revue is held at what used to be a general store in town. The event is called the Colony Jamboree. The evening begins at 6 P.M. and ends at 10 P.M. so that "everyone can wake up in time to go to church the next morning."

Coweta Bill Bright, evangelist and founder of Campus Crusade for Christ, was born here in 1921. The town of Coweta was a Creek Indian town in which a Presbyterian minister set up a mission school in 1850. The Presbyterian missionary, Robert M. Loughridge, and his wife are buried near Haskell, where they had begun a boarding school for Creek children.

Dougherty Four miles east of Price Falls in this little crossroads is where Roy Rogers and Dale Evans were married. Today it is better known as the home of the Catfish Kitchen and Steak House (Hwy. 110), which has a fabulous weekend buffet.

Enid On the eastern edge of the city is Phillips University (100 N. University Ave.), a school affiliated with the Christian Church (Disciples of Christ), set on 36 acres. Just south of the school is the Lake View Assembly Grounds, where Enid's annual Easter morning service is held.

Fairview Oklahoma's largest population of Mennonites is in this area. The Major County Historical Museum (1.5 miles east of town on Rte. 58) shows historical artifacts. On the weekend after Thanksgiving the Mennonite Relief Sale is held on the County Fairgrounds, beginning with a chicken dinner on Friday night and ending with a quilt auction on Saturday night with more than 100 homemade quilts auctioned off.

Grand Lake Six miles south in the town of Disney is the Picture in Scripture Amphitheatre, which stages the biblical story of Jonah and the whale.

Also in the area is Har-Ber Village (3.5 miles west of town on Har-Ber Rd.) with about a hundred reconstructed buildings and shops along with various displays. Lendonwood Gardens (west of Main St. on Har-Ber Rd.) houses one of the largest collections of chamaecyparais in the nation. Besides the main garden, there is also an English Terrace Garden and a Japanese Garden.

Lawton Geronimo, the Apache leader, died at Fort Sill near here and is buried in the Old Post Cemetery. He surrendered to the U.S. military in 1886 and later converted to Christianity, joining the Dutch Reformed Church. The Old Stone Corral contains relics of frontier days. Also here is the Geronimo Guardhouse where Indian warriors were kept. The Old Post Chapel at Fort Sill is one of the oldest houses of worship still in use in the state.

An Easter Sunday Pageant is held on Easter weekend at the Wichita Mountains National Wildlife Refuge, which is one of the most beautiful areas of the state. The wildlife is plentiful and the scenery is breathtaking. You can see bison, longhorn cattle, and other animals at home here. It's also the best place in Oklahoma for hiking, rock climbing, and mountain biking.

> *There, by the Ahava Canal, I proclaimed a fast, so that we might humble ourselves before our God and ask him for a safe journey for us and our children, with all our possessions.*
>
> EZRA 8:21

A stone amphitheater comprised of 20 rock buildings was constructed in the 1930s by the Works Progress Administration. It was meant to resemble Jerusalem. Now it is called the Holy City of the Wichitas (1212 W. Gore Blvd.).

Muskogee In 1882 a Methodist missionary magazine, *Our Brother in Red,* was published here with both English and Creek language sections. In a few years it became a weekly. It was the first publication of its kind, seeking to minister to both Native American and white constituents.

Norman The McFarlin Methodist Church (University Blvd. and Apache St.) is an imposing structure. Neo-Gothic in design, the exterior has a plain white stone simplicity, but the interior is richly ornamented with hand-carved walnut woodwork.

281

Oklahoma City Oklahoma is cowboy country, crisscrossed by cattle trails like the Chisholm Trail. Oklahoma City is still home to the country's largest live cattle auction, held every Monday morning at the Stockyards, 2500 Exchange Ave. Admission is free—but wear blue jeans and a cowboy hat if you want to blend in.

You can see an extensive collection of western artifacts at the National Cowboy Hall of Fame and Western Heritage Center (1700 N.E. 63d St.). A Rodeo Hall of Fame is also on site, and the Children's Corral gives kids the opportunity to try their hand with bedrolls, saddles, and lassos.

Frontier City Theme Park (11501 N.E. Expressway) is a 70-acre western-style amusement park that includes five roller coasters, livery stables, and staged western gunfights. Music groups entertain visitors daily all summer long, and fireworks displays are common on summer evenings.

Crossroads Cathedral (8901 S. Shields Blvd.), associated with the Assemblies of God, has more than 5,000 worshipers on an average Sunday morning in its services and thus ranks as one of the largest churches in the state.

Pawhuska It's called the Cathedral of the Osage, but its proper name is the Immaculate Conception Catholic Church (1314 N. Lynn St.). It was constructed in 1920, although World War I slowed down the arrival of the stained glass windows the church had ordered from Munich. Most of the windows are of saints and biblical figures, but one shows Christopher Columbus meeting with Native Americans and another shows a Jesuit priest surrounded by members of the Osage tribe. The Jesuit priest had established a school and mission among the Osage in Kansas.

Ponca City In 1926 when a local oilman wanted to honor pioneer women, he asked 12 leading sculptors to submit bronzes of what an archetypal pioneer woman would look like. The winner was Bryant Baker, who depicted a determined-looking woman with a Bible tucked under her arm, wearing a bonnet and leading a little boy. Critics didn't think much of it, but it is called the *Pioneer Woman* and this 17-foot-high bronze statue now stands on Monument Ave. in Ponca City.

Shawnee This town of 26,000 is the home of Oklahoma Baptist University (500 W. University St.), a Southern Baptist school with 2,000 students. The school was founded in 1911, having its first classes in the basement of the First Baptist Church and at Convention Hall.

The town takes pride also in being the birthplace of Jim Thorpe, the great Native American athlete, the birthplace of astronaut Gordon Cooper, and the birthplace of Brewster Higley, the physician who wrote "Home on the Range." (See Thorpe also under Jim Thorpe, Pa.)

The Mabee-Gerrer Museum of Art (1900 W. MacArthur Dr.) has a diversified display with art from various periods of history and artifacts from Egyptian, Babylonian, Grecian, Roman, and Persian periods. It is housed at St. Gregory's College on W. MacArthur Dr. The collection of art was begun by a monk in the early 1900s and now includes paintings by Whistler, Rembrandt, and Raphael as well as such artifacts as Egyptian mummies.

The Sacred Heart Mission, seven miles east of Asher on Hwy. 39 is where mystery writer Tony Hillerman once served as an altar boy.

Tahlequah This town, some 70 miles east of Tulsa, marks the end of the Cherokee tribe's 1838 forced march along the Trail of Tears from North Carolina, Georgia, and Tennessee to the Indian Territories. Today Tahlequah is the home of the Cherokee tribe's capitol building. The Cherokee Heritage Center (four miles south on Hwy. 82 and Willis Rd.) chronicles the history of the Cherokees. Also on site are the Cherokee National Museum; the Ancient Village of Tsa-la-Gi, where costumed tribal members demonstrate basketweaving, pottery, stickball games, and other Cherokee traditions; and Adams Corner, a re-created pioneer village from the 1800s.

Tulsa Oral Roberts University (7777 S. Lewis Ave., about six miles south of downtown) was founded here in 1965 by noted healing evangelist Oral Roberts, who was born in Ada, Oklahoma. The previous year Roberts had a dream in which God commanded him, "Build Me a university." Roberts built more than a university; he built Tulsa's most frequented tourist attraction. At the heart of the campus is the 200-foot glass and steel Prayer Tower, where the visitors center is located. The campus also features a seven-story diamond-shaped library and graduate center complex, a symphony hall, a chapel, carillon, and television production studio. A media presentation is available for viewing.

The Boston Avenue United Methodist Church on S. Boston Ave. is done in art deco style, the first large-scale use of the style in church buildings. It features a 225-foot tower and several smaller towers.

283

The Victory Christian Center in Tulsa (7700 S. Lewis Ave.), with 6,500 in average Sunday morning attendance, is one of the larger churches in the nation.

The Philbrook Museum (off Rockford Rd., at the end of 27th Pl.) contains some interesting art. In the West Gallery *The Adoration of the Child* by Biagio d'Antonio da Firenze is displayed so dramatically that it captures your attention. Baroque paintings are in the East Gallery. The Philbrook has produced for youngsters "A Philbrook Gallery Guide for Children and their Parents," suggesting activities tied to the exhibits and ways to make the museum a family affair.

The Fenster Museum (1223 E. 17th Pl.) is nearby. This museum is dedicated to Jewish art. Of note is a curtain that is said to have hung before the ark, an exquisite tapestry handworked in colored silk. A separate room houses Jewish costumes and ceremonial clothes.

Vian North of town is the Dwight Mission (Rte. 2), which was established in 1830 by Presbyterian missionaries. Until World War II it operated as an Indian school. Some of the buildings still stand along with a reconstruction of a cabin. It now operates as a Presbyterian camp and retreat center.

Watts Near this town not far from Siloam Springs, Arkansas, is the site of the Cherokee Baptist Mission, established in 1839. Rev. Evan Jones and his son set up six churches with a membership of 1,200 Indians. In 1844 a mission printing press published the first issue of *The Cherokee Messenger,* printed in the Cherokee characters invented by Chief Sequoyah.

■SOUTH DAKOTA

Tourist Info
Phone 800-S-DAKOTA
Web sites
  Entire state   www.state.sd.us/tourism
  Aberdeen   www.aberdeencvb.com
For a complete list of updated links, visit www.christiantraveler.com

Aberdeen According to local tradition, the first Methodist congregation here dragged in planks and placed them on empty beer
barrels to provide seating at what was known as Brock's Tent Hotel.
That was in 1881. Later a small chapel and then a larger church
were built. Today's First United Methodist Church was finished
in 1905 and was built in an eclectic revival adaptation of the
Byzantine style. It's located on S. Lincoln St. and Fifth Ave.

Built in 1884, the Finnish Apostolic Lutheran Church (four
miles east of Frederick) is one of the oldest and best preserved
examples of 19th-century Apostolic Lutheran pioneer churches
in South Dakota. It is located near the North Dakota state line.

Storybook Land and Land of Oz (2216 24th Ave. NW) fit well
in Aberdeen because this was the city that L. Frank Baum, author
of *The Wizard of Oz,* called home. Incidentally, Baum memorabilia is in the local Alexander Mitchell Library (519 S. Kline St.).
In Storybook Land various children's stories are re-created. The
Land of Oz is a theme park that features Dorothy's farmstead, a
children's zoo, a pony-ride concession, and even a Yellow Brick
Road. It is open from April 15 to October 15.

De Smet This town was named after Father Pierre Jean de Smet,
a missionary who traveled throughout the West in the early 1800s
and who wrote several books about his experiences in eastern
South Dakota. (See de Smet also under Hazelwood, Mo.; Casper,
Wyo.; and Kettle Falls, Wash.)

Six of the books in the *Little House on the Prairie* series by Laura
Ingalls Wilder are also set in this town, where she lived for 15
years. The Ingalls family moved to De Smet in 1879 and lived there
first in a shanty, then in a farmhouse, and later in a house that Pa
built. The shanty and town house are open to the public and
include period furnishings and other memorabilia mentioned in
the books. A pageant, showing scenes from Wilder's *These Happy
Golden Years,* is held the last weekend in June and the last two
weekends in July each year. (See Wilder also under Burr Oak, Iowa;
Spring Valley and Walnut Grove, Minn.; Mansfield, Mo.; Pepin,
Wisc.; and Independence, Kans.)

Flandreau This town was first settled in 1869 by 25 Christian
Santee Sioux families, and its First Presbyterian Church is the
oldest continuously operating church in the state.

Hot Springs The fossilized remains of ancient mammoths at the Mammoth Site (one block north of the US 18 Bypass) will intrigue both young and old. Discovered in 1974, the site is believed to contain up to 100 mammoths and 29 other species in the sink-hole, which was their ancient watering hole.

Hoven Located some 50 miles west of Aberdeen, this little town would not be remarkable but for one thing: the Cathedral of the Prairies. This masterpiece of Romanesque architecture is more formally known as St. Anthony of Padua Catholic Church (536 Main St.), and was completed in 1921. It was patterned after a 1,000-year-old church in Ruhmann-felden, Bavaria. This tower-ing structure can be seen for miles, thus earning its nickname, the Cathedral of the Prairies.

Ipswich Just west of Aberdeen on US 12 is this small, quaint town. The community library is a charming stone structure, and the First Baptist Church (305 Main St.) exhibits some of the finest fieldstone architecture in the state.

Madison For 42 years, the Chautauqua summer programs drew people here to Lake Madison for lectures, concerts, plays, and debates. Now the Smith-Zimmerman State Museum on the Dakota State University Campus houses the Chautauqua collec-tion. The museum is open daily. (See also Chautauqua, N.Y., and other Chautauqua-inspired sites under Ridgecrest, N.C.; Sac City, Iowa; Lake Side, Ohio; and Boulder, Colo.)

Also in Madison is Prairie Village, which replicates a pioneer town, including a sod house, a log cabin, and an 1893 steam carousel.

Mitchell You have to see it to believe it, but here, 60 miles west of Sioux Falls, is the world's only Corn Palace (604 N. Main St.). More than 750,000 people visit it yearly. Each summer, follow-ing precise directions, crews apply the corn kernels, 3,000 bushels of them, to form mosaics covering the outside and inside of the building. (Old-timers call it the world's biggest bird feeder.) The first Corn Palace was built in 1892 and each year it is rebuilt and has attracted international attention. Since 1937 it has had Moorish-inspired minarets, turrets, and kiosks. Even if the build-ing is closed to visitors when you arrive, it's worth a detour to check out the exterior. And while it is . . . well . . . corny, it is a truly unique testament to the state's agricultural wealth.

At Mitchell's Dakota Wesleyan University, more than 700 artifacts are displayed in seven buildings in the state's largest museum called Friends of the Middle Border Museum. Among the buildings are the 1909 Farwell Methodist Church, an 1885 one-room school, and an 1886 Italianate home, which was built for the cofounder of the Corn Palace.

Pickstown Fewer than 200 people live here, but alongside them is the huge Fort Randall Dam, 10,700 feet long and 165 feet high, and at the base of the dam is the Fort Randall Historic Site. Fort Randall was a military outpost established in 1856 to keep peace between white settlers and the Sioux Indians. The only visible sign of the fort is the 1875 Fort Randall Chapel, which has been worn down through the years.

Rapid City Bear Country U.S.A. (eight miles south of Rapid City on US 16) is a drive-through wildlife park featuring black bears, wolves, and other North American wildlife. There is also a walk-through area with bear cubs, wolf pups, and other baby animals. There is certainly no substitute for seeing animals in the wild, but it is on the way to Mt. Rushmore, and your children will enjoy the opportunity to see the animals up close.

The Black Hills have been the battlefield for Americans and Native Americans over the course of our nation's history. The clash of these two resident cultures is strikingly portrayed in two of the nation's grandest monuments. Separated by only 20 miles distance, Mt. Rushmore (on US 16) honors four U.S. presidents, and the Crazy Horse Memorial honors the great Lakota warrior who defeated Custer at Little Bighorn. Mt. Rushmore's four granite presidential faces, Washington, Jefferson, Theodore Roosevelt, and Lincoln, were completed in 1941 by Gutzon Borglum. The 60-foot-high heads were supposed to be accompanied by 465-foot bodies, but work on the project ceased as the country entered World War II. There is an impressive lighting ceremony in the evening, which you can watch from the amphitheater. Admission is free.

The size of Rushmore will astonish you—until you see Crazy Horse (on US 16/385). All four of the presidents' heads could fit inside Crazy Horse's face. The project was begun in 1947 by sculptor Korczak Ziolkowski as a rebuttal to Mt. Rushmore, and the work is carried on today by his ten children. The memorial is not yet finished. When it is, it will be the world's largest sculpture at 563 feet.

Near the two memorials are Wind Cave (US 385) and Jewel Cave (US 16) National Monuments. Wind Cave was discovered in 1881 by Tom Bingham, who noticed the sound of wind escaping from the cave's tiny natural entrance. The wind blew his hat off when he got close, and so the cave was named. Wind Cave is known for its "boxwork," a honeycomb surface of calcite covering the walls. There are five different tours of the cave, but make sure you are in good physical condition before taking them. Each tour has more than 150 stairs. The Garden of Eden tour is the least strenuous. Bring a jacket regardless of the outside air temperature.

Great Places for Family Fun

✔ Horseback riding in Theodore Roosevelt National Park, North Dakota

✔ Camping in Custer State Park, Custer, South Dakota

✔ Wall Drug Store, Wall, South Dakota

Jewel Cave is a striking contrast to Wind Cave. Its walls are covered with calcite crystals from which the cave got its name. This cave's tours are more strenuous than those of Wind Cave. The half-mile Scenic Tour includes 723 stairs and the Spelunking Tour is limited to ten people ages 16 and up. Participants of the latter tour must be able to fit through an opening only eight inches by two feet in size. You can get more information from the visitors center.

The Norwegian Chapel-in-the-Hills (south of Rapid City off Hwy. 44 at 3788 Chapel Lane) is an exact copy of the famous 800-year-old Borgund Church in Norway. Its intricate wood carvings, dragon heads, and ingenious construction attract thousands of tourists each year. During the summer months, vesper services are held at 8 P.M.

Storybook Island on Sheridan Lake Rd. is a free fairyland park and Rapid City's most popular attraction. It features fountains, trains, castles, live animals, and a children's theater.

Rockport Hutterites, an Amish-like group that emigrated from Russia in the 1870s, came first to South Dakota, then moved to Canada during World War I, and then began moving back to the United States in the 1930s. Some moved to Montana, others back to Rockport, which is near the town of Alexandria. (See Hutterites also under Yankton, S.D.; Lewistown, Mont.; and St. Jacobs, Ont.)

St. Francis The St. Francis Mission (350 S. Oak St.) in the Rosebud Reservation was so successful that at one time it had the largest Indian mission school in America. On the campus of the St. Francis Mission and School is the Beuchel Memorial Lakota Museum. Father Beuchel, a Jesuit priest, deciphered the Lakota language and wrote a Bible history as well as grammar guides in that language.

Sioux Falls You'd hardly expect to see any of Michelangelo's work in Sioux Falls. But you will—well, full-scale replicas anyway. A full-scale cast of Michelangelo's *David* sits in Fawick Park (2d Ave. and 10th St.). You can see the only existing cast of Michelangelo's *Moses* on the grounds of Augustana College (30th St. and Grange Ave.).

Spearfish The *Black Hills Passion Play* is put on by more than 200 actors and actresses three times a week (Tuesdays, Thursdays, and Sundays). It can be seen from mid-June through late August. The annual play was begun here in 1939 and is now a permanent Black Hills institution. It is held in a 6,000-seat outdoor amphitheater on I-90. Phone 605-642-2646 for details. (For other Passion plays, see Lake Wales and St. Augustine, Fla.; Atlantic Beach, N.C.; Gadsden, Ala.; Eureka Springs, Ark.; Ruston, La.; Gatlinburg, Tenn.; Bloomington and Zion, Ill.)

Vermillion The University of South Dakota is here and its campus boasts the Shrine to Music Museum (Clark and Yale Sts.). In the museum are more than 6,000 musical instruments, including a 1693 Stradivarius violin, a 1785 French harpsichord, ivory lutes from Elizabethan times, and a nine-foot-tall slit drum from the South Pacific.

Wessington Springs It doesn't seem as if they belong here but Shakespeare Garden and Anne Hathaway Cottage (501 Alene Ave. N) are open to the public during daylight hours. You can even call ahead and have some English tea.

Yankton The African Methodist Episcopal Church on Cedar St. was built in 1885 by former slaves and is the oldest black church in the Dakotas.

North of Yankton near Olivet is the Wolf Creek Colony, the second-oldest Hutterite community in the state. Wolf Creek

Industries, one of the Hutterites' recent business ventures, now takes orders for furniture and lumber. Unlike the Amish, the Hutterites do not reject technology, but they live communally, and there are about 35 colonies in the state. (See Hutterites also under Rockport, S.D.; Lewistown, Mont.; and St. Jacobs, Ont.)

Southwestern States

A MIX OF NATIVE AMERICAN, MEXICAN, and cowboy spices gives the Southwest a unique flavor. The big cities of Dallas and Phoenix long to be recognized as cosmopolitan high-tech centers, which is a point well taken. But most visitors to the area want sagebrush and salsa.

Nevada was once settled by Mormon pioneers and Spanish padres, but you may not have guessed that; that part of the state's reputation has not held up. But you can take advantage of cheap airline tickets to the gambling meccas of Las Vegas and Reno and head from there into the natural beauty around Lake Mead and Lake Tahoe. Christian history is beautifully preserved in San Antonio, Texas, and you can't miss with the natural beauty throughout the Southwest. If God's creativity doesn't impress you here, nothing will.

■ARIZONA

Tourist Info
Phone 888-520-3433
Web site
 Entire state   www.arizonaguide.com
For a complete list of updated links, visit www.christiantraveler.com

Apache Junction Three miles north of town on Mammoth Mine Rd., the Goldfield Ghost Town offers mine tours, gold panning, gunfights, and specialty shops within view of the Superstition Mountains. A narrow gauge railroad goes around the ghost town.

Bisbee Dawson Trotman, founder of the Navigators, was born here in 1906. The Navigators, founded in 1943, grew from a Bible study for sailors to an international organization now based at Glen Eyrie, near Colorado Springs. It is known for its emphasis on discipleship and Scripture memorization.

Flagstaff In 1894 Percival Lowell established an astronomical observatory here and then spent the rest of his life working and looking out into space. Today the Lowell Observatory (1400 W. Mars Hill Rd.) has five telescopes that have been used in breakthrough studies of the outer planets. You can enjoy the museum with hands-on astronomy exhibits and, on clear summer nights, look through a 100-year-old telescope to see what Lowell may have seen.

The Riordan Mansion State Park includes a 13,000-square-foot mansion built by local lumber merchants Michael and Timothy Riordan. The Riordans did much for Flagstaff, building the Catholic church, library, power company, and phone company.

Fountain Hills The fountain of Fountain Hills is supposedly the tallest in the world with a 560-foot jet of water shooting above the town for 15 minutes every hour on the hour, except when it gets too windy.

Grand Canyon National Park How can you describe the Grand Canyon in three lines? Perhaps it's best to admit that it is indescribable and go on.

On the trail, you can see plaques with inscriptions from Mother Basilea Schlink (Lutheran) at the Watch Tower at Desert View, at the head of Bright-Angel Trail, and outside Hermit's Rest Gift Shop.

Jerome Several things in this town are unique. One is its Sliding Jail (US 89A), which because of underground dynamiting, has ended up 225 feet from where it was built. Another is the Powder Box Church out on Douglas Rd. It is so named because it was constructed out of dynamite boxes. Maybe it has something to do with the gospel being the power of God.

Lake Havasu City London Bridge, which once spanned the Thames River in London, now crosses a man-made channel of the Colorado River in the Arizona desert. The bridge was purchased in 1963, dismantled stone by stone, and then reconstructed in this recreational and retirement community. There are now more than 50 British-style shops that comprise the English Village that is located near the bridge.

> *You will go out in joy and be led forth in peace; the mountains and hills will burst into song before you, and all the trees of the field will clap their hands.*
>
> ISAIAH 55:12

Mesa The Word of Grace Church (655 E. University Dr.) has been growing rapidly and is now one of the larger churches in the area. Gary Kinnaman, who has written several books, serves as the pastor.

Phoenix The Phoenix Zoo (455 N. Galvin Pkwy.), spread over more than 125 acres, is a wonderful park. An African savanna and a tropical rain forest are among the featured exhibits. All told, there are more than 1,300 mammals, birds, and reptiles. The Arizona Trail features plants and animals of the Southwest. The Children's Trail presents small animals from around the world and a barnyard petting area. But don't count on seeing any polar bears; polar bears don't like Phoenix for some reason. Bring your hat, sunglasses, and sunscreen; it can get awfully hot.

The Heard Museum (22 E. Monte Vista Rd.) is internationally renowned for its outstanding collection of Native American pieces. Interactive exhibits, a multimedia show, and live demonstrations add to the experience. As well as housing ancient pieces, the museum features the work of modern Native American artists and exhibits designed to appeal to children.

This city has two mega-churches with average attendance of 10,000 or more. They are First Assembly of God and North Phoenix Baptist. Bethany Bible Church (6060 N. 7th Ave.) is another large church in Phoenix with a strong emphasis on the study of Scripture.

The Hall of Flame Museum of Firefighters (6101 E. Van Buren St.) in Papago Park houses one of the largest collections of fire fighting equipment in the world, dating back to 1725. A play area for children is included.

In Heritage Square (6th and Monroe Sts.) are eight restored buildings containing a variety of exhibits, a museum, and restaurants. One of the houses, the Stevens house, includes the Arizona Doll and Toy Museum, with antique dolls and toys from around the world.

GREAT PLACES FOR FAMILY FUN

✔ The Grand Canyon, Arizona, from any angle and at any time of day

✔ Skiing Lake Tahoe, Nevada

✔ Spelunking in Carlsbad Caverns National Park, New Mexico

The Mystery Castle (800 E. Mineral Rd.) near South Mountain Park was started in the 1930s as a dream castle for a little girl. By the time it was completed 15 years later, it was an 8,000-square-foot home built of native stone and a conglomeration of scavenged materials. It has 18 rooms, 13 fireplaces, and a small chapel where weddings are often performed.

The Pioneer Arizona Living History Museum (on Pioneer Rd., 12 miles north of Phoenix) has more than 20 original and reconstructed buildings. Among the buildings in this quaint little village are a church, opera house, schoolhouse, a Victorian mansion, and a stagecoach station.

Prescott Prescott Pines Camp and Conference Center (855 E. Schoolhouse Gulch Rd.) is a Christian conference grounds two hours north of Phoenix. It is located 6,100 feet up in the Bradshaw Mountains.

St. David If you would like to spend a quiet weekend at a monastery, the Holy Trinity Monastery on the San Pedro River is something you might consider. But it probably won't be quiet in

May and November when up to 12,000 people come because of the arts and crafts fair that serves as the monastery's main fundraising event. Other than that, you can spend your time birdwatching (because it's a bird sanctuary too), meditating, and visiting the fascinating shop in the small town.

Scottsdale The Out of Africa Wildlife Park (9736 N. Fort McDowell Rd.) features leopards, mountain lions, and tigers. There is also an Arizona exhibit that includes wolves, bears, and cougars.

Sedona The Chapel of the Holy Cross (780 Chapel Rd.), built in 1956, is situated between two sandstone mountain peaks. A 90-foot cross dominates the structure. Open daily, it provides scenic views of the area.

Tempe Grace Community Church of the Valley (1200 E. Southern Ave.) is a large independent church with more than 4,000 members and a Sunday school of more than 3,000. It also operates a preschool and grade school.

Big Surf (on N. McClintock St.) has a variety of water-based activities, with its man-made waves and beaches. It includes 15 water slides and 3 activity pools.

Tombstone Most of the city's historic buildings are located in the same area, clustered around Allen St. Among them are St. Paul's Episcopal Church (3d and Safford Sts.), which was built in 1882; the Crystal Palace, which was one of the more luxurious saloons in the West; and the *Tombstone Epitaph* building, where the oldest continuously published paper in Arizona is still being published. The first editor chose the name for the newspaper believing that a "tombstone is never complete without its epitaph."

Because of your great compassion you did not abandon them in the desert.

NEHEMIAH 9:19

The O.K. Corral (Allen St.), where the Earp-Clanton gunfight took place in 1881; the adjacent Historama, which provides an animated introduction to the town; and the Rose Tree Inn Museum (4th and Toughnut Sts.) are all close by. The latter features the world's largest rose bush, which covers more than 8,000 square feet.

Tubac Originally a mining town but now an art colony, more than 80 arts and crafts stores have opened in the revived town. While you're there, take time out to visit the old mission in town. (See Tumacacori National Historical Park.)

Tucson Old Tucson Studios (201 S. Kinney Rd.) is a replica of Tucson in the 1860s and served as the filming location for more than 300 westerns since 1939. A fire destroyed the entire complex in 1995, but it has since been rebuilt and is open to visitors as a theme park with western shows, games, rides, shops, and food.

The Arizona-Sonora Desert Museum (2021 N. Kinney Rd.) has more than 200 live animals and 1,200 species of plants that are indigenous to the area.

The DeGrazia Gallery in the Sun (6300 Swan Rd. in the foothills of the Santa Catalinas) exhibits the deeply religious work of artist Ted De Grazia. Next to the gallery is the Museum in the Sun, an open-air chapel, which he built and decorated with frescoes.

Mission San Xavier del Bac (nine miles south on I-19) was built by the Franciscans between 1783 and 1797, though the mission itself goes back to 1692. The mission is called the White Dove of the Desert, because the white stucco covering the adobe bricks makes the whole church shimmer in the desert light. It is an impressive example of Spanish mission architecture and is the oldest Catholic church in the country still serving the community for which it was built. Its beautiful painted statues, carvings, and frescoes are must-sees.

The Pima Air and Space Museum (1000 E. Valencia Rd.) displays more than 200 vintage aircraft, showing the history of aviation. Included is a plane used by Presidents John F. Kennedy and Lyndon B. Johnson.

The Casas Adobes Baptist Church (2131 W. Ina Rd.) and Christ Community Church (7801 E. Kenyon Dr.) are two of the larger churches in the city.

The Saint Augustine Cathedral (192 S. Stone Ave.), built in 1896, is modeled after the Cathedral of Queretaro in Mexico. Above the entry is a bronze statue of Saint Augustine.

El Tiradito (S. Granada and W. Cushing Sts.) is listed on the National Register of Historic Places and has long been important to Tucson Catholics. The shrine is dedicated to a sinner who was buried on unconsecrated ground at this spot. Though no one knew who the sinner was, people began burning candles for him, and candles are still being burned at the shrine.

Tumacacori National Historical Park The park (19 miles north of Nogales at 1891 E. Frontage Rd.) preserves the abandoned Mission San Jose de Tumacacori. Around 1800 Franciscans began building the present adobe church but it was never completed. A self-guided tour includes the church and cemetery as well as a patio garden and mortuary chapel. Visitors can also tour a museum displaying objects related to the Spanish missions and the indigenous people.

Williams The Grand Canyon Railway provides round-trip excursions to the South Rim of the Grand Canyon aboard the restored 1923 Harriman coaches, pulled by turn-of-the-century steam trains. On board there are strolling musicians and refreshments. The train leaves at 9:30 A.M. and returns at 5:30 P.M. with a three-and-a-half hour stopover at the canyon. Phone 800-843-8724 for details.

Window Rock Eight miles north of Gallup, this community is capital of the Navajo Reservation. You will find the Navajo Tribal Museum (Rte. 264) and the Navajo Nation Zoological and Botanical Park here too.

The St. Michaels Historical Museum (2.5 miles west of Window Rock on Rte. 264), located in the St. Michaels Mission, displays the work of the Franciscan Friars in the Navajo Nation. The museum is housed in the original mission building, which has been restored to its 1898 appearance.

■NEVADA

Tourist Info
Phone 800-NEVADA-8
Web sites
  Entire state   www.nevadatravel.net
  Las Vegas   www.lasvegas24hours.com
  Reno/Lake Tahoe   www.playreno.com
For a complete list of updated links, visit www.christiantraveler.com

Nevada's tourist trade is thought by most to be almost entirely involved with gambling, and unfortunately there's a lot of truth to that statement. Any tourist information you get from the state is likely to include lists of casinos that are eager to get your money. Finding inexpensive airfare into the cities is not difficult, nor is it difficult to find very inexpensively priced lodging and meals. So if you aren't offended by all the casinos that clutter Las Vegas's and Reno's streets, those cities can serve as home bases from which to explore Nevada's more heavenly natural beauties. But be aware that you will not be able to ignore the state's gambling industry— it's everywhere—and the city streets often have vending machines displaying newspapers with barely dressed women gracing the front pages. Unless you get outside the main thoroughfares, the only chapels you are likely to see will be wedding chapels. If you have young children, you may want to avoid the cities altogether.

Austin This town was built in a high mountain canyon dubbed Pony Canyon because a retired Pony Express rider made the initial silver discovery here in 1862. The Catholic church here is the oldest in the state and the Methodist church (now the town hall) has been in use since 1866. Both are on Rte. 50. The Austin Baptist Church/RV Park is probably the only combination church/RV park in the country. The park office doubles as a Sunday school room.

Beatty The Rhyolite State Historic Site is one of the most photographed ghost towns of the West. It includes the Bottle House, the old railroad depot, and concrete ruins of the rest.

Boulder City St. Jude's Ranch for Children (100 St. Jude's St.) is known not only for its ministry but also for its beautiful Holy Family Chapel. It includes artwork by Salvador Dali. It also has a miniature car museum.

Lake Mead Cruises depart from the Lake Mead Marina (seven miles east of Boulder City on Lakeshore Dr.) and provide a 90-minute sightseeing cruise to Hoover Dam on the paddle wheeler *Desert Princess*.

Carson City The Children's Museum (813 N. Carson St.) has hands-on exhibits that will help your children learn while having fun at the same time.

The Nevada State Museum (600 N. Carson St.) not only features Nevada's history but also contains a full-size replica of a ghost town and an underground mine.

Elko The Western Folklore Center (501 Railroad St.) is dedicated to the preservation of western ranch culture and so the almost-world-famous Cowboy Poetry Gathering is held here. If you haven't heard of it, it explains why it is still *almost* world famous. But 10,000 people come each year to celebrate it.

Nearby in the little village of Lamoille is the historic Church of the Crossroads, built in 1910. The Ruby Mountains and Lamoille Canyon have been called Nevada's Yosemite because of the impressive peaks and glacier-carved cliffs.

Henderson The Ethel M Chocolate Factory and Cactus Garden (2 Cactus Garden Dr.) is an interesting combination, but it may be the only place in the world where you can have a tour to see how delicious chocolates are made and then walk out to see more than two acres of 350 kinds of cacti.

> Who cuts a channel for the torrents of rain, and a path for the thunderstorm, to water a land where no man lives, a desert with no one in it?
>
> JOB 38:25–26

Near the Chocolate Factory is Kidd's Marshmallow Factory (1180 Marshmallow Lane). You get a complimentary sample at the end of the self-guided tour.

Lake Mead About 35 miles outside Las Vegas, Hoover Dam was constructed in the 1930s, truly an engineering marvel in its day. Tours into the 727-foot-high dam are conducted daily. *Note:* During the tour you will find that puns on the words *dam* and *damn* are common. The sensitive are forewarned.

The water backed up by the Hoover Dam created Lake Mead, the largest man-made lake in the western hemisphere with more than 500 miles of shoreline. This is an extremely popular place to enjoy boating, fishing, and swimming. And not a casino in sight!

Lake Tahoe Ponderosa Ranch (100 Ponderosa Ranch Rd.) was the home of the old *Bonanza* TV western series with the Cartwrights. It has the ranch house, a western town with an 1870 country church, and a collection of antique automobiles, carriages, and farm equipment.

The Heavenly Aerial Tram (top of Ski Run Blvd.) will give you a five-minute tram ride to an elevation of 8,250 feet, where you will get a spectacular view of Lake Tahoe.

Las Vegas If you are planning to spend the night in Las Vegas, there are a couple of casinos that offer attractions youngsters will enjoy. Admission is free, but don't be mistaken: These places hope to persuade you to make a brief stop at their slot machines.

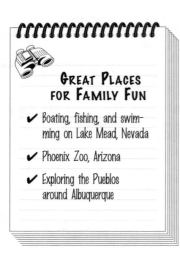

GREAT PLACES FOR FAMILY FUN

✔ Boating, fishing, and swimming on Lake Mead, Nevada

✔ Phoenix Zoo, Arizona

✔ Exploring the Pueblos around Albuquerque

Circus Circus (2880 Las Vegas Blvd. S) caters to families with children. Their indoor big top offers nonstop free circus acts, with tightrope walkers and trapeze artists soaring overhead. The hotel also has a midway with carnival games and a five-acre indoor amusement park called Grand Slam Canyon, home of the world's largest indoor roller coaster. But then how many indoor roller coasters are there?

The Mirage (3400 Las Vegas Blvd. S) is a 670-million-dollar palace with a volcano that erupts regularly in the front yard, a towering waterfall, lagoons, and tropical plants. Indoor you'll see live tigers in a glassed-in den. And Caesar's Palace (3570 Las Vegas Blvd. S) is an opulent casino, which is built to resemble an ancient Roman streetscape. (But be careful—those lusty Romans apparently didn't wear much.)

For a truly family-friendly experience, skip the Strip and head to Wet 'n' Wild (2310 Paseo del Prado), a 26-acre amusement park with every water ride you can imagine. The Lied Discovery Children's Museum (833 Las Vegas Blvd. N) is one of the nation's largest children's museums with more than 100 hands-on exhibits.

Treasures of Russia (3700 Flamingo Rd.) displays more than 1,150 Imperial pieces from the Peterhof State Museum near St. Petersburg, Russia. Included are porcelains, paintings, tapestries, and religious artifacts.

One of the larger Protestant churches in the city is First Presbyterian (1515 W. Charleston Blvd.).

Reno Boomtown's Family Fun Center (I-80 at Boomtown) provides a variety of family things to do from miniature golf, carousel and Ferris wheel rides, to the movies.

May Arboretum (Rancho San Rafael Park, 1502 Washington St.) has ten acres with twelve diverse theme gardens, including a rose garden and a songbird garden. Admission is free.

The May Great Basin Adventure (same location as the above) is a children's park with farm animals, dinosaurs, log flume, and pony rides. Admission is $3 for adults, $2 for children.

The National Automobile Museum (10 Lake St. S) contains more than 200 cars in period street scenes.

Sparks Wild Island (250 Wild Island Ct.) is northern Nevada's largest family amusement complex. It includes a water park, a 36-hole mini–golf course, bumper cars, and a giant game center.

Virginia City The Virginia & Truckee Railroad (Washington and F Sts.) will give you a narrated 35-minute steam train ride through the heart of the historic Comstock mining region.

The Castle (70 South B St.) was built by a mine superintendent in 1868. It's a Victorian mansion that was once referred to as the "house with silver doorknobs."

Washoe Valley The Bowers Mansion (4005 Hwy. 395) was built in 1864 for the first millionaires of the Comstock Lode. It has since been refurbished with many original pieces.

■NEW MEXICO

Tourist Info
Phone 800-SEE-NEWMEX
Web sites
   Entire state   www.newmexico.org
   Albuquerque   www.abqcvb.org
   Santa Fe   www.santafe.org
For a complete list of updated links, visit www.christiantraveler.com

Acoma This pueblo, also known as Sky City, is one of the oldest continuously inhabited sites in the country. It dates back to 1150, and by the time Coronado came in 1540, it was well established. To get into the pueblo, you must first register at the visitors center at the base of the mesa. There is a registration fee and an additional charge if you take photos. San Esteban Del Rey Mission, which is the largest of the early southwestern missions, dates from 1620. It's remarkable that all the construction material was carried up the mesa. Once you see it, you will realize how remarkable that is!

Alamogordo This town made headlines in 1945 when it was announced that the first man-made atomic explosion took place at the White Sands Missile Range near here. The Space Center (two miles northeast of US 54) and the Clyde Tombaugh Space Theater are well worth a stop.

Children and not just a few fathers may be equally interested in seeing the Toy Train Depot (1991 N. White Sands Blvd.), which features hundreds of models and toy train displays housed in an old train depot.

Albuquerque This city was founded in 1706 in what is now the Old Town. Facing the Old Town Plaza is the historic San Felipe de Neri Church (2005 N. Plaza NW). The church has been enlarged over the years, but the original structure remains, its massive adobe walls looking just as a New Mexican church should. The adobe houses surrounding San Felipe have been converted into charming shops, restaurants, and galleries.

Children will enjoy the Albuquerque Biological Park, which encompasses the Rio Grande Zoo (903 10th St. SW), the Albuquerque Aquarium, and the Rio Grande Botanic Garden (both at 2601 Central Ave. SW). The Aquarium's Eel Cave is especially popular. The Rio Grande Zoo is home to over 1,000 animals, including koalas, which are rarely seen in American zoos. Admission is $4.25.

The Albuquerque Children's Museum (800 Rio Grande Blvd.) features arts and cultural exhibits, a computer lab, an art room, and the ever-popular Bubble Room, where kids can enclose themselves in a giant bubble.

Sandia Peak Aerial Tramway (located on Tramway Blvd. northeast of Albuquerque) is a year-round attraction. Nearly three miles long, it is one of the world's longest, giving you a spectacular view of the Sandia Mountains. Sandia Peak is a popular spot for balloonists, so you may see some take off as you ascend via the tramway. The ascent takes about 18 minutes.

And speaking about balloons, the Albuquerque International Balloon Fiesta is the nation's most well-known hot-air balloon festival. It's also the world's largest, featuring hundreds of beautiful balloons. The event is held annually in early October.

Isleta Pueblo (13 miles south of the city off US 85) is a prosperous community with a church that was originally built by Juan de Sala. It was burned during the Pueblo Rebellion of 1680 and later rebuilt. Its lovely sanctuary and altar are worth seeing.

The largest Protestant church in the area is Hoffmantown Baptist (8888 Harper Dr. NE) with attendance averaging over 3,000.

Boys Ranch Located near Grants, the New Mexico Boys Ranch, Inc. (774 Hwy. 304), contains a boys' ranch, a girls' ranch, and a youth ranch—all Christian residential child care centers for children from troubled backgrounds. Families for Children is an adoption and foster care agency, located at the ranch as well.

Carlsbad The Living Desert Zoo and Gardens State Park (1504 Miehls Dr.) is a 1,100-acre indoor/outdoor museum of the Chihuahuan Desert's plants and animals. It has more than 60 animal species that are indigenous to the area.

The Million Dollar Museum is a collection of early Americana including a 25,000-dollar doll collection and 31 antique European doll houses. It is displayed in a ten-room museum. The museum is located just outside the entrance to Carlsbad Caverns National Park—a million-dollar display of another sort.

Chama The Cumbres & Toltec Scenic Railroad, New Mexico Express, goes round-trip to Osier, Colorado, on an 1880s narrow gauge steam railroad. Trips are made daily from Memorial Day to mid-October.

Chimayo This town is an example of an old-style protected Spanish colonial village. Ortega's Weaving Shop (53 Plaza del Cerro) is a neat place to find goods. Weavers from a long line of weavers make blankets, rugs, purses, vests, and coats.

Cimarron Five miles south of town is the Philmont Scout Ranch (Rte. 1), a 140,000-acre expanse donated to the Boy Scouts of America in 1938 by the founder of the Phillips Petroleum Company.

Farmington Navajo Missions, Inc. (2103 W. Main St.), an inter-denominational work, is headquartered here. It focuses on helping dependent Navajo children and also ministers through a Christian radio station, print shop, and Christian bookstore.

Glorieta The Glorieta Conference Center, operated by the Southern Baptists, is located here about 18 miles northeast of Santa Fe (just off I-25). It's a year-round Christian conference facility, which accommodates nearly 3,000 in the summer and nearly 2,000 in the winter. It is also available for family vacations with a variety of activities for all ages. Phone 505-757-6161 for details.

Los Alamos The area is best known for the nuclear research the federal government conducted here during and after World War II. The scientific laboratories are still a classified installation.

The Jemez State Monument marks the place where a Spanish mission was built by Franciscan missionaries in 1621. In the visitors center you will find anthropology and archaeology exhibits. The mission is 13 miles north of Jemez Pueblo in the town of Jemez Springs.

Santa Fe The heart of Santa Fe is its historic Plaza, established in 1607. Once the end of the Santa Fe Trail, today the Plaza is lined with shops, restaurants, and galleries. Facing the Plaza is the oldest public building in the United States, the adobe Palace of the Governors, which today is the home of the State History Museum.

One block east of the Plaza is the fabulous French-Romanesque St. Francis Cathedral (231 Cathedral Pl.). Santa Fe's first archbishop, Jean Baptiste Lamy, is buried here. The statue *La Conquistadora (Our Lady of the Conquest)* was carried to Santa Fe in 1692 by Don Diego de Vargas. The St. Francis Cathedral and its archbishop were fictionalized by Willa Cather in her classic *Death Comes for the Archbishop.* (See Cather also under Red Cloud, Neb.)

The famous Miraculous Staircase is in the Loretto Chapel (211 Old Santa Fe Trail), a Gothic chapel built by the Sisters of Loretto, who were the first religious women to come to New Mexico. The staircase was built to solve the problem of how to get to the choir loft. It is a circular stairway 22 feet high, built without central support. It has 33 steps and it makes two complete 360-degree turns. It is certainly an engineering feat, but some of the faithful will tell you that the staircase was built by St. Joseph himself and that's why it is so miraculous.

Just down the street is the adobe San Miguel Mission (De Vargas St. and Old Santa Fe Trail). Built about 1625 by Tlaxcala Indians, the mission church is the oldest church still in use in the continental United States. Glass windows over the altar look down over the original altar built by Native Americans. The mission also contains priceless statues and paintings. One treasure is the San Jose Bell, believed to have been cast in Spain in 1356, almost 650 years ago.

The Cristo Rey Church is the largest adobe structure in the country. It has beautiful old stone altar screens. It is located on Canyon Rd., where many artists have now taken up residence.

The Sanctuario de Guadalupe (on Guadalupe St.), built around 1785, is an adobe church museum featuring notable Spanish Colonial art.

The Santa Fe Children's Museum (1050 Old Pecos Trail) has many interactive exhibits and highlights a greenhouse with reptiles, four bubble exhibits, and a rock-climbing wall.

The oldest house in the United States is just down the street from the San Miguel Mission on De Vargas St. It was built about 1200. The building was originally part of a pueblo complex.

Santa Fe is home to two of America's largest festivals. In the heat of August the nation's largest Indian Market fills the plaza as tribes from across the country put up over 500 exhibits of fine arts and crafts. Then, early

> Since I have been longing for many years to see you, . . . I hope to visit you while passing through and to have you assist me on my journey there, after I have enjoyed your company for a while.
>
> ROMANS 15:23–24

in September, the three-day Fiesta de Santa Fe celebrates Don Diego De Vargas's peaceful reconquest of New Mexico in 1692, marking the end of the Pueblo Rebellion. The festival is marked by street dancing, processions, and lots of good food.

Socorro The most unusual thing about the Old San Miguel Mission in this town is that its walls are five feet thick. The restored building was built originally in 1598.

Taos In the 17th century, Spanish missionaries and farmers brought Christianity to the local Native Americans by working

305

and farming alongside them. Today the farming and ranching community south of Taos, Ranchos de Taos, is the site of the magnificent San Francisco de Asis Church. It is truly one of the Southwest's most splendid Spanish churches. Built early in the 1700s, its interior is adorned with art objects, images of saints, and a large figure of Christ. In the rectory is Henri Ault's painting *The Shadow of the Cross.* In certain light, Christ appears to be carrying a cross, and at other times, the cross is invisible. Generations of artists have received inspiration from this mission, as have countless numbers of Christians.

The Taos Pueblo (two miles north of town) is home of the Taos Tiwa-speaking Indians, whose pueblo dwelling is one of the oldest continuously inhabited dwellings in the United States. This community predates Christopher Columbus's discovery of the new world by over 200 years. Unlike many other Native American tribes, these people were not evicted by the U.S. government and have remained in this location for centuries.

■Texas

Tourist Info
Phone 800-888-8839
Web sites
  Entire state   www.traveltex.com
  Amarillo   www.amarillo~cvb.org
  Arlington   www.arlington.com
  Austin   www.austintexas.org
  Dallas   www.dallascvb.com
  East Texas   www.easttexasguide.com
  Galveston   www. galvestontourism.com
  Houston   www.houston-guide.com
  San Antonio   www.sanantoniocvb.com
  Waco   www.wacocvb.com
For a complete list of updated links, visit www.christiantraveler.com

Amarillo Some 38 miles northwest of the city is Cal Farley's Boys Ranch (3301 E. 10th Ave.). Located on 10,000 acres, it was established in 1939 as a ranch home for troubled and needy boys.

More than 400 boys between the ages of 4 and 19 now live and work here. Visitors are welcome to tour the grounds.

Arlington Six Flags over Texas (off I-30) was the nation's first Six Flags park and is home to the Texas Giant roller coaster, in addition to loads of other thrills. The park features festivals and special events all year long. One of particular interest to Christians is the annual Christian Youth Days, featuring contemporary Christian musicians of national renown. The annual event, now in its 23d year, is generally held around Easter weekend. Across from Six Flags is Wet 'n' Wild, an amusement park devoted to water recreation.

For a different kind of musical experience, you can visit Johnnie High's Country Music Revue (you are in Texas, after all). Twenty different acts include singing, dancing, musicians, and comedians every weekend in a family-friendly theater atmosphere. Friday nights feature gospel music, and weekends in December feature Christmas shows every evening.

Austin At the University of Texas at Austin, the Harry Ransom Humanities Research Center has a Gutenberg Bible on display as well as several collections of rare books and manuscripts. The Photography Collection, with more than five million prints and negatives, includes the world's first photograph and 3,000 pieces of antique photographic equipment.

Hyde Park Baptist Church has a Sunday school of more than 3,000, which makes it the largest in the city.

Blanco Five miles west of town is the Christ of the Hills monastery, where pilgrims come for services and to visit a Virgin Mary shrine.

Brenham The Texas Baptist Historical Center has exhibits relating to Sam Houston and to the history of Texas Baptists (intersection of FM 390 and 50). The Center was formerly the church where Houston was converted and baptized. A century-old church bell is also here.

Saint Clare Monastery Miniature Horse Ranch is located nine miles northeast and has a miniature carousel and carriage displays. It's a 98-acre ranch run by resident cloistered nuns who breed, train, and sell gentle miniature horses. The sisters of the Order of Saint Clare are now known as among the top breeders of tiny horses.

Brownsville The Gladys Porter Zoo at Ringgold and Sixth Sts. is considered one of the top ten zoos in the United States. The 31-acre spread contains 1,800 different mammals, reptiles, and birds. It also has a children's zoo.

Brownwood The Douglas MacArthur Academy of Freedom on the campus of Howard Payne University includes the Hall of Christian Civilization, with one of the largest murals in Texas; the Mediterranean Hall, with a reproduction of the Rosetta Stone; and the MacArthur Exhibit Gallery, with memorabilia of the World War II general. Howard Payne University is a Southern Baptist school.

Corpus Christi The World of Discovery features replicas of the *Nina, Pinta,* and *Santa Maria,* the ships of Christopher Columbus's historic voyage. The replicas were built by the Spanish government for the 500th anniversary. You can see Columbus's quarters and go below decks of the *Santa Maria.* The museum includes a hands-on children's area with a shrimp boat, bird costumes, video phones, and other attractions.

Crystal City You may wonder why this town has a large statue of Popeye the Sailor in front of its city hall, but it makes sense when you know that the town also calls itself the Spinach Capital of the World.

Dallas The Biblical Arts Center (7500 Park Lane) includes a 124-foot-by-20-foot painting depicting the miracle at Pentecost. There is also a life-size replica of the garden tomb of Christ. Dramatic 30-minute sound and light presentations are made every hour at half past the hour. The East Gallery features changing exhibits, ranging from ancient archaeological artifacts to contemporary spiritual art. The purpose of the museum is to use art to help people envision places, events, and people of the Bible.

The Dallas Zoo (621 E. Clarendon St.) features more than 1,400 mammals, reptiles, and birds on 70 acres. It also has a one-mile monorail ride. Animals roam freely on six naturalistic habitats.

The Dallas World Aquarium (1801 N. Griffin St.) is a large multilevel aquarium that can't be beat. The huge rain forest exhibit with its bats, penguins, crocodiles, and birds make the rain forest come alive.

Although Dallas would prefer to be thought of as a cosmo-politan, trendy city, most people associate the city with cowboys. If you are one of the latter, don't leave Dallas without visiting the Mesquite Rodeo (1818 Rodeo Dr.). This nationally televised rodeo is one of the most competitive in the country. Shows are scheduled on April through October weekends.

Several Baptist churches in the city area have large average attendances. First Baptist (1707 San Jacinto St.), which was pastored for many years by C. A. Criswell, is the largest. Prestonwood Baptist (15720 Hillcrest Rd.) is only slightly smaller, followed in size by Concord Missionary Baptist (3410 S. Polk St.).

The largest church of another denomination is Highland Park Presbyterian (3821 University Blvd.), with about 4,000 in average attendance.

Two nationally known Christian preachers and authors have based their ministries in Dallas. T. D. Jakes is the pastor of The Potter's House (6777 W. Kiest Blvd.), one of the nation's fastest growing mega-churches with 21,000 members. The church is also home to T. D. Jakes Ministries. Tony Evans is pastor of the Oak Cliff Bible Fellowship (1808 W. Camp Wisdom Rd.). It has about 3,000 members. Evans is a best-selling Christian author and is also known throughout the nation for his powerful speaking.

GREAT PLACES TO ENJOY GOD'S CREATION

✔ Floating down the Rio Grande in Big Bend National Park, Texas

✔ Horseback riding through Palo Duro Canyon State Park, Texas

✔ Watching the bison pass through the Tallgrass Prairie Reserve, Oklahoma

C. I. Scofield, editor of the Scofield Reference Bible, founded the Scofield Memorial Church here (7730 Abrams Rd.), as well as the Central American Mission.

Dallas Theological Seminary was founded by an associate of Scofield, Lewis Sperry Chafer, in 1924, three years after Scofield's death. Today, with a variety of advanced programs, it is one of the larger seminaries in the country.

The Dallas Baptist University on Mountain Creek Pkwy. incorporates a Corrie ten Boom Museum in its library.

Denison Besides being the birthplace of Dwight D. Eisenhower, this city is also the location of the Grayson County Frontier Village, with more than a dozen renovated buildings dating back to the mid or late 1800s. The Frontier Village covers more than 18 acres on the southwest edge of town.

Denton The Little Chapel in the Woods (Bell and University Sts.) is considered one of the country's finer architectural achievements. Built in 1939, it was the work of architect O'Neil Ford.

El Paso El Paso is an old city, established by the Spanish in 1598. Remnants of that old Spanish religious history can still be seen today. The Spanish Mission Ysleta on Old Pueblo Rd. was built in 1681, making it the oldest Spanish mission in the Southwest and oldest community in Texas. Originally the mission was in Mexico, but when the Rio Grande shifted, it found itself in Texas. Technically it is the Mission Nuestra Senora del Carmen. Another three miles down the Trail is the Socorro Mission, also founded in 1682, with ornate, hand-hewn roof beams. And then another five miles will bring you to the San Elizario Presidio fort and chapel (1770). The fort was built to protect the missions. The chapel is an active church with a lovely courtyard.

Fort Worth The Fort Worth Zoo (in Forest Park at 1989 Colonial Pkwy.) has a huge number of animals—over 5,000—including a rare Komodo dragon and a white tiger.

The Fort Worth Botanic Gardens (3220 Botanic Garden Dr., off University Dr., west of downtown) contains thousands of kinds of flowers, plants, and trees. In the Rose Garden alone are over 3,500 rose bushes.

Southwestern Baptist Theological Seminary, located here, is the largest seminary in the country.

Galveston Galveston Island is famous for its sparkling Gulf-coast beaches and temperate weather. A great family destination, Galveston also offers horseback riding, miniature golf, unique shopping, fishing, and golf. The island has a beautiful historic district, including a number of churches, which can be toured during the annual Sacred Places Tour, held in late January.

The Blessing of the Shrimp Fleet is usually held the first weekend after Easter. In Cajun shrimper tradition, Catholic priests are called in to bless the shrimp trawlers for the spring harvest.

Glen Rose On Fridays and Saturdays from June through October, *The Promise* is performed at the Texas Amphitheatre (just off Hwy. 67). The musical drama presents the life of Jesus Christ.

Goliad Most of us recognize the phrase "Remember the Alamo," but probably few of us know that the battle cry was actually, "Remember the Alamo! Remember Goliad!" Although Goliad, located about 80 miles southeast of San Antonio, has played an important part in Texas history, its role is relatively obscure today. The Presidio La Bahia (Hwy. 183), built in 1749, is considered the world's finest example of a Spanish frontier fort. It is the only Texas Revolution site with its original 1836 appearance. The massacre that occurred here represents the largest single loss of life in the cause of Texas Independence and inspired the cry "Remember Goliad!"

There are several historic missions here. The Mission Nuestra Senora del Rosario, or Mission Rosario for short, was founded in 1754 by Franciscan missionaries. The ruins are located about six miles west of the city of Goliad off US Hwy. 59.

Mission Rosario was built to serve the Karankawa Indians, who had abandoned an earlier Spanish mission, Mission Espiritu Santo, founded in 1722. After Mission Espiritu Santo was abandoned, the missionaries moved to the present site, along the San Antonio River near Goliad. From that location, Mission Espiritu Santo served the local population and was an agricultural center for 110 years, longer than any other mission in Texas. During that time, the mission supplied not only its own needs, but those of other Spanish colonial settlements as far away as Louisiana and was the first large cattle ranch in Texas.

Gonzales The first shots for Texas independence were fired here in 1835. Today the Gonzales Pioneer Village, with ten reconstructed buildings from before 1900, including an 1870s church, helps to recall the history. The village is located one mile north of the city.

Groom Standing tall above the flat prairie just west of town is a cross 190 feet tall that can be seen almost 20 miles away. The arms of the cross are 110 feet wide, and the structure, including its foundation, weighs 2.5 million pounds. The cross is at the intersection of I-40 and FM 295.

Houston Hermann Park features 388 acres of beautifully landscaped grounds that are home to museums, gardens, paddleboats, and golfing. The Houston Museum of Natural Science is at the northern entrance, offering exhibits on gemstones and petroleum, a butterfly center, planetarium, IMAX theater, and hands-on displays. And if that isn't enough, you can find at the southern end the Houston Zoological Gardens. Especially popular are the zoo's rare white tigers.

The city's most popular attraction is Space Center Houston (as in "Houston, we have a problem"), which is actually not in Houston but 20 miles south in Clear Lake at 1601 NASA Rd. This is the active Mission Control Center for the nation's space program. Space Center Plaza re-creates life on the deck of a space shuttle. The Kids Space Place allows children to ride on the lunar rover and try out tasks in the Apollo command module. Johnson Space Center, which is next door, includes a visit to Mission Control and laboratories that simulate weightlessness.

Houston is known for its mega-churches. One of the largest Southern Baptist churches in the world is Second Baptist in this city. First Baptist (844 Fortune St.) is only slightly smaller. The First United Methodist Church (1320 Main St.), with Dr. William Hinson as pastor, is one of the largest Methodist churches in the country. Lakewood Church (Independent, at 7317 E. Houston Rd.) is another large church with average attendance well over 5,000 on Sunday mornings.

Architecturally speaking, there are two other Houston churches worth noting and they are as different from one another as they could be. The Rothko Chapel (3900 Yupon St.) is an octagonal ecumenical church, with walls adorned by 14 Mark Rothko paintings. At first look these are simply black canvases, but when you come close, you will see subtle shadings of color. Outside the chapel is the sculpture *Broken Obelisk,* which symbolizes the life and assassination of Martin Luther King Jr.

If the dark minimalist paintings of the Rothko Chapel aren't your cup of tea, visit the Byzantine Fresco Chapel Museum (4011 Yupon St.). Frescoes from a 13th-century chapel have been preserved here. The dome and apse were rescued from thieves and restored under the direction of the Greek Orthodox Church and the Republic of Cyprus.

Ninety miles north of downtown Houston and situated in the piney woods of East Texas is Cho-Yeh Camp and Conference Center (2200 S. Washington Ave. in the town of Livingston), owned and operated by the Presbyterian denomination. The center, established in 1947, encompasses approximately 300 acres of forests, streams, and lakes. The name literally means "place of tall pines," but it has come to be translated "the place where faith grows."

Kerrville The Y.O. Ranch, 22 miles southwest of town on Hwy. 41W, used to be 550,000 acres but it has shrunk to 40,000 acres. For the past 30 years the owners have been breeding "exotic" game here like blackbuck antelope, addax, Persian ibex, and oryx. They also have emu, ostrich, rhea, giraffe, and zebra. Guest cottages are available for visitors who want to stay a day or two.

The Howard E. Butt Foundation Camp, founded by the grocery store chain owner, is located here. Associated with it is Laity Lodge (719 Earl Garrett St.), which is a retreat center that brings in outstanding Christian speakers.

GREAT PLACES FOR FAMILY FUN

✔ Astroworld/Waterworld, Houston, Texas

✔ The beaches of South Padre Island, Texas

✔ The annual Native American Powwow at the Tulsa Fairgrounds

Longview LeTourneau University here is a Christian four-year liberal arts college, with strong specialization in engineering, technology, and business administration. Displays on campus contain early scale models of earthmoving equipment invented by R. G. LeTourneau, who founded the university.

For more than 40 years the Longview Welding Company (1108 W. Marshall Ave.) has boldly displayed the sign: "Hell Is Forever/Jesus Wants to Save You/ Repent and Be Converted." Now it has become a town landmark.

Nacogdoches The city of Nacogdoches (and we dare you to say that three times fast) is home to the Pine Creek Lodge, a camp and conference center in forested eastern Texas. Several lodges are available to accommodate various sizes of groups, whether for banquets, retreats, or just a weekend away. Visitors can enjoy a pool, driving range, hot tubs, hiking, or fishing. Phone 409-560-6282.

New Braunfels The world's largest Hummel collection is located in this German town at the Hummel Museum on Main Plaza. The New Braunfels collection contains more than 300 figurines.

Odessa The Globe Theatre here is a replica of England's Globe Theatre and it has been designed for performances of Shakespeare's dramas. During January and February, there is a Shakespeare Festival, and during the remainder of the year, there are other theatrical performances. Nearby is the Ann Hathaway Cottage Archival and Shakespeare Library with many books, costumes, and furnishings relating to Shakespeare.

Panna Maria This little town, located about 55 miles southeast of San Antonio, is the first Polish settlement in the nation. Founded by a Polish Franciscan monk and missionary who wanted to bring his countrymen to Texas, Panna Maria's first Polish settlers arrived in 1854. Its Church of the Immaculate Conception (just off Hwy. 87), built in 1856, is still an active church. St. Joseph's School, which was built in 1868, is just down the street and now houses the local historical museum.

Pittsburg This town is famous for possessing the Ezekiel Airship, a replica of a 1902 airplane that supposedly was airborne a year before the Wright Brothers made their flight. Its inventor, a part-time Baptist preacher, got his idea from the biblical prophet Ezekiel. The preacher raised 20,000 dollars, sold stock in the company, and built his ship. Unfortunately it was destroyed during shipment to the St. Louis World's Fair in 1904. The replica can be seen at Warwick's Restaurant on Marshall St.

San Antonio As conquistadors of centuries ago explored new lands for "God, Gold and Glory," the church played an integral part in colonization and dominion over vast New World empires. Missions were often the first permanent Spanish settlements in new areas. More than just frontier churches, the missions also served as vocational and educational centers, economic enterprises, and regional trade centers. The missions in and around San Antonio are examples of this. Altogether these San Antonio missions formed the greatest concentration of Catholic missions in North America and formed the foundation for what is today the thriving city of San Antonio.

Founded by Spanish missionaries in 1691, the city's first mission is also the country's most famous: Mission San Antonio de Valero. We know it better as the Alamo. Although the Alamo was built for religious purposes, your visit there will highlight its political and cultural importance to Texas. The historic chapel (one of the most photographed facades in America) and barracks contain guns and other equipment used by William Travis, Davy Crockett, James Bowie, and other famous Texas heroes. To learn more about the Alamo's role in Texas history, visit the Alamo IMAX theater in the Rivercenter mall (849 E. Commerce St.).

But the Alamo is only one of five Spanish missions in the city. The other four are encompassed in the San Antonio Missions National Historic Park and connected by a seven-mile bike trail. Mission San Jose is known as the Queen of the Texas Missions, and its famous rose window is considered one of the finest pieces of Spanish Colonial ornamentation in the country. Mission Concepcion is best known for its beautiful frescoes. Mission San Juan was an agricultural center, supplying produce that helped support the missions. The chapel and its lovely bell tower are still in use. Mission Espada, the southernmost mission, included the best preserved segments of the historic aqueducts that were part of the missions' irrigation system for watering crops.

San Fernando Cathedral (Commerce and Flores Sts.) is best known as the site where Santa Ana raised his flag to intimidate the Alamo defenders. In the end Texas would claim victory.

San Antonio's leading tourist attraction is the Riverwalk, or Paseo del Rio. Built a full story below street level, it is three miles of scenic stone pathways lining both banks of the San Antonio River. You can ply the waters on river taxis or charter boats as well. A great place to eat, shop, and spend the night, the Riverwalk is also the center of many festivities, like the annual Fiesta River Parade in April, the Holiday River Parade in November, and Las Posadas, a traditional Mexican reenactment of Mary and Joseph's search for lodging in Bethlehem.

Children enjoy the San Antonio Zoo (3903 N. St. Mary's St.) with its 3,600 animals. The third largest in the nation, it is widely acclaimed and has a reputation for its successful captive breeding. The Children's Zoo features a boat ride past an everglades exhibit and an educational rain forest exhibit.

Sea World of Texas is the largest of the four Sea Worlds in the United States and is becoming one of the city's top tourist spots. It is also the largest marine life theme park in the world, occupying over 250 acres at Ellison Dr. and Westover Hills Blvd.

There are several Protestant churches with nationally known ministers: Oak Hills Church of Christ (8308 Fredericksburg Rd.) is where best-selling author Max Lucado preaches most every Sunday.

The Trinity Baptist Church (319 E. Mulberry Ave.), which Buckner Fanning pastors, is a popular church with more than 4,000 in attendance on a typical Sunday morning. Television evangelist John Hagee is pastor of the Cornerstone Church here (18755 Stone Oak Pkwy.).

Bible Study Fellowship, which administers a five-year Bible study program throughout the country, is headquartered on Blanco Rd. here.

Tyler For many years half of the roses grown commercially in the United States came from the Tyler area. That is no longer true, but the city still has its Municipal Rose Garden where 500 rose varieties are cultivated.

THE SPANISH MISSIONS IN SAN ANTONIO

In 1690 a group of Spanish padres headed to Texas to bring the gospel to the new frontier. In all, 38 missions were founded in the state. San Antonio is home to five of these classic church communities, which are now preserved in the San Antonio Missions National Historic Park. While all five of the missions served similar functions, the National Park Service has assigned interpretive themes to each mission, highlighting a particular role performed by Spanish missions throughout the Southwest.

Mission San Antonio de Valero, popularly known as the Alamo, was the earliest of the local missions, established in 1691. "The Cradle of Texas Liberty," this mission was the site of an infamous battle that kindled Texans' desire for freedom. The Alamo is the only mission that is no longer an active parish church. Its political and military history has eclipsed its religious origins.

Of the other four missions, San Jose has received the most reconstruction, providing a glimpse of how this "Queen of the Texas Missions" looked originally. Mission Concepcion is one of the oldest unrestored stone churches in the United States. Mission San Juan's church was never completed, but its original compound is well preserved. Finally, Mission Espada, its original adobe church in ruins, was replaced in the 1800s and features an interesting Moorish-style gateway.

Visitors to San Antonio will see the Spanish padres' legacy permeating all of San Antonio: in its historic missions, its Mariachi masses, its annual Fiesta San Antonio, its art galleries and museums, and its candlelit Las Posadas Christmas processions.

Waco Unfortunately Waco has become known in recent years for the showdown between the U.S. government and David Koresh's cult. But there is much more to Waco than that.

Just outside the Waco city limits is the Homestead Heritage Traditions Crafts Village (off I-35 at FM 308 and 933). Visitors can follow a self-guided tour to watch artisans create wheel-thrown pottery, handmade furniture, wrought iron, and dried herb bouquets, and then top the visit off with a sandwich and homemade ice cream.

One of the largest church-related schools in the country (and the largest Baptist university in the world) is Baylor University here, affiliated with the Southern Baptist Convention. One of its treasures is its collection of materials relating to Robert and Elizabeth Barrett Browning, contained in its Armstrong Browning Library. The library also has 56 stained glass windows depicting the famous pair's poetry.

St. Francis on the Brazos Catholic Church (301 Jefferson Ave.) has a celebrated rose window, a replica of the window in the more famous San Jose Mission in San Antonio. Christmas on the Brazos (river) is an annual event worth visiting as well.

Rocky Mountain States

THE ROCKIES CONSTITUTE A GIANT WRINKLE in the North American continent, stretching 3,000 miles from northern Alberta to New Mexico. Only 5 percent of the U.S. population lives in the area commonly called the Rocky Mountain states, but millions flock here every year to hike, camp, ski, and generally enjoy the outdoors.

There are a number of evangelical Christian organizations clustered around Colorado Springs and they welcome visitors. And there are many sites in Salt Lake City related to the religious persecution of the Mormons and their subsequent settling of the city and its state. But Utah has plenty to offer besides the Mormon sites in Salt Lake City. Like the rest of the Rocky Mountain states, from Glacier in northern Montana to Zion in southern Utah, every bend in the road offers new opportunities to take your eyes off the road and gaze at the spectacular view. But we wouldn't advise it!

■COLORADO

Tourist Info
Phone 800-COLORADO
Web sites
  Entire state   www.colorado.com
  Colorado Springs   www.coloradosprings-travel.com
  Denver   www.denver.org
  Grand Junction   www.grand-junction.net
For a complete list of updated links, visit www.christiantraveler.com

Alamosa The Cumbres & Toltec Scenic Railroad, Colorado Limited, departs from nearby Antonito on its round-trip excursion to Osier on an 1880s narrow gauge steam railroad. On the trip you pass through mountain scenery, including the Phantom Canyon and the Toltec Gorge. Phone 719-376-5483 for schedules and pricing information.

Aspen During the summer, the Silver Queen Gondola goes to the top of Ajax Mountain each day and at the top provides nature walks, led by a naturalist. Besides that, free classical concerts are given by the Aspen Music Institute on most Saturdays during the summer. For gondola information, phone 800-525-6200.

At the Music Tent or at Harris Concert Hall the Aspen Music Festival presents classical concerts nightly during the summer months. Phone 970-925-3254 for a schedule.

Boulder Chautauqua Park (900 Baseline Rd.) was founded in 1898 as part of the movement that sought to bring culture and spiritual life to rural areas of the country. Summer concerts and a silent film series are presented at the exposed-wood auditorium, and lectures and other performances are given at the Community House. From the 26-acre park, hiking trails lead to the surrounding mountains and plains. (See also Chautauqua, N.Y., and other Chautauqua-inspired sites under Ridgecrest, N.C.; Sac City, Iowa; Lake Side, Ohio; and Madison, S.D.)

Celestial Seasonings Tour of Tea (4600 Sleepytime Dr.) provides tours of the company's headquarters. The facility produces 50 varieties of tea, and the tour includes marketing, research, tea-

319

tasting, a walk-through of the production and packaging facilities, plus the aromatic mint room.

The University of Colorado Museum (15th and Broadway) has a lot of exhibits about the natural history of the southwestern United States and it also includes a hands-on children's room and slide show.

Burlington At the Kit Carson County Carousel, 46 hand-carved animals adorn the antique carousel, so you can choose from a lion, giraffe, camel, or another exotic creature for your ride. The carousel is located on the fairgrounds.

The Old Town Museum on 14th St. is a collection of re-created buildings, including a schoolhouse, church, jail, and soda fountain.

Canon City The Holy Cross Abbey (2951 E. Hwy. 50), about two miles east of town, is a Benedictine monastery with a Tudor-Gothic–style chapel. In a basement room is a Native American museum with artifacts from plains tribes. Tours are available.

The Royal Gorge is a magnificent canyon with cliffs that rise more than 1,000 feet above the Arkansas River. The suspension bridge here is the highest in the world. The Royal Gorge Incline Railway, which is the world's steepest, takes you down 1,550 feet to the bottom of the canyon, and a 2,200-foot aerial tramway transports you across the canyon.

Before the mountains were born or you brought forth the earth and the world, from everlasting to everlasting you are God.

PSALM 90:2

Colorado Springs The United States Air Force Academy (about five miles north of the city) is worth visiting if only to tour its Cadet Chapel. It is 150 feet high and can be seen for miles. The futuristic multispired chapel is divided into three sections, the main floor being a Protestant sanctuary, and the lower level separated into Catholic and Jewish worship areas. Note that the end of each pew is sculpted to resemble an airplane propeller. Don't miss the fabulous mosaic artwork in the Catholic section, as well as the three-dimensional cast taken from the famous Shroud of Turin, believed by some to be Christ's burial shroud. Looking face-to-face into what may be Jesus' likeness is a very awe-inspiring experience. The chapel is open every day, and worship services on Sunday mornings are open to the public.

The Cheyenne Mountain Zoo (4250 Cheyenne Mountain Zoo Rd.) is unique in several ways. It gives you an opportunity to see more than 100 endangered species and other animals. In addition, there are special programs for children, including Preschool Discovery (ages 3 to 5) and camp (ages 6 to 11).

The largest church in the area is First Presbyterian (219 E. Bijou St.), with a Sunday school of close to 2,000 on an average Sunday.

This city now is home for many Christian organizations. Among them are Young Life, the Christian Booksellers Association, Compassion International, International Students, the International Bible Society, and the Christian and Missionary Alliance.

Focus on the Family (8605 Explorer Dr.), headed by well-known speaker/author James Dobson, is also here. The Focus on the Family Welcome Center includes interactive displays, a theater with a 20-minute video, and a children's area. A guided 45-minute tour of the building includes the broadcast studio and an overview of the ministry.

Glen Eyrie, located at 3820 N. 30th St., near exit 146 off I-25, is owned by the Navigators. Glen Eyrie, built by the founder of the D&RG Railroad in 1905, is a Tudor-style sandstone castle with 67 rooms, 30-foot vaulted ceilings, and 24 fireplaces. Each tile in the red roof of the castle was individually wrapped and sent from England. Now a conference center, it is open to all groups. The scenic surroundings cover 750 acres. Castle tours are given daily at 1 and 3 P.M. in the summer.

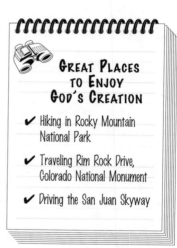

GREAT PLACES TO ENJOY GOD'S CREATION

✔ Hiking in Rocky Mountain National Park

✔ Traveling Rim Rock Drive, Colorado National Monument

✔ Driving the San Juan Skyway

The Colorado Springs Symphony Orchestra offers free concerts in area parks in July and August, and the United States Air Force Academy offers free band concerts at the Academy on Sunday afternoons in July and August.

Como This former railroad town, eight miles north of Fairplay, is now a ghost town with a number of old buildings. Three distinctive buildings include an 1881 roundhouse built by the Denver, South Park & Pacific Railroad; the Como Community Center; and the 1882 Catholic church.

Crested Butte In this town there are four historic buildings that remind you of its mining camp origin. They are the Elk Mountain Lodge, dating from 1881, the Union Congregational Church, dating from 1883, the Old Town Hall, also from 1883, and a unique two-story outhouse.

Cripple Creek The Cripple Creek and Victor Narrow Gauge Railroad on E. Carr St. offers a four-mile, 45-minute, narrated trip behind a steam locomotive through an area of abandoned mines.

Denver Denver has America's only downtown amusement park. Elitch Gardens is 58 acres filled with 28 thrill rides, lakes, lagoons, flower gardens, and fun for everyone. Recently it added a ten-acre water adventure park, called Island Kingdom, which offers a dozen high-speed water slides, an action river ride, and a 28,000-square-foot wave pool.

If it's only water fun that you want, you can visit Water World (88th and Pecos Sts. in Federal Heights), America's largest family water park, featuring 32 attractions on 60 landscaped acres. Besides the expected twisting water slides, you will enjoy two wave pools and white-water rafting adventures.

The Children's Museum of Denver (2121 Crescent Dr.), in addition to science and computer labs, provides Kidslope, which is an artificial ski slope where professionals offer two-hour ski lessons to children. Instruction is also available for snowboarding and in-line skating. Kids can visit a working television station and work in a child-sized grocery store.

An ocean in Denver? That's what the creators of Ocean Journey have tried to build in a new interactive park linked to the Children's Museum. Exhibits combine the qualities of an aquarium with an interactive experience that has a special emphasis on the interconnectedness of the earth's ecosystems. An outdoor trout stream, a coral reef aquarium, ocean fog, and sea spray are all features that add to the unique experience of Ocean Journey.

The Denver Zoo (in the City Park on E. 23d St., between York St. and Colorado Blvd.) is home to more than 3,500 animals and is consistently rated one of the nation's top ten zoos. The new Primate Panorama is especially fun, offering an up-close look at gorillas. Tropical Discovery re-creates a rain forest journey.

The Denver Museum of Natural History (2001 Colorado Blvd.) is the fifth-largest museum of its kind, with a huge assortment of dioramas, dinosaurs, gems, and other exhibits. Prehistoric Journey traces life on earth from its beginning, while the Hall of Life offers hands-on health science exhibits. There is also an IMAX theater and planetarium on site.

The Denver Art Museum (100 W. 14th Ave.) is truly a world-class museum, housing over 40,000 pieces. Its display of 17,000 Native American art objects is considered by many to be one of the finest collections of its kind in the world. The six-story "vertical" museum was designed specifically to accommodate totem poles and period architecture.

The Denver Museum of Miniatures, Dolls and Toys at 1880 Gaylord St., includes antique as well as modern dolls and toys and historic dollhouses and teddy bears.

Trinity United Methodist Church (1820 Broadway), the oldest church in the city, was established in 1859. Its stained glass windows were made in Chicago in 1888. Its 4,200 pipe organ was also built in 1888. Above the organ are 66 small lights, which symbolize the 66 books of the Bible.

GREAT PLACES FOR FAMILY FUN

✔ White-water rafting anywhere in Colorado

✔ Canon City's Royal Gorge

✔ Skiing at Winter Park

Denver Seminary (3401 S. University Blvd.), associated with the Conservative Baptist movement, is the largest seminary in the state.

At the Mother Cabrini Shrine on Cabrini Blvd. is a 22-foot statue of Christ at the top of a 373-step stairway. From this vantage point you also have a unique view of the city of Denver.

Estes Park From 420 E. Riverside Dr. two enclosed ten-person tram cars take you to the summit of 8,700-foot Prospect Mountain. The round-trip will take an hour.

Georgetown The Georgetown Loop Railroad tour leaves from the Devil's Gate boarding area (Georgetown exit 228 off I-70). A 1920s steam-powered train takes you through silver-mining country. You can also tour the Lebanon Silver Mine if you wish. Phone 303-569-2403 for reservations and information.

Golden Heritage Square is a re-created 1880s town but it also includes amusement rides, an alpine slide, and many shops. At the music halls, you can see humorous adaptations of Victorian melo-dramas, and the chuck wagon presents an Old West–style supper and show Wednesday through Saturday.

Manitou Springs Miramont Castle (9 Capitol Hill Ave.) is a unique 46-room mansion, built in 1895 by a sick French priest who came to the area because of the purported value of the mineral waters here. The mansion he built incorporates nine architectural styles. It has two-foot-thick walls and a 200-ton sandstone fireplace.

The Pikes Peak Cog Railway has been popular with tourists for more than a century. The new Swiss-built trains run like clock-work on the three-and-a-quarter-hour round-trip, including a 40-minute orientation at the top of Pike's Peak. Trains leave from the Cog Railway Depot at 515 Ruxton Ave. daily during the months of May through November. When it's very clear, you can see Denver 75 miles to the north.

Morrison Tiny Town and Railroad (S. Turkey Creek Rd.) is a minia-ture children's village on a ten-acre site. Begun in 1915, it includes a toy store, church, ice cream shop, newspaper office, and much more with 100 buildings in all. Everything is one-sixth actual size. Visitors can ride a miniature steam train through the town.

Pueblo The Rock Canyon Water Slide (Pueblo Reservoir Blvd.) offers a beach, water slide, bumper boats, and paddleboats.

Sangre de Cristo Arts and Conference Center (N. Santa Fe Ave.) has four galleries with changing art displays and a children's museum with hands-on exhibits.

Silverton The Old Hundred Gold Mine Tour (five miles east of town on Rte. 110) will take you on an electric mine train into the heart of 13,700-foot Galena Mountain. Narrated tours will tell you all about mining as well as offering historical and geological insights. Gold panning on the surface is included in this one-hour trip.

Sterling The Overland Trail Museum (on Rte. 6) contains a num-ber of historic exhibits, including an evangelical church, a school-house, print shop, and general store. Picnic facilities are available.

Vail Next to the Gerald R. Ford Amphitheater is the Betty Ford Alpine Gardens, which contain more than 500 different kinds of alpine and subalpine plants. The Perennial Garden has more than 1,500 varieties of plants, and the Mountain Meditation Garden combines Asian design and philosophical elements with Rocky Mountain plantings.

■IDAHO

Tourist Info
Phone 800-VISIT-ID
Web sites
  Entire state   www.visitid.org
  Boise   www.boise.org
For a complete list of updated links, visit www.christiantraveler.com

Boise The city of Boise lays claim to more museums per capita than any other city in the United States. Julia Davis Park, located next to the Boise River, is home to two of those museums, as well as the Boise City Zoo. The two museums, both free, are the Idaho State Historical Museum, where you will see Old West artifacts, and the Boise Art Museum, which features both historical and contemporary art.

At the edge of Julia Davis Park is The Discovery Center, a hands-on science museum offering a see-and-do learning environment with over 150 interactive exhibits.

The Old Idaho Territorial Penitentiary (2445 Old Penitentiary Rd.) is no longer a prison but another museum. And just up the road from there, you can tour a number of themed gardens at the Idaho Botanical Gardens (2355 Penitentiary Rd.). On display are Idaho native plants and a garden for children. A less formal collection of plant life can be seen at the Morrison Knudsen Nature Center (600 S. Walnut Ave.), with its exhibits of wetlands, plains, high-desert, and mountain ecosystems.

If you want to get an overview of the city, try the Boise Tour Train (9824 W. Gurdon Ct.), which leaves from the depot across from the rose garden in Julia Davis Park. It will give you a one-hour narrated tour of the historic and downtown areas of the city.

The World Center for Birds of Prey (seven miles south on Flying Hawk Lane) features exhibits about birds of prey and lets you view live falcons and eagles.

The First United Methodist Church (the Cathedral of the Rockies), which dates from 1872, covers a city block on Franklin St. The present Gothic structure is the third building of the congregation and contains impressive stained glass windows.

The Boise Christian Center (Cole Rd.), where U.S. Representative Helen Chenoweth attends, is a vigorous church in the area.

Cataldo The Cataldo Mission located in Old Mission State Park is the oldest standing building in Idaho. Built in 1854, it has foot-thick walls and was built without any nails by Jesuit priests and Native American converts. The mission served as a learning center and home of the Coeur d'Alene Indians, a stopover for westward settlers, a haven for the sick, and a supply and post office. If you peek behind the altar area, you can see little handprints (no doubt, belonging to inquisitive Native American children) in the dried mud. If you happen to be in the area in July, you will have to visit Cataldo Mission Fair, when artisans display pioneer crafts and give demonstrations.

Clyde On Sunday evenings throughout the summer, Gospel on the Green services are held alternately in the towns of Arco and Clyde.

Coeur d'Alene Nestled in the pine-covered hills surrounding a beautiful lake of the same name, Coeur d'Alene is one of the most beautiful towns in the state. Here you can enjoy lakefront dining, a 3,300-foot floating boardwalk, and resort hotels. The town attracts sailors, snow skiers, water-skiers, and golfers—there are 30 golf courses within an hour's drive. If you're a golfer, you will want to check out the Coeur d'Alene Resort course, with its famous 14th hole, the world's only floating green.

Lake Coeur d'Alene Cruises depart from the city dock at Independence Point, leaving at 1:30 and 4:00 P.M.

The New Life Community Church (6100 W. Hayden Ave.) of nearby Rathdrum was listed by *Charisma* magazine as one of the fastest-growing churches in the nation.

Kellogg The Silver Mountain Gondola (off I-90, exit 49) is believed to be the world's largest single-stage gondola. On an enclosed tram you go 3.1 miles in 19 minutes, rising 3,400 feet from the base level. From there you can take a chair lift to 6,300-

foot Kellogg Peak, where you can see deer, mountain lions, and eagles, as well as panoramic views.

Ketchum It's a 100-year-old mining town but today it features more than 80 restaurants, 20 art galleries, and a variety of shops. There are also 30 miles of paved trails for walking, cycling, or roller blading in the summer and for cross-country skiing in the winter. Author Ernest Hemingway is buried in the Ketchum cemetery.

Montpelier In this town located in the southeast corner of the state is the new National Oregon Trail Visitors Center, at the junction of US 89 and 30. The center has maps and other information about the Oregon Trail.

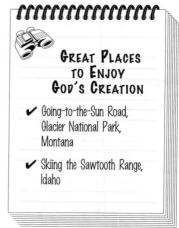

GREAT PLACES TO ENJOY GOD'S CREATION

✔ Going-to-the-Sun Road, Glacier National Park, Montana

✔ Skiing the Sawtooth Range, Idaho

Sandpoint Pend Orielle Lake is Idaho's largest and stretches about 40 miles. Two-hour guided boat tours of the area are available. Phone the Sandpoint Chamber of Commerce for names of tour operators and other information: 800-800-2106.

Silverwood The Silverwood Theme Park (15 miles north of Coeur d'Alene on US 95) is an amusement park in the old mining town of Silverwood. It features two old-fashioned wooden roller coasters, a narrow gauge steam train, live theater, family shows, and a wild animal park, as well as a late 19th-century mining town. It's open in summer months only.

Spalding Presbyterian missionary Henry Spalding built a mission near here in 1836 to reach the Nez Perce Indians. His mission included Idaho's first printing press, sawmill, and gristmill. The Spalding Site is a quarter mile east of town and represents the second mission built by the missionary.

Twin Falls The Perrine Memorial Bridge spans the spectacular Snake River Gorge. A mile east of the bridge is where the daredevil Evel Knievel attempted to leap across the chasm in 1974.

There are pedestrian walkways along the bridge that give you great views of waterfalls and sheer cliffs.

Wallace The Sixth Street Melodrama in the 1899 Lux Building is exactly that, with audience participation encouraged. Its aim is to present family-style entertainment.

The Sierra Silver Mine Tour (420 Fifth St.) lets you view silver mining in an hour-long tour. You are guided through a tunnel where you see equipment in operation and techniques used in mining silver ore.

■MONTANA

Tourist Info
Phone 800-847-4868
Web sites
  Entire state   www.visitmt.com
  Billings   www.billingscvb.visitmt.com
For a complete list of updated links, visit www.christiantraveler.com

Ashland The St. Labre Indian School in town was established in 1884 by Franciscan missionaries. Today the visitors center, museum, and gallery all feature interesting exhibits of Cheyenne heritage and art.

Bannack This ghost town (west of Dillon) has been preserved virtually intact. It was the site of Montana's first major gold rush in 1862 and it became Montana's first territorial capital. Today Bannack is a quiet park, managed by the state. A visitors center acquaints guests with life in the 1860s. The walking tour introduces you to Sheriff Henry Plummer's gallows, the first jail, and the Methodist church where circuit rider "Brother Van" preached. Late in July Bannack celebrates its history with Bannack Days, a special weekend, including a frontier church service along with gold panning, buggy rides, a rifle shoot, and frontier arts and crafts.

Bigfork The Big Sky Bible Camp is an interdenominational Bible camp located on McCaffery Rd. and operating throughout the summer.

Big Sky The Big Sky Ski and Summer Resort is a lively village that serves as a great home base for outdoor enthusiasts. It's a year-round playground featuring everything from hiking to white-water rafting to skiing and snowmobiling. Gondola rides with spectacular views of the area are available in the summer. Take a hike in the Lee Metcalf Spanish Peaks Wilderness, and for a tremendous view of Lone Mountain, stop by Soldier's Chapel, built in 1955 as a World War II memorial. It might be a good idea to stop there anyway.

Billings Montana's largest city, Billings is a business hub as well as a cultural, medical, educational, and entertainment center. You will enjoy the Western Heritage Center (2822 Montana Ave.), which features "Our Place in the West," a social history of the Yellowstone Valley.

The Pictograph Cave State Park will remind you how short-lived the European American's history in this country has been. The remains of a prehistoric native culture can be viewed here—rock paintings that are visible from a short, paved trail near the cave. More than 30,000 artifacts from this park have been identified.

Your children will enjoy Zoo Montana (2100 S. Shiloh Rd.), which is a combination zoological and botanical garden, specializing in northern latitude temperate species. It also has a sensory garden and a children's zoo and is open from mid-April to mid-October.

Glacier Camp and Retreat Center offers quiet solitude on a 75-acre rustic site on Flathead Lake, less than an hour from Glacier National Park. Their office in town is located at 100 24th St. W.

Bozeman The Museum of the Rockies (600 W. Kagy Blvd.) is associated with Montana State University and showcases 4.5 billion years of northern Rocky Mountain history. Features include paleontology exhibits, a hands-on dinosaur playroom, planetarium shows, and history exhibits.

Butte This city was once known as "the richest hill on earth," the site of copper, gold, and silver mines. The miners who uncovered that wealth donated a portion of their earnings to build the St. Lawrence Church in 1897. Hand-carved altars, some made of marble and brass, and 40 frescoes make this church a beautiful option for Sunday morning worship. The cost to build in 1897 was 25,000 dollars.

North of the city on Rte. 1, in the Anaconda Pintler Wilderness area, is St. Timothy's Chapel. The view of the Georgetown Lake area from the chapel is spectacular.

East of Butte, situated 8,500 feet above sea level and perched atop the Continental Divide, is Our Lady of the Rockies, a 90-foot statue of St. Mary. Tours are available during the summer months, but you can see the exterior at any time of the year. It's just too large to miss.

Deer Lodge This city is the home of the Montana Prison, and you may not want to "do time" here, but the Grant-Kohrs Ranch National Historic Site is a fun place for the family. In the 19th century this was the headquarters for a huge cattle empire that grazed cattle in four states and Canada. It is located on the northern outskirts of town. Besides the bunkhouse, the elegant ranch house, and other buildings, you'll see livestock grazing here.

Also in Deer Lodge is a place called Yesterday's Playthings, which is a Toy Museum, featuring more than a thousand dolls that span a century. This museum, as well as several others, including a Law Enforcement Museum and Frontier Montana, are in the Old Prison Museum Complex at 1106 Main St.

I will lead them beside streams of water on a level path where they will not stumble.
JEREMIAH 31:9

Great Falls To understand the Lewis and Clark expedition, you should visit the Lewis and Clark National Historic Trail Interpretive Center here. It is the newest addition to the many interpretive sites along the Lewis and Clark Trail. It is situated about midway on the trail, along the banks of the Missouri River overlooking Black Eagle Falls. A film by Ken Burns, the creator of the popular PBS series *The Civil War,* is presented, and the exhibits focus on the relations between the explorers and the Indian tribes, as well as the month-long portage around the five falls in the Missouri River near Great Falls. (See Lewis and Clark also under Washburn, N.D., and Astoria and Portland, Ore.)

Helena Maybe you don't expect to see such a cathedral in the Old West, but you have to admit that the Rocky Mountains setting certainly enhances its beauty. The Cathedral of St. Helena (530 N. Ewing St.) is modeled after the Cathedral of the Sacred Heart in Vienna, with twin spires rising 230 feet into the air. Its stained glass comes from Bavaria, and its white marble altar from Italy.

Lewistown The Hutterites are an Amish-like sect that emigrated from Russia to the Dakotas after 1870. However, their pacifism and aloofness caused them problems during World War I and they moved to Canada to avoid military conscription. A few years later, when Canada started to impose limitations on land ownership, they began moving back to the Dakotas and Montana. Today there are about 40 colonies, each with a population of between 50 and 100 people, living in central and north central Montana. It was in the Lewistown area that they established their first colony in 1937 and many Hutterites still live here. Although many of them, unlike the Amish, drive cars and use telephones, most of them do not use buttons, but, rather, use hooks and eyes. They also shun television and musical instruments. (See Hutterites also under Rockport and Yankton, S.D., and St. Jacobs, Ont.).

Missoula This town of 43,000 residents is Montana's third-largest city and its cultural center. There is much for all ages here, including the Memorial Rose Garden (Brooks St.) with more than 2,500 rose bushes, a Carousel for Missoula experience for the kids, and the Snowbowl Summer Chairlift Ride, a 22-minute lift that takes you up 7,000 feet. The ride is located in a popular ski area 12 miles northwest of town, and from 7,000 feet you can get a good look at the majestic scenery. Phone 406-549-9777 for more information.

The carousel is something special. It is the first fully hand-carved carousel to be built in America since the Great Depression. Hundreds of volunteers worked to design, carve, sand, and paint ponies and gargoyles, piece together stained glass windows, and raise funds to build a location for the finished project. So visit the carousel in Caras Park, downtown on the Clark Fork River, and be appreciative of all the labor that went into it.

The National Bison Range just north of town in the village of Moiese is where you can view not only bison but also elk, deer, antelope, and bighorn sheep through your car windows.

And don't forget old St. Francis Xavier Church (420 W. Pine St.), built in 1889, the year that Montana became a state. It is outstanding for its graceful steeple, paintings, and stained glass.

St. Ignatius This town outside Polson was originally a Catholic mission, built cooperatively with the local Native Americans. The town's St. Ignatius Church was established in 1854, after St. Mary's Church in Stevensville was forced to close. St. Ignatius was orig- inally a simple wooden chapel, but late in the 19th century a large brick church was erected. Its walls and ceilings are enhanced with 58 murals by Brother Joseph Carignano showing scenes from Bible history. St. Ignatius is the old- est continuously operating mission in Montana and is a favorite among photog- raphers because of its beautiful setting. The Mission Range of mountains provides a striking backdrop for the mission.

GREAT PLACES FOR FAMILY FUN

✔ Horse packing at the White Tail Ranch, Ovando, Montana

✔ White-water rafting Idaho's Salmon River

✔ Skiing or mountain biking around Whitefish, Montana

Stevensville The story of St. Mary's Mis- sion here begins in 1823 when 24 Iroquois Indians, employed by the Hudson Bay Company, settled in as trappers among the Flathead tribe in the Bitterroot Valley. The Iroquois people had been introduced to Christianity some 200 years earlier and spoke with the Flatheads of white men who wore long black gowns, carried crucifixes, and instructed people in how to know God. The Flatheads and their neighbors, the Nez Perce, became so intrigued that they sent four delegations to St. Louis to obtain their own Black Robe. And so St. Mary's was established. In the first year the Jesuits baptized 700 Indians. Word spread of the Black Robes' arrival, and soon Indians from sur- rounding tribes came to the head priest, Father Ravalli, who was also a physician, surgeon, pharmacist, architect, artist, and sculp- tor. St. Mary's became a center for training in religion, academics, music, and trade skills. Today you can tour the old buildings of St. Mary's Mission and remember the fascinating history.

Virginia City This and neighboring Nevada City are two authen- tically preserved and restored mining camps from the 1860s gold rush era (Rte. 287, between Butte and Yellowstone Park). Chil- dren can try gold panning here. Nightly during the summer, the Virginia City Players offer 19th-century melodrama. Period build- ings are also on display.

West Glacier Glacier National Park joins with Waterton Lakes National Park in Canada to make up the Waterton/Glacier International Peace Park with more than 50 glaciers. On Sunday there are worship services at more than a dozen locations.

Five miles from Glacier National Park is Shiloh Valley near the town of Coram. Owned by a Christian couple, Shiloh Valley offers vacation lodging in a secluded setting.

West Yellowstone In the winter this is known as the snowmobile capital of the world, but the National Geographic IMAX theater is open year-round and it will give you a graphic introduction to Yellowstone Park. It won't substitute for the real thing, of course, but it's a different way to experience the park, especially if you can't get deep into the backcountry for one reason or another. The Grizzly Discovery Center nearby is an educational facility devoted to the preservation of bears and wolves.

Wibaux This gateway to eastern Montana has a rich history. The Wibaux County Museum Complex (Orgain St.) provides an introduction. Also on Orgain St. is St. Peter's Catholic Church, with its stained glass and lava rock exterior. It was built in 1885 through the generosity of Pierre Wibaux himself.

■UTAH

Tourist Info
Phone 801-538-1030
Web sites
  Entire state   www.utah.com
  Salt Lake City   www.visitsaltlake.com
For a complete list of updated links, visit www.christiantraveler.com

Utah was founded by Mormons seeking refuge from the severe religious persecution they had experienced out East. On July 24, 1847, Brigham Young looked out over the Salt Lake Valley and announced to his ragged band of pioneers, "This is the place." So Salt Lake City was founded, and indeed Utah. If there were any doubts that Utah bears the legacy of that emigration, statistics prove otherwise. Over 70 percent of the state's population is Mormon today.

THE MORMONS IN UTAH

The Mormon church was founded in 1830 by Joseph Smith in Fayette, New York. These Latter-day Saints, as they called themselves, had religious beliefs that were outside mainstream Christian tradition and they were often feared and hated for their differences. Persecution and antagonism pushed the Mormons west, to Ohio, Missouri, and eventually to Nauvoo, Illinois. While there, the group prospered and grew until a new wave of antagonism surfaced. Hostilities escalated until Joseph Smith and his brother Hyrum were killed, while in prison, by an angry mob. The following year adversaries burned more than 200 Mormon homes and farm buildings.

So the Mormons moved west, as did some 400,000 other Americans. From 1846 to 1869 more than 70,000 Mormons traveled along the Mormon Pioneer Trail, one of the nation's greatest mass migrations. They were a unique part of the nation's westward expansion, in that they did not go voluntarily, but were driven by their desire to find a place where they could worship in peace.

On July 24, 1847, Brigham Young looked out over the Salt Lake Valley and announced to his ragged band of pioneers, "This is the place." So Salt Lake City was founded, and indeed Utah. Reminders of the Mormons' presence are everywhere within Salt Lake City, including the famous Mormon Tabernacle and its choir. But the evidence of Mormon influence extends the entire length of the Mormon Pioneer Trail, from small settlements established along the way to the wagon ruts in the rock.

Historic Christianity differs from Mormon theology on basic doctrines. But whatever your view of Mormon tenets, their strong commitment to family and an honest work ethic deserve respect. Large numbers of American businesses have relocated to Salt Lake City in recent years for just those reasons.

If viewing Mormon sites isn't your thing, Utah still has plenty to offer. The Great Salt Lake is the most saline body of water on earth except for the Dead Sea. Water flows into the lake but it has no outlet. This traps minerals and salts, making for an interesting swimming experience. The water is so buoyant that no one has ever drowned here.

Skiing is extremely popular. The Wasatch Mountains and Park City are Utah's premier ski destinations, with powder that can compete with any other place in the country. Or visit God's creation in the south of the state and see the national parks that are sometimes referred to as the "Fab Five": Arches, Bryce Canyon, Canyonlands, Capitol Reef, and Zion.

Bluff Father Harold Lieber, an Episcopalian missionary, came into this canyon country in southeastern Utah in 1943. He established St. Christopher's

Episcopal Mission to reach the Navajo Indians. He built a school, chapel, and other buildings. Visitors are welcome. It is located two miles northeast of Bluff.

Cedar City The Utah Shakespearean Festival is held here on Southern Utah University campus during the summer months. Day care services are provided on the festival grounds. Six evening performances are rotated so there is a new play performed every evening and there are matinees in the afternoons. Evening performances are preceded by Elizabethan music, juggling, magic, and storytelling.

GREAT PLACES TO ENJOY GOD'S CREATION

✔ Enjoying the landscape's colors in Arches National Park

✔ Hiking the trails in Bryce Canyon National Park

✔ Walking to the hanging gardens near Weeping Rock, Zion National Park

Corinne Five miles west of Brigham City on the way to the Golden Spike National Historic Site is the little town of Corinne. For many years it was called the "Gentile" (non-Mormon) capital of Utah. The Methodist Church at S. Sixth and Colorado Sts., dating from 1870, is believed to be the first non-Mormon church built in the state.

Golden Spike National Historic Site On May 10, 1869, railroad tracks from the Atlantic seaboard and the West Coast were joined at this spot, as a transcontinental railroad linked the East with the West. The visitors center relives that historic moment when the Golden Spike was driven in. Each May 10 there is a festive celebration of the occasion, and in August there is a Railroaders Festival here.

Kanab Because hundreds of films and TV episodes have been filmed in the area, it is logical that Frontier Movie Town should be located here on Center St. It features a western town, museum, and original movie sets from a variety of productions. You can also enjoy a dinner and western show.

Moab A variety of motorboat, jetboat, and rafting experiences are available along the Colorado River. At one section the river is gentle enough for even amateur rafters to navigate by themselves.

A motorboat "Canyonlands at Night" tour includes a sound and light show on the way back.

Ogden The Abbey of Our Lady of the Holy Trinity is a community of 30 Trappist monks. In its chapel and reception area, the monks explain their work. They produce bread, honey, and farm products. The abbey is located four miles southeast of Huntsville at 1250 S. 9500 East.

Park City The Park City Silver Mine Adventure is an elevator trip down into a 1,500-foot shaft; then you go on a narrow gauge train 3,500 feet into mine shafts to explore the mine's inner workings. Guides explain the mining process.

Provo At 246 N. 100 East St. is the McCurdy Historical Doll Museum, which has 3,000 dolls costumed according to various themes. Among them are Women of the Bible, Folk Dresses of the World, First Ladies of America, and American Indian Dolls. The museum is open afternoons, Tuesday through Saturday.

Salt Lake City The Mormon presence is felt nowhere more strongly than in Salt Lake City and in the smaller cities surrounding the capital. In the center of the city is Temple Square, the heart of Mormonism. It's a ten-acre square, pleasant and beautifully landscaped. The Mormon Temple is on the east side, and the Mormon Tabernacle is on the west. The many-spired Temple is off-limits to non-Mormons, but the Tabernacle is open to the public, as are the visitors centers, which are filled with Mormon history.

The Mormon Tabernacle, built in 1867, is so accoustically sensitive that a pin dropped in one end of the building can be heard 175 feet away at the other end. Almost synonymous with the Tabernacle in many people's minds is the Mormon Tabernacle Choir. Members of the choir are chosen based on their musical competence and personal character, and occasionally on family tradition. Sunday morning broadcasts and Thursday Tabernacle Choir rehearsals are open to the public. The choir is accompanied by a massive 11,623 pipe organ, and visitors can enjoy twice-daily organ recitals (except Sundays). In the summer months there are also frequent concerts at Assembly Hall, located next to the Tabernacle.

Whether you are Mormon or not, you'll enjoy the free elevator ride up to the top of the Saints Office Building (50 E. North Temple St.). It's the highest skyscraper in the city. From here you can take in fabulous views of the Great Salt Lake and the Wasatch Range.

If you are interested in tracing your family's genealogy, you may want to visit the Family History Library at 35 N. West Temple St. Mormons have specialized in genealogical research because, if they discover who their ancestors are, they believe they can be baptized by proxy for them and thereby seal them for all eternity (if the spirit of the ancestor consents). The library is open to the public and the staff will answer all your questions.

The Pioneer Memorial Museum (300 N. Main St.), next to the capitol, has personal items that belonged to the area's earliest settlers. These items include tools, carriages, toys, and dolls, as well as information about the early Mormon leaders.

Hansen Planetarium (15 S. State St.), also on capitol hill, is an impressive turn-of-the-century building. Visitors can enjoy wonderful free exhibits, including a moon rock and laser shows set to classic rock music.

Every Tuesday and Friday evening in the hot summer months, the Temple Square Concert Series conducts free outdoor concerts in Brigham Young Historic Park. Visitors can enjoy everything from classical music to rock and roll.

GREAT PLACES FOR FAMILY FUN

- ✔ Dinosaur National Monument
- ✔ Skiing at Alta near Salt Lake City
- ✔ Swimming (floating) in the Great Salt Lake

North of downtown at 840 N. 300 West (US 89), the Children's Museum is a hands-on experience, whether it is implanting an artificial heart in a dummy, piloting a 727 jet trainer, or using computers. There are also handicap-awareness simulations, which give children the opportunity to know what it feels like to live with a disability. Children are challenged to take a wheelchair through an obstacle course and to walk through a "blind room."

The Lagoon Amusement Park and Pioneer Village is 16 miles north of Salt Lake City (off I-15 on Lagoon Dr.) and has roller coaster rides, a giant Ferris wheel, and other midway favorites. A beach provides water slides and landscaped pools. Pioneer Village lets you interact with the past through its authentic 19th-century buildings, stagecoach and steam train rides, and a variety of exhibits.

The Abravanel Concert Hall (23 W. South Temple St.) glitters with gold leaf, crystal chandeliers, and brass railings. Its acoustic design makes it one of the best concert halls in the world.

While Mormons (or technically, members of the Church of Jesus Christ of Latter-day Saints) comprise a large percentage of the population of Utah, Christian denominations have their representatives here too. Although it is now independent, Westminster College (1840 S. 1300 East) was begun as a Presbyterian boys preparatory school in 1875 and became a Presbyterian college around the turn of the century. Its concerts and theater performances are open to the public.

First Presbyterian Church is located at 347 E. Temple St., and the Roman Catholic Cathedral of the Madeleine is nearby at 331 E. Temple St.. The Cathedral is open daily and presents concerts Sunday evenings in spring and summer.

Vernal Near this city and crossing over the Colorado border is Dinosaur National Monument, established in 1915. Paleontologist Earl Douglass unearthed a large collection of fossilized dinosaur bones here some seven years earlier. Many more have been discovered since then. Children will especially enjoy watching modern-day paleontologists at work under the roof of the visitors center, carefully picking away at massive bones that still lie entombed in the surrounding rock. There is a sense of discovery here, as well as the opportunity to watch real scientists at work.

■WYOMING

Tourist Info
Phone 800-225-5996
Web site
 Entire state   www.wyomingtourism.org
For a complete list of updated links, visit www.christiantraveler.com

Buffalo Carousel Park (655 Hart St.) features a renovated 1925 Spillman carousel, with reproductions of bucking horses. It also has the Cloud Peak Ferris Wheel, which was built during the 1930s. The high ride will give you a good view of the Bighorn Mountains and the Cloud Peak Wilderness Area.

Casper St. Anthony's (1st and Center Sts.) was the first Catholic church in Casper, founded in 1898. The present structure is a bit more recent; it was dedicated in 1920. The square bell tower, tile roof, round arched windows, and corbel tables more closely resemble Italian churches than western American ones.

In the North Casper Park complex on Bryan-Evansville Rd., you can see an interpretive sign associated with a historic ferry that was built to assist travelers in crossing the North Platte River. It was an important aid for many settlers. The ferryboat consisted of two 30-foot cottonwood logs covered with planks to carry wagons. The ferry operated at different locations from 1847 to 1851. No traces of the crossing remain at the park, but there is a replica of the ferry at Fort Casper.

GREAT PLACES FOR FAMILY FUN

✔ Camping on Jenny Lake, Grand Teton National Park

✔ The prairie dog towns scattered around Devil's Tower National Monument

✔ Hiking in Yellowstone National Park

The Historic Trails Expeditions departing from Fort Casper (4001 Fort Casper Rd.) feature a wagon train, which travels along the actual ruts of the California, Oregon, and Mormon Trails. Or if you prefer, you can ride horses, as the Indians did, along the trails.

Just southwest of Casper is Independence Rock, an important landmark for the wagon trains on their way west. The rock was so named by an early group who arrived on July 4. As other bands of emigrants passed the rock, it became clear that meeting this landmark by Independence Day was an important milestone, because it meant that the settlers would probably reach their destinations before winter set in. Further reason for celebration was the rock's proximity to the refreshing waters of the Sweetwater River, a great stopover point. Settlers who reached Independence Rock carved their names and dates on its smooth surface, as much a register for those who would follow as it was graffiti. Father Pierre Jean de Smet, a famous Jesuit missionary, appropriately nicknamed the place "The Register of the Desert" in 1840. Many of those names can still be read. (See de Smet also under Hazelwood, Mo.; De Smet, S.D.; and Kettle Falls, Wash.)

Cheyenne During Cheyenne's Frontier Days, the last week in July every year, the town doubles in size as people come from across the country to participate in the world's largest outdoor rodeo competition. Visitors will also enjoy free pancake breakfasts at the Chamber of Commerce, parades, big-name country music concerts, and square dancing. Of course, you should be forewarned that any time during June and July "a gunfight is always possible" in Cheyenne, and the Cheyenne Gunslingers fulfill that threat at W. 16th and Carey Sts., shooting one another with blanks every Monday through Friday evening at 6 P.M. and every Saturday at "high noon." You may want to visit their soda saloon at 218 W. 17th St.

The Old West Museum (in Frontier Park, 4610 N. Carey Ave.) houses a large collection of western memorabilia, including 125 carriages. During Frontier Days, top western wildlife and landscape artists from across the country exhibit their work at this museum. Guided tours are geared toward children.

St. Mark's Episcopal Church (1908 Central Ave.), completed in 1893, and First United Methodist Church (18th and Central Ave.), built in 1894, are both landmarks in the city.

Two-hour summer trolley tours, which take you to the Old West Museum and F. E. Warren Air Force Base, as well as downtown Cheyenne, are available. The trolley departs from the Cheyenne Area Tourist Center at 10:30 A.M. and 2:30 P.M. each day. Admission is $6.50 for adults.

Cody Many visitors consider Cody merely a point along the path to Yellowstone's east entrance. But if you're interested in the history of the American West, you really ought to see the Buffalo Bill Historical Center. It includes the Buffalo Bill Museum, a Plains Indian Museum, the Whitney Gallery of Western Art, and the Cody Firearms Museum, boasting the world's largest collection of American firearms.

Evanston Four churches line Center St. in this Uinta Mountain town: United Presbyterian, built in 1902; the United Methodist church, built in 1929; the Roman Catholic church, built in 1939; and the Baptist church, built in 1892.

Grand Teton National Park The Chapel of the Transfiguration has become one of Wyoming's most photographed scenes. Episcopal services are held during the summer. Behind the altar of the 1925 log chapel a wall of glass permits a broad view of the towering saw-toothed Teton range. The chapel is located four miles north of Jackson at US 26/191/89, inside Grand Teton National Park. The national park has more than 200 miles of trails.

Green River Green River's oldest church is St. John's Episcopal Church, a wood frame building erected in 1892. The town is the starting point for John Wesley Powell's descent of the Colorado River in 1869. At Expedition Island you can see the place where his ten-man crew launched their four wooden boats into the water.

Jackson Hole Jackson Hole's permanent population is only 4,500 but it has about 2,200 motel rooms and hundreds of camping and RV spaces. It also has traffic problems. Although Jackson has become increasingly popular as a retreat for the wealthy, locals are determined not to allow what they refer to as "Aspenization."

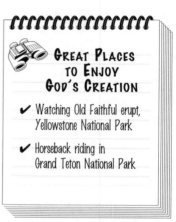

GREAT PLACES TO ENJOY GOD'S CREATION

✔ Watching Old Faithful erupt, Yellowstone National Park

✔ Horseback riding in Grand Teton National Park

Raised wooden sidewalks and old-fashioned storefronts make you wonder if Jackson is a Wild West movie set. The St. John's Episcopal Church, finished in 1915, is one of a handful of buildings that looks and is historic. It is a dignified log building with an unusual stockade-type bell tower.

A variety of river trips is offered, from white-water rafting to scenic float trips on calmer waters. When it comes time to settle down, check out Granite Hot Springs (south of Jackson off US 181 and ten miles into the Bridger-Teton National Forest). You'll find a creekside campground, a hot springs pool, hiking trails, and great scenery.

Three miles north of town is the National Elk Refuge (2820 Rugius Rd.). A herd of more than 7,000 elk hole up here in the winter months. You can take horse-drawn sleigh trips to see the elk from mid-December through March.

Kemmerer This is a high-elevation desert coal town, but its claim to fame is that it was the home of J. C. Penney, the retail chain magnate. He began with a small retail outlet here in Kemmerer in 1902, with an original investment of 500 dollars, and then expanded and expanded and expanded. The homestead of this

Christian businessman now sits at 107 J. C. Penney Drive, and it's worth a visit.

Lander In nearby Atlantic City (and no one is sure how it got its name) is the St. Andrews Episcopal Church, built in 1911. It has a wood stove dating to 1893.

The Sinks Canyon State Park is near Lander. It has a series of waterfalls and cascades that is reached by a 1.5-mile foot trail through a river gorge.

Laramie Railroad aficionados as well as the entire family will enjoy Laramie's scenic railroad. It crosses the plains to Centennial, stops for an hour so passengers can visit a museum, and then climbs to Albany, before returning to Laramie via Foxpark. Phone 307-742-9162 for details.

The Wyoming Territorial Park is a good family visit too. It includes a Frontier Town and the Territorial Prison.

Rawlins The France Memorial Presbyterian Church (Cedar and 3d Sts.) was built in 1882, making it one of the oldest structures in the area.

The Wyoming Frontier Prison here, which replaced the Territorial Prison in 1901, was used until 1981, and is open throughout the summer.

Riverton The Riverton Museum contains reconstructions of many frontier buildings, including a church, school, post office, dentist's office, and bank.

Yellowstone National Park There is a great deal for any family to enjoy here, and a favorite area is around Old Faithful. Most of the trails here are quite short, but if you want a longer trail, go to the Midway Geyser Basin and walk the three-and-a-quarter-mile Fairy Creek Trail.

States of the Pacific

THE PACIFIC STATES CONTAIN the most diversity of any of the groupings in this book. Yet they do share a number of things in common. All owe much of their survival to the Pacific Ocean, which they share. All of the Pacific states have strong native cultures, from the Inuit tribes of Alaska to the Polynesians of Hawaii to the Native Americans along the mainland's West Coast. And all of these states are home to some of this country's most spectacular natural beauty. Christian travelers may find that their most spiritual experiences will be found not in any man-made locations but rather in this region's glorious outdoors.

There are man-made treasures as well. Make time in your schedule to visit one of the remaining Spanish missions dotting the California landscape. Stretching from Sonoma south to San Diego, they are well worth a detour.

■ALASKA

Tourist Info
Phone 907-465-2012
Web sites
  Entire state   www.visitalaska.org
  Anchorage   www.anchorage.net
  Inside Passage   www.alaskainfo.org
  Juneau   www.juneau.com
For a complete list of updated links, visit www.christiantraveler.com

Anchorage Since you probably don't want to enter the Iditarod, you may prefer to take your family on an hour-long float trip on the Matanuska River. You may also like the experience of panning for gold, and that is something else you can do within an hour from downtown Anchorage. Or you can go from Anchorage by bus or by railway to Denali National Park

The Alaska Experience Theater (705 W. 6th Ave.) provides a good overview of the state. A 40-minute film, "Alaska the Greatland," is projected on a 180-degree screen. The film was made from planes, river rafts, and trains, so it gives you a good panorama of Alaska's splendor.

The Alaska Zoo (at milepost 2 on O'Malley Rd.) is a good place to see local wildlife, including some animals that are generally difficult to spot.

GREAT PLACES FOR FAMILY FUN

✔ Totem Bight State Historical Park near Ketchikan

✔ Discovering great scenery and wildlife in the Kenai Fjords

✔ Skiing in the Alyeska Resort south of Anchorage

Chugach National Forest Big Game Alaska (Seward Hwy., milepost 79) is a 100-acre drive-through wild animal park, and it gives you the opportunity to see musk oxen, buffalo, Sitka blacktail deer, moose, and reindeer.

You can take a one-hour narrated Portage Glacier Cruise (you board about 5.5 miles east of milepost 79 on the Seward Hwy.). You will be taken to within 300 yards of the Portage Glacier and view sections of the glacier breaking off into the ocean below.

Eklutna In 1830 Russian missionaries came here to convert the Athabascan Indians and they built the St. Nicholas Russian Orthodox Church. The log structure still stands (Glenn Hwy., milepost 28) and is still used for services.

Fairbanks Yes, they have theme parks in Alaska. Alaskaland (Airport and Peger Rds.) includes early 20th-century buildings, live shows, an aviation museum, some Christian rock on the loudspeakers, but not many rides.

Fairbanks is the home of the University of Alaska (501 Yukon Dr.). Worth seeing is the university's museum. The collection includes a 36,000-year-old mummified steppe bison, a whale skull, dinosaur fossils, and ivory carvings. In summer the museum's daily programs focus on Alaska's northern Native groups. You are allowed to touch and explore Native masks and tools, animal skins, and historic artifacts.

Juneau St. Nicholas Russian Orthodox Church (on 5th St.) is a must-see. The hexagonal and onion-domed church was constructed in 1894 and holds rows of icons and a fabulous altar. It is the oldest original Russian church in Alaska. Services are held every weekend and are conducted in English, Old Slavonic, and Tlingit.

Bus tours can take you to view the impressive Mendenhall Glacier or visit the Chapel by the Lake at Auke Lake. This is one of the larger Protestant churches in the state.

The Alaska State Museum (395 Whittier St.) is an excellent introduction to the history and culture of Alaska's four major native groups: Tlingit, Athabascan, Aleut, and Inuit.

Kenai At the Holy Assumption Russian Orthodox Church (Mission St., off Overland), not only do you get an understanding of the Russian heritage of the area, but you also get a wonderful view of the Kenai inlet.

Ketchikan The Totem Heritage Center (601 Deermount St.), perched on a hill over the city, has 33 totem poles for various villages. It is the largest collection of authentic totem poles in the United States.

Kodiak The Baranof Museum (101 Maine Way) is the oldest Russian structure in Alaska, and for that matter it is the oldest wooden structure on the West Coast, built around 1793. The oldest parish in Alaska is the Russian Orthodox Church here, which dates from 1794. Its old church bells are still rung by hand.

Ninilchik This small village—population 750—is an old Russian fishing village with an interesting old church, the Holy Transfiguration of our Lord Orthodox Church, built in 1901.

RUSSIAN ORTHODOX IN ALASKA

Economic and strategic interests in Alaska brought Europeans from England, Spain, France, and Russia. But Russia quickly won the upper hand and established fur trading outposts all along the Alaska coastline. With those outposts came Russian Orthodox priests whose mission was not only to minister to the Russian settlers in the area but to deliver the gospel to the native peoples.

In 1791 these Russian settlers established Fort St. Nicholas Redoubt at the mouth of the Kenai River. While the Orthodox priests worked from chapels within this important fort and from other outposts, it wasn't until 1845 that Father Nikolai Militov was able to establish a permanent parish in Kenai. Thousands of local Indians would hear the Word and be baptized, and the familiar Russian onion domes would soon dot the Alaskan skies.

Alaska's oldest existing Russian church is the small St. Nicholas Russian Orthodox Church in Juneau. The hexagonal and onion-domed church was constructed in 1894 and holds rows of icons and a fabulous altar. Services are held every weekend and are still conducted in Old Slavonic as well as in English and Tlingit. Other interesting churches include the Holy Assumption of the Virgin Mary Russian Orthodox Church in Kenai and St. Michael's Cathedral in Sitka.

Palmer The Musk Ox Farm (two miles north at milepost 50) is said to be the only musk ox domestication project in the world, and we believe them. The animals are valued for their underwool, which is knitted by Eskimos and is eight times warmer than wool.

Not far away is the Reindeer Farm (11 miles on the Old Glenn Hwy.). Here you can feed and pet the reindeer if you wish.

Sitka Sheldon Jackson College is a Presbyterian College located here. Sheldon Jackson, a missionary who worked his lifetime with the Eskimos, is remembered by a museum that has exhibits on his ministry as well as on Eskimo, Aleut, and Indian life. It is one of the best museums in Alaska for native artifacts and history.

St. Michael's Cathedral (Lincoln St.) with its onion-shaped dome is a Sitka landmark. Built in 1848 and rebuilt in 1966, it has an extensive collection of Russian Orthodox art, including enameled porcelain and wedding crowns.

The Russian Bishop's House, just two blocks down Lincoln St., is a log building constructed in 1842. It is one of the few remaining Russian colonial buildings in America. It is open to visitors in summer only.

Valdez Residents here remember well what happened on two Good Fridays: In 1964 Valdez had a devastating earthquake on Good Friday, and in 1989 the city had the devastating Valdez oil spill on Good Friday. The town is rebuilding again, and if you want to talk more about it, check out the Valley Christian Book and Coffee Shoppe (126 Pioneer Dr.), where you can order soup-in-a-sourdough bowl or have a bagel with cream cheese at the same time you are reading a Christian book. Make sure you don't spill any coffee. They don't like spills in Valdez.

■CALIFORNIA

Tourist Info
Phone 800-GO-CALIF
Web sites
Entire state   www.gocalif.ca.gov
Long Beach   www.lbacvb.org
Los Angeles   www.lacvb.com
Monterey   www.monterey-travel.org
San Diego   www.sandiego.org
San Francisco   www.sfbayarea.com
San Jose   www.sanjose.org
San Luis Obispo   www.visitslo.com
For a complete list of updated links, visit www.christiantraveler.com

Anaheim The big attraction in Anaheim is certainly Disneyland, nicknamed "the happiest place on earth." The park was clearly not designed for the number of visitors that come here, and consequently the park feels busier than its more heavily visited cousin Disney World in Orlando. But Disney does know how to entertain in style, and visitors can't help but enjoy themselves. Disneyland now has eight theme parks. Mickey's Toontown, almost a suburb of Fantasyland, is the latest addition.

347

Azusa Azusa Pacific College, an interdenominational evangelical school in this town east of Los Angeles, has been growing rapidly in the past two decades.

Berkeley The Bade Institute of Biblical Archaeology (1798 Scenic Ave.), associated with the Pacific School of Religion, is devoted to the archaeology of Palestine. Its biblical collection has documents from the 5th to 18th centuries. The museum is open Monday through Friday.

GREAT PLACES TO ENJOY GOD'S CREATION

✔ Denali on a cloudless day, Denali National Park

✔ Glimpses of wildlife in Wrangell-St. Elias National Park

✔ Cruising through Glacier Bay National Park

Buena Park Knott's Berry Farm (8039 Beach Blvd.) is smaller and more manageable than Disneyland. It began as a real farm, and when Mrs. Knott started selling her boysenberry pies and chicken dinners during the Depression, it got the whole thing going. Now there are over 165 rides, attractions, shops, shows, and restaurants. In addition to thrill rides like Montezooma's Revenge, Jaguar!, and Boomerang, visitors can enjoy a pioneer village with working artisans. Besides that, it is now the official home of Snoopy and the Peanuts characters. And don't forget to shop for the boysenberry pies that made Mrs. Knott famous.

Carmel The Carmel Mission, or more properly Mission San Carlos Borromeo del Rio Carmel (Rio Rd. and Rte. 1), is one of the loveliest missions in the state. It was the second mission founded by Father Junipero Serra in 1770 and the place where he chose to be buried. (See Father Serra also under San Diego, San Francisco, San Juan Capistrano, San Luis Obispo, and Santa Cruz.)

The Biblical Garden at the Church of the Wayfarer (Lincoln St. and 7th Ave.) contains trees and plants mentioned in the Bible and that are indigenous to the Holy Land. A 32-rank pipe organ provides quarterly concerts. Stained glass windows in the sanctuary depict biblical as well as local scenes.

Fremont Mission San Jose Chapel and Museum (43300 Mission Blvd.), founded in 1797, is elegant inside with crystal chandeliers, murals, and religious paintings.

Fresno Near Fresno is the Hume Lake Christian Camp and Bible Conference facility, which is open throughout the year. The camp is located at 5545 E. Hedges Ave.

Fullerton Writer and pastor Charles R. Swindoll was minister at the First Evangelical Free Church (2801 Brea Blvd.) from 1971 to 1994, when he became president of Dallas Theological Seminary.

Garden Grove This is the home of both the Crystal Cathedral (12141 Lewis St.) and the TV program *Hour of Power,* founded by Dr. Robert H. Schuller. The Crystal Cathedral, made of 10,000 panes of glass, is 120 feet high. In addition, the Crean Tower contains the Arvella Schuller Carillon and the Mary Hood Prayer Tower. Tours are provided for visitors through the massive 18-million-dollar facility, which includes grounds, arboretum, and cathedral. *The Glory of Easter* and *The Glory of Christmas* are special dramatic spectaculars, telling the gospel stories, in March and April and in November and December each year at the cathedral.

Glendale Forest Lawn Memorial Park (1712 S. Glendale Ave.) displays a trilogy of huge paintings portraying the three most dramatic moments in the life of Christ: the crucifixion, the resurrection, and the ascension. Jan Styka's *Crucifixion* at 45 by 195 feet is one of the world's largest religious oil paintings. Forest Lawn also has reproductions of some of Michelangelo's greatest works. The museum at the park displays all types of coins mentioned in Scripture and also has a gem collection. Buried here are some of Hollywood's most famous celebrities, including Clark Gable, George Burns, and Sammy Davis Jr.

Hollywood Universal Studios (at the junction of Hollywood and Ventura Freeways) makes it possible for you to experience the parting of the Red Sea. A tour tram waits for the waters to part, then drives through. Five-hour tours through the movie/TV studios are available.

The Hollywood Bowl (2301 N. Highland Ave.) has concerts on Tuesdays, Thursdays, and weekends from early July to mid-September. It has been a Los Angeles tradition since 1922.

The First Presbyterian Church of Hollywood (1760 N. Gower St.) has long been an evangelical stronghold in this movie-minded city. Henrietta Mears, who founded Gospel Light Publishing, was director of Christian education here and was a key influence in the lives of such Christian leaders as Bill Bright and Richard Halverson.

Joshua Tree National Park Situated in the hot Mojave desert, Joshua Tree National Park and its namesake trees received their name from the Mormon pioneers who crossed the desert in the 19th century. Apparently the Mormons thought the trees' crooked limbs looked like the Old Testament leader beckoning his people into the Promised Land. It's an interesting story, but don't expect that you will recognize these trees as Joshua or any other human. Perhaps it was the heat.

La Canada If you want to get away from the hustle and bustle of L.A., try the Descanso Gardens (1418 Descanso Dr.), nestled below an umbrella of California live oaks. It is the largest camellia forest in the world, and that is not to mention the lilac grove and the large azalea patch. A 45-minute tram ride will take you through it all.

La Mirada Biola University and Talbot Seminary (both at 13800 Biola Ave.) had their roots in Los Angeles, and when Biola moved out to this suburb, it adopted the initials of its old name, Bible Institute of Los Angeles.

The Far East Broadcast Company, which operates Christian radio stations around the world, is headquartered here at 15700 Imperial Hwy.

Lompoc La Purisma Concepcion was once a picturesque community of over 1,000 Native Americans, priests, and soldiers. Its 20,000 cattle, efficient agricultural system, and ten-acre vineyard formed a model of self-sufficiency and gave the mission a favorable reputation throughout California. But tragedy destroyed most of the mission. In 1812 a series of violent earthquakes followed by floods and heavy rains destroyed La Purisma. Despite attempts at rebuilding, the mission never regained its former status.

Today's visitor to La Purisma Mission State Historic Park will find the mission rebuilt as it was in its glory days. The 900-acre grounds of La Purisma comprise the only mission in California that is complete with a church, a cemetery, living quarters, a kitchen, and gardens. The tools and equipment commonly used during mission times are on view, and on designated weekends costumed interpreters take up the tasks that were once commonplace here. La Purisma is located on Rte. 246, two miles northeast of Lompoc. Admission is free.

Los Angeles The Los Angeles Zoo (located within Griffith Park at 5333 Zoo Dr.) allows you to get oriented to its 113-acre spread with a Safari Shuttle that encircles the zoo. This zoo, which is divided geographically so that the 2,000 animals are separated according to continent, is consistently counted among the nation's best.

El Pueblo de Los Angeles State Historic Park preserves a number of historic buildings of Spanish and Mexican origin. The Sepulveda House is the location of the visitors center, which offers free walking tours. Beginning in the Old Plaza, you make your way toward the Avila Adobe, the oldest house in the city, which now is done in concrete instead of its original adobe to meet earthquake precautions. Then go on to the Old Plaza Church (on North Main St. at the Plaza), which is the oldest church in Los Angeles. It was completed in 1822 and still ministers to an active parish.

First Baptist Church (760 S. Westmoreland Ave.) has rose windows patterned after the

THE SPANISH MISSIONS OF CALIFORNIA

Father Junipero Serra, an enthusiastic Franciscan priest, had plans for a chain of missions running along the California coast. In 1769 the padre began with San Diego, and thus began the Camino Real, or the Royal Road. Stretched out over 600 miles, from just north of the Mexican border to just north of San Francisco, each mission was designed to be one day's walk from the next, stopping points for traveling padres.

The padres established 21 missions in all, many of which became the foundations of California's biggest and most important cities: San Diego, Los Angeles, San Francisco, and San Jose among them. Beyond establishing supply outposts, the missions introduced cattle, sheep, and horses as well as old-world skills and business practices. Not only did the meatpacking and wine and fruit production trades provide food for missions, they also helped pay operating expenses. The missions became educational, social, and religious centers for the local people.

Modern-day visitors can get a glimpse of life in those early missions at many different locations. The real jewels include Santa Barbara, La Purisma Concepcion, and Santa Ines. Many of the mission churches continue to function as active parishes and celebrate their history with colorful festivals, featuring mariachi music, dancing, and lots of food.

351

windows of the Chartres cathedral in France, and its gold leaf embossed ceiling is patterned after an Italian palace.

St. John's Church (514 E. Adams Blvd., east of Figueroa) is an Episcopalian church patterned after an 11th-century church in Toscanella, Italy. On the west side of the clerestory is a Martin Luther King Jr. window, dedicated in 1977.

St. Sophia Cathedral (1324 S. Normandie St.) has large-scale murals, gilded woodwork, and crystal chandeliers in its interior. It is Greek Orthodox.

Edward V. Hill, powerful black pastor born in a Texas log cabin, has been pastor of the Greater Mount Zion Baptist Church (4925 Compton Ave.) since 1961.

Aimee Semple MacPherson founded the International Church of the Foursquare Gospel (910 W. Sunset Blvd.) in 1927. She was the first woman to preach on the radio in 1920, bought a radio station in 1924, and founded a Bible college in 1926.

Mission Viejo The vision of Pastor Rick Warren has developed Saddleback Valley Community Church (23456 Madero #100) into a very unique outreach. The church keeps outgrowing its facilities and its Sunday morning attendance is now in the thousands.

Mount Hermon The Mount Hermon Camp and Conference Center offers Bible conferences throughout the year (just off Hwy. 17). It has gained an excellent reputation not only across the state but across the nation. Facilities are available for rental, for families, retreats, or reunions. Phone 888-MH-CAMPS for details.

Napa The Christian Brothers (4401 Redwood Rd.), famous for their wine of the same name, are actually a monastic teaching order. They began making wine for communion use, and theirs was the only winery allowed to continue operations during Prohibition. Today the Christian Brothers carry on the tradition of wine making. They also operate a retreat and conference center

---

GREAT PLACES TO ENJOY GOD'S CREATON

✔ Horseback riding through King's Canyon National Park

✔ Sitting inside a hollow tree, Sequoia National Park

✔ Watching the sun rise from Key's View, Joshua Tree National Park

---

here and offer Sunday worship services on site that are open to the public.

Palo Alto The beautiful 8,000-acre campus of Stanford University located here was built to honor the son of Jane and Leland Stanford, who died of typhoid. Tours of the campus include Memorial Church, a nondenominational golden chapel with stained glass windows and beautiful mosaic walls that look like those of an Eastern Orthodox church.

Pasadena Fuller Theological Seminary, one of the largest seminaries in the country, is located here.

The Lake Avenue Congregational Church (393 N. Lake Ave.), with an average attendance in excess of 3,000, is a well-known evangelical church in this area.

The Harambee Christian Family Center, begun by John and Vera Mae Perkins in 1982, is a ministry to neighborhood families. Since 1995 the center has included a prep school. Now administered by two of their children, the ministry is located on Navarro Ave. in Northwest Pasadena. (See Perkins also under Jackson and Mendenhall, Miss.)

Rancho Mirage The Children's Museum in the Desert (42-501 Rancho Mirage Lane) is unique in its simplicity. Because the building was once a dentist's office, the museum has separate little rooms each emphasizing a different vocation.

Redding The Prosellis Bowl (Eureka and Vine Sts.) is nicknamed the Little Hollywood Bowl because free concerts are held here every Tuesday and Friday in the summer.

Riverside Harvest Christian Fellowship (6115 Arlington Ave.), pastored by Greg Laurie, has been a rapidly growing church. Its average attendance is in the thousands.

Sacramento If you like trains, be sure to visit the California State Railroad Museum (2d and I Sts.) It's the largest interpretive museum of its kind in the nation. The museum is spread over 100,000 square feet and there are 35 locomotives stored in it. Kids will be interested in the 1929 Pullman passenger car and the mail-sorting car.

If you want to move around the city, investigate the horse-drawn wagon and carriage rides, located throughout Old Sacramento. If you prefer water, try out the historic paddle wheeler *Spirit of Sacramento* from Front and L Sts. A one-hour narrated voyage is fun for everyone.

The Capital Christian Center (Assemblies of God, at 9470 Micron Ave.) is the largest church in the city with average attendance around 6,000.

St. Paul's Episcopal Church (15th and J Sts.) is Sacramento's oldest congregation. The church features beautiful Tiffany stained glass windows.

San Bernardino The National Children's Forest, 3,400 acres in the San Bernardino National Forest, was developed so that kids—especially those with handicaps—could enjoy nature. Many children have participated in its development, helping to design educational exhibits and trails, and helping to maintain the forest.

San Diego The San Diego Zoo in Balboa Park is world renowned, with its more than 4,000 animals and 800 species, including the rarely seen koala. It has the largest number of parrots and parrotlike birds ever assembled. It also has an enormous botanical garden, housing one of the world's largest collections of subtropical plants.

In Balboa Park free organ concerts are given on Sundays at the Spreckels Organ Pavilion, an outdoor concert area. The pipe organ is said to be the largest outdoor organ in the world.

Sea World is practically as well known as the zoo. The chief attraction is the four-ton killer whale known as Shamu, but everyone will enjoy the sharks, penguins, and dolphins. Located at 1720 S. Shores Rd., Mission Bay, it is really a theme park dedicated to sea creatures.

If you prefer to see your animals looking just a bit wilder, visit the San Diego Wild Animal Park, just north of town in Escondido. Endangered animals roam freely through huge habitats designed to re-create their natural surroundings. Most of the 800-acre park can be reached only by way of a one-hour monorail tour. The experience really duplicates being in a wild setting. The chief drawback is that some animals are so far away that they cannot be easily viewed.

In 1769 Father Junipero Serra and a band of Spanish soldiers established a fort and mission in the area of the city now known as Old Town. Thus began San Diego. Presidio Park is central to the historical area, with its Serra Museum (2727 Presidio Dr.). The massive adobe fort is not the original, but was erected in 1929 on the site of the first structure. In 1774 Father Serra moved his mission about six miles away to its current location (10818 San Diego Mission Rd. in Mission Valley). The mission, called Mission Basilica San Diego de Alcala, was destroyed by earthquakes in 1803 and subsequently rebuilt. It is still an active church with masses held daily and contains a chapel, gardens, a reconstruction of Father Serra's living area, and a small museum. (See Father Serra also under Carmel, San Francisco, San Juan Capistrano, San Luis Obispo, and Santa Cruz.)

The Museum of Creation and Earth History, sponsored by the Institute of Creation Research here, collects evidence to refute evolution. It is associated with Christian Heritage College. Both are located in El Cajon, off US 8, east of San Diego.

GREAT PLACES FOR FAMILY FUN

✔ Sea World, San Diego

✔ Disneyland, Anaheim

✔ San Diego Zoo

The Christian Community Theater (1546 Pioneer Way, El Cajon) is one of the largest community theaters in the San Diego area. It puts on four different dramatic presentations each year in addition to its Christmas spectacular.

The Lamb's Players Theatre in Coronado is one of San Diego's leading professional theaters. It performs year-round in a 350-seat auditorium in Coronado. The Lamb's Players are a Christian company but they offer a mix of religious and secular performances.

San Francisco If you are in San Francisco, you have to ride on a cable car; it's almost as good as riding on a roller coaster. There are three different lines that still operate on the 12 miles of track.

Pier 38 is a fun place to visit, and for youngsters there is nothing better than Waterfront Park, stretching from Piers 35–41, where they'll find a little bit of everything.

Depending on your mood, a trip to Alcatraz, a.k.a. the Rock, is a memorable time, because we all have heard so much about it. The tour takes you through the buildings, cellhouse, and grounds. Because stairs are involved—lots of them—be prepared with good walking shoes.

Ripley's Believe It or Not! Museum (175 Jefferson St.) has 2,000 or more exhibits, like the smallest violin ever made and tiny roller skates that actually work. Close by is the Guinness Museum of World Records (235 Jefferson St.) and there you will see the shoes worn by the smallest woman and the tallest man.

The Exploratorium (3601 Lyon St.) is sometimes called "The Playful Museum," and you may find it difficult to drag your kids (or your spouse) away. Over 700 hands-on exhibits are there to help you and your family learn more about light, color, sound, motion, language, touch, electricity, and almost everything. *Scientific American* has called it the "best science museum in the world."

Next door to the Exploratorium is the Palace of Fine Arts, built of remnants from the 1915 Panama Pacific Exposition. It's an impressive place.

Another multifeatured museum is the California Academy of Science, located in Golden Gate Park (bordered by Fulton St. and Lincoln Way). It contains an aquarium, planetarium, laserium, Discovery Room (for the younger set), and the unique SafeQuake Ride to help you experience an earthquake safely.

The San Francisco Zoo (Sloat Blvd. and 45th Ave.) is a zoo that is like none other. Other zoos may have just as many of this or that (except koalas), but the way that this was put together has made it user-friendly for every member of the family.

Grace Cathedral (1100 California St.) is the largest Gothic building west of the Mississippi. The cathedral's bronze doors were made from castings of Ghiberti's famous *Gates of Paradise* in the Baptistery in Florence. In fact the castings are such an exact match that they were used to restore the originals. Inside, murals combine scenes from various saints' lives with events from San Francisco's and the country's history.

Old Saint Mary's Cathedral (660 California St.) is California's first cathedral. Noontime concerts are given every Tuesday and Thursday at 12:30 P.M.

Mission Dolores, founded by Father Junipero Serra, is over 200 years old and thought to be the oldest building in the city. Founded in 1776, the mission was originally named Mission San Francisco in honor of St. Francis of Assisi, as was the city of San Francisco itself. However, due to its proximity to Laguna de Nuestra Senora de los Dolores (the Lagoon of Our Lady of Sorrows), the mission soon became known as Mission de los Dolores. Visitors may walk through the building and grounds, and masses are still held daily.

The lovely flowered cemetery was featured in Alfred Hitchcock's film *Vertigo*. (See Father Serra also under Carmel, San Diego, San Juan Capistrano, San Luis Obispo, and Santa Cruz.)

San Jose The Children's Discovery Museum (180 Woz Way) is designed for children 3 to 13 years old, and it has things like the Doodad Dump and Gilliland Global Communications, which are fun to do and educational as well.

It's questionable how educational the Winchester Mystery House is (525 S. Winchester Blvd.). The heiress to the Winchester rifle estate built the place and it has staircases leading nowhere and a switchback stairway that has seven turns and 44 steps but rises only nine feet. She thought that if she built a baffling house, it would baffle the spirits that were trying to kill her. She died anyway, in 1922.

El Pueblo de San Jose de Guadalupe was the first California settlement under Spanish rule when the city was established in 1777. Today restored 19th-century and mission-style buildings remind visitors of San Jose's Spanish roots.

The Cathedral Basilica of St. Joseph (90 S. Market St.) was built in 1877 and has extraordinary stained glass windows and murals.

San Juan Capistrano Mission San Juan Capistrano is called "the Jewel of the Missions." Father Junipero Serra established the mission in 1776, but a more elaborate church was built by 1806. An earthquake ravaged it and today only the Serra Chapel is left from the original. The chapel is the oldest building in the state and still serves as an active Catholic church. Even better known than the chapel is the fact that swallows keep returning to Capistrano on March 19 every year. No one knows why they keep coming back to the mission. After all, it's a 6,000-mile trip from Goya, Argentina, where they spend the winter. (See Father Serra also under Carmel, San Diego, San Francisco, San Luis Obispo, and Santa Cruz.)

San Luis Obispo The beautiful San Luis Obispo Mission, founded in 1772 by Father Junipero Serra, still serves as the parish church in this lovely seaside town. The mission itself—rebuilt after the original building was destroyed—is quite simple and small, with wooden pews and wood-beamed ceilings. Outside is a small quiet garden. (See Father Serra also under Carmel, San Diego, San Francisco, San Juan Capistrano, and Santa Cruz.)

San Marino The Huntington Library, Art Collections, and Botanical Gardens (1151 Oxford Rd.) are all worth visiting. The library has a Gutenberg Bible, one of only three animal-skin copies in the United States; the art collections are invaluable; and the 130-acre botanical gardens are a succession of beauties.

San Simeon The Hearst Castle (just off Rte. 1, north of Cambria) is incredible. Its rooms—more than 100 of them—serve as museum space for the William Randolph Hearst collection.

Santa Ana Calvary Church (1010 N. Tustin Ave.), which sprang up from the Jesus People revival of the 1970s, is now one of America's largest churches, with 12,000 in attendance on a typical Sunday. Pastor Chuck Smith has ministered there from the start, and now there are many Calvary Chapels across the country.

Santa Barbara Built in 1786, Mission Santa Barbara (E. Los Olivos and Lagune Sts.) is sometimes called the Queen of the California Missions, because it is the best preserved. The original living quarters of the missionaries are now museum rooms. The church displays examples of 18th- and 19th-century Mexican art. The mission was the tenth of 21 Franciscan missions built in the state.

The Santa Barbara Trolley is a fun way to see the city and a good way to get oriented. It stops at Mission Santa Barbara and by the Botanic Gardens (1212 Mission Canyon Rd.).

Whale watching is often a satisfying venture here. The Museum of Natural History (2559 Puesta del Sol Rd.) has special excursions led by naturalists, but with binoculars (and even without) you can often spot whales from the shore.

Westmont College (955 La Paz Rd.) is an interdenominational school, located on a lovely campus in the south end of the city. It has a student body of about 1,300.

Santa Clara Great America Theme Park is best known for the Grizzly, which is the favorite ride of teenagers. But there are six theme areas here, each with rides, shows, shops, and restaurants. Management tries to have enough for all ages to keep the entire family happy.

Santa Cruz Roaring Camp and the Big Trees Narrow Gauge Railroad is located in Felton (six miles north of Santa Cruz via

Graham Hill Rd.). The place is covered with redwoods, and you will find a real steam logging train, which is supposed to remind you of the Bret Harte story, "The Luck of Roaring Camp." The train ride up the mountain takes about 75 minutes and the tracks are steep.

Santa Cruz was another of Father Serra's missions. Established in 1791, it no longer exists. The name is Spanish for "holy cross." (See Father Serra also under Carmel, San Diego, San Francisco, San Juan Capistrano, and San Luis Obispo.)

Santa Monica In the Santa Monica Mountains above Bel Air is the new J. Paul Getty Museum and Getty Center (1200 Getty Center Dr.). The museum includes most of oil billionaire Getty's art collection, housed in five pavilions. Of special interest is the large Rembrandt collection, the Impressionist paintings, and Renaissance drawings. The three-acre Central Garden is a living work of art that changes with the seasons.

Sequoia–King's Canyon National Parks Make sure you see the General Grant Tree and the General Sherman Tree, which are the two largest living things on earth. Sherman is 274 feet tall and between 2,500 and 3,000 years old. King's Canyon was named in 1805 by Spanish explorers who discovered the area on Epiphany, the day traditionally associated with the visit of the kings to the infant Jesus.

Solvang Santa Ines Mission was designed as a way station for padres traveling between the Santa Barbara and La Purisma missions, as well as an outpost for the local Indian population. Like La Purisma in nearby Lompoc, Santa Ines has been plagued by earthquakes. The existing church and its attached wing are only a fraction of the size of the original mission. But Santa Ines is still worth a visit. Resting in a picturesque valley, its compact size, lovely gardens, and wonderful historical museum rank this mission a favorite for many. Santa Ines is located on Rte. 246 just outside Solvang. Admission is $3.

Sonoma The town of Sonoma is best known as the heart of California's wine country, but its beginnings were as a Spanish mission. The northernmost in a long chain of missions, the Sonoma Mission (E. Spain and 1st Sts.) was built in 1826. An adobe church stands on the site, located within the Sonoma State Historic Park.

Sun Valley Author and Bible teacher John MacArthur is the pastor of the Grace Community Church (13248 Roscoe Blvd.), which has an average attendance of 8,000 in its services.

Valencia Just north of Los Angeles, the Six Flags Magic Mountain (Magic Mountain exit off I-5) has 100 or so rides, a petting zoo, live shows, and a crafts village. Besides its breathtaking roller-coaster rides, it is known for its flume rides and was one of the first theme parks to have them. Young and old can always find something fun to do here.

Van Nuys Jack Hayford is the well-known minister of The Church on the Way (14300 Sherman Way), which has reached out effectively to many people in the entertainment business. In addition to the large congregation, Hayford has a weekly TV program.

Victorville The Roy Rogers/Dale Evans Museum (15650 Seneca Rd.) is located here, with souvenirs of their personal and professional lives. Roy died in 1998, but Dale still lives here. The museum is located on the edge of the Mohave Desert. (See Roy Rogers also under Portsmouth, Ohio.)

Yosemite About four miles before you enter the park on Rte. 41 in the town of Fish Camp is the Yosemite Mountain–Sugar Pine Railroad. It's a logger steam train that is both historic and scenic. The train runs every day from mid-April to mid-October. Phone 559-683-7273 for more information.

■HAWAII

Tourist Info
Phone 800-GO HAWAII
Web site
  Entire state   www.visit.hawaii.org
For a complete list of updated links, visit www.christiantraveler.com

Hawaii

Hilo The Lyman Museum (276 Haili St.) is named for the Reverend David Lyman, who came to Hawaii with his wife as missionaries before 1840. The museum is worth visiting in its own right, but next to it is the large missionary house in which the Lymans lived. With seven children, the Lymans needed a big house. In addition, they boarded some Hawaiian youngsters who lived in their attic. You might be interested in Sarah Lyman's melodeon, rocking chair, and china dishes.

Also on Haili St. are three churches, which is why it was once called Church Row. St. Joseph's, in a Spanish-mission design, was built in 1919; Haili Church, resembling a New England barn, was built in 1859; and Central Christian Church, in a Victorian style, was built in the early 1900s.

Honaunau On Painted Church Rd. is St. Benedict's Painted Church. It's a Catholic church known for its interior done by a Belgian Catholic priest in 1899. The walls are painted with a series of biblical scenes to help native Hawaiians who couldn't read. The ceiling is a Hawaiian sky with clouds and birds, and the wall behind the altar resembles a Gothic cathedral in Burgos, Spain. The tin-roofed church still holds services on Sunday and still sings hymns in Hawaiian.

Kailua You'll have a different look at the water when you ride the *Nautilus II,* a 34-passenger semisubmersible craft. You sit in a glass-windowed room beneath the surface of the water and look out at the fish as the boat edges along the reef. It leaves from Kailua Pier. Or you might opt for the more conventional 16-passenger glass-bottom boat for an hour-long ride.

Kapaau Shortly after Protestant missionaries Elias and Ellen Bond came here in 1841, they started building the Kalahikiola Church (near the 24-mile marker half a mile east of the Kamehameha statue). Damaged in an earthquake in 1973, it has since been restored.

Kona Hawaii's first Christian church was established on Kailua Bay in 1820, shortly after the first Christian missionaries landed here. In 1836 the temporary structure was replaced by the current Mokuaikaua Church, which has walls of lava rock held together with mortar of sand and coral lime. Pews and pulpit are made of koa. The church steeple is still the highest structure here at 112 feet. On display in the back of the church is an eight-foot

model of the ship *Thaddeus,* which brought the first Congregational missionaries to Hawaii.

St. Michael's Church, the pink church opposite Waterfront Row,
replaced an earlier thatched chapel that was the first Catholic
church on this island.

Also here is an independent Hawaiian Congregational church
called the Kealaokamalamalama Church. It is a green and white
building, and its interior looks typically Hawaiian with tropical
flowers and a rainbow painted across the wall.

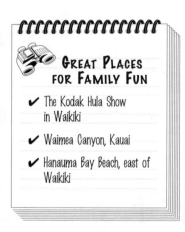

**GREAT PLACES
FOR FAMILY FUN**

✔ The Kodak Hula Show
in Waikiki

✔ Waimea Canyon, Kauai

✔ Hanauma Bay Beach, east of
Waikiki

Incidentally, the first coffee trees were
introduced to Hawaii by missionaries in
1827. After growing in sales throughout
the 19th century, the coffee production
dropped dramatically in the 20th century
until the popularity of gourmet coffees
increased sales of Kona bean coffee. Most
of the coffee trees are in South Kona.

Puna On Hwy. 130 at the 20-mile marker
is a little white Catholic church called The
Star of the Sea Painted Church. It is
painted imaginatively to make it look
something like a grand cathedral. Father
Damien was with the parish before he
moved to Molokai and the leprosy colony
there. A stained glass window commemorates him. (See Father
Damien also under Honolulu and Kalaupapa Peninsula, Molokai.)

Kauai

Hanalei This is the site of the Waioli Mission (on Kuhio Hwy.),
which was founded by Christian missionaries in 1837. Hanalei
is also known for less sacred reasons. It is the legendary home of
Peter, Paul, and Mary's "Puff the Magic Dragon."

The Old Lutheran Church (just south of the intersection of
Hwy. 56 and Hwy. 50) doesn't look unusual from the outside, but
go inside and you will see the difference. When German immigrants came here in the late 1800s, they designed their church to
look like the boat that brought them here. So the floor slants like

the deck of a ship and the balcony looks like a captain's bridge
and there are ship lanterns hanging from the ceiling.

Waimea All the churches here are lined up alongside each other.
You have Imiola Congregational Church, built in 1838, replacing
a grass hut built in 1830. Imiola means "seeking salvation." In
the graveyard is the burial site of missionary Lorenzo Lyons, who
spent 54 years here.

Alongside the Congregational church is the Ke Ola Mau Loa
Church, which is an all-Hawaiian church. There are also houses
of worship for Buddhists, Baptists, and Mormons on the row.

Maui

Hana The Wananalua Congregational Church (south of the Hotel
Hana-Maui) was built in 1838 replacing an earlier grass church.
It has thick walls of lava rock and coral mortar and it resembles
an ancient Norman church more than what you would expect in
Hawaii.

During the last years of his life Charles Lindbergh, the noted
aviator, made his home here and died of cancer on Maui in
1974. He is buried in a simple grave marked with small U.S.
flags in the graveyard of Palapala Hoomau Congregational
Church, a mile south of Oheo. The church, which dates from
1864, is known for its window painting of a Polynesian Christ
dressed in the red and yellow feather capes worn by Hawaii's
noblest chiefs.

Kihei David Malo was one of the first graduates of Lahainaluna
Seminary in Lahaina and he became the first Hawaiian ordained
to the Christian ministry. The church that he built after gradua-
tion from seminary is at 100 Kulanihakoi St. Much of the church
has been dismantled, but open-air services are still held here on
Sunday mornings.

Next to the library (131 S. Kihei Rd.) is the Keolahou Congregational Hawaiian Church, built in 1920. Many of the Ton-
gans who live on Maui are members here and services are held in
the Tongan language on Sunday afternoons.

The Keawalai Congregational Church (190 Makena Rd., south
of the Makena Landing) dates to 1832 and is one of Maui's earliest

missionary churches. The current building, however, dates to 1855. Services are held with a mix of Hawaiian and English.

Lahaina The oldest building in Lahaina is the Baldwin House, built in 1834. It is next to the Masters' Reading Room at Front and Dickinson Sts. Dwight Baldwin was a missionary doctor who made the trip to Hawaii with his wife around the Horn of South America. It took them 161 days to get here from Connecticut. The house is now a museum and still holds the china and furniture they brought with them on the journey. It also has the Baldwins's Steinway piano. With walls 24 inches thick, the house is cool all year round.

The Wainee Church (535 Wainee St.), built in 1832, was the first stone church built in Hawaii and it played a vital role in the conversion of the island to Christianity. The present building is the fourth to stand in this general location. It is now called the Waiola Congregational Church and holds regular Sunday services.

Holy Innocents' Episcopal Church (561 Front St.) is decorated in Hawaiian fashion. On the front of the altar is a painting of a fisher in an outrigger canoe and Hawaiian farmers harvesting taro and breadfruit, no doubt free adaptations of some of the gospel narratives. Over the altar is a Hawaiian *Madonna and Child*.

Lahainaluna Seminary, which is now Lahaina's public high school (at the end of Lahainaluna Rd.), was the first U.S. educational institution west of the Rockies. It was founded by missionaries in 1831. On the grounds is Hale Pai, which was the site of the first printing press in Hawaii. The main purpose of the missionary press was to print the Bible, but other books were printed here too, including the first Hawaiian botany book and Hawaii's first newspaper. Examples of early books are on display.

Your family might want to do some whale watching while you are in Hawaii, and whale sightings are guaranteed on the non-profit Pacific Whale Foundation cruises that leave from both Maalaea and Lahaina. They use a 50-foot sailboat, a 65-foot catamaran, or a 53-foot motorboat, so you can take your choice.

GREAT PLACES TO ENJOY GOD'S CREATION

✔ The spouting calderas in Hawaii Volcanoes National Park

✔ Camping in Haleakala National Park

✔ Whale watching off the Maui coast

Wailuku The oldest Congregational church in Maui is the Kaahu-manu Church (West Main and High Sts.). When Queen Kaahu-manu decided to get rid of her temple idols and become a Christian, she visited this area and asked that a new church be built with her name on it. The old clock in the steeple, which was brought from New England around the Horn, still keeps accurate time.

The Bailey House (up Iao Valley Rd. from the church) was the home of Missionary Edward Bailey, who built the present church building.

Molokai

Kalaupapa Peninsula This has been a leprosy settlement for more than a century. Today it is administered by the U.S. National Park Service and the State Department of Health.

In 1865 King Kamehameha V, alarmed by the spread of leprosy on the islands, signed a law banishing people with leprosy to this peninsula. Father Damien arrived here as a missionary in 1873. Today fewer than 100 patients live here. The only access to the peninsula is by mule trail, by air, or by a two-mile hike, and unless you are with a guided tour you can't get in.

St. Philomena Church here is better known as Father Damien's Church. (See Father Damien also under Honolulu and Puna, Hawaii.)

Oahu

Haleiwa The Liliuokalani Protestant Church is named after the Hawaiian queen who attended services here during the summer. The church congregation dates from 1832, but the current building was built in 1961. Services were conducted in Hawaiian until the 1940s. The sundial clock here was given by the queen in 1892, and it shows the hour, day, month, and year as well as the phases of the moon. Since the queen's name has 12 letters, her name replaces the numerals on the clock face.

Honolulu Two statues are near the state capitol building at Beretania and Richards Sts. The statue of Queen Liliuokalani, who wrote the Hawaii constitution and the popular hymn *Aloha Oe*, stands between the capitol and Iolani Palace. Directly in front of

AMERICAN MISSIONS IN HAWAII

In 1820 the first group of American missionaries arrived in Honolulu from New England, having traveled by ship from Boston around the South American Horn to Hawaii. They brought plenty of provisions with them, including a mission house—a prefabricated building that still stands today. It is the oldest wooden structure on the islands.

Those first missionaries were Protestants, but they would soon be followed by Catholics, Mormons, and others from America and Europe. Whatever the differences between the groups—and there were serious differences—all of the missionaries had profound effects on the culture and future development of the Hawaiian Islands. They converted the Hawaiian language into a written alphabet and promoted literacy. They became advisers to the Hawaiian rulers and were influential in liberalizing the government. They were strong advocates of public education. They introduced the coffee tree to the Islands. And they were instrumental in having Christianity, both Protestant and Roman Catholic branches, declared the national religion.

There are many reminders of the missionaries' strong influence in Hawaii. One of the oldest Catholic cathedrals in the United States is the Cathedral of our Lady of Peace in Honolulu. It was constructed of coral blocks. Hawaii's first Christian church is in Kona, built of lava rock. Another interesting church is in Honaunau. The walls are painted with a series of biblical scenes to help native Hawaiians who couldn't read. The ceiling is painted to resemble the Hawaiian sky with trees and birds, and the congregation still sings Hawaiian hymns in its Sunday services.

the capitol, however, is a statue of Father Damien, the Belgian priest who volunteered to work among the lepers of Molokai and died of leprosy at age 49, 16 years later. (See Father Damien also under Puna, Hawaii, and Kalaupapa Peninsula, Molokai.)

St. Andrew's Cathedral (Alakea and Beretania Sts.) was built by King Kamehameha V in 1867, although it was his father and mother who founded the Anglican church in Hawaii nine years earlier and had the dream for the cathedral. When Kamehameha IV died on St. Andrew's Day in 1865, his son picked up the vision and thought it appropriate to name the church after the day on which his father died. The western facade of the church is formed by a large stained glass window, in the right section of which is a depiction of the Reverend Thomas Staley, the first Anglican bishop of Hawaii.

One of the oldest Catholic cathedrals in the United States is the Cathedral of our Lady of Peace (Beretania St. and Fort St. Mall). Older than St. Andrew's Church, it was built of coral blocks in 1843. Father Damien was ordained here in 1864.

Known as the "Westminster Abbey of Hawaii," the Kawaihao Church (Punchbowl and King Sts.) is the oldest church on the island. It was built on the location where the first missionaries constructed a grass thatch church soon after they arrived in 1820. The grass thatch church, measuring 54 by 22 feet, seated 300 people on lauhala mats. The present church is a more typically New England–style Congregational church, and it was built between 1838 and 1842 from 14,000 giant coral slabs. The clock, installed in 1850 still keeps accurate time. The cemetery behind the church is where many of the early missionaries are buried. Generations of Hawaiian royalty have been coronated, married, and eulogized in this church. Sunday services are held in Hawaiian.

The original Christian mission to Hawaii was called the Sandwich Islands Mission, and three of the original buildings of the mission headquarters still stand at the Mission Houses Museum (553 S. King St.). They date from 1821 to 1841. The oldest one, called the Frame House, was a prefab wooden house the missionaries brought with them when they came by ship from Boston around the South American Horn to Hawaii. This is now the oldest wooden structure on the islands.

At the north end of Chinatown is the Foster Botanical Garden (entrance on Vineyard Blvd.). The garden is laid out with groupings of palms, orchids, plumerias, and poisonous plants. The garden is home to many unusual and rare plants and trees, including the cannonball tree, the sausage tree, and the double coconut palm that can produce 50-pound nuts.

Kaneohe The largest botanic garden on the island is Hoomaluhia, which is spread over 400 acres. Trees and shrubs from tropical areas around the world adorn this preserve, and that's what it is— a preserve more than a landscaped garden. Admission is free.

Makapuu Sea-Life Park makes a good family stop. It has a 300,000-gallon oceanarium in which 4,000 sea creatures—including sharks and stingrays—enjoy themselves. Then at the Ocean Science Theatre, trained dolphins, penguins, and sea lions perform regularly. If you wish, you can feed the sea animals. You can also investigate the *Essex,* which is a 70-foot replica of a whaling vessel. And across the road is the fabled Makapuu Beach, where you and your family can picnic.

Pearl Harbor Hawaii's most visited attraction is Pearl Harbor, where more than 1.5 million people come each year. It is also the most famous historic spot in Hawaii. The visitors center includes a museum and a theater as well as a memorial at the site of the sunken USS *Arizona*. The Navy offers free one-hour tours of the memorial, but be sure to arrive early. The free tickets are usually gone by noon. And be aware that very young children are not admitted.

Waikiki The International Market Place (230 Kalakaua Ave.) is just east of the pink 1921 Royal Hawaiian Hotel. Under the shade of a spreading banyan tree the outdoor bazaar offers a little island authenticity to the dozens of souvenir and T-shirt stands.

The Waikiki Aquarium, also on Kalakaua Ave., is a great way to become acquainted with local marine life. The aquarium features more than 300 species of fish and aquatic animals.

The Honolulu Zoo (151 Kapahulu Ave.) is at the Diamond Head end of Waikiki. This is not a large zoo by any means, but the 40-acre spread is so lushly planted that it is certainly one of the country's prettiest.

Waimea The St. Peter and Paul Church (northern side of Waimea Bay) is an unlikely Catholic church indeed. It was originally a rock-crushing plant, built to supply gravel for the construction of a highway. After the highway was built and the building was abandoned, the Catholic church converted it into a chapel.

■ OREGON

Tourist Info
Phone 800-547-7842
Web sites
  Entire state   www.traveloregon.com
  Oregon Shakespeare Festival   www.orshakes.org
  Oregon state parks   www.prd.state.or.us
  Portland   www.pova.com
  Southwest Oregon   www.crater-lake.com
For a complete list of updated links, visit www.christiantraveler.com

Ashland Near California's border, the town of Ashland is an unlikely but world-famous venue for Shakespeare. The Oregon Shakespeare Festival (15 S. Pioneer St.) is the largest Shakespeare festival in the United States and has performances daily (except Monday) from mid-February through the end of October. Incidentally, the Methodist Church deserves credit for getting this started. Years ago, the church's adult education program launched a Chautauqua series, bringing lectures, concerts, and theater to town. A hall was built to accommodate the crowds. In the 1930s the crowds had disappeared and all that was left was the auditorium. Then a local drama teacher, who thought the empty auditorium resembled drawings he had seen of Shakespeare's Globe Theatre, convinced the townspeople to take it over and start a Shakespeare Festival, which has been an annual event since 1935. More than 100,000 visitors now attend the festival every year. The town has a good climate, lots of bed and breakfast places, and great restaurants. What more could Shakespeare lovers ask? If you want to go, you will need to purchase your tickets six months in advance, because the festival is popular. Phone 541-482-4331 for more details.

Astoria This was the end of the line for Lewis and Clark in 1805 and they wept for joy on finally seeing the Pacific Ocean. Founded in 1811, the town is believed to be the first official settlement established by the United States on the West Coast. Today Astoria's Victorian homes, busy waterfront, rolling hills, and frequent fog remind visitors of a small version of San Francisco. The Astoria Column, 125 feet tall and perched atop Coxcomb Hill, is modeled after Trajan's Column in Rome, a reward for those who make the climb up 164 spiral stairs—as if the magnificent view of the ocean, the Columbia River, and the Coast Range weren't enough! (See Lewis and Clark also under Washburn, N.D.; Great Falls, Mont.; and Portland, Ore.)

Baker City The St. Francis Cathedral (1st and Church Sts.), built in the early 1900s, is a Gothic Revival building, constructed of volcanic tuff from local quarries.

Beaverton Beaverton Foursquare Church, under the ministry of Ron Mehl, may be the largest Protestant church in the state. The church is at 13565 S.W. Walker Rd.

Brownsville The Living Rock Studios (911 Bishop Way West) is an amazing structure built with 800 tons of rock. It is inlaid with pioneer wagon-wheel rims, an American Indian mortar and pestle, fool's gold, and coffee jars filled with crystal. If you

369

go downstairs, you will see a series of illuminated biblical pictures. Upstairs you will see the owner's carvings on display.

Cannon Beach The Cannon Beach Conference Center is a Christian organization that has gained a reputation as an outstanding conference in a prime location. The center offers conference and retreat facilities as well as accommodations for the whole family. For information, phone 503-436-1501.

Eugene For two weeks every summer Bach's sacred melodies grace the city of Eugene. The annual Oregon Bach Festival features some of the country's most impressive musicians in a Baroque extravaganza. Visitors can enjoy Bach's concerti and cantatas, as well as selections from other classical composers. Concerts are held beginning the last week of June at the Hult Performing Arts Center (1 Eugene Center) and at the University of Oregon's Beall Concert Hall.

Every animal of the forest is mine, and the cattle on a thousand hills. I know every bird in the mountains, and the creatures of the field are mine.

PSALM 50:10–11

While in Eugene, spend a day at the Saturday Market (8th Ave. and Oak St.). Many colorful venders display crafts, clothing, jewelry, and artwork, among other things, including music, from April through November.

Florence About five miles north of the city are the Sea Lion Caves, a great stop for family members of any age. A huge vaulted chamber is home to hundreds of sea lions, many of which weigh a ton or more, and they are close enough to be easily viewed.

McMinnville Linfield College (American Baptist) was founded here in 1849. The music department offers frequent concerts throughout the year. On the 100-acre campus is the Renshaw Art Gallery.

Medford Harry and David's Original Country Store (1314 Center Dr., Suite A) is located in Harry and David's Country Village (exit 27 off I-5). This is where those catalogs come from that want to sell you fruits, nuts, candies, and other gift items. Next door is Jackson & Perkins, the rose people, who sell more roses than anyone else in the world.

The Applegate Christian Center (7590 Hwy. 238) in Jacksonville is a vigorous church with more than 4,000 in weekly attendance.

Newburg The Quakers made their first settlement west of the Rockies here and established Pacific Academy (George Fox College since 1949) in 1885. In the first graduating class was Herbert Hoover, who became the 31st president of the United States (not a bad start for a young school). See displays at the Hoover building and in Brougher Museum.

The Hoover-Minthorn House (115 S. River St.) is the boyhood home of Herbert Hoover and the oldest remaining in Newburg. Hoover's uncle helped to raise him here between 1884 and 1889.

Newport The village of Newport is a charming seaport, with fishing boats, art galleries, and seafood markets. But another reason to visit Newport is its fabulous Oregon Coast Aquarium (2820 Ferry Slip Rd. SE). The six-acre complex contains everything oceanic, from bullfrogs to sea otters. Outdoor pools, cliffs, and caves are fun to explore, and there are indoor galleries devoted to Oregon's coastal habitats and native marine life.

Oregon City The Aurora Colony was a strange 19th-century cult led by Dr. William Keil, a Prussian who had emigrated to the United States in 1931. He brought his followers out West along the Oregon Trail in 1855. For several years his colony was very successful. It owned 16,000 acres of land and developed many businesses. They shared all property and had little social contact with the outside world, except to sell their products. However, they were known for their singing and their band. After Keil's death in 1877, the group was gradually assimilated into the community. Today you can see the artifacts of the group in the Old Aurora Colony Museum (15 miles southwest of Oregon City on 2d St. NE in Aurora).

Portland Portland is called the Rose City and one of the reasons is the International Rose Test Gardens, one of the oldest rose gardens in the nation (S.W. Park Pl. and Vista Ave.). It is the testing grounds for the American Rose Society, and over 400 rose varieties are seen here.

The Grotto (N.E. 85th Ave. and Sandy Blvd.) is a renowned Catholic sanctuary that is visited by more than 150,000 guests each year. At its center is a marble replica of Michelangelo's famous *Pietà*. From the manicured gardens of the upper level, you can see panoramic vistas of the Columbia River Valley, the Cascade Range, and Mount St. Helens. Its Meditation Chapel was featured on the cover of *Architecture* magazine.

Portland's Children's Museum (3037 S.W. Second Ave.) is a "please touch" museum designed for kids up to age ten. A variety of activities are offered, including a child-sized grocery store and a water room full of interactive displays.

The Old Church (1422 S.W. 11th Ave.) was built in 1882 and is a prime example of the Carpenter Gothic architectual style. Its rough-cut lumber, tall spires, and original stained glass windows are impressive. Consider attending a free concert, hosted by the church every Wednesday at noon.

The Oregon Historical Society Museum and Library (1200 S.W. Park Ave.) has an impressive exhibit of photographs, artifacts, and records of Oregon's last two centuries, including interactive displays on Oregon, Willamette, and Portland. You'll recognize the building when you see it. Huge murals of Lewis and Clark and the Oregon Trail frame the building's entrance. Admission is $6. (See Lewis and Clark also under Washburn, N.D.; Great Falls, Mont.; and Astoria, Ore.)

The Metro Washington Park Zoo (4004 S.W. Canyon Rd.) is known for its meticulously re-created natural animal habitats. Indigenous Northwest animals are especially worth visiting. Recently the zoo has been noticed for its successful elephant breeding program.

New Hope Community Church (11731 S.E. Stevens Rd.) is one of the largest in the state with average worship attendances of 5,000 or more.

Mercy Corps International (3030 S.W. 1st Ave.), which responds to international emergencies and sets up self-help programs, is headquartered in Portland.

Multnomah School of the Bible (8435 N. Glisan St.), Warner Pacific College (2219 S.E. 68th Ave.), and Western Conservative Baptist Seminary (5511 S. Hawthorne Blvd.) are three well-known evangelical schools that have their main campuses here.

The Willamette Shore Trolley (311 N. State St. in Lake Oswego) gives a 90-minute, 13-mile round-trip scenic tour along the Willamette River in a vintage trolley.

Redmond The Crooked River Railroad Company (5252 S.W. 6th St.) gives you a theme-based train ride and a meal at the same time. They specialize in murder mysteries and staged train robberies, in the middle of a cowboy breakfast or a Saturday night dinner.

GREAT PLACES FOR FAMILY FUN

✔ Cannon Beach, Oregon

✔ Mt. Hood National Forest, Oregon

✔ Whidbey Island, Washington

Salem In 1840 Jason Lee, a Methodist missionary, started a mission here, calling it Salem, a place of peace. In 1842 a school to train children of white settlers was established, called the Oregon Institute. By 1853 the school had been chartered as Willamette University and it became the oldest university in the West. In 1851 Salem became the territorial capital.

At the Willamette University Library (900 State St.) is the Mark O. Hatfield Library. Hatfield was a Conservative Baptist who had a distinguished career in the U.S. Senate and served on the boards of several Christian organizations. The library contains his public papers.

Mission Mill Village is a five-acre village complex (1313 Mill St. SE), housing a number of restored pioneer houses, including the home of Jason Lee, which was built in 1841, and an old church. Each of these is as it was in the 1840s.

In Turner, just seven miles south of Salem on Rte. 5, is the Enchanted Forest (8462 Enchanted Way), worth a stop for the kids. It has attractions like a crooked house and Alice in Wonderland's rabbit hole. Plays are performed in an outdoor theater.

Nearby is the Benedictine Mt. Angel Abbey (840 S. Main St., Mt. Angel), which is noted for the gardens of the Queen of Angels Monastery, a part of the abbey. The abbey's library is noteworthy for its rare handprinted books. There is also a newly remodeled museum, focusing on the Russian Old Believer community.

Northwest of Salem in Amity is the Brigittine Monastery (23300 Walker Lane, Amity), where you can buy homemade fudge and truffles if you wish to indulge.

The Dalles Old St. Peter's Church (3d and Lincoln Sts.) is the city landmark. Built in 1898, it has a weather vane rooster on its steeple cross that has become The Dalles's symbol. Besides looking at the rooster, you should also go inside the old church and look at its stained glass windows and its pipe organ.

The first white settlers here were Methodist missionaries, and Pulpit Rock (12th and Court Sts., behind the high school) is where they first preached to Native Americans in 1838. Local Easter services are still held here.

Winston The Winston Wildlife Safari (I-5, exit 119) has 600 acres and 600 animals. There are large herds of animals from Africa, Asia, and North America, including giraffes, bison, moufflon sheep, emus, and antelope. So drive slowly.

Yachats South of Waldport in the central coast area is this charming little town (pronounced Ya-hots). At 3d and Pontiac Sts. you will find the Little Log Church. It has only a handful of white pews and is heated by a pioneer stove. Outside is a lovely garden. It's worth a photo or two on the outside and then a moment or two to sit inside and worship.

■WASHINGTON

Tourist Info
Phone 800-544-1800
Web sites
  Entire state   www.tourism.wa.gov
  Seattle   www.seeseattle.org
  Spokane   www.spokane-areacvb.com
  Washington state parks   www.parks.wa.gov
For a complete list of updated links, visit www.christiantraveler.com

Blaine The Peace Arch is a 67-foot arch that strides the border of the United States and Canada. The arch is set in a landscaped park that you can enter from either country. On the second Sunday of June each year is a Peace Arch Celebration, honoring the fact that the U.S.–Canadian border is the longest undefended border in the world.

Chehalis The historic Claquato Church (three miles west on Rte. 6), built in 1858, is the oldest church in the state, still in good condition. Its pews and pulpit are handmade. If you're interested in going inside, you can get the keys at the residence across the street.

Ephrata The Grant County Pioneer Village and Museum (742 Basin St. N) has more than 20 buildings, both original and restored, including church, schoolhouse, barbershop, and bank, and displays that trace the early history of the area.

Kettle Falls The St. Paul's Mission (12 miles northwest of Colville near the intersection of US 395 and the Columbia River, in the Coulee Dam National Recreation Area) was built by Native Americans under the direction of Father Pierre Jean de Smet. A chapel, built in 1845, was followed by a log church in 1847. After that fell into disuse, the church was restored into the present structure in 1939. The mission is located behind the Kettle Falls Historical Center. (See de Smet also under Hazelwood, Mo.; De Smet, S.D.; and Casper, Wyo.)

As you enter Kettle Falls, you may notice a sign that says, "1324 Friendly People and 1 Grouch." Who's the grouch? Each year the town grouch is elected as part of a fund-raising event. It costs 25 cents to vote.

La Conner If you like flowers, you will like La Conner. Its flower fields rival those of the Netherlands, which it emulates. Even if you miss the tulip and daffodil season in the spring, you can visit the English country gardens of La Conner Flats (1598 Best Rd.) at other times of the year.

Leavenworth This town has been made into a Bavarian village, complete with oom-pah bands and alpine scenery. Of course, the scenery has always been here, thanks to the Cascades, but the rest was launched in 1965, and it's a lot of fun with pastry shops, wood carvings, and, during the summer, free concerts and dancing exhibitions in the city park.

Marysville The Tulalip Reservation (six miles northwest on Rte. 506) is the location of St. Anne's Church, built in 1904—with its old mission bell—and the Native American Shaker Church.

Oak Harbor Immigrants from the Netherlands settled here amid the oak trees of Whidbey Island in the 1890s. Today Holland Gardens

(500 Ave. W and 30NW) is a big attraction especially during Holland Happening the last weekend of April, when tulips and daffodils decorate the grounds. Throughout the year, gardens of flowers and shrubs along with the white windmill make this an attractive place to visit.

Olympic National Park You can take a paddle wheeler cruise on the *Storm King* during the summer from mile 233 on US 101. It's a 90-minute cruise departing from the Storm King General Store. Phone 360-452-4520 for information and reservations.

GREAT PLACES TO ENJOY GOD'S CREATION

✔ Getting wet in the Hoh Rainforest, Olympic National Park, Washington

✔ Viewing Mt. Ranier National Park, Washington

✔ Hiking in Crater Lake National Park, Oregon

Oysterville The town hasn't changed much since 1880, when oyster production was at its peak. The entire town is now in the National Register of Historic Places because of all its well-preserved Victorian homes. The 1892 Oysterville Church looks the same as it did a century ago. By the way, an oyster plant is still in business at the docks on Pacific St. if you want to investigate.

Port Gamble Port Gamble Church (dating from 1870 and modeled after a church in East Machias, Maine) is the elegant focal point in this interesting company town, and it is a company town built by Pope & Talbot, a forest products and land development firm. The company has restored the old homes and now the entire town has been declared a historic area. The oldest of the homes is the Thompson House, built in 1859.

Port Townsend Founded in 1851, much of this city has been designated a National Historic Landmark area with more than 70 Victorian houses and other buildings. The Trinity Methodist Church (Jefferson and Clay Sts.) was built in 1871 and is the state's oldest standing Methodist church. In a small museum in the church is the Bible of the church's first minister.

Redmond Just outside of Seattle in this suburban area is one of the fastest-growing churches in the country, the Overlake Christian

Church (9900 Willows Rd. NE). You may want to visit and see what makes it so popular.

The oldest building in Kirkland is the 1891 Peter Kirk Building (7th Ave. NE and Market St.). It is a turreted structure, built by one of the town's founders.

Seattle The Monorail and the Space Needle are two Seattle institutions that introduce you to the city. The Monorail provides you with a scenic ride between Center House and Westlake Center in downtown Seattle. The Space Needle is a 605-foot tower, with an observation deck at the 520-foot level. Here you can get a great view of the entire area. You can also eat dinner at one of the revolving restaurants, although they are a bit pricey. It takes more than $5 for a 41-second elevator ride to the top. If nothing else, the Needle serves as a useful landmark if you ever get lost—it can be seen from anywhere in the city.

The Seattle Aquarium (at Pier 59 near Union St.) is an extremely popular destination. Visitors flock to the underwater dome, which features Puget Sound fish and animals, including sea otters, harbor seals, and fur seals. Also on exhibit are re-created salt marshes and tide pools in outdoor tanks.

Pioneer Square was the home of the first Seattleites, and although the buildings are quite old, they are not original. A fire in 1889 destroyed most of the original wood frame structures, and the area was rebuilt in brick. After a period of decline, the buildings were once again restored in the 1970s. This is an attractive place to shop and have a bite to eat, but the area becomes a bit rowdy with drinkers after dark.

The Seattle Center is a 740-acre complex that was originally built for the 1962 Seattle World's Fair. There are lots of attractions in the area, including an amusement park, theaters, museums, and shops. The Pacific Science Center has a planetarium and an IMAX theater. Also on site is the Children's Museum, with hands-on displays that re-create home life around the world. The programs, exhibits, and workshops here will appeal to all ages.

If you like to stay on the ground, try the Alaska Way Trolley, which will take you up and down the waterfront for about a dollar or less. And if you prefer water, take a ride on the ferry across Puget Sound and back. You'll have a great view of Seattle and if it's perfectly clear, you will be able to see the Olympic Mountains and Mt. Rainier.

The Museum of Flight (9404 S. Marginal Way, ten miles south of Seattle, next to Boeing Field) is a six-story building that contains a replica of the Wright Brothers' first glider, the first Air Force F–5 supersonic fighter, the world's fastest jet, and much more.

The Woodland Park Zoo (5500 Phinney Ave. N) is rated as one of the best in the country. It features 92 acres of highly realistic habitats for its animals, including a tropical rain forest, two gorilla exhibits, an Asian elephant forest, and an African savanna. The Alaska-themed Northern Trail is especially worthwhile.

The Washington Park Arboretum (2300 Arboretum Dr. E) is a 200-acre expanse with 5,500 different plant species. At the southern end of the arboretum is the Japanese Gardens, which is a 3.5-acre formal garden.

The St. James Cathedral (Ninth and Marion Sts.) was built in neo-Baroque style in 1907, and the Trinity Episcopal Church (609 Eighth Ave.), which dates back to 1891, is a stone church looking like an English country parish church.

University Presbyterian (4540 15th Ave. NE) is a mega-church here with both Sunday school and church attendances above 3,000. It has been known for the outstanding ministers it has had in its pulpit, including Earl Palmer and Bruce Larson.

A little smaller but also growing churches in Seattle are Calvary Fellowship (23302 56th Ave. W) and Mt. Zion Baptist (1634 19th St.).

Seattle Pacific University, affiliated with the Free Methodist denomination, is located just northwest of the downtown area. It has about 3,300 students.

Sedro Woolley You'll enjoy a ride on the Lake Whatcom Railway (11 miles north on Rte. 9 in Wickersham). It gives you a seven-mile, round-trip steam train ride in antique Northern Pacific passenger cars through the countryside.

Spokane Riverfront Park (507 N. Howard St.) is Spokane's center and a great place to spend several hours with your family. Developed for the 1974 World's Fair, the park comprises 100 acres, covering several islands in the Spokane River, and includes the Spokane Falls. Within the park, you can see an IMAX film, go ice skating (in winter only), or visit the small amusement park area with a number of children's rides and the beautiful Looff Carousel, hand-carved in 1909 and a local landmark.

The Cathedral of St. John the Evangelist (Episcopal) is a stunning sandstone Gothic structure at 1125 S. Grand Blvd. Recitals on its 49-bell carillon are given Thursdays and Sundays and recitals on its Aeolian-Skinner organ are given at other times.

Whitworth College (300 W. Hawthorne Rd.), a Presbyterian school with an evangelical commitment, is located on a 200-acre campus here. It has about 2,000 students enrolled in more than 40 majors. Concerts are presented frequently throughout the year.

This year about 100 million Father's Day cards will be purchased, all because of a 27-year-old woman in Spokane. In 1909 Sonora Smart Dodd, who had lost her father when she was 16, was listening to a Mother's Day sermon and wondering why there was no corresponding day to honor fathers. So she started promoting the idea. At first, she was laughed at, but the Spokane Ministerial Association and then the local YMCA began to support the idea and it spread. Orator William Jennings Bryan promoted it, and in 1914 Congress passed a resolution proclaiming the first national Father's Day.

Tacoma The Enchanted Village and Wild Waves Water Park (36201 Enchanted Pkwy S in Federal Way) rate high with families. The village is a family entertainment park with rides, a wax museum, and an antique toy and doll museum. The water park is what you would expect from a water park in a major city like Tacoma.

Never Never Land (5400 N. Pearl St.) is located in a forest area, and the fairy-tale characters that come out of the forest here will delight your kids.

The oldest church in the city is St. Peter's (Episcopal). Located at 2910 Starr St., it was built in 1873. To get to Tacoma, the organ and the half-ton bell had to be shipped around Cape Horn.

World Vision International (34834 Weyerhaeuser Way S), the world's largest Christian international relief organization, is now located in Federal Way, near the Sea-Tac airport. World Vision oversees development projects in more than 100 countries but is perhaps best known for its ministry to orphans.

Lakewold Gardens (12317 Gravelly Lake Dr.) ranks among the top private gardens in the Northwest. On the ten-acre estate, you find hundreds of rhododendrons and exotic trees, besides a formal garden with fountains and statuary.

Walla Walla The Whitman Mission National Historic Site (seven miles west on US 12) remembers Marcus and Narcissa Whitman, Presbyterian missionaries who came in 1836 to minister to the Native Americans in the area. Eleven years later, when a measles epidemic ravaged a Cayuse Indian village, Whitman, a doctor, was blamed for spreading the disease and he, his wife, and twelve others were slain in what is known as the Whitman Massacre.

"Though the mountains be shaken and the hills be removed, yet my unfailing love for you will not be shaken, nor my covenant of peace be removed," says the LORD, who has compassion on you.

ISAIAH **54:10**

Whitman College in Walla Walla also remembers the slain missionaries. Nearby, Fort Walla Walla Park (755 Myra Rd.) re-creates the pioneer days with 14 historic buildings and a pioneer museum.

CANADA

Eastern Provinces

EASTERN CANADA IS DEFINED largely by the Atlantic Ocean. Rugged coastal cliffs smooth into white sandy beaches that soon become rugged cliffs again. You'll find a wide array of ethnicities in eastern Canada, which makes for countless cultural opportunities. People of British, French, Scottish, German, African, Jewish, Greek, and Native Canadian heritage, even descendants of Yankee Loyalists who fled following the American Revolution, all call Eastern Canada their home.

Many of Canada's oldest settlements exist in Eastern Canada, and Christians will appreciate the old Canadian churches that are here as well. Consider worshiping in one of many historic Catholic and Presbyterian churches in the area, built in the days when the Acadians and Scotch Presbyterians were the dominant ethnic and religious groups.

▲ New Brunswick

Tourist Info
Phone 800-561-0123
Web sites
  Entire province   www.gov.nb.ca/tourism
  Fredericton   www.city.fredericton.nb.ca
For a complete list of updated links, visit www.christiantraveler.com

---

Barachois The Historic Church of St. Henri de Barachois (at Rtes. 133 and 930) is believed to be the oldest Acadian wooden church in North America. It was built in 1824 but since then has been restored and made into a museum and cultural center.

Caraquet The Acadian Historical Village (about six miles west on Rte. 11) is a re-creation of an early 18th-century settlement. Forty-two buildings have been moved to this location and have been restored. These authentic structures include a church, school, cobbler's shop, general store, homes, farms, and more.

Dorchester St. James Church (on Hwy. 106 at 4967 Main St.) was built in 1884 but it is now used as a museum to house a variety of antique tools, such as spinning wheels and pedal lathes. Occasionally, demonstrations on carding, spinning, and weaving are given here.

Fredericton The Christ Church Cathedral (Church St. between King and Brunswick Sts.) dates from 1853. It was patterned after a church in Norfolk, England, and is styled in decorated Gothic architecture.

Grande-Anse It's not large; fewer than 1,000 people live here, but the Museum of the Popes (Rte. 11) makes it a place of interest, especially for Catholics. The museum was founded in 1985, the year after the Pope visited Moncton. The portrait gallery features portraits of all 264 popes, but the main feature is the intricate model of the Vatican, which takes up much of the central hall; the top of the dome is six feet tall.

Moncton The city's oldest building is the Free Meeting House (20 Mountain Rd.). There is nothing fancy about it—no steeple or bell—but it was dedicated in 1821 and has been used by several denominations since then. Notice the box pews inside.

Until 1974 the Lutz Mountain Heritage Museum (3143 Mountain Rd.) was known as the Second Moncton Baptist Church. It now contains pioneer artifacts and genealogical records.

Magic Mountain Water Park (Magnetic Hill Park at exit 488 of the Trans-Canada Hwy.) has eight water slides, a wave pool, whirlpool, and miniature golf course. It is open in July and August.

The Magnetic Hill (next to Magic Mountain) is one of those optical illusions where it looks as if you are going downhill—but if you put your car in neutral, it will move backwards.

Sackville It's not a large town but it is proud of its heritage. It claims to have Canada's first Baptist church and also is the place where, in 1875, an academic degree was conferred on a woman for the first time anywhere in the British Empire. The Sackville United Church, built in 1876, is a white-steepled building with stained glass windows.

St. Andrews The Grenock Presbyterian Church (Montague and Edward Sts.), built in 1824, is quite amazing. The pulpit and the platforms were constructed without nails, thanks to a design of perfect proportions.

Saint John Rockwood Park here is a recreational area of more than 2,000 acres and ranks as one of Canada's largest municipal parks. Included is a children's animal farm, gardens, an 18-hole golf course, and much more.

Trinity Church (115 Charlotte St.) contains the Royal Coat of Arms of King George III, which was smuggled out of the Boston State House by Loyalists during the American Revolution. The church was built originally in 1791, and then after a fire, rebuilt in 1880.

St. Stephen Crocker Hill Studios and Gardens (Prince William St. and Ledge Rd.) is an art gallery surrounded by gardens containing more than 100 kinds of herbs. From the gardens you can see ospreys, loons, seals, and bald eagles on the St. Croix River.

▲ NEWFOUNDLAND

Corner Brook It's probably not worth your going clear across the province to see, but if you are in the area, you, and especially the children, will be intrigued by the Sticks and Stone House (12 Farnell's Lane). The man who built it spent 25 years decorating the interior with Popsicle sticks, pop can lids, and radiator grills from old cars. He called it folk art.

Harbour Grace This is one of Newfoundland's oldest and most historic towns. In the 19th century it was the province's second-largest community; in the 20th century it was the takeoff point for early transatlantic aviators like Wiley Post and Amelia Earhart. Though fires have ravaged many of the older buildings, three historic structures remain: St. Paul's Anglican Church, built in 1835, the jail, and the courthouse.

> The LORD had said to Abram, "Leave your country, your people and your father's household and go to the land I will show you."
>
> GENESIS 12:1

St. Anthony Sir Wilfred Grenfell, converted through the ministry of evangelist Dwight L. Moody in England, became a medical missionary to Labrador and Newfoundland in 1892, starting a string of hospitals and nursing stations. He was knighted by King George V in 1927. In the center of the town of St. Anthony is the Grenfell House museum, which has artifacts and exhibits about his life and work. In the hospital nearby are murals depicting scenes from Grenfell's life.

St. John's This might be the oldest city in North America. John Cabot sailed into the harbor here on June 27, 1497, the feast day of John the Baptist, and hence the name of the city.

The Anglican Cathedral of St. John the Baptist (Gower St. at Church Hill) was begun in 1847, but after the Great Fire of 1892, it was restored to its present grandeur. Today it stands as one of the loveliest examples of Gothic architecture on the continent.

The Basilica Cathedral of St. John the Baptist (Military Rd. at Harvey and Bonaventure Sts.) is built in the shape of a Latin cross and dates from 1841.

The Old Garrison Church (St. Thomas's, on Military Rd.), built in 1836, is one of the oldest wooden churches in the city. Originally it was used by the army and it still displays the Hanoverian coat of arms. British troops were stationed in St. John's until 1970.

The Fluvarium (C. A. Pippy Park off Prince Philip Dr.) takes you down three stories and lets you look underwater into a stream. In fact it's the only place on the continent where you can do so. You can see the trout swimming by; unfortunately, you can't reach through the glass to catch them. There are also exhibits and interpretive programs.

Wiltondale The Pioneer Village (Hwy. 430, south of Hwy. 431) has a country church, a store, a schoolhouse, a barn, and a house—just about all you need in a pioneer village, depicting rural life in the late 1800s in the province.

▲NOVA SCOTIA

Tourist Info
Phone 800-565-0000
Web site
  Entire province   www.explore.gov.ns.ca
For a complete list of updated links, visit www.christiantraveler.com

Antigonish St. Ninian's Cathedral (St. Ninian's St.) is a limestone and sandstone Roman basilica–style building, completed in 1874. The towers rise 125 feet high. In the rear of the cathedral is a painting of St. Ninian.

Baddeck This is where Alexander Graham Bell lived his final years. The Alexander Graham Bell National Historic Site (east end of Hwy. 205) houses a museum commemorating his life and work. During July and August, there are special programs for children. About 2.5 miles from town is Bell's summer home, but it is closed to the public because his descendants continue to live there. Both Bell and Mrs. Bell are buried there.

Barrington The Old Meeting House Museum (2408 Hwy. 3) is Canada's oldest nonconformist house of worship still in existence, which means that it wasn't associated with the Church of England (the Anglican Church). Built in 1765, it is a New England–style meetinghouse, and guides in period costumes are available to explain its history. Admission is by donation.

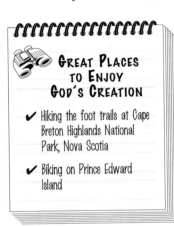

GREAT PLACES TO ENJOY GOD'S CREATION

✔ Hiking the foot trails at Cape Breton Highlands National Park, Nova Scotia

✔ Biking on Prince Edward Island

Church Point St. Mary's Museum (Hwy. 1) was a church before it became a museum, and as a church it ranked as one of the largest wooden ones on the continent. Featured in the museum are photographs, paintings, religious artifacts, and a decorated painted ceiling.

Clementsport The Old St. Edward's Loyalist Church (Hwy. 1) goes back to 1795. It was built using hand-hewn beams, fixtures, hinges, and plaster made of clam shells.

Grand Pré The Church of the Covenanters (Hwy. 101, exit 10) was built in 1790 by New Englanders. The church has box pews, sounding boards, and a pulpit that almost reaches the ceiling.

The stone church (a short drive east of Wolfville) at the Grand Pré National Historic Site is the presumed site of the original church here. The present church was built in 1922. Evangeline Bellefontaine, the fictional heroine of Longfellow's epic poem, was supposedly born here, and there is a statue of her in the garden. The park and church were established in memory of the town's Acadian settlers, who were deported from 1755 to 1763 to other British colonies throughout North America. (See Longfellow also under Portland, Maine; Sudbury Center, Mass.; and Haddonfield, N.J. See Acadians also under Lafayette and St. Martinville, La.)

Halifax The Discovery Centre (1593 Barrington St.) is an interactive science center to help children develop in math, physics, chemistry, and other scientific fields.

The Chapel of Our Lady of Sorrows (Holy Cross Cemetery at South and S. Park Sts.) is a small chapel that was built in one day. The date was August 31, 1843, and 2,000 men were involved in the huge endeavor. One of the stained glass windows dates from 1661.

The Old Dutch Church (Brunswick and Garrish Sts.) is the first Lutheran church in Canada. Built in 1756 by German settlers, it measures only 20 by 39 feet.

St. Paul's Church (1749 Argyle St.) is the oldest Protestant church in Canada. It was built in 1750 and the walls are covered with interesting tablets.

The Public Gardens, designed in 1875, are reputed to be among the finest Victorian gardens in Canada. Free concerts are given Sunday afternoons at 2 P.M. in July and August.

New Glasgow Magic Valley (six miles west on Hwy. 104) is a pleasant family stop with a Storybook Village and Old MacDonald's Farm, as well as a variety of rides.

Pictou The Burning Bush Centre-Museum (off Hwy. 106 on Prince St.) can trace its lineage back to 1786 when a Scottish Presbyterian minister organized a congregation. This building was finally built and it became the First Presbyterian Church. Documents and artifacts of the Women's Missionary Society of the Atlantic Provinces are housed here.

The first church in the county was the Loch Broom Log Church (off Hwy. 104, exit 20 to Rte. 376), built in 1787. It's a simple log church overlooking the river.

St. Ann's This is the heart of the Gaelic community and at its center is Gaelic College, the only college of its kind in North America. During the summer you can see various Highland arts and crafts, like Highland dancing, bagpipe playing, hand weaving of tartans, and Gaelic singing. On campus, the Great Hall of the Clans Museum depicts the history and culture of Scotland from its earliest days.

387

Sydney Saint Patrick's Museum (end of the Government Wharf) is the oldest Roman Catholic church on Cape Breton Island. It was built in 1828.

▲ Prince Edward Island

Tourist Info
Phone 888-PEI-PLAY
Web site
 Entire province   www.gov.pe.ca
For a complete list of updated links, visit www.christiantraveler.com

Cap-Egmont They are not exactly dream houses, but The Bottle Houses (Hwy. 11) are certainly unusual. Three buildings are built out of 25,000 bottles of various shapes and sizes. One is a chapel and another is a six-gabled house. The surrounding grounds feature rock gardens.

Cavendish If you have read *Anne of Green Gables* by Lucy Maud Montgomery, you may feel you know Cavendish already. Mark Twain called Anne "the dearest and most loveable child in fiction since the immortal Alice." The author, Lucy Montgomery, is buried in the Cavendish cemetery. The Green Gables House (west of Hwy. 13 on Hwy. 6) is part of Prince Edward Island National Park and is furnished in Victorian style.

Enchanted Lands (on Hwy. 6, one mile west of the junction of Hwys. 6 and 13) consists of The Enchanted Castle, King Tut's Tomb, and River of Adventure miniature golf. Nearby is The Great Island Adventure Park, which is an outdoor science theme park. Besides that, there is Rainbow Valley with the Children's Farm and Anne of Green Gables Land, so every member of the family should find something of interest in Cavendish.

Charlottetown William and Robert Harris were both important figures in Canada a century ago. William was an architect and Robert was a painter. They combined forces in building the All Souls Chapel or St. Peter's Cathedral here and you can check out the results (at the corner of Rochford Sq. and Rochford St.).

Confederation Centre of the Arts (Grafton and Queen Sts.) is another place where you can check on the works of Robert Harris. The art gallery's collection of 15,000 works of Canadian art includes 7,500 paintings, watercolors, drawings, and letters by Harris. Perhaps you could say that he was prolific! The gallery also includes the handwritten manuscripts by Lucy Maud Montgomery, author of *Anne of Green Gables*. During the summer, musical productions of *Anne of Green Gables* are presented on stage here.

GREAT PLACES FOR FAMILY FUN

✔ Metro Toronto Zoo

✔ Skiing the Laurentians, Quebec

✔ The ring of beaches around Prince Edward Island

St. Dunstan's Basilica (Great George St.) is built in the form of a Gothic cross and its triple spires are a landmark in Charlottetown.

St. James Presbyterian Church (Fitzroy and Pownal Sts.) features stained glass windows and relics from the island of Iona, where Scotland was first introduced to Christianity.

Hope River St. Ann's Church Lobster Suppers are served Monday through Saturday from 4 to 9 P.M. The church hall is located just off Rt. 224 between Rtes. 6 and 13. Lobster suppers are now an institution on the north shore of Prince Edward Island, but St. Ann's Church was the first to do it.

Kensington The Woodleigh Replicas and Gardens (on Hwy. 234) displays 30 large-scale models of castles and cathedrals from Great Britain, in the midst of ten acres of English country gardens. Daily bagpipe performances are presented in July and August.

New London The birthplace of Lucy Maud Montgomery (Hwy. 20 at Clifton Corner) contains personal items including her scrapbooks and her wedding dress.

Tignish The Church of St. Simon and St. Jude (Church and Maple Sts.) is notable because of its pipe organ, the largest of four wooden tracker-action organs in Canada. It was built in 1882.

Montreal

Toronto

Central Provinces

ONTARIO AND QUEBEC ARE HOME to over half of Canada's population of 29 million people, the vast majority of whom live near the U.S. border. And although we've found it convenient to group the two provinces together in this book, the citizens of the two provinces may not appreciate the pairing. Ontario is largely Anglo in its heritage, while Quebec is largely French, and every so often threats of a Quebec secession are raised.

Language and culture are not the only differences between Ontario and Quebec; Christians will find differences of faith as well. Must-see sites in Quebec are Catholic, including the fabulous cathedrals in Montreal and Quebec City, among the finest on the continent. Christian sites in Ontario tend to be Protestant, including the Mohawk Church near Brantford and the Mennonite communities near Kitchener and Waterloo.

▲ ONTARIO

Tourist Info
Phone 800-ONTARIO
Web sites
  Entire province   www.travelinx.com
  Ottawa   www.tourottawa.org
  Toronto   www.tourism-toronto.com
  Windsor   www.city.windsor.on.ca
For a complete list of updated links, visit www.christiantraveler.com

Brantford This is called the Telephone City because it is the location of the Alexander Graham Bell Homestead. Bell lived here with his family between 1870 and 1881, when he made the world's first long-distance telephone call to Paris. That's not Paris, France, but Paris, Ontario, eight miles away. Most of the furnishings in the homestead are authentic.

Joseph Brant, for whom the town was named, was a Mohawk chief who brought together members of the Six Nations Confederacy into Canada after the American Revolution. In gratitude, King George III built the Mohawk Church (292 Mohawk St.). Its name was changed to His Majesty's Chapel of the Mohawks in 1904. This simple, white frame building is the oldest Protestant church in Ontario and the only Indian Royal Chapel in existence. It has eight stained glass windows depicting the history of the Six Nations people.

Dresden They call it Uncle Tom's Cabin, and this "Uncle Tom" was the Reverend Josiah Henson, an ex-slave who purchased 200 acres here and founded a vocational school for runaway slaves in 1841. Besides the main cabin you can also see a church dating to the 1850s, a museum containing rare books and documents, a smokehouse, and farming and logging equipment.

Hamilton The African Lion Safari (12 miles west of the city off Hwy. 8) is a drive-through wildlife park with rail and cruise boat excursions, petting zoo, and daily animal and bird shows.

A little tamer is the Royal Botanical Gardens (Plains Rd.), which has 5 major gardens and 30 miles of trails. It claims to have the world's largest collection of lilacs, besides two acres of roses and a variety of everything else.

Kingston There's always something going on at Fort Henry (Hwy. 2, just east of town). All summer long the Fort Henry Guard and its goat mascot named David parade and perform 19th-century drills and musters. Usually the performance includes music and a marching display by a fife and drum band and a mock battle with artillery support.

Kitchener-Waterloo These two towns have merged so as to be almost indistinguishable from each other. Settled around 1800 by Swiss-German Mennonites from Pennsylvania, this region has become more secular, but not any less German. There is a mammoth glockenspiel downtown by Speakers' Corner, and every October the twin cities celebrate Oktoberfest.

London Storybook Gardens (929 Springbank Dr.) is on the Thames River (where else?) in the 281-acre Springbank Park. Your youngsters will see a castle, storybook characters, and a zoo. Besides that, it is a very inexpensive children's theme park because it is run by the city's Public Utility Commission.

Maple Canada's Wonderland (off Hwy. 400) is a theme park featuring three dozen rides. Open from May through September, it's a 370-acre park with a musical theater, aquarium, and lots of restaurants.

Moose Factory Island Don't try to get here by car, but if you do manage the trip by train and boat, you will find that it is 186 miles north of Cochrane, which is called the gateway to the Arctic. Moose Factory Island was the site of the second Hudson Bay Company trading post, established in 1672, and it has a unique church, St. Thomas Anglican Church on Front Rd. In the floor of the church are holes to let floodwater out and to ventilate the foundation. It seems that when the church was being built in 1864, the foundation floated away in a spring flood. Somehow the holes in the floor may keep that from happening again. By the way, the altar cloths and lectern hangings are of moose hide decorated with beads.

Newmarket Eleven miles outside of the Toronto city limits is a Quaker meetinghouse, the first church erected in the lands north of Toronto, and it has been on the west side of Rte. 11 (Yonge St.) since 1810.

Niagara Falls It may be that the most exciting way to see the falls is from the decks of the *Maid of the Mist* (5920 River Rd.), which has been operating since 1846. You get a little wet, but it gives you and the family something to talk about. However, if you want to stay dry, experience the falls in the IMAX theater (6170 Buchanan St.), with its six-story-high screen.

Ottawa The National Gallery of Canada (380 Sussex Dr.) is a fabulous glass-towered building, housing one of the premier collections of Canadian art in the world. Of special interest to Christians is the reconstructed Rideau Convent Chapel, a classic example of French Canadian 19th-century architecture with the only neo-Gothic fan vaulted ceiling on the continent.

The oldest church in this capital city is the Notre Dame Basilica (St. Patrick St.), consecrated in 1846. Its spires dominate the skyline.

The Changing of the Guard on the Parliament Hill lawn is a colorful half-hour ceremony held daily from late June to late August. The parade of 125 soldiers assembles at 9:30 A.M. and marches up Elgin St., reaching the hill at 10 A.M. The ceremony includes inspection of dress and weapons. The colors are marched before the troops and then saluted.

In the evenings, there is a sound and light show against the backdrop of the Parliament buildings. Two performances are given each night, one in English and one in French.

Ottawa's biggest event of the year is its Canadian Tulip Festival in May, when 200 varieties of tulips are arrayed around public buildings, monuments, and homes in the area.

Port Hope Near here is a monument saying, "Four miles north, in Pengally's Cemetery, lies the philanthropist and author of this great masterpiece, written at Port Hope." Above the inscription are the words of the hymn "What a Friend We Have in Jesus" and the name of the author, Joseph Scriven. Though he came from a prosperous background in Ireland, he had only limited possessions. He worked for people who could not afford to pay him and gave away what little he had. When he heard that his mother was dying in Dublin, he expressed regret that he could not be with her and he enclosed the words of this song. Later, when a friend saw the words in Scriven's small bedroom and asked if Scriven had written the words, he got the reply, "The Lord and I did it between us."

St. Jacobs This and the nearby town of Elmira are in the heart of Mennonite and Hutterite country in Ontario. To learn more about the Old Order Mennonite community here, visit the Meetingplace Interpretation Center (Hwy. 8). The St. Jacobs Farmers' Market and Flea Market is open on Thursdays and Saturdays. There are also more than 100 shops in the area that offer antiques and hand-crafted quilts. (See Hutterites also under Rockport and Yankton, S.D., and Lewistown, Mont.)

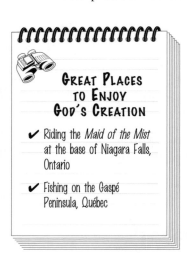

GREAT PLACES TO ENJOY GOD'S CREATION

✔ Riding the *Maid of the Mist* at the base of Niagara Falls, Ontario

✔ Fishing on the Gaspé Peninsula, Québec

Sharon About 25 miles north of Toronto is the community of Sharon, which was established by a Quaker splinter group called the Children of Peace. Sometimes they were known as the Davidites because their leader was David Willson. Central to their community was the Temple of Peace, which was intended to show their beliefs through its architecture. The temple was 3 stories high, symbolizing the Trinity, and had 12 supporting pillars, bearing the names of the apostles. After Willson died in 1866, interest in the temple started to wane, and followers began to lose heart. However, it has been partially restored, and there is a museum owned by the Sharon Temple Museum Society (18974 Leslie St.).

Stratford In 1953 the Stratford Shakespearean Festival was launched and has become a world-famous theatrical event, attracting 400,000 people a year to this town on the Avon. The Stratford Festival hosts music, opera, and drama with a special emphasis, of course, on Shakespeare. There actually are three theaters in town, which offer a variety of productions. Whether or not you see a play here, the town is worth seeing in its own right, with its quaint flower-lined streets, cozy bed and breakfast establishments, and lots of great shopping and restaurants. The ticket office is at 55 Queens St.

Toronto The CN Tower (301 Front St.) at 1,815 feet is called the world's tallest freestanding structure, outdoing the Empire State Building, which is a mere 1,250 feet. If you go to the observation deck or to the revolving restaurant, Top of Toronto, you can get a great view of the area. On a good day you may even be able to see Niagara Falls, 62 miles away. Then check out the Tour of the Universe, which starts at the base of the tower. This will take you down in the elevators where you will be led by guides and by robots through computerized passport controls and video screens into a 40-passenger "spaceship" that will give you a tour of the galaxy. Pretty impressive!

The Ontario Science Center (northeast of downtown on Don Mills Rd.) is a fascinating science museum that the entire family will enjoy. It is hands-on with a variety of exhibits that demonstrate the wonders of modern technology.

The Metro Toronto Zoo (Meadowvale Rd., north of Hwy. 401) is actually 22 miles northeast of downtown Toronto. It's a world-class zoo, no doubt about it. It's estimated that it would take visitors four full days to see everything in this 710-acre layout. The zoo is obviously very spread out, which makes for more separation between animals and regions and for happier animals; unfortunately it also makes for sore feet. Consider renting a stroller if you have young children. An electrically powered train moves silently among the animal exhibits and can accommodate strollers and wheelchairs. Choose those areas you're most interested in and hit them first. If you need suggestions, head for the enclosed climate-controlled pavilions located in each region, including Indo-Malayan, African, and Eurasian. But don't let its size stop you—this is one great zoo!

Ontario Place (855 Lakeshore Blvd. W) is a 96-acre recreation complex opened in 1971. The Children's Village is the most creative playground you will find anywhere, but there is much more than that to enjoy here.

Casa Loma (1 Austin Terrace) is hard to describe. Its builder, Sir Henry Pellatt, wanted to build a medieval castle, and so he did, complete with Elizabethan-style chimneys, Rhineland turrets, secret panels, a great hall with a 60-foot ceiling, and an 800-foot tunnel to the stables. Why is it called Casa Loma? Who knows? Maybe because of the Spanish tile in the stables.

Black Creek Pioneer Village (12 miles north of downtown Toronto at the corner of Jane St. and Steeles Ave.) is a reproduction of a rural Victorian community of the 1860s. Roblin's Mill continues to grind wheat, powered by a large waterwheel, and costumed artisans demonstrate their trades, from weaving to clock making to tinsmithing.

Harry A. Ironside, best known as pastor of the Moody Memorial Church in Chicago for 20 years, was born in Toronto to Plymouth Brethren parents and read the Bible through 14 times before he was 14 years old.

Jarvis Street Baptist Church (130 Gerrard St. E) provided the pulpit for Fundamentalist leader T. T. Shields from 1910 until his death. Shields gained national attention through his strong views in *Gospel Witness,* which he edited.

Knox Presbyterian Church (630 Spadina Ave.) has had a strong evangelical presence in the community for many years.

In 1994 a revival called the Toronto Blessing broke out in the Toronto Airport Christian Fellowship. In its first years the controversial revival was characterized by "holy laughter." Thousands of seekers came from across the continent to get in on the blessing. Believers meet today in the Asian Trade Center.

Winchester This town was the birthplace of George Beverly Shea, America's beloved singer, who has worked with Billy Graham for more than fifty years. He is also known for writing the song, "I'd Rather Have Jesus," which he penned when he was 23.

▲ QUÉBEC

Tourist Info
Phone 800-363-7777
Web sites
  Entire province   www.tourisme.gouv.qc.ca
  Montréal   www.tourism-montreal.org
  Québec City   www.quebecregion.com
For a complete list of updated links, visit www.christiantraveler.com

Baie Ste-Catherine The Centre d'Interprétation et d'Observation de Pointe-Noire (one mile south of the Tadoussac ferry dock) is a good place to observe marine mammals and especially beluga whales. From the interpretation center you can walk down stairways to a platform from which you will have a good view of the fjord and the St. Lawrence River.

Cap-de-la-Madeleine Thousands of Roman Catholics come to the Shrine of Notre-Dame-du-Cap (just south of Hwy. 138 at 626 rue Notre-Dame) each year. The Madonna here is Canada's national shrine to Mary.

Grand-Metis The Metis Gardens (on Hwy. 132) display more than 1,000 kinds of trees, flowers, and shrubs and rank among eastern Canada's finest gardens. Rhododendrons and crab apples are colorful in early summer and then lilies and roses are abloom after that.

Hemmingford The Park Safari (on Hwy. 202) is a 200-acre family-oriented park. The drive-through wildlife section has African, European, Asian, and North American divisions, and there are four walk-through areas. In addition, there are mechanical rides, a soft play area for children, and a Magic Creek for tube rides.

Kahnawake The Saint François Xavier Mission and the Shrine of Kateri Tekakwitha are at the center of the Iroquois reservation here. In the church is the tomb of an Iroquois maiden, Kateri Tekakwitha, who has been beatified by the Vatican and may become the first North American Indian saint.

Montréal The Basilique Notre-Dame-de-Montréal (Notre Dame Basilica), at 116 rue Notre-Dame Ouest, is one of the most beautiful churches in North America. The first church built here under that name was a bark-covered structure built in 1642. Three times it has been torn down and rebuilt, each time larger and more ornate. The existing building was constructed in 1829, a massive 3,800-seat neo-Gothic cathedral designed by James O'Donnell, who started the project as a Protestant and converted to Catholicism during the construction. One of the cathedral's twin towers holds the continent's largest bells. Stained glass windows, a beautiful blue vaulted ceiling studded with thousands of 24-carat gold stars, and one of North America's largest organs are a few of this cathedral's gems. If you want to hear all 7,000 of the organ's pipes in action, you have to attend the 11 A.M. mass on Sundays and listen closely to the recessional.

Chapelle Notre-Dame-de-Bonsecours (400 rue St-Paul Est) was dedicated to the Virgin Mary in 1657 by Ste. Marguerite Bourgeoys, Montréal's first schoolteacher, later canonized. It became known as a sailor's church, and small wood models of sailing ships hang from the ceiling reminding visitors of the fact. In 1998 a massive renovation project revealed several priceless murals that had been hidden behind glued-on paintings. If you aren't afraid of heights, climb the precarious bell tower for a fabulous view of the Vieux-Port.

The Cathedral of Marie-Reine-du-Monde (1085 rue de la Cathédrale) is the seat of the Roman Catholic archbishop of Montréal. It is a one-third–scale replica of St. Peter's Basilica in Rome. It was built between 1870 and 1894.

There's a lighted cross atop Mont Royal Park, and it is there because Maisonneuve, the founder of Montréal, promised that if God would spare the colony during the flood of December 25, 1642, he would put a cross at the top of the mountain. Horse-drawn vehicles are allowed up there, and from a chalet on the mountain you get a good view not only of Montréal but also of the St. Lawrence River and of the New York Adirondacks.

Christ Church Cathedral (535 rue Ste-Catherine Ouest) was built in 1859 and is the main church of the Anglican diocese of Montréal. In the late 1980s the diocese leased the land and air rights surrounding the church. The developers then built La Maison des Cooperants, the office tower located behind the cathedral, and a huge retail complex, Les Promenades de la Cathédrale. The beautiful church features frequent organ recitals and concerts.

St. George's (1100 rue Stanley) is a beautiful neo-Gothic structure, the prettiest Anglican church in Montréal. Built in 1872, St. George's dim interior has a beamed wooden ceiling and beautiful stained glass.

A church rarely visited by tourists is St. Patrick's Basilica (460 boul. René-Levesque Ouest). Built in 1847, it is one of the best examples of the Gothic Revival style in Canada. The church is decorated in muted colors. Over the sanctuary, the vaulted ceiling is covered with green and gold mosaics. The pulpit has panels depicting the apostles, and a huge lamp with six-foot-high angels hangs over the main altar.

Olympic Park is where the city played host to the 1976 summer Olympics, and there is much there to see. The Olympic Tower is 623 feet high and you can reach it by a funicular. The Biodome is a museum of the environment in which four ecosystems are explored.

St. Joseph's Oratory (3800 chemin Queen Mary) is one of the city's most important religious shrines and it is also one of the world's largest basilicas. It was the dream of Brother André, who had a simple wooden chapel here, where he prayed for hundreds of people. The tomb of Brother André is in the oratory.

The Montréal Royal City Tour, departing from the Tourist Center (1001 Dorchester Sq.) will give you a bilingual tour of the downtown area. If you wish to go by water, try Le Bateau-Mouche tour from the Jacques Cartier Pier. It's a glass-roofed, Paris-style riverboat that will give you a 90-minute, bilingual look at the waterfront and skyline.

Rafting Montréal (8912 boul. LaSalle) has a Family Discovery Trip, which explores calmer channels than the normal white-water rafts go on.

THE FRENCH CATHOLICS IN MONTRÉAL

Over 450 years ago, in 1535, the French explorer Jacques Cartier first came to the place the Algonquin Indians called, "Kebek," or "where the river narrows." Along with the subsequent explorers and fur trappers came a number of French missionaries, intent on evangelizing the native peoples and establishing a solid religious base for the colonists.

The settlers who arrived in 1642 in present-day Montréal had especially great religious designs. They hoped to do nothing less than establish a new Christian society, naming their settlement Ville-Marie in honor of St. Mary. Two French women were particularly busy: Jeanne Mance, a French noblewoman, and Marguerite Bourgeoys. The Religieuses Hospitalières de St-Joseph, a nursing order founded by Mance, is the oldest nursing group in the Americas. The women also established the colony's first school and a world-renowned teaching order.

In 1760 Montréal fell to the hands of the British. The Seven Years' War—known to Americans as the French and Indian War—saw the end of French control of Canada. But Montréal's religious roots remained strong. The island city remained the property of French clerics for almost another century. The aristocratic French priests, the Sulpicians, administered the colony and recruited colonists until 1854. Today they still run the Basilique Notre-Dame-de-Montréal.

Today's visitors to Montréal cannot miss the influence of those early French missionaries. The city appears more French than North American and is home to some of the most beautiful cathedrals on the continent. Two of the city's largest tourist attractions are dedicated to Christ's earthly parents. Don't miss the Basilique Notre-Dame-de-Montréal, built in honor of Christ's mother, Mary, or the Oratoire St-Joseph, built in honor of Christ's earthly father, Joseph.

The hymn "My Jesus I Love Thee" was written by a 16-year-old boy in this city in 1862. The young man, William Featherston, died before his 27th birthday and apparently never wrote another hymn.

Québec City The basilique Notre-Dame-de-Québec (16 rue Buade) is Québec City's most famous basilica. Its parish is the oldest in North America, dating from 1647. The interior of the basilica is beautifully ornate, with gold leaf decorating the ceiling and stained glass windows. The basilica's large crypt was Québec City's first cemetery; over 900 people are buried here. In the summer visitors can enjoy the daily indoor sound and light show, *Act of Faith*, which recounts the history of the city and the church. Admission to the basilica is free; the show costs $7.

The Holy Trinity Anglican Cathedral (31 rue des Jardins) was built in 1804 on the site of a previous church and became the first Anglican Cathedral outside the British Isles. The present church was constructed by order of King George III of England, and a portion of the balcony remains for the exclusive use of the reigning British sovereign or his or her representative.

Another historic church is the Eglise St-Jean-Baptiste, located at 410 rue St-Jean. Seven varieties of Italian marble were used in the interior, and the church's 36 stained glass windows are stunning.

St. Andrew's Presbyterian Church (106 rue Ste-Anne) was built in 1810. The interior is interesting with its high sidewall pulpit and its unique arrangement of pews and balcony.

The Couvent des Ursulines (Ursuline Convent), at 18 rue Donnacona, operates North America's oldest school for girls, founded in 1639 by two French nuns. The private school is not open to visitors, but there are two sites here that are open to the public. The Musée des Ursulines (Ursuline Museum) offers an interesting look at over 100 years of convent life under French rule, including magnificent works of ornate embroidery. Visitors may also tour the Chapelle des Ursulines. The chapel's interior is original, sculpted over a period of ten years in the early 18th century. Look for the votive lamp that was lit in 1717 and has never been extinguished. Admission to the museum is $3. The chapel is free.

Château Frontenac (1 rue des Carrières) is Québec City's most famous landmark. The fabulous green copper-roofed castle stands on the site of what was once the headquarters of New France. The castle owes its name to the Comte de Frontenac, governor of New

France in the late 17th century. Château Frontenac was built as a magnificently luxurious hotel in 1893 and continues to operate as such today. Visitors are welcome to tour the hotel, even if they are not spending the night.

Rock Island Have a unique experience and go to the Haskell Free Library and Opera House (Church St.). It lies directly on the international border of Canada and the United States. In fact the stage of the opera house is in Canada and the seats are in the United States.

Ste-Adèle The town is a writers' and artists' colony, but it also has the delightful Seraphin Village Museum and The Wonderland (both on Hwy. 117). The museum is a re-creation of a village of the 1880s, with life-sized mannequins, live animals, a miniature train, and costumed staff. The Wonderland presents fairy-tale–inspired settings, costumed characters, a wading pool, and water games.

Ste-Anne-de-Beaupré The Basilica of Ste-Anne-de-Beaupré attracts more than a million pilgrims and visitors each year. Next to the shrine is the Scala Sancta, a replica of the 28 steps that Jesus supposedly ascended to meet Pilate in Jerusalem.

Near the basilica is the Cyclorama of Jerusalem. This is a cylindrical painting 46 feet high and 361 feet around, painted in Munich, depicting events in Jerusalem, on Calvary, and in the surrounding countryside at the time of the crucifixion.

Sillery The Old Jesuit House (2320 chemin du Foulon), built about 1637, is one of the oldest in Canada and now contains a historical museum along with arts and crafts.

Villa Bagatelle (1563 chemin Saint-Louis) is a restored villa surrounded by a formal garden in which more than 350 kinds of flowers are displayed.

Vancouver

Winnipeg

Western Provinces

WESTERN CANADA COMPRISES A VAST AREA, stretching from the beautiful Pacific coast through the Canadian Rockies and into the prairie provinces. Yet in spite of the huge geographical span, well under half of Canada's population lives here. British Columbia is blessed with stunning coastline and mountains; it is consequently blessed with most of the tourist trade in this region as well. The remaining provinces are less touristed and often more interesting for that very reason. A travel experience in the prairie provinces will be warm and genuine.

The religious history of the area parallels that of Canada's neighbor to the south. Much of western Canada was settled by groups of persecuted Christians who headed west in the hope of leading peaceful lives, free of conflict and true to their consciences. You'll find that communities of Mennonites, Hutterites, Doukhobors, and others have left their subtle religious imprint throughout the region.

▲ ALBERTA

Tourist Info
Phone 800-661-8888
Web sites
  Entire province   www.discoveralberta.com
  Calgary   www.tourism-calgary.org
  Edmonton   www.gov.edmonton.ab.ca
For a complete list of updated links, visit www.christiantraveler.com

Banff Both the Banff Sulphur Mountain Gondola Lift and the Lake Louise Gondola are spectacular ways to see Banff and Lake Louise respectively. At the top of each is an observation deck.

The Cascade Rock Gardens that encircle the Banff Park's administration buildings have a series of rock terraces, displaying an unusual assortment of flowers, plants, and shrubs.

Calgary Calgary Tower (101 9th Ave. SW) is a good place to start your tour of Calgary, whether you choose to dine at the revolving restaurant or not. The observation deck is 626 feet above the city and in the clear air you can almost see forever.

Calaway Park (six miles west on Hwy. 1) is a 69-acre amusement park with 21 rides, live musical shows, miniature golf, and a picnic area.

The Calgary Zoo, Botanical Gardens, and Prehistoric Park (1300 Zoo Rd. NE) are well worth seeing. They are located on St. George's Island in the middle of the Bow River. This is Canada's second-largest zoo with more than 1,400 animals, some rare and/or endangered, and the gardens have more than 10,000 plants. The Canada Wilds section focuses on endangered Canadian ecosystems. The Prehistoric Park features 22 dinosaur recreations in exhibits designed to resemble their original habitats.

The Heritage Park Historical Village (1900 Heritage Dr. SW) is located on a 60-acre site that shows you what life was like a century ago. About 70 percent of the buildings are originals that have been moved to the park. An antique steam train circles the park, and a 200-passenger stern-wheeler cruises on Glenmore Reservoir.

Canmore In the early part of the 20th century Ralph Connor was a best-selling Christian novelist who lived in western Canada. His books aren't read much anymore, but one church that he helped start still bears his name. It's the Ralph Connor Memorial United Church on 8th St. It was built in 1890 and is now a Provincial Historic Site.

Drumheller Just west of town along the north Dinosaur Trail is the Little Church, to which 150,000 visitors come each year. It is a small chapel, so it means that only six of those 150,000 can get in at a time.

Dunvegan This was a fur-trading post in the nineteenth century and it was also the location of one of the first Roman Catholic missions in the state. You can see the church, the 1885 St. Charles Mission, and the 1889 mission rectory.

Edmonton You go back to school, way back to school, when you visit the Edmonton Public Schools Museum (99th Ave. at 104th St.). It is located in a 1904 brick schoolhouse. Also on the grounds is the first public school in Alberta, built in 1881.

The Space and Science Center (142d St. and 112th Ave.) presents laser light shows on its 75-foot domed ceiling. The giant-screen IMAX theater, the largest planetarium theater in Canada, engulfs you and gives you a fresh appreciation for God's creation of the heavens. There are also games and interactive displays here.

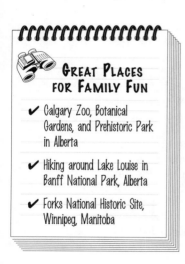

GREAT PLACES FOR FAMILY FUN

✔ Calgary Zoo, Botanical Gardens, and Prehistoric Park in Alberta

✔ Hiking around Lake Louise in Banff National Park, Alberta

✔ Forks National Historic Site, Winnipeg, Manitoba

The West Edmonton Mall (87th Ave. and 170th St.) will entice you inside even if you didn't plan to do any shopping on your vacation. It is a combination shopping mall and amusement park with 800 stores and services, 19 movie theatres, 100 eateries, and 5 major attractions. It claims to be one of the world's largest indoor malls. As for the rides, there are 23 of them, and besides that there is a World Waterpark with one of the world's largest indoor wave pools.

Lac La Biche In 1853 a mission was started here and it played a major role in the settlement of the area. The Lac La Biche Mission (five miles north on Mission Rd.) has recently been restored, and on the site are a church, schoolhouse, and convent.

Lethbridge The Nikka Yuko Japanese Garden (in Henderson Park) incorporates five different types of traditional Japanese gardens into its design. Hostesses in kimonos conduct tours.

Medicine Hat They call it the World's Tallest Tepee (Hwy. 1 and South Ridge Dr.) and they may be right. It is about 22 stories high, and if you have seen one taller than that, let us know. The tepee was used in the 1988 Olympics in Calgary and afterwards it was moved here on the Saamis Archaeological Site.

St. Albert Father Albert Lacombe came here in 1852, playing the role of a peacemaker between tribes and between Indians and the railroad people. He helped the Indians develop the first farms of the area. Father Lacombe Chapel (7 St. Vital Ave.) is a log chapel, honoring the priest's role as spiritual leader, peacemaker, and negotiator.

Next door is the Vital Grandin Centre. It was the residence of the first Catholic bishop in the province. Completed in 1887, it still houses several priests—they live on the second floor, which is off-limits to visitors—but there is a museum on the first floor and a private chapel you can view.

Stettler It's called the Alberta Prairie Railway Excursion and it operates from the Stettler train station at 47th Ave. and 47th St. What you get is a steam-powered train ride, a buffet-style, home-cooked meal at your destination, and a good look at the Alberta countryside on the way.

Three Hills One of the Canadian schools that is best-known to evangelicals in the United States is Prairie Bible College in this small village of 3,300 residents. The school has been operating since 1922 and has always had a strong emphasis on the deeper spiritual life and on foreign missions. The largest building on campus is a 2,500-seat auditorium, which becomes the Prairie Tabernacle church on weekends.

Three Hills is also the home of GuZoo Animal Farm, which has a motley collection of exotic animals from Siberian tigers to cougars and bobcats.

▲BRITISH COLUMBIA

Tourist Info
Phone 250-953-2680
Web sites
  Entire province   www.travel.bc.ca
  Vancouver   www.tourism-vancouver.org
  Victoria   www.travel.victoria.bc.ca
For a complete list of updated links, visit www.christiantraveler.com

Alert Bay The Anglican Church here (Front St.) was erected in 1881, and its stained glass windows show an interesting blend of Indian and European cultures.

One of the world's largest totem poles is near the Indian Big House (Mavis Ave.), and if you like totems, you can see a lot more of them at the Nimpkish Burial Ground at the other end of town.

Barkerville Believe it or not, this gold rush town once had the largest population north of San Francisco and west of Chicago. Of course, it didn't have much competition in those days. It has now been restored and contains about 125 reconstructed buildings, including the Barkerville Hotel and St. Saviour's Church. At the Theatre Royale you can see some old-fashioned melodrama most every night through Labor Day, and if you wish, you can pan for gold at Eldorado Mine. We can't guarantee you'll find any.

Castlegar The Doukhobor Historic Village (just off Rte. 3A W) is a replica of the communal settlement of the Russian immigrants who lived here in the early part of the century. The Doukhobors are pacifists who had trouble finding a place where they were appreciated. Initially they were in Saskatchewan but in the early part of the twentieth century, some of them moved to Castlegar and Grand Forks. The Doukhobor Bridge spans the Kootenay River, and just on the other side of it is the tomb of their leader, Peter Verigin. (See Doukhobors also under Grand Forks, British Columbia, and Veregin, Saskatchewan.)

Fort St. James Our Lady of Good Hope Church, built in 1873, is one of the oldest churches in the province. The mission, however, was founded at the fort three decades earlier. Services continue to be held here.

Grand Forks The Mountain View Doukhobor Museum (Hardy Mountain Rd.) is a 1912 Doukhobor communal farmhouse. (See Doukhobors also under Castlegar, British Columbia, and Veregin, Saskatchewan.)

Harrison Hot Springs The Kilby Historic Store and Farm (215 Kilby Rd.) is a living history museum, taking visitors back to the British Columbia of the 1920s. Tour the general store and farm buildings of the Kilby family and other pioneers and visit the orchards, barn, and dairy house on the grounds.

GREAT PLACES TO ENJOY GOD'S CREATION

✔ Driving along the Icefields Parkway, Alberta

✔ Hiking in Glacier National Park, British Columbia

✔ Viewing Takakkaw Falls in Yoho National Park, British Columbia

Hope Another of the province's oldest churches is Christ Church (Anglican) built here in 1859.

Remember When Doll Museum (10 miles west in Laidlaw on Hwy. 1) is a fascinating nostalgic stopping place.

Kamloops In the late 19th century Roman Catholic missionaries and the Kamloops Indian band built St. Joseph's Church (north on Mount Paul Way, then west to end of Chilcotin St.). The building has been recently renovated and its religious artifacts restored.

Wanda Sue is the name of a stern-wheeler that offers two-hour narrated cruises on the Thompson River. Food is available. The ship leaves from the end of 10th Ave.

Kelowna South of town and right on Benvoulin Rd. is the Father Pandosy Mission, established in 1859 by Father Pandosy. It was the first white settlement in the area, the first Roman Catholic mission in the interior of the province, the first school,s and it produced the first fruit and vine crops.

Langley Trinity Western University (7600 Glover Rd.), associated with the Evangelical Free Church, is located in this suburb of Vancouver.

Maple Ridge The oldest church in the province is probably St. John the Divine (Anglican), which is located just west on Hwy. 7. The church was built downstream in 1859 and then moved intact to its present location in 1882.

Mission This Vancouver suburb got its name because a Roman Catholic mission was built here in 1861 to serve the Indian tribes. Today there is a Mission Museum (33201 Second Ave.) with pioneer and Indian artifacts, and the Westminster Abbey (about a mile east and a half-mile north on Hwy. 7). The abbey is managed by Benedictine monks.

Revelstoke The Enchanted Forest (20 miles west on Hwy. 1) features 300 figurines in a natural forest setting. It is open daily from May 15 to September 15.

At the Three Valley Gap Ghost Town (12 miles west on Hwy. 1) you will see more than 20 relocated historic buildings, including a church, schoolhouse, and general store. Live performances of a musical show are presented almost every night.

Vancouver Queen Elizabeth Park (off Cambie St.) includes a lovely arboretum and garden. You get some magnificent views of the city thrown in, just because the park is on the highest point in Vancouver.

Also in South Vancouver (37th and Oak Sts.) are the Vandusen Botanical Gardens, which is something like the Butchart Gardens of Victoria, only smaller. If you are there in May, you may never want to get beyond the parking lot, where rhododendron grow in profusion. Vandusen has more than 1,000 varieties of these flowering shrubs.

Children will love the Kids Only Market (1496 Cartwright St., on Granville Island). The market has two floors of shops selling dolls, music, toys, arts and crafts supplies, science kits, and other kids stuff.

Christ Church Cathedral (690 Burrard St.), built in 1889, is the oldest church in the city. The tiny church is built in Gothic style, with buttresses, arched windows, and beautiful stained glass that make it look very European. The interior, on the other hand, is very Canadian, crafted of local Douglas fir and cedar. Choral evensong, carols, and Gregorian chants are frequently sung here. Notice also the special tableau of the crucifixion.

St. Andrew's Wesley Church (1012 Nelson St.) is a Gothic building with a great many stained glass windows.

Holy Rosary Cathedral (646 Richards St.) is worth seeing for its stained glass windows and worth hearing for its bell ringing, which takes place Tuesday evenings and Sunday mornings.

Regent College, a graduate school of Christian studies, is affiliated with the University of British Columbia. Some outstanding scholars of the evangelical world have served on the faculty here, including J. I. Packer and Eugene Peterson.

Vernon North of town at 9380 Hwy. 97, the O'Keefe Historic Ranch offers you a look at a turn-of-the-century cattle ranch. The late 19th-century Victorian-style mansion is furnished with period antiques. Visitors can also visit the Chinese cooks' house, St. Anne's church, a display of the Shuswap and Okanagan Railroad, a general store, a blacksmith shop, and a restaurant and gift shop.

Victoria Butchart Gardens (13 miles north, off Hwy. 17) are a world-renowned horticultural wonder with each season bringing out its own splendor. Something like 35,000 new bulbs and 100 new roses are tested in the nurseries each year. The gardens contain a Rose Garden, Japanese Garden, Italian Garden, and more.

GREAT PLACES FOR FAMILY FUN

✔ Whale watching off the coast of Vancouver Island, British Columbia

✔ The tramway up Whistlers Mountain, Jasper, Alberta

✔ The Gold Rush town of Skagway, the Yukon

Christ Church Cathedral (Quadra and Rockland Sts.) is an Anglican church that reminds you of a Gothic church of the Middle Ages. This building, completed in 1986, is one of Canada's largest cathedrals. It is the third church on this site. The first church was built in 1856. Free choral recitals are offered at 6 P.M. Saturdays in July and August.

In the Empress Hotel on Humboldt St. is Miniature World, which uses animation, lighting, and sound effects to bring 80 highly detailed miniature scenes to life. Included are two of the world's largest dollhouses and a futuristic space diorama.

▲ MANITOBA

Tourist Info
Phone 800-665-0040
Web sites
  Entire province   www.travelmanitoba.com
  Winnipeg   www.tourism.winnipeg.mb.ca
For a complete list of updated links, visit www.christiantraveler.com

More than 40 farms in Manitoba open their homes to visitors who can choose to help out around the farm or else do nothing and just relax. Guests may eat all or some meals with the family. For more information, contact the Manitoba Country Vacations Association, c/o Bob Front, R.R. 1, Elm Creek, Man. R0G 0N0; 204-436–2599.

Brandon The Thunder Mountain Waterslide (five miles off Hwy. 1 on Hwy. 459) has a variety of slides, including twister slides, a tube slide, and a speed slide, as well as a two- and three-person river raft ride.

Carberry The noted artist and naturalist Ernest Thompson Seton got much of his inspiration from this area. The Seton Centre (116 Main St.) features artwork and photographs depicting his life and philosophy.

The Spirit Sands Covered Wagon Tours are covered wagon rides that last from 90 minutes to overnight. Visitors travel through the Spirit Sands and the Devil's Punch Bowl areas. Phone 204-827-2800 for reservations and pricing information.

Churchill This is Canada's northernmost subarctic sea port on Hudson Bay. If you want an unusual experience, sign up for a Tundra Buggy Tour (124 Kelsey Blvd.). You will be taken in a specially designed vehicle for crossing the tundra to view the polar bears in the Cape Churchill Wildlife Management Area. During the summer, eco-tours, birding, and naturalist tours are offered.

Cooks Creek The Immaculate Conception Church (three miles north on Hwy. 212) features onion domes and the icon of Our Lady of Perpetual Help. Alongside the church is a replica of the Grotto of Lourdes, France.

Lockport Two miles south on River Road Heritage Pkwy. is the oldest Anglican stone church west of the Great Lakes. Worshipers still use the buffalo-hide–covered kneelers. The rectory was one of the first stone houses in the settlement and contains exhibits depicting local history and the early missionaries.

Selkirk St. Peter's Dynevor Church (about four miles northeast of town off Hwy. 59) was built in 1853, replacing the original church built in 1836. Anglican missionaries were seeking to reach out to the Saulteaux Indians.

Steinbach About 30 miles southeast of Winnipeg, Steinbach is populated with the descendants of Mennonites who fled religious persecution in late 19th-century Europe. The Mennonite Heritage Village (on Rte. 12, one mile north of town) is a 40-acre complex depicting Mennonite life. Between 1874 and 1880 about 7,000 Ukrainian Mennonites emigrated to this area. During World War I, Manitoba banned unregistered schools and that caused an exodus of Mennonites to Mexico and Uruguay. But then another flood of emigrants came after the Communist Revolution in Russia. The museum shows the life of the Mennonites. Guides demonstrate wheat grinding, blacksmithing, and old housekeeping practices. Occasionally you can hear the people conversing in the Mennonite German dialect. A restaurant on the grounds serves inexpensive and authentic Mennonite specialties, and if you've experienced Mennonite cooking, that's enough reason to drop in.

The Steinbach Bible College is a Mennonite school located here.

Swan River Christ Church (Edwards Ave.) is an Anglican church founded in 1840 by the first native Indian ordained to the Anglican ministry. It contains hand-hewn furnishings made by ships' carpenters in 1847.

Winnipeg St. Boniface Cathedral (av. de la Cathédrale and av. Tache) was built in 1972 within the shell of a 1908 building that was burned in 1968, and that 1908 basilica had been a replacement for an earlier one built in 1819. The area was home to the largest French-speaking community in western Canada, founded as Fort Rouge in 1783, and was an important fur-trading outpost. When a group of Roman Catholic priests arrived, the settlement was renamed St. Boniface. Some of the early religious articles of worship are housed in the nearby St. Boniface Museum, the oldest structure in Winnipeg, built in 1846, and the largest oak log building in North America. Interesting artifacts include an altar made of papier-mâché and the first church bell in western Canada.

Assiniboine Park (2355 Coydon Ave.) is spread over 393 acres so there is plenty of room for picnicking, playing, and biking. There is also ample room for a miniature railway, a duck pond, an English garden, a cricket pitch, and a conservatory. The Leo Mol Sculpture Garden has more than 30 bronze sculptures. Besides that, there is room for a 98-acre zoo, which is home to more than 1,200 animals.

The Prairie Dog Central is a 1900s steam-era train that operates weekends from June to September. It takes you on a two-hour, 36-mile round-trip from Winnipeg north and gives you a good feeling of the prairie.

During the summer there are also cruise ships that provide a variety of cruises on the Red and Assiniboine Rivers.

The Fun Mountain Water Slide Park (four miles east on Hwy. 1 east) offers 10 slides as well as bumper boats and a kids' playground.

At the Manitoba Children's Museum, kids can explore a 1952 diesel locomotive and passenger coach and get a behind-the-scenes look at a TV studio.

▲ SASKATCHEWAN

Tourist Info
Phone 877-2ESCAPE
Web site
  Entire province   www.sasktourism.com
For a complete list of updated links, visit www.christiantraveler.com

---

As in Manitoba, many farm families open their homes to visitors. Some operate like bed and breakfasts, but others give opportunities to work on the farm or to ride their horses and do other interesting things. For more information, write to Beatrice Magee, Saskatchewan Country Vacations, PO Box 654, Gull Lake, Sask. S0N 1A0; 306-672-3970.

Caronport Briercrest Bible College, one of the larger evangelical schools in Canada, is located here.

Gravelbourg The Cathédrale Notre-Dame de l'Assomption (Main St.) was founded in 1918 and its founding pastor painted the lovely interior murals.

Lloydminster In 1903 the Reverend Isaac Barr led a group of settlers here. Their first settlement was in what is now Weaver Park (Hwy. 16E at 44th St. and 45th Ave.), and restored buildings mark the location. The Barr Colony Heritage Cultural Centre shows household items and furniture of the early colonists and also their first church as well as a school dating from about 1906. Adjoining the museum is the Imhoff Gallery, which displays about 250 religious and historical paintings by Bernhard Imhoff, whose murals adorn many North American churches and public buildings. (See Imhoff also under Muenster.)

Moose Jaw The Sukanen Ship, Pioneer Village and Museum (eight miles south of Moose Jaw on Hwy. 2) does indeed house a ship. It was being built by a Finnish settler who intended to sail back to his native country from Moose Jaw, which is about 2,000 miles from the Atlantic Ocean, to say nothing about the distance from Finland. He thought, however, he could get there by the Saskatchewan River and Hudson Bay. Fortunately (or unfortunately), he never finished his ship. In the pioneer village here is an early Moose Jaw church.

Muenster St. Peter's Abbey (a half-mile east on Hwy. 5) gives you information for a walking tour of the abbey and about monastic life and work.

St. Peter's Cathedral (a half-mile north on Hwy. 5) is a virtual gallery of Berthold Imhoff paintings. The walls and ceiling are lined with his work, which incorporates 80 life-size figures. (See Imhoff also under Lloydminster.)

Prince Albert About an hour north of Saskatoon is this town of about 35,000 residents, founded by Presbyterian minister James Nisbet in 1866. The log church Nisbet built is now in Kinsmen Park.

Regina Buffalo Days, the big time of the year in Regina, is usually held the first week of August. Shop owners and professional people alike dress in Old West style, as the city celebrates the time when buffalo roamed the area.

The RCMP Training Academy and Museum is located in Regina on 11th Ave. W. As any Canadian will tell you, RCMP stands for the Royal Canadian Mounted Police. In the museum you will trace their interesting history since their founding in 1874. A tour also goes to the chapel, and if you are there at the right time, you can observe the training of the cadets. At 12:45 P.M. each weekday is the Sergeant Major's Parade and that's a highlight you shouldn't miss if you are in the area. Admission is free.

The Canadian Bible College (4400 4th Ave.), associated with the Christian and Missionary Alliance, is located here.

Saskatoon Two small denominational colleges and two small seminaries are located here. They are Central Pentecostal College (1303 Jackson Ave.), College of Emmanuel and St. Chad (Episcopal, 1337 College Dr.), Lutheran Theological Seminary (114 Seminary Cresc.), and St. Andrew's College (a seminary of the United Church, 1121 College Dr.).

Museum Ukraina (202 Ave. M South), located next to the St. George's Ukrainian Greek Catholic Cathedral, gives tours portraying Ukrainian civilization from prehistoric times. Information on the cathedral is available next door.

Gladys' Doll Wonder World Museum (2.5 miles north on Hwy. 12) has more than 800 new and antique dolls and furnishings in 150 realistic settings.

Veregin The National Doukhobor Heritage Village (across the tracks south of Hwy. 5) is made up of the original prayer home and several reconstructed villages to show how Doukhobors lived in the early 1900s. The name Doukhobor means "spirit wrestler" in Russian, signifying the importance of the interior life in its struggle for relationship with God. In the late 19th century Peter Verigin, the Doukhobor leader, arranged for many of his followers to come to Canada with him. About 7,400 came. Among the beliefs of the group were a communal society, pacifism, vegetarianism, the role of inner illumination, and the place of morality over ritual. (See Doukhobors also under Castlegar and Grand Forks, British Columbia.)

Amy Eckert and **Bill Petersen** have combined many years of travel experience with many hours of research to provide you with *The Christian Traveler's Companion*. Even so, you may know of destinations that the authors missed. If you would like to submit ideas for the next edition of *The Christian Traveler's Companion: The USA and Canada,* please share them with us.

Would you like to add your name to our mailing list? You will receive free information of interest to Christian travelers as well as advance notices of upcoming *Christian Traveler's Companions*. Send your name and mailing address and any inquiries to:

> *The Christian Traveler*
> P.O. Box 1736
> Holland, MI 49422
> info@christiantraveler.com

Or visit our Web site at www.christiantraveler.com for regular updates and additional Christian travel information.